SOCIAL GOALS IN THE CLASSROOM

Social Goals in the Classroom is the first volume to comprehensively examine the variety of students' non-academic goals and motivations within the classroom.

Each expertly written chapter defines and investigates a particular aspect of students' social objectives before addressing related findings on academic performance, interpersonal outcomes, and directions for future research. Presented in three succinct and comprehensive parts, this book reviews, expands upon, and theoretically synthesizes current research on the many different social goals to offer readers a thorough understanding of non-academic desires and their consequences on learners' educational experiences.

Situated in evidence-based theory as well as real-world contexts such as ethnicity, sexual orientation, and social media, this insightful collection – ideal for graduate students, teachers, and researchers – explores how students' social motives influence their academic performance and peer relationships.

Martin H. Jones, PhD, is Associate Professor of Educational Psychology at the University of New Mexico, USA.

SOCIAL GOALS IN THE CLASSROOM

Findings on Student Motivation and Peer Relations

Edited by Martin H. Jones

NEW YORK AND LONDON

First published 2020
by Routledge
52 Vanderbilt Avenue, New York, NY 10017

and by Routledge
2 Park Square, Milton Park, Abingdon, Oxon OX14 4RN

Routledge is an imprint of the Taylor & Francis Group, an informa business

© 2020 Taylor & Francis

The right of Martin H. Jones to be identified as the author of the editorial material, and of the authors for their individual chapters, has been asserted in accordance with sections 77 and 78 of the Copyright, Designs and Patents Act 1988.

All rights reserved. No part of this book may be reprinted or reproduced or utilised in any form or by any electronic, mechanical, or other means, now known or hereafter invented, including photocopying and recording, or in any information storage or retrieval system, without permission in writing from the publishers.

Trademark notice: Product or corporate names may be trademarks or registered trademarks, and are used only for identification and explanation without intent to infringe.

Library of Congress Cataloging-in-Publication Data
A catalog record for this title has been requested

ISBN: 978-1-138-60451-3 (hbk)
ISBN: 978-1-138-60450-6 (pbk)
ISBN: 978-0-429-46845-2 (ebk)

Typeset in Bembo
by Taylor & Francis Books

 Printed in the United Kingdom by Henry Ling Limited

I dedicate this book to my adviser, Joyce M. Alexander, PhD. Thank you for our countless conversations, your wisdom, and your patience.

CONTENTS

List of Tables	*ix*
List of Contributors	*x*
About the Editor	*xi*
Acknowledgements	*xii*

PART I
Overview

1

1 The Social Side of Classrooms: Introducing Social Goals and
the Book's Purpose **3**
Martin H. Jones

2 Social Goals: A Historical Overview **8**
Ronnel B. King and Dennis M. McInerney

PART II
Social Goals

35

3 Academic or Social Focus Toward School **37**
Martin H. Jones, Alexandra Tonigan and Gülay Güler

4 Social Achievement Goals **53**
Sungok Serena Shim and Allison M. Ryan

5 Social Dominance Goals **74**
Sarah M. Kiefer

viii Contents

6 Prosocial Goals 93
Christi Bergin

7 Revenge Goals 111
Kristina L. McDonald

8 Cool Goals 131
Rhonda S. Jamison and Travis M. Wilson

9 Popularity/Antisocial Goals 154
David B. Estell

PART III
Social Goals in Context 171

10 Social Goals in Context: Asian Students 173
Kara A. Makara

11 Social Goals in Context: African American Students 192
James M. Ford, Jr. and Leigh M. Harrell-Williams

12 Social Goals in Context: Latinx Students 206
Angela M. Labistre Champion and Francesca López

13 Social Goals in Context: Sexuality and Gender Diversity 221
Tara S. Hackel and Kristopher M. Goodrich

14 Social Goals in Context: Social Media 237
Gaëlle Ouvrein, Karen Verswijvel and Lies De Kimpe

PART IV
In Conclusion 255

15 Social Goals: Conclusions and Future Directions 257
Martin H. Jones

Index 266

TABLES

2.1 Definitions and Operationalizations of Social Goals according to the Three Goal Traditions	13
3.1 Age and Academic and Social Focus in Fall 2011 and Spring 2012: Correlations and Descriptive Statistics	41
3.2 Student Reports of Academic and Social Foci and Achievement Goal Orientations in School from Fall 2011: Correlations and Descriptive Statistics	42
3.3 Student Reports of Academic and Social Foci and Achievement Goal Orientations in School from Fall 2011: Linear Regression	42
3.4 Academic and Social Focus and Student Engagement Fall 2011: Correlations and Descriptive Statistics	43
3.5 Academic and Social Focus and Student Engagement Fall 2011: Regression	43
4.1 Cross-domain concurrent correlations among goals	59
8.1 Study 1: Latent Correlations between Coolness and Social Goals	141
8.2 Study 1: Longitudinal Stabilities in Coolness and Social Goals	142
8.3 Study 1: Longitudinal Cross-lagged Paths between Coolness and Social Goals	142
8.4 Study 2: Latent Correlations between Coolness and Social Goals	146
8.5 Study 2: Longitudinal Stabilities in Coolness and Social Goals	147
8.6 Longitudinal Cross-lagged Paths between Coolness and Social Goals	147
14.1 Types of Social Relationships (five-point Likert scale)	240
14.2 Self-disclosure	241

CONTRIBUTORS

Christi Bergin University of Missouri
Lies De Kimpe University of Antwerp
David B. Estell Indiana University, Bloomington
James M. Ford, Jr. University of Memphis
Kristopher M. Goodrich University of New Mexico
Gülay Güler University of New Mexico
Tara S. Hackel University of New Mexico
Leigh M. Harrell-Williams University of Memphis
Rhonda S. Jamison University of Maine at Farmington
Martin H. Jones University of New Mexico
Sarah M. Kiefer University of South Florida
Ronnel B. King The Education University of Hong Kong
Angela M. Labistre Champion University of Arizona
Francesca López University of Arizona
Kara A. Makara University of Glasgow
Kristina L. McDonald University of Alabama
Dennis M. McInerney The Education University of Hong Kong
Gaëlle Ouvrein University of Antwerp
Allison M. Ryan University of Michigan
Sungok Serena Shim Ball State University
Alexandra Tonigan University of New Mexico
Karen Verswijvel University of Antwerp
Travis M. Wilson Oberlin College

ABOUT THE EDITOR

Dr. Martin H. Jones is Associate Professor of Educational Psychology in the Department of Individual, Family and Community Education at The University of New Mexico. Dr. Jones' research centers on how friends affect academic motivation and academic achievement, especially in underserved student populations. He received his bachelor's degree in social studies education at Purdue University and his master's and PhD in educational psychology at Indiana University, Bloomington. He currently serves on multiple editorial boards and publishes regularly on how peer interactions inside school might alter students' desire to learn and, ultimately, achieve greater academic success.

Correspondence should be addressed to Martin H. Jones, Department of Individual, Family and Community Education, MSC 05 3040, 1 University of New Mexico, Albuquerque, NM 87131. E-mail: martinjones@unm.edu

ACKNOWLEDGEMENTS

For Chapters 1 and 3, Martin H. Jones would like to acknowledge the hard work of the SMAART lab at the University of New Mexico.

In Chapter 8, Rhonda S. Jamison and Travis M. Wilson are grateful to the children, teachers, and school principals who contributed to their project. Their research was supported by a grant from the Spencer Foundation to the second author (Grant #201500085).

The author of Chapter 9, David Estell, passed away on February 19, 2019. His chapter is dedicated to his daughters Eleanor and Lily.

In Chapter 14, the work by Gaëlle Ouvrein, Karen Verswijvel, Lies De Kimpe was supported by the Research Foundation - Flanders (FWO): G047415N.

PART I

Overview

1

THE SOCIAL SIDE OF CLASSROOMS

Introducing Social Goals and the Book's Purpose

Martin H. Jones

Think back to when you were in grade school. You may remember the classroom as a place where you learned math, social studies, and other academic disciplines. You may also remember that the classroom was a place where you met friends, pursued romantic interests, and worried about whom you sat with at lunch. Both then and now, students come to the classroom with a mix of academic learning goals as well as desires to interact socially with their friends, classmates, and teachers. These are often social goals, or the psychological reasons behind why students socially interact during school. Not only do students come to a learning setting with their own social goals, but teachers, administrators, and others involved in any given learning setting hold their own social desires apart from the learning experience. For example, teachers may come to the learning setting with a desire to be liked, or feared, by students and fellow teachers, maintain social control of the classroom, and build positive rapport with their students. As students and teachers naturally comingle their social and learning goals, the learning setting becomes an environment not strictly for learning.

Often, teachers, parents, and community members presume that a school classroom is a place centered on learning. The presumption is that schools and individual classroom exist as a way to educate youth. While not untrue, this presumption does not consider that students are housed within a social setting (i.e., a classroom or virtual learning environment). Students' classroom experiences include motives not directly related to learning, but, rather, to the "social side" of the classroom. The "social side" of the classroom includes the sometimes overlooked parts of the schooling experience that are not directly linked to academic content, or may be only partially linked to academic learning (e.g., extracurricular activities). The social side of the classroom entails the many interpersonal interactions within a classroom or learning setting. This may be between classmates, between students and instructors, or among teachers. These interpersonal interactions often involve personal motives. For example, two students desire a romantic relationship, while another student plots revenge for an aggressive comment made by a student at lunch. These interpersonal interactions occur within a learning setting, and can affect learning, but these social interactions are not directly part of academic instruction. These interpersonal desires are students' social goals.

Defining Social Goals

As a general definition, social goals in the classroom are one or more psychological desires for non-academic outcomes occurring in formal and informal learning settings that a person can consciously or unintentionally use. The emphases on this definition are threefold. First, social goals constitute a psychologically desired outcome, or a purposeful approach to obtaining some type of social consequence. Social goals are inherently psychological in nature as individuals hold preferences, beliefs, values, past experiences, and opinions about what they want from a social interaction. Second, social goals exist within a classroom or learning setting. Social goals may also happen outside of the learning setting, but this book will focus mostly on social goals within learning environments. Third, social goals can exist apart from academic desires as well as co-exist within academic pursuits. There are times when students employ social goals along with their academic goals, but social goals can also be unrelated to academic pursuits.

Social goals can include, but are not limited to, making friends, developing prosocial behaviors, becoming popular, and socially controlling the classroom. Social goals lead to a range of outcomes from affecting academic performance to bullying classmates. Some of these outcomes may be specifically desired and strived for by the student, whereas individuals' social goals can also produce unintended consequences by the student. The individual may hope that a new friendship emerges, a romantic relationship develops, or that one becomes more popular, but these goals could also hurt existing friendships, hurt a friend's feelings, or result in bullying.

Purpose of this Book

Social goal research stands at a crossroads. As seen in Chapter 2, the earliest forms of social goal research emerged several decades ago. Over these past decades, a variety of social goal studies emerged across different psychological and sociological academic journals. These studies demonstrated a growing interest by researchers to understand why students pursue social interactions in school as well as the consequences of pursuing these social interactions. What followed these publications was the creation of several different psychological constructs trying to explain why students pursued these social interactions in school. Unfortunately, these articles often used the same terminology of "social goal" despite those articles utilizing different social behaviors (i.e., prosocial goals and social dominance goals could both be labeled as social goals, though they are quite different). Thus, our current understanding of what is a social goal often varies by how a given article operationally defined the social goal used within the manuscript. This book hopes to move past the current gridlock of defining what is a social goal by expanding and furthering the extant social goal literature.

The first step in moving past the social goal terminology roadblock is understanding that there is more than one social goal. "Social goal" is a more general term for what includes several specific social pursuits, which are housed under the label of being a social goal. Each of these social pursuits constitutes its own social goal. Thus, a social goal is not a singular psychological entity, but rather many social goals exist. The book explores several of these social goals in greater depth (Chapters 3 through 9). These chapters are not exhaustive in their inclusion of all social goals, but rather represent social goals that have some prominence in the extant literature. Further, each of the social goals is unique, but they all branch from the same premise of understanding why individuals might desire social interactions inside school.

As social goals present themselves inside schools, social goals might also be specific to the given context in which the goal appears. That is, social goals do not exist within psychological and social vacuums, but reciprocally interact with individuals' social settings. These social settings come with their own specific socio-cultural contexts. Each context is unique with their own specific values, problems, and social rules. By delving into these social contexts, findings present a deeper understanding of how social goals operate as well as showing the interactive nature of context with social goals. How social goals are present within different contexts are more greatly explored in Chapters 10 through 14.

By understanding the cultural contexts, and acknowledging that multiple social goals exist, the field may begin moving forward. This book also attempts to move the field forward by utilizing two specific tactics. First, authors had freedom to expand and "fill-in" certain discussions whenever extant literature did not currently exist to support a topic or area. This choice hopefully encouraged the authors to think about progressing the field and providing a logical roadmap for future research, though empirical findings may not currently be present to support the given argument. Second, each chapter in this book presents areas of future research for the given social goal and context. The final chapter provides a more general discussion of future areas of social goal research and a brief discussion of what social goal research might entail in the year 2040. The freedom to write about current gaps in the literature and imagine the future of social goal research may propel social goal research past the current crossroads. Thus, this book's purpose is describing the current state of social goal research, while urging the field toward a much richer understanding of students' social goals.

Social Hierarchies and Interactions in School

Understanding how social goals function in school likely involves understanding the social dynamics inherent within schools. Schools include a variety of different social players: teachers, students, administrators, community members, maintenance staff, and even parents coming into the school to help classrooms or on field trips. Social players have an opportunity to use social goals with each other. Teachers may have certain social goals, such as exerting social dominance over their class or appearing cool to other teachers. At the same time, students can have social goals, such as exerting social dominance over their teachers and appearing cool to classmates.

Social players inside schools typically exist within coherent patterns or social hierarchies. Most schools contain a series of nested levels organized by classrooms, grade levels, school building, and then school districts. Social goals likely occur within and across each level of this hierarchy. Most social goal research exists within the classroom level when research occurs in elementary schools. In middle and high schools, social goal research may happen within classrooms, but also appears inside a given school grade and across the whole school. Still, most social goal research involves the most basic level of interpersonal interactions within classrooms.

Inside classrooms, the social hierarchy still exists on multiple nested levels. The first level is the individual, who will hold one or more social goals. The next level includes dyadic relationships. Dyadic relationships are between two people. These dyadic relationships may be reciprocal friendships (i.e., both dyadic members agree that the other is a friend) or between non-reciprocal friends (e.g., two classmates that are not friends, but may sit near each other). Next, groups of friends merge together to form peer groups. A peer group may vary in size and tightness of social bonds, but peer groups generally comprise multiple friendships that hold some type of homophily, or similarity, across members. Peer groups then reside within a larger social network. A social network is everyone that an individual may come into contact with, such as an elementary student's classroom or the entire school for high school students. Across the social network and down to dyadic relationships, students have opportunities for utilizing their social goals with their peers.

Social Goals in Action

Students must navigate the learning experience of a classroom, while also managing their own social goals. Anecdotally, I experienced the dual navigation of social and learning goals while watching the high school men's basketball state tournament. Besides the cheerleaders and athletes on the basketball court, there were high school seniors sitting in the front of the student section leading cheers and motivating the student section, with first year students sitting in the back and not leading any cheers. The position of students, the social roles and social expectations of the students, and why the students were even present within the basketball arena demonstrate how social goals intermingle with academic pursuits. It was a school-sponsored basketball tournament involving students, but the basketball game offered little direct academic content to the students. Still, the students were co-regulating learning and social goals. This became apparent as the game lasted late into the night, which meant that the students chose between sleep and supporting the school's basketball team. Further, as most of these students were younger than 18, parents likely gave explicit or implied permission of some type to have their children attend the sporting event. Hence, students, teachers, parents, and even administrators are complicit in developing an environment where students co-regulate their academic interests and their own social goals.

In turn, these academic and social goals lead to specific outcomes. Some of the students may have gained or lost popularity by leading cheers. Younger basketball team members became more popular when scoring points for their team. The loss of sleep may interfere with the students' ability to learn and perform well in school. The students' social goals had both academic and interpersonal consequences.

Other extracurricular activities demonstrate the entangled nature of academics and social goals. The United States' secondary schools often have clubs or organizations loosely associated with academic content areas. For example, high schools can have foreign language clubs. The purposes for many foreign language clubs are learning and practicing the language. Foreign language clubs may have outings to local restaurants serving food from the given country where the language is spoken or even taking trips to visit a given country. There is learning involved in these outings, but there are also social goals at play too. Students may have friends or romantic partners in the foreign language club, and these friendships and intimate relationships may dissolve or grow during the outings. While students are learning a foreign language, they are also exercising social goals in developing relationships with their classmates.

In Summary

Whether in academically connected extracurricular organization, a sporting event, classroom, or any other learning setting, students hold both academic and social goals concurrently. At times, an academic goal or a social goal may come to greater prominence, such that a social goal may be more utilized than a learning goal, but the social side of the classroom persists. This book propels this discussion forward as each chapter discusses a given social goal or context, offers a definition, presents the social goal's academic and interpersonal outcomes, and offers areas of future research. By attuning to students' social goals, researchers may further understand how the social side of the classroom alters students' learning and affects interpersonal interactions in school, which may ultimately explain students' success.

2

SOCIAL GOALS

A Historical Overview

Ronnel B. King and Dennis M. McInerney

Introduction

Anna wants to help her friends with their homework (*prosocial goal*), while Jose wants to do well in school in order to please his parents (*social approval goal*). Pat wants to develop and deepen bonds with her friends (*social development goal*), while Richard is concerned with appearing cool and hanging out with popular peers (*social demonstration approach*). All these students are pursuing different types of social goals. Social goals occur quite frequently in the classroom setting and loom large in students' psyches (Dowson & McInerney, 2001, 2003). However, despite their ubiquity and psychological salience, social goals have not received sufficient attention in the educational psychology literature.

Social goals are key motivational constructs that are proximally related to learning and socio-emotional well-being (Ryan & Shim, 2006; 2008; Urdan & Maehr, 1995; Wentzel, 2000). Numerous qualitative studies have shown that students usually pursue different types of social goals and endorse them to a strong degree (Bernardo, 2008; Dowson & McInerney, 2001, 2003; King & McInerney, 2019; Lemos, 1996; Wentzel, 1991a). While the bulk of the research on goals in the educational psychology literature has focused on achievement goals (mastery vs. performance goals), research has shown that social goals predict a significant amount of variance in key outcomes even after taking into account the variance explained by the more commonly examined achievement goals (e.g., King, McInerney, & Watkins, 2010; 2012, 2013; Ryan, Hicks, & Midgley, 1997; Shim, Cho, & Wang, 2013; Wentzel, 1996). In certain cases, social goals are even more powerful predictors of key outcomes compared to achievement goals (King & McInerney, 2019; King, McInerney, & Watkins, 2012, 2013; Wentzel, 1996).

Despite the importance and ubiquity of social goals, theoretical and empirical understanding of social goals has lagged behind that of the more commonly researched achievement goals such as mastery and performance goals. The social goal literature is generally characterized by several problematic issues.

First, there is a lack of definitional precision: social goals can be considered as "fuzzy but powerful constructs" (Pintrich, 1994, p. 139). Researchers adopt different definitions of social goals, and sometimes create their own idiosyncratic operationalizations of social goals. This phenomenon makes theoretical integration very difficult. While there is reasonable (if far from complete) agreement among achievement goal researchers about the definition of mastery and performance goals, the same could not be said for social goals. Second, different researchers usually study social goals within their own theoretical framework with little attempt to synthesize across frameworks. This has resulted in a fractionated literature that is nearly impossible to summarize. A multiplicity of theoretical positions is not necessarily a problem, and most topics that receive vigorous research attention may in fact be characterized by disagreements among various theorists. However, in the field of social goals, multiple conceptualizations of social goals are being researched in parallel but not interacting with each other or engaging in productive debates. Third, there is a lack of agreement on the types of social goals that should be investigated with different researchers focusing on different types of social goals.

It is our hope that the first step towards theoretical advancement in social goal research is to recognize the multiplicity of theoretical perspectives that dominate social goal research. This chapter has several major aims. First, we conduct a historical overview of social goal research and trace its origins from drive theories and later on the social cognitive approach. Second, we review the three key social goal research traditions, mapping out their conceptual parameters, and review relevant studies undertaken within each tradition. Lastly, we proffer key substantive and methodological recommendations to help social goal theorizing move forward.

Historical Underpinnings

Drive paradigm

More than half a century ago, researchers understood motivation as a drive, an internal state, need or condition that impels individuals toward action. Needs were assumed to reside largely within the individual and were described as trait-like. The conceptualization of motivation as a drive evolved from earlier theories of motivation that emphasized the satisfaction of basic physiological needs such as hunger and thirst (Woodworth, 1918). However, as the limitations of a purely physiological approach were recognized, scholars broadened the range of drives they examined to include learned drives such as need for power, achievement, and affiliation.

The work on drives reached its summit in the early 1960s in the work of Atkinson (1964) and McClelland (1961). In the work of McClelland and Atkinson, which we refer to in this chapter as the McClelland-Atkinson model. According to this model, one's motive to achieve is driven in large part by a stable personality trait called the Need for Achievement, usually abbreviated as nAch. It is associated with the intrinsic desire to perform well against a standard of excellence than extrinsic rewards (Atkinson, 1964; McClelland, 1961).

The McClelland-Atkinson model assumed that some individuals are higher in nAch than others. Although their model also took cognitive factors into account such as the perceived probability of success and incentive value (whether an individual values achievement in the relevant domain), the crucial variable was nAch. Researchers measured the nAch construct using projective responses to selected Thematic Apperception Test (TAT) cards as well as self-report surveys. nAch has been observed to predict high levels of performance (Epstein & Harackiewicz, 1992).

Aside from need for achievement, individuals also varied with regard to their Need for Affiliation (nAff) which can be seen as precursors of social goals in modern educational psychology research. McClelland (1961) defined nAff as the desire for "warm, close relationships with other people" (p. 161). Achievement motivation researchers assumed that need for affiliation is detrimental to achievement. As Friis and Knox (1972) wrote, "The drive that is most often mentioned by nAch theorists as being the least compatible with nAch is the need for affiliation (nAff) (p. 1214). Schneider and Green (1977) found that high school students scoring high in nAch and low in nAff earned higher grades, spent more time studying and less on socializing. They also obtained higher grades compared to those who were high in both nAch and nAff. The incompatibility of nAch and nAff was also reflected in the construction of the NachNaff Scale which is a 30-item forced choice questionnaire that asks respondents to select either an achievement or affiliation-oriented response from self-descriptive adjectives.

However, later scholars have critiqued drive theories as limited because they are not sensitive enough to the role of situational factors, an inevitable result of understanding needs as trait-like. Drive theories also fail to model adequately the dynamic nature of motivation as something that changes across time.

Goal paradigm

With the advent of the cognitive revolution in psychology, motivation scholars paid increasing attention to goals as a more productive unit of analysis. Goals are usually defined as internal representations of desired states (Austin & Vancouver, 1996). In the educational psychology literature, achievement goals have usually dominated the research conversation. Achievement goals emerged from the work of Carole Ames, Carol Dweck, Martin Maehr, and John Nicholls each of whom lead independent research programs at the University of Illinois. They began meeting regularly in the late 1970s and thereafter a series of papers emerged which would become foundational for the achievement goal approach (Maehr & Nicholls, 1980; Nicholls & Dweck, 1979) (see also Murayama, Elliot, & Friedman, for a historical overview of these developments). The achievement goal perspective focuses on competence-related strivings and is encapsulated in the pursuit of mastery and performance goals.

Much (though not all)[1] of contemporary theorizing on social goals emerged as an attempt to widen the lens of achievement goal researchers and address its shortcomings. Social goal researchers recognize the need to put the social aspects of the classroom into the center stage (Juvonen & Wentzel, 1996). More often than not social goal researchers argued that the dominance of the achievement goal approach may perhaps have the unintended consequence of focusing solely on the competence-related dimensions of schooling and less emphasis on its social-related dimensions. We give a few verbatim examples from prominent social goal researchers who have eloquently articulated this view:

> Thus, it is reasonable to suggest that students' social orientations are not peripheral to their academic performance and achievement. Rather, these orientations may directly influence students' psychological processes as they strive toward academic achievement. For this reason, both practitioners and researchers need to take seriously the possibility that diverse social orientations to learning may impact students' achievement. Social goals may actually be more salient and predictive of students' global motivation and achievement than either mastery or performance goals. In other words, it is possible that researchers have got it wrong in putting the emphasis on mastery and performance goals ... Social motivation is still backstage; it may need to be moved front stage in researchers' thinking about what really motivates students.
>
> *(Dowson & McInerney, 2001, pp. 40–41)*

> Research on students' achievement goals conducted over the last two decades has largely focused on two types of goals: task goals and ability goals ... However, as research on students' social relationships and social motives has demonstrated, students have other reasons for engaging in, or failing to engage in, academic work ... As Juvonen and Weiner (1993) have noted, theories of motivation have generally given scant attention to the influence of social relationships on academic achievement motivation. Similarly, achievement goal theorists have typically ignored social goals in their studies of motivation.
>
> *(Urdan & Maehr, 1995, p. 214)*

> In numerous studies achievement-oriented goals have been linked to learning-related outcomes (see, Ames & Ames, 1989; Maehr & Pintrich, 1991). However, in only a few studies have researchers examined links between students' goals to achieve social outcomes and classroom-related social competence ... there appears to be merit in expanding the present, somewhat restricted, focus on students' academic goal orientations to include a more general consideration of outcomes that students might be trying to achieve at school. Clearly, research on students' goal orientations toward academic achievement has contributed

enormously to the understanding of links between student motivation and academically relevant outcomes. However, an examination of the varied and often multiple outcomes that students are trying to accomplish at school can also provide important information for understanding relations between students' goals and their actual academic accomplishments.

(Wentzel, 1994 p. 173, p. 180)

Three traditions of social goal research

Although social goal researchers were united in terms of what they thought as the limitations of goal theory with its focus on competence-related strivings, they developed independent research programs to address these limitations. These research programs have coalesced into three distinct research traditions identified by Kiefer and Ryan (2008) as the goal content approach, the social-academic or goal complex approach, and the social achievement goal approach. Below, we elaborate on these social goal traditions, map out their parameters, and review the relevant empirical evidence. Table 2.1 shows how researchers within the three traditions defined and operationalized social goals.

Goal content approach

The goal content approach is one of the most common ways to conceptualize achievement goals. Wentzel defines the goal content approach as focusing on the "cognitive representation of what it is an individual is trying to achieve in a given situation" (Wentzel, 2000, pp. 105–106). Social goals, as defined within this research tradition, therefore, pertain to specific social outcomes that students are trying to pursue.

Wentzel's work

The primary proponent of the goal content approach is Wentzel (1989, 1993, 1994, 1998) who explicitly elucidated the distinction between the goal content approach from the more common achievement goal model. She (Wentzel, 1993) wrote, "in contrast to other approaches that assess goal orientations reflecting how and why academic achievements are pursued (i.e., achievement goal approach), the present approach focused on the content of students' goals and how often students try to pursue various types of goals at school" (p. 6). Wentzel typically measured social goals by asking students how often they try to accomplish certain social outcomes. She identified two types of social goals which influence classroom motivation and behavior, namely, *social responsibility goals* and *prosocial goals*. Social responsibility goals are defined as students' willingness to meet social demands or expectations, while prosocial goals are defined as students' willingness to share and help peers.

TABLE 2.1 Definitions and Operationalizations of Social Goals according to the Three Goal Traditions

Publication	Social goal	Definition	Sample item
Tradition 1: Goal content approach			
Wentzel's work			
Wentzel, 1994	Prosocial goal	"students efforts to share and to help peers with social problems and efforts to share and help classmates with academic problems" (Wentzel, 1994, p. 175)	How often do you try to help kids when they have a problem?
	Social responsibility goal	"how often students try to keep promises and commitments made to peers and to follow classroom rules" (Wentzel, 1994, p. 175)	How often do you try to do what your teacher asks you to do?
Personal investment theory			
McInerney & Ali (2006)	Social affiliation goal	"interest in belonging to a group when doing schoolwork"	"I prefer to work with other people at school rather than work alone"
	Social concern goal	"Concern for other students and a willingness to help them with their school work"	I like to help other students do well at school"
Self-determination theory's Goal Content Theory			
Grouzet et al. (2005)	Social affiliation	"to have satisfying relationships with family and friends"	"I will have a committed intimate relationship""
	Social concern	"to improve the world through activism or generativity"	"I will assist people who need it, asking nothing in return"
Tradition 2: Social-academic goal approach			
Dowson & McInerney (2004)	Social affiliation	"wanting to achieve to enhance a sense of belonging to a group" (Dowson & McInerney, 2004, p. 295)	I want to do well at school so that I can feel close to my group of friends
	Social approval	"Wanting to achieve to gain the approval of peers, teachers, and/or parents" (p. 296)	I try to do well at school to please my teachers

(Continued)

14 Ronnel B. King and Dennis M. McInerney

TABLE 2.1 (Cont.)

Publication	Social goal	Definition	Sample item
	Social concern	"Wanting to achieve academically to be able to assist others in their academic or personal development" (p. 296)	I do my best at school so that I can give my friends help with their schoolwork
	Social responsibility	"Wanting to achieve to maintain interpersonal commitments, meet social role obligations, or follow social and moral rules" (p. 296)	I want to do well at school to show that I am being a responsible student
	Social status	"Wanting to attain wealth and/or position in school and/or later life" (p. 297)	I do well at school so that I can get a high-paying job later on
Tradition 3: Social achievement goal approach			
Ryan & Shim (2006)	Social development	"concerns a focus on developing social competence ... learning new things, growth, and improvement. Success would be judged by whether one is improving social skills, deepening the quality of relationships, or developing one's social life in general" (Ryan & Shim, 2006, p. 1247)	"I feel successful when I learn something new about how I relate to other people"
	Social demonstration approach	"focus on demonstrating social competence and gaining from others positive judgments that one is socially desirable" (Ryan & Shim, 2006, p. 1247)	"It is important to me to have cool friends"
	Social demonstration avoidance	"focus is on avoiding doing something that would incur negative judgments from others and indicate social undesirability" (Ryan & Shim, 2006, p. 1247)	I try not to goof up when I am out with people

Wentzel (1991) found that social responsibility goals were positively correlated with academic achievement, and these effects were partially mediated by responsible behavior. Wentzel (1996) also found that a composite score of prosocial and social responsibility goals served as a good predictor of effort in English classes even when academic motivation variables were taken into account. It was interesting to note that when mastery goals, performance goals, intrinsic value, and self-efficacy alongside social goals were entered into the regression equation, only social goals positively predicted effort in English classes. Social goals were also positively related to other academic outcomes such as self-efficacy, intrinsic value, and mastery goals. More importantly, social goals were also positively related to both concurrent English grades and English grades two years later.

Wentzel has made social goals a key centerpiece of her work. However, there are other researchers who have studied social goals using the goal content perspective. These researchers cast a broader goal net and studied multiple types of goals under broad theoretical frameworks. We review these theoretical approaches below.

Personal investment theory

One of the earliest theoretical frameworks to explicitly include social goals is personal investment theory. Personal investment theory assumes that all individuals possess resources such as knowledge, skills, time, and energy. However, individuals differ in terms of where they choose to invest themselves and their resources. The theory is interested in answering the questions, why, when and how do individuals invest time, talent, and energy in a particular activity.

Personal investment theory is multi-faceted and posits that the decision to invest oneself in an activity depends on three key components. The first is *sense of self* (Who am I?)-refers to the more or less organized collections of perceptions, beliefs, and feelings about who one is. The second critical component refer to *facilitating conditions* (What are the available options?) –refers to the social-contextual environment within which a person is situated that makes certain options more available and salient in contrast to other less appealing alternatives. Facilitating conditions include socio-cultural norms, opportunities, and options that an individual perceives in a given situation. The third key component are *perceived goals* (What do I want?) and refers to reasons or purposes for engaging in a task. These goals include mastery, performance, social, and extrinsic goals. We focus only on social goals for the purposes of this chapter.

Personal investment researchers have focused on two types of social goals: social affiliation which pertain to the desire to affiliate and work with others in class and social concern goals which pertain to the desire to help others (King, McInerney, & Watkins, 2012). In general, studies have found these goals to be positively related to a wide range of learning-related outcomes (King & Ganotice, 2014a, 2014b; King, McInerney, & Nasser, 2017)

Motivational systems framework

Ford's Motivational Systems Framework (Ford, 1992; Ford & Nichols, 1991; Ford & Smith, 2007) is another theoretical perspective that includes social goals. It is a broad motivational theory that specifies different types of personal goals that individuals could pursue in life. Ford conceptualized motivation as an emergent phenomenon that depends on the interactions among goals, personal agency beliefs, and emotions. Of particular interest to this paper would be the goals component. Ford proposes six superordinate goal categories that direct human action: (1) integrative social relationship goals, (2) self-assertive social relationship goals, (3) affective goals, (4) cognitive goals, (5) task goals, and (6) subjective organization goals.

The first two goal categories-integrative social relationship and self-assertive social relationship goals – can be defined as social goals and we focus on these two categories. Ford argues that these superordinate goals can be further subdivided into more specific goals. For example, integrative social relationship goals can be further broken down into:

Belongingness goal (wanting to build and maintain friendships, intimacy, and a sense of community)
Social responsibility goal (wanting to keep interpersonal commitments and meeting role obligations)
Equity goal (wanting to promote equality, fairness, and justice)
Resource provision (wanting to give support, assistance, and validation to others)

Self-assertive social relationship goals can also be further classified into the following:

Individuality (wanting to feel unique and different from others)
Self-determination (wanting to experiencing a sense of freedom to make one's choices)
Superiority (wanting to compare favorably to others in terms of status or success)
Resource acquisition (wanting to obtain approval, support, assistance, and advice from others)

Though Ford's Motivational Systems Framework is ambitious in scope, unfortunately very few studies have applied this to the educational psychology context and not enough empirical evidence has accumulated to shed light on how these social goals play out in the school setting.

Self-determination Theory's Mini-theory: Goal Content Theory

Self-determination theory (SDT) is a macro-theory of human motivation that consists of five interlocking mini-theories (Ryan & Deci, 2000). Of particular interest in this review is the goal content mini-theory. Kasser was one of the pioneer SDT researchers who started to focus on life goals or aspirations that people pursue (see Kasser, 2002; Vansteenkiste, Lens, & Deci, 2006) and this work is encapsulated in the goal content mini-theory. SDT researchers have examined the correlates of both intrinsic and extrinsic life goals.

Intrinsic life goals include goals for personal growth, close relationships, community contribution, and physical health. Extrinsic goals include aspirations for money, fame, and image. The intrinsic goals for close relationships and community contribution can also be construed as social goals. Intrinsic goals satisfy basic psychological needs for autonomy, competence, and relatedness and lead to higher levels of psychological adjustment. In contrast, extrinsic goals are unrelated to need satisfaction and can actually detract from its fulfillment (Vansteenkiste, Soenens, & Duriez, 2008). Studies have found that intrinsic goals including the social goals for close relationships and community contribution are associated with better learning outcomes.

Social-academic approach

The social-academic or goal complex approach gained prominence in the literature through the groundbreaking paper of Urdan and Maehr (1995), and developed in response to the need to put social goals on equal conceptual footing with achievement goals which the authors defined as academic reasons for wanting to do well in school. Another impetus for the development of the social-academic goal approach was a perceived shortcoming of the existing goal content approach.

Urdan and Maehr (1995) wrote, "Wentzel, when asking students how often they try to accomplish something without asking them why, may have measured something more than or different from goals. Specifically, she may have included self-regulatory processes and acts of compliance with students' thoughts and desires about outcomes of behavior" (p. 216). Social-academic goal researchers wanted a greater degree of precision in the measurement of social goals.

Urdan and Maehr (1995) argued that achievement goals usually focus on competence-related reasons for pursuing academic tasks. Thus, they claimed that social goals can be defined as social reasons for pursuing academic-related tasks. This approach actually represents a "hybrid of social-academic goals" (Kiefer & Ryan, 2008, p. 417) and focuses on wanting to achieve academically for a variety of social reasons. This approach emphasizes a goal complex wherein the academic goal of doing well in school is undertaken in order to serve higher-order social purposes.

Dowson and McInerney (2001, 2003, 2004) carried out the most extensive work on social-academic goals. Using a blend of quantitative and qualitative approaches, they identified five types of social-academic goals that students typically pursue: *social affiliation* (wanting to achieve in school in order to enhance a sense of belonging, e.g., "I want to do well in school so that I can feel close to my group of friends"), *social approval* (wanting to achieve in school in order to gain the approval of parents and teachers, e.g., "I try to do well at school to please my teachers"), *social concern* (wanting to achieve in school in order to help others, e.g., "I want to do well at school so that I can help other students with their work"), *social responsibility* (wanting to achieve in school in order to follow moral norms, e.g., "I want to do good schoolwork because other people expect it of me"), and *social status* (wanting to achieve in school in order to attain status, e.g., "I want to do well at school so that I can have lots of money later on").

King et al. (2012) investigated the various types of social-academic goals among secondary school students and found that social-academic goals positively predicted behavioral, emotional, and cognitive engagement even after controlling for the effects of mastery and performance goals. In particular, social concern, social responsibility, and social status goals were strong positive predictors of the engagement. Wolters, Denton, York, and Francis (2013) examined social-academic goals among adolescent students and found that social responsibility, social approval, and social affiliation goals were positively correlated with intrinsic motivation, importance of school, and utility value of school.

Social achievement goal approach

The social achievement goal approach pioneered by Ryan and Shim (2006, 2008) is the latest addition to the social goal literature. Researchers using the social achievement goal approach focus on how students define social competence and their standards for achieving their desired level of social competence. Social goals within this tradition are called social achievement goals and three types of goals have been identified: *social development goals* which focus on developing social competence (e.g., "I like it when I learn better ways to get along with friends"), *social demonstration approach goals* which focus on demonstrating social competence and being seen as socially desirable by others (e.g., "It is important to me that other kids think I am popular"), and *social demonstration avoidance goals* which focus on avoiding appearing socially incompetent (e.g., "When I am with other kids I don't want to be made fun of").

Social achievement goal research is heavily indebted to both the goal content literature and the achievement goal literature. A. Ryan, the leading proponent of this approach, started her foray in social goals using the goal content approach (Ryan et al., 1997). Later, she attempted to apply the insights of achievement goal theory to the domain of social competence which led to the development of the social achievement goal construct. Achievement goals have typically been examined in relation to academic competence, and the social achievement goal approach was the first attempt to use the achievement goal model to study social competence representing a novel theoretical development.

Social achievement goal researchers have shown that social development goals are associated with various indices of psychological adjustment and well-being, while social demonstration avoid goals are associated with negative psychological outcomes. For example, Shim and Ryan (2012) found that social development goals positively predicted social competence and prosocial behavior. Social demonstration avoid goals were linked to aggressive, socially anxious, and internalizing behaviors. Social demonstration approach goals showed a mixed profile, exhibiting a positive relationship with both adaptive (e.g., social competence, popularity) and maladaptive outcomes (e.g., aggressive behavior, socially anxious behavior).

Social achievement goals have also been found to be related to students' emotional experiences (Shim, Wang, & Cassady, 2013). Students who pursued social development goals were more likely to experience positive emotions such as love and joy and less likely to experience negative emotions such as fear, anger, shame, and sadness. Conversely, those who pursued social demonstration avoidance goals were more likely to experience negative emotions such as fear, shame, and sadness, and less likely to experience positive emotions such as joy. Social demonstration approach goals was not significantly correlated with most of the emotions measured.

Social development goals have been found to be positively related to social self-efficacy (Shim & Finch, 2013). Social demonstration approach and social demonstration avoidance goals were both strongly correlated with social worry. Aside from social-achievement goal researchers, those who conduct research using the goal content and social-academic goal approaches have also conducted preliminary studies on the relationship between social goals and adjustment outcomes. For example, using the goal content approach, Wentzel et al. (2007) found that a composite score of prosocial and social responsibility goals were positively correlated with empathy and perspective-taking. Prosocial goals were positively correlated with prosocial behavior (Wentzel et al., 2004).

Directions for Future Research

To summarize, there are three distinct research traditions on social goals. From a chronological perspective, the first to gain traction in the literature was the goal content approach which focuses on *what* social outcomes students are trying to pursue. It was followed by the social-academic approach which focuses on *social reasons* for wanting to do well in school. The most recent addition to the social goal literature is the social achievement goal approach which focuses on *social competence* and how students define social competence. The three social goal approaches have rich historical inter-connections. However, they also have fine-grained conceptual distinctions in the way they define social goals as well as the types of social goals they focus on.

Having reviewed the historical origins of social goal research and having mapped out the different social goal traditions in educational psychology, we now have a clearer knowledge base to articulate substantive issues that social goal researchers need to contend with to move the research agenda forward. We proffer nine key questions which may need to be addressed.

How are the different types of social goals related to each other?

The three different social goal traditions in educational psychology define social goals in different ways. For example, the social goals in self-determination theory and the motivational systems framework seem to be more general orientations towards life while the research by Wentzel and social-academic researchers seem to be more specific to the school context. How do these different varieties of social goals relate to each other and more broadly to other competence-related achievement goals?

What are the antecedents of different social goals?

Much of the research on social goals has focused on the effects of social goals on a wide range of academic outcomes. Much less research has focused on the antecedents of social goals. Earlier, we highlighted the possible role of both individual difference variables and social-contextual factors in social goal pursuit. Identifying the antecedents of social goals is an important direction for future research. If researchers could identify the antecedents of social goals, then suitable intervention programs could be created to facilitate the adoption of adaptive types of social goals.

How do social goals change across time?

School motivation has been found to decline for many students as they move from earlier grades to higher grades (Anderman & Maehr 1994; Anderman et al. 1999; Balfanz, Herzog & MacIver 2007). The declining levels of motivation has been attributed by some researchers to the stresses of puberty that adolescent students face as well as to the lack of fit between the psychological needs of adolescents and the affordances of the school environment (e.g. Eccles et al., 1993).

Regardless of what causes the motivational decline, this decline seems to be widespread across cultures (e.g., Wang & Pomerantz, 2009) and has been documented for a wide range of motivational constructs (Dotterer, McHale, & Crouter, 2009; Fredricks & Eccles, 2002; van de gaer, De Fraine, Pustjens, De Munter, & Onghena, 2009). It is possible that certain types of social goals may also decline. Pomerantz, Qin, Wang, and Chen's (2011) study provides indirect evidence for this possibility. They found that adolescent students' sense of responsibility toward their parents declined during the 7th and 8th grades, at least for the American students. Although not directly assessing social goals, the decline in sense of responsibility may also be reflective of a decline in students' pursuit of social responsibility goals in the academic setting. Studies that show increases in delinquent behavior across the adolescent years also seem to provide partial support for the assumption that adaptive types of social goals may decline as students get older (Compas, Hinden, & Gerhardt, 1995).

Not all social goals, however, may decline during adolescence. It is possible that social demonstration approach and social demonstration avoidance goals may increase in salience during the adolescent years given the heightened concern of adolescents towards how their peers view them at this age (LaFontana & Cillessen, 2010). Moreover, these particular social goals may also spike during transitions such as the transition from elementary to middle school or from high school to university given that students must renegotiate their identities when they enter a new context (Bellmore, Villarreal, & Ho, 2011).

Throughout different developmental stages, the meaning of different types of social goals may also vary. For example, in primary school, social responsibility goals may just pertain to following what the teacher says (e.g., not cheating, not talking to one's seatmates, finishing one's homework.). However, when students are in the university, social responsibility may take on a somewhat different meaning (e.g., being a good citizen). Aside from following norms set up by the teacher, it may also involve more abstract moral commitments that could (possibly) transcend or take precedence over the rules that the teacher has set in class. For example, it is possible that a mature adult who holds a social responsibility goal could report a teacher who engages in dishonest behavior (e.g., accepting bribes or ignoring cases of student cheating).

To date, we still lack knowledge about the developmental trends associated with social goals. However, there are compelling theoretical reasons to assume that the developmental trajectories of different types of social goals will vary. Empirical studies are needed to give psychologists a more detailed account of how social goals change across time.

What role does culture play in the development of social goals?

Cultures have been found to influence a wide range of psychological processes. They also exert a large influence on determining which goals are important and which ones are not (Schwartz, 1992). For example, in individualist cultures more independent types of goals such as goals for self-determination and agency are more highly valued. In collectivist cultures, on the other hand, goals for conformity and belongingness may be more salient (Schwartz, 2004).

Given this, it is possible that cultures may also influence the types of social goals that students pursue in school. Cross-cultural psychologists have argued that social goals as a whole may be more salient in collectivist cultures where interdependent self-construals are more prevalent (Cheng & Lam, 2013; King & McInerney, 2014; King et al., 2012). Peoples from collectivist cultures are more likely to incorporate others in their self-schemas which may predispose them to endorse social goals more strongly compared to their counterparts in individualist cultures. However, actual research that compares cultures in terms of endorsement of social goals is still lacking.

It is possible that social goals may have different nomological networks depending on the socio-cultural context. Cheng and Lam's (2013) study presents intriguing evidence that the effects of certain types of social goals may vary depending on the cultural context. For example, they found that social approval goals were not that harmful among collectivists but led to self-handicapping for individualists.

Should social goals be bifurcated into their approach-avoidance dimensions?

Achievement goal theory which focuses on mastery and performance goals has profited much from untangling performance approach from performance avoidance goals (Linnenbrink-Garcia et al., 2012). Later renditions of the theory have also argued for the necessity of bifurcating mastery goals into mastery approach and mastery avoidance goals. Earlier studies which did not make a clear distinction between approach and avoidance mastery and performance goals have led to conceptual confusion and inconsistent findings.

To date, social goal research has not yet fully incorporated approach-avoidance distinctions. Thus far, only studies that use the social achievement goal approach as well as a few other scattered studies have systematically included approach and avoidance dimensions of social goals. The majority of existing social goal studies only focus on approach forms of goals by default (e.g., Dowson & McInerney, 2004; Wentzel, 1994). Other studies have aggregated both approach and avoidance items (e.g., Miller et al., 1996) into an overall scale. Future studies may need to systematically incorporate the approach-avoidance distinction in their research. Given the importance of the approach-avoidance distinction in goal psychology and the larger motivational literature, there are strong theoretical reasons to suggest that bifurcating social goals into their approach and avoidance components would led to substantial theoretical and empirical dividends. However, there is also a need to consider whether approach and avoidance-worded items are actually understood to be such by participants. While researchers typically make the approach-avoidance distinction, participants may not interpret these items in the same way (e.g., Urdan & Mestas, 2006). Thus, in-depth qualitative studies are needed to examine whether participants are able to understand the researchers' intentions.

What happens when there is conflict among multiple social and non-social goals?

Despite the acknowledgment that multiple-goal pursuit is the norm, and not the exception, educational psychologists have rarely examined what happens when multiple goals are in conflict. Research has shown that 47 percent of individuals regularly fail to enact their goals thereby demonstrating the ubiquity of goal conflict (Sheeran, 2002). How will a student decide to allocate his time for example when the social goal of hanging out with friends (social intimacy goal) conflicts with the goal of mastering the material (mastery approach goal)?

Research on motivational conflict in the educational setting has been pioneered by Hofer and his colleagues (Hofer, 2007; Hofer, Kuhnle, Kilian, Marta, & Fries, 2011). They usually focused on situations wherein students are torn between leisure and study. Though they did not frame their research in terms of social goals, the academic-leisure choices could easily be rephrased in goal terminology as a conflict between different types of goals. Future research on social goals should account for how individuals would choose among competing goals and how, and how they allocate their resources as a result of this choice. Applying this to the realm of social goals, researchers can explicitly measure goal conflict by asking participants to rate the relative salience of different goals. Making multiple social (and academic) goals salient at the point of measurement can facilitate a more accurate prediction of what students will actually do. For example, one can envision researchers asking participants to answer how important it was for them to (a) spend time with their peers (social affiliation goal) or (b) to spend time mastering the course materials (mastery approach goal) and examine how individuals will allocate their resources to one or another type of goal.

What levels of analyses should we adopt when doing research on social goals?

It is ironic to see that social goals, despite their social nature are usually measured at the level of an individual. For example, researchers typically ask individuals how much they try to pursue a certain type of social goal. However, it is equally likely that social goals could exist at the group level. In the achievement goal literature, researchers have recognized the utility on focusing on two-levels of analysis – the individual and the class. Students are usually asked to rate their own achievement goal orientations; they are also asked to assess the classroom goal structures which could be seen as achievement goals that operate at the level of the classroom. Bandura's (2001) research on efficacy has similarly profited from adopting a multi-level focus by focusing on one's own sense of agency (i.e., self-efficacy) and the agency of one's group (i.e., collective self-efficacy).

In a similar manner, perhaps one can study social goals both at the individual level and at the level of groups. This group level social goal could be measured by directly asking students about the perceived social goals of their group. A possible sample item would be, "Students in our group try to share information with each other" (prosocial goals at the group level). Another alternative for measuring group-level social goals would be to aggregate the individual-level social goals of students who are part of a certain group. Group-level social goals may lead to a distinct set of group outcomes and are empirically distinct from social goals measured at the individual level. Imagine, for example, two groups who are working on a collaborative learning task. Group A may have a higher overall level of prosocial goals compared to Group B. This might lead to higher levels of team performance, interpersonal trust, and satisfaction with the collaborative learning in Group A. The overall prosocial goal of the group is empirically distinct from the social goals situated at the individual level. To date, we know of no existing study that has actually measured social goals at the group level.

Can we design intervention programs to develop adaptive types of social goals?

None of the major researchers from the three social goal traditions have used interventionist methods to change students' social goals. This is lamentable given that social goals have crucial impact on several key learning and well-being outcomes. Social goals may be perceived as un-modifiable. However, correlational studies have shown that they are strongly related to the social context (King & Ganotice, 2014a; Spera & Wentzel, 2003). Thus changing aspects of the social context may lead to subsequent changes in social goals. Moreover, brief experimental procedures have also been shown to be successful in modifying students' social goal pursuit (Cheng & Lam, 2013). Taken together, these provide strong evidence for the malleability of social goals which leads to the

What other outcomes can social goals account for?

We believe social goal research could become most useful if it can present a set of unique processes and outcomes most (or more) reliably explained or predicted by social (than academic) goals. Introducing such process and outcomes will help establish social goals as independent predictors in their own right, rather than subsidiary predictors to academic goals of important student outcomes. In the section on the antecedents and consequences of social goals, we elaborated on the academic and non-academic outcomes that researchers have examined in relation to social goals. However, there are many other types of outcomes that could be investigated. Psychological adjustment, nature of peer relations, task-related interaction, and school affect, for example, are good candidates given their close association with interpersonal relationships.

Conclusion

Social goal research is still in its nascence compared to the more well-developed literature on achievement goals and other competence/task-related constructs. Examining social goals is crucial given that humans are social beings and school is an inherently social setting. Social goals are an important part of students' lives and educational psychologists should turn their attention to this powerful yet neglected construct. However, research on social goals is fractionated and would benefit from some form of theoretical integration. In this chapter, we attempted to give some order to the fragmented social goal literature by tracing the historical origins and mapping out the different research traditions on social goals. We proffered some recommendations and directions for future research that could move social goal theorizing forward.

Note

1 Self-determination theory's goal content perspective pioneered by Tim Kasser and Martin Ford's Motivational Systems Framework are rooted in a different theoretical tradition from achievement goal research.

References

Anderman, E. M. (2011). Educational psychology in the twenty-first century: Challenges for our community. *Educational Psychologist, 46*, 185–196.

Anderman, L. H. (1999). Classroom goal orientation, school belonging and social goals as predictors of students' positive and negative affect following the transition to middle school. *Journal of Research and Development in Education, 32*, 89–103.

Anderman, L. H., & Anderman, E. M. (1999). Social predictors of changes in students' achievement goal orientations. *Contemporary Educational Psychology, 24*, 21–37.

Anderman, E. M., & Maehr, M. L. (1994). Motivation and schooling in the middle grades. *Review of Educational Research, 64*, 287–309.

Anderman, E. M., Maehr, M. L., & Midgley, C. (1999). Declining motivation after the transition to middle school: Schools can make a difference. *Journal of Research and Development in Education, 32*, 131–147.

Atkinson, J. W. (1957). Motivational determinants of risk taking behavior. *Psychological Review, 64*, 359–372.

Austin, J. T., & Vancouver, J. B. (1996). Goal constructs in psychology: Structure, process, and content. *Psychological Bulletin, 120*, 338–375.

Bailey, K. D. (1994). *Typologies and taxonomies: An introduction to classification techniques.* Newbury Park, CA: Sage.

Balfanz, R., Herzog, L., & MacIver, D. J. (2007). Preventing student disengagement and keeping students on the graduation path in urban middle-grades schools: Early identification and effective interventions. *Educational Psychologist, 42*(4), 223–235.

Bandura, A. (2001). Social cognitive theory: An agentic perspective. *Annual Review of Psychology, 52*, 1–26.

Baumeister, R. F., & Leary, M. R. (1995). The need to belong: Desire for interpersonal attachments as a fundamental human motivation. *Psychological Bulletin, 117*, 497–529.

Bellmore, A., Villarreal, V. M., & Ho, A. Y. (2011). Staying cool across the first year of middle school. *Journal of Youth and Adolescence, 40*, 776–785.

Bernardo, A. B. I. (2008). Individual and social dimensions of Filipino students' achievement goals. *International Journal of Psychology, 43*(5), 886–891.

Berndt, T. J. (1999). Friends' influence on students' adjustment to school. *Educational Psychologist, 34*, 15–28.

Bipp, T., Steinmayr, R., & Spinath, B. (2008). Personality and achievement motivation: Relationship among Big Five domain and facet scales, achievement goals, and intelligence. *Personality and Individual Differences, 44*, 1454–1464.

Bobko, P., & Russell, C. (1991). A review of the role of taxonomies in human resource management. *Human Resource Management Review, 1*, 293–316.

Boekaerts, M. (2009). Goal directed behavior in the classroom. In K. Wentzel & A. Wigfield (Eds.), *Handbook on motivation at school* (pp. 105–122). New York andLondon: Routeledge.

Boekaerts, M., de Koning, E., & Vedder, P. (2006). Goal-directed behaviour and contextual factors in the classroom: An innovative approach to the study of multiple goals. *Educational Psychologist, 41*, 33–51.

Boekaerts, M., Smit, K., & Busing, F. (2012). Salient goals direct and energise students' actions in the classroom. *Applied Psychology*, 61, 520–530.

Boon, H. J. (2007). Low- and high-achieving Australian secondary school students: Their parenting, motivation, and academic achievement. *Australian Psychologist*, 42, 212–225.

Brechwald, W. A., & Prinstein, M. J. (2011). Beyond homophily: A decade of advances in understanding peer influence processes. *Journal of Research in Adolescence*, 21, 166–179.

Bruner, J. (1990). *Acts of meaning*. Cambridge, MA: Harvard University Press.

Cattell, R. B. (1957). *Personality and motivation structure and measurement*. New York: World Press.

Chan, D. W. (2008). Goal orientations and achievement among Chinese gifted students in Hong Kong. *High Ability Studies*, 19(1), 37–51.

Chang, W. C., & Wong, K. (2008). Socially oriented achievement goals of Chinese university students in Singapore: Structure and relationships with achievement motives, goals and affective outcomes. *International Journal of Psychology*, 43(5), 880–885.

Chen, C., & Zhang, L. (2011). Temperament, personality and achievement goals among Chinese adolescent students. *Educational Psychology*, 31(3), 339–359.

Cheng, R. W.-Y., & Lam, S.-F. (2013). The interaction between social goals and self-construal on achievement motivation. *Contemporary Educational Psychology*, 38, 136–148.

Coleman, J. S. (1961). *The adolescent society*. New York: Free Press.

Compas, B. E., Hinden, B. R., & Gerhardt, C. A. (1995). Adolescent development: Pathways and processes of risk and resilience. *Annual Review of Psychology*, 46, 265–293.

Corker, K. S., Oswald, F. L., & Donnellan, M. B. (2012). Conscientiousness in the classroom: A process explanation. *Journal of Personality*, 80, 995–1028.

Costa, P. T., & McCrae, R. R. (1992). Normal personality assessment in clinical practice: The NEO Personality Inventory. *Psychological Assessment*, 4, 5–13.

Day, E., Radosevich, D. J., & Chasteen, C. S. (2003). Construct- and criterion-related validity of four commonly used goal orientation instruments. *Contemporary Educational Psychology*, 28(4), 434–464.

Debacker, T. K., & Nelson, R. M. (2008). Achievement motivation in adolescents: The role of peer climate and best friends. *The Journal of Experimental Education*, 76, 170–189.

DeShon, R. P., & Gillespie, J. Z. (2005). A motivated action theory account of goal orientation. *Journal of Applied Psychology*, 90, 1096–1127.

Dotterer, A. M., McHale, S. M., & Crouter, A. C. (2009). The development and correlates of academic interests from childhood through adolescence. *Journal of Educational Psychology*, 101, 509–519.

Dowson, M., McInerney, D. M. (2001). Psychological parameters of students' social and work avoidance: A qualitative investigation. *Journal of Educational Psychology*, 93, 35–42.

Dowson, M., & McInerney, D. M. (2003). What do students say about their motivational goals? Towards a more complex and dynamic perspective on student motivation. *Contemporary Educational Psychology*, 28, 91–113.

Dowson, M., & McInerney, D. M. (2004). The development and validation of the Goal Orientation and Learning Strategies Survey (GOALS-S). *Educational and Psychological Measurement*, 64(2), 290–310.

Eccles, J. S., Midgley, C., Wigfield, A., Buchanan, C. M., Reuman, D., Flanagan, C., & MacIver, D. (1993). Development during adolescence: The impact of stage-environment fit on young adolescents' experiences in schools and in families. *American Psychologist*, 48, 90–101.

Elliot, A. J. (1999). Approach and avoidance motivation and achievement goals. *Educational Psychologist*, 34, 169–189.

Elliot, A. J., Gable, S. L., & Mapes, R. R. (2006). Approach and avoidance motivation in the social domain. *Personality and Social Psychology Bulletin*, 32(3), 378–391.

Elliot, A. J., & Thrash, T. M. (2002). Approach-avoidance motivation in personality: Approach and avoidance temperaments and goals. *Journal of Personality and Social Psychology*, 82, 804–818.

Fleisher, M. S., Edwards, B. D., Woehr, D. J., & Cullen, K. L. (2011). Further evidence of the efficacy of frequency-based personality measurement. *Journal of Research in Personality*, 45, 535–548.

Ford, M. E. (1992). *Motivating humans*. Newbury Park, CA: Sage.

Ford, M. E., & Nichols, C. W. (1991). Using goal assessments to identify motivational patterns and facilitate behavioral regulation. In M. Maehr & P. Pintrich (Eds.), *Advances in motivation and achievement, Vol. 7: Goals and self-regulatory processes* (pp. 57–84). Greenwich, CT: JAI Press.

Ford, M. E., & Smith, P. R. (2007). Thriving with social purpose: An integrative approach to the development of human functioning. *Educational Psychologist*, 42, 153–171.

Fredricks, J. A., & Eccles, J. S. (2002). Children's competence and value beliefs from childhood through adolescence: Growth trajectories in two male-sex-typed domains. *Developmental Psychology*, 38(4), 519–533.

Friis, R. H., & Knox, A. B. (1972). A validity study of scales to measure need achievement, need affiliation, impulsiveness, and intellectuality. *Educational and Psychological Measurement*, 32, 147–154.

Gable, S. L. (2006). Approach and avoidance social motives and goals. *Journal of Personality*, 74, 175–222.

Giota, J. (2010). Multidimensional and hierarchical assessment of adolescents' motivation in school. *Scandinavian Journal of Educational Research*, 54(1), 83–97.

Gonzalez, A. L., & Wolters, C. A. (2006). The relation between perceived parenting practices and achievement motivation in mathematics. *Journal of Research in Childhood Education*, 21, 203–217.

Goodenow, C., & Grady, K. E. (1993). The relationship of school belonging and friends' values to academic motivation among urban adolescent students. *The Journal of Experimental Education*, 62, 60–71.

Gordon, M. S., & Cui, M. (2012). The effect of school-specific parenting processes on academic achievement in adolescence and young adulthood. *Family Relations*, 61, 728–741.

Gottfried, A. E., Fleming, J. S., & Gottfried, A. W. (2001). Continuity of academic intrinsic motivation from childhood through late adolescence: A longitudinal study. *Journal of Educational Psychology*, 93, 3–13.

Grouzet, F. M. E., Kasser, T., Ahuvia, A., Dols, J. M. F., Kim, Y., Lau, S., Ryan, R. M., Saunders, S., Schmuck, P., & Sheldon, K. M. (2005). The structure of goal contents across 15 cultures. *Journal of Personality and Social Psychology*, 89, 800–816.

Harackiewicz, J. M., Barron, K. E., Carter, S. M., Lehto, A. T., & Elliot, A. J. (1997). Predictors and consequences of achievement goals in the college classroom: Maintaining interest and making the grade. *Journal of Personality and Social Psychology*, 73, 1284–1295.

Hergovich, A., Sirsch, U., & Felinger, M. (2002). Self-appraisals, actual appraisals, and reflected appraisals of preadolescent children. *Social Behavior and Personality*, 30, 603–611.

Hijzen, D., Boekaerts, M., & Vedder, P. (2006). The relationship between the quality of cooperative learning, students' goal preferences, and perceptions of contextual factors in the classroom. *Scandinavian Journal of Psychology*, 47(1), 9–21.

Hofer, M. (2007). Goal conflicts and self-regulation: A new look at pupils' off-task behaviour in the classroom. *Educational Research Review*, 2, 28–38.

Hofer, M. (2010). Adolescents' development of individual interests: A product of multiple goal regulation. *Educational Psychologist*, 45, 149–166.

Hofer, M., Kuhnle, C., Kilian, B., Marta, E., & Fries, S. (2011). Motivational interference in school-leisure conflict and learning outcomes: The differential effects of two value conceptions. *Learning and Instruction*, 21(3), 301–316.

Huang, C. (2012). Discriminant and criterion-related validity of achievement goals in predicting academic achievement: A meta-analysis. *Journal of Educational Psychology*, 104, 48–73.

Hulleman, C. S., Schrager, S. M., Bodmann, S. M., & Harackiewicz, J. M. (2010). A meta-analytic review of achievement goal measures: Different labels for the same constructs or different constructs with similar labels? *Psychological Bulletin*, 136, 422–449.

Hustinx, P. W. J., Kuyper, H., van der Werf, M. P. C., & Dijkstra, P. (2009). Achievement motivation revisited: New longitudinal data to demonstrate its predictive power. *Educational Psychology*, 29(5), 561–582.

Jackson, S. E. (1981). Measurement of commitment to role identities. *Journal of Personality and Social Psychology*, 40, 138–146.

Jacobs, J. E., Lanza, S., Osgood, D. W., Eccles, J. S., & Wigfield, A. (2002). Changes in children's self-competence and values: Gender and domain differences across grades one through twelve. *Child Development*, 73(2), 509–527.

Jarvinen, D. W., & Nicholls, J. G. (1996). Adolescents' social goals, beliefs about the causes of social success, and satisfaction in peer relations. *Developmental Psychology*, 32, 435–441.

Jeanne Horst, S., Finney, S. J., & Barron, K. E. (2007). Moving beyond academic achievement goal measures: A study of social achievement goals. *Contemporary Educational Psychology*, 32, 667–698.

Johnson, D. W., & Johnson, R. T. (2009). An educational psychology success story: Social interdependence theory and cooperative learning. *Educational Researcher*, 38, 365–379

Kasser, T. (2002). Sketches for a self-determination theory of values. In E.L. Deci and R. M. Ryan (Eds), *Handbook of self-determination research* (pp. 123–140). Rochester, NY: University of Rochester Press.

Kasser, T., & Ryan, R. M. (1996). Further examining the American dream: Differential correlates of intrinsic and extrinsic goals. *Personality and Social Psychology Bulletin*, 22, 281–288.

Kasser, T., & Ryan, R. M. (2001). Be careful what you wish for: Optimal functioning and the relative attainment of intrinsic and extrinsic goals. In P. Schmuck, & K. M. Sheldon (Eds.), *Life goals and well-being: Towards a positive psychology of human striving* (pp. 116–131). Ashland, OH: Hogrefe and Huber.

Kiefer, S. M., & Ryan, A. M. (2008). Striving for social dominance over peers: The implications for academic adjustment during early adolescence. *Journal of Educational Psychology*, 100(2), 417–428.

King, R. B., & Ganotice, F. A. (2014a). The social underpinnings of motivation and achievement: Investigating the role of parents, teachers, and peers on academic outcomes. *The Asia-Pacific Education Researcher*, 23, 745–756.

King, R. B., & Ganotice, F. A. (2014b). What's happening to our boys: A personal investment analysis of gender differences in student motivation. *The Asia-Pacific Education Researcher*, 23, 151–157.

King, R. B., Ganotice, F. A., & Watkins, D. A. (2012). Cross-cultural validation of the Inventory of School Motivation (ISM) in the Asian setting: Hong Kong and the Philippines. *Child Indicators Research*, 5(1), 135–153.

King, R. B., Ganotice, F. A., & Watkins, D. A. (2014). A cross-cultural analysis of achievement and social goals among Chinese and Filipino students. *Social Psychology of Education*, 17(3), 439–455.

King, R. B., & McInerney, D. M. (2014). Culture's consequences on student motivation: Capturing universality and variability through personal investment theory. *Educational Psychologist*, 49, 175–198.

King, R. B., & McInerney, D. M. (2019). Family-support goals drive engagement and achievement in a collectivist context: Integrating etic and emic approaches in goal research. *Contemporary Educational Psychology*, 58, 338–353.

King, R. B., McInerney, D. M., & Nasser, R. (2017). Different goals for different folks: A cross-cultural study of achievement goals across nine cultures. *Social Psychology of Education*, 20, 619–642.

King, R. B., McInerney, D. M., & Watkins, D. A. (2010). Can social goals enrich our understanding of students' motivational goals? *Journal of Psychology in Chinese Societies*, 10, 1–16.

King, R. B., McInerney, D. M., & Watkins, D. A. (2012). Studying for the sake of others: The role of social goals on academic engagement. *Educational Psychology*, 32(6), 749–776.

King, R. B., McInerney, D. M., & Watkins, D. A. (2013). Examining the role of social goals in school: A study in two collectivist cultures. *European Journal of Psychology of Education*, 28, 1505–1523.

Kirschner, P. A. (2001). Using integrated electronic environments for collaborative teaching/learning. *Research Dialogue in Learning and Instruction*, 2, 1–10.

Kordik, A., Eska, K., & Schultheiss, O. C. (2012). Implicit need for affiliation is associated with increased corrugator activity in a non-positive, but not in a positive social interaction. *Journal of Research in Personality*, 46, 604–608.

Kuroda, Y., & Sakurai, S. (2011). Social goal orientations, interpersonal stress, and depressive symptoms among early adolescents in Japan: A test of the diathesis-stress model using the trichotomous framework of social goal orientations. *The Journal of Early Adolescence*, 31(2), 300–322.

LaFontana, K. M., & Cillessen, A. H. N. (2010). Developmental changes in the priority of perceived status in childhood and adolescence. *Social Development*, 19, 130–147.

Lee, J. Q., McInerney, D. M., Liem, G. A. D., & Ortiga, Y. P. (2010). The relationship between future goals and achievement goal orientations: An intrinsic-extrinsic motivation perspective. *Contemporary Educational Psychology*, 35(4), 264–279.

Lemos, M. S. (1996). Students' and teachers' goals in the classroom. *Learning and Instruction*, 6, 151–171.

Leondari, A., & Gonida, E. (2007). Predicting academic self-handicapping in different age groups: The role of personal achievement goals and social goals. *British Journal of Educational Psychology*, 77(3), 595–611.

Liem, G. A. D., Lau, S., & Nie, Y. (2008). The role of self-efficacy, task value, and achievement goals in predicting learning strategies, task disengagement, peer relationship, and achievement outcome. *Contemporary Educational Psychology*, 33, 486–512.

Liem, G. A. D., Martin, A. J., Porter, A. L., & Colmar, S. (2011). Sociocultural antecedents of academic motivation and achievement: Role of values and achievement motives in achievement goals and academic performance. *Asian Journal of Social Psychology*, 15(1), 1–13.

Linnenbrink-Garcia, E., Middleton, M. J., Ciani, K. D., Easter, M. A., O'Keef, P. A., & Zusho, A. (2012). The strength of the relation between performance-approach and performance-avoidance goal orientations: Theoretical, methodological, and instructional implications. *Educational Psychologist*, 47, 281–301.

Madill, R. A., Gest, S. D., & Rodkin, P. C. (2014). Students' perceptions of relatedness in the classroom: The roles of emotionally supportive teacher-child interactions, children's aggressive-disruptive behaviors, and peer social preference. *School Psychology Review*, 43(1), 86–105.

Magnusson, D. (2003). The person approach: Concepts, measurement models, and research strategy. In S. C. Peck & R. W. Roeser (Eds.), *New directions for child and adolescent development: Person-centered approaches to studying development in context* (No. 101, pp. 3–23). San Francisco: Jossey-Bass.

Maehr, M., & Nicholls, J. (1980). *Culture and achievement motivation: A second look*. In N. Warren (Ed.), *Studies in cross-cultural psychology* (Vol.2, pp. 221–267). New York: Academic Press.

Martin, A. (2003). Boys and motivation: Contrasts and comparisons with girls' approaches to schoolwork. *Australian Educational Researcher, 30*, 43–65.

Martin, A. J. (2004). School motivation of boys and girls: Differences of degree, differences of kind, or both? *Australian Journal of Psychology*, 56, 133–146.

McCabe, K. O., van Yperen, N. W., Elliot, A. J., & Verbraak, M. (2013). Big Five personality profiles of context-specific achievement goals. *Journal of Research in Personality*, 47, 698–707.

McClelland, D. C. (1973). Sources of n achievement. In D. C. McClelland & R. Steele (Eds.), *Human motivation: A book of readings* (pp. 252–276). Morristown, NJ: General Learning Press.

McClelland, D. C. (1987). *Human motivation*. Cambridge: Cambridge University Press.

McCrae, R. R., & Costa, P. T. (1997). Personality trait structure as a human universal. *American Psychologist*, 52, 509–516.

McCrae, R. R., & John, O. P. (1992). An introduction to the five-factor model and its applications. *Journal of Personality*, 60, 175–215.

McInerney, D. M. (2008). Personal investment, culture and learning: Insights into school achievement across Anglo, Aboriginal, Asian and Lebanese students in Australia. *International Journal of Psychology*, 43(5), 870–879.

McInerney, D. M., & Ali, J. (2006). Multidimensional and hierarchical assessment of school motivation: Cross-cultural validation. *Educational Psychology*, 26(6), 717–734.

McInerney, D. M., & Liem, G. A. D. (2009). Achievement motivation in cross-cultural context: Application of personal investment theory in educational settings. In A. Kaplan, S. A. Karabenick, & E. V. De Groot (Eds.), *Culture, self and motivation: Essays in honor of Martin L. Maehr* (pp. 213–241). Charlotte, NC: Information Age Publishing.

Mcinerney, D. M., & Sinclair, K. E. (1991). Cross cultural model testing: Inventory of school motivation. *Educational and Psychological Measurement*, 51(1), 123–133.

McInerney, D. M., Roche, L., McInerney, V., & Marsh, H. W. (1997). Cultural perspectives on school motivation: The relevance and application of goal theory. *American Educational Research Journal*, 34(1), 207–236.

Meece, J. L., & Miller, S. D. (1999). Changes in elementary school children's achievement goals for reading and writing: Results of a longitudinal and an intervention study. *Scientific Studies of Reading*, 3, 207–229.

Miller, R. B., Greene, B. A., Montalvo, G. P., Ravindran, B., & Nichols, J. D. (1996). Engagement in academic work: The role of learning goals, future consequences, pleasing others, and perceived ability. *Contemporary Educational Psychology*, 21, 388–422.

Mouratidis, A., & Michou, A. (2010). Self-determined motivation and social achievement goals in children's emotions. *Educational Psychology*, 31(1), 67–86.

Mouratidis, A. A., & Sideridis, G. D. (2009). On social achievement goals: Their relations with peer acceptance, classroom belongingness, and perceptions of loneliness. *The Journal of Experimental Education*, 77(3), 285–307.

Murphy, P. K., & Alexander, P. A. (2000). A motivated exploration of motivation terminology. *Contemporary Educational Psychology*, 25, 3–53.

Murray, H. A. (1938). *Explorations in personality*. New York: Oxford University Press.

Nicholls, J. G., & Dweck, C. S. (1979). A definition of achievement motivation. Unpublished manuscript, University of Illinois.

Ouano, J. A., & Pinugu, J. N. (2012). Social goals of Filipino adolescents: Do they contribute to student life satisfaction? *International Journal of Research Studies in Psychology*, 1(3), 43–51.

Pajares, F., & Graham, L. (1999). Self-efficacy, motivation constructs, and mathematics performance of entering middle school students. *Contemporary Educational Psychology*, 24, 124–139.

Patrick, H., Hicks, L., & Ryan, A. M. (1997). Relations of perceived social efficacy and social goal pursuit to self-efficacy for academic work. *The Journal of Early Adolescence*, 17(2), 109–128.

Payne, S. C., Youngcourt, S. S., & Beaubien, J. M. (2007). A meta-analytic examination of the goal orientation nomologicalnet. *Journal of Applied Psychology*, 92, 128–150.

Pintrich, P. R. (1994). Continuities and discontinuities: Future directions for research in educational psychology. *Educational Psychologist*, 29, 137–148.

Pomerantz, E. M., Qin, L., Wang, Q., & Chen, H. (2011). Changes in early adolescents' sense of responsibility to their parents in the United States and China: Implications for academic functioning. *Child Development*, 82, 1136–1151.

Rawsthorne, L. J., & Elliot, A. J. (1999). Achievement goals and intrinsic motivation: A meta-analytic review. *Personality and Social Psychology Review*, 3, 326–344.

Reeve, J. (2009). Why teachers adopt a controlling motivating style toward students and how they can become more autonomy supportive. *Educational Psychologist*, 44, 159–178.

Rodkin, P. C., Ryan, A. M., Jamison, R., & Wilson, T. (2013). Social goals, social behavior, and social status in middle childhood. *Developmental Psychology*, 49(6), 1139–1150.

Rose, A. J., & Rudolph, K. D. (2006). A review of sex differences in peer relationship processes: Potential trade-offs for the emotional and behavioural development of girls and boys. *Psychological Bulletin*, 132, 98–131.

Roussel, P., Elliot, A. J., & Feltman, R. (2011). The influence of achievement goals and social goals on help-seeking from peers in an academic context. *Learning and Instruction*, 21(3), 394–402.

Rudolph, K. D., Abaied, J. L., Flynn, M., Sugimura, N., & Agoston, A. M. (2011). Developing relationships, being cool, and not looking like a loser: Social goal orientation predicts children's responses to peer aggression. *Child Development*, 82(5), 1518–1530.

Ryan, R. M., & Deci, E. L. (2000). Self-determination theory and the facilitation of intrinsic motivation, social development, and well-being. *American Psychologist*, 55, 68–78.

Ryan, A. M. (2001). The peer group as a context for the development of young adolescent motivation and achievement. *Child Development*, 72, 1135–1150.

Ryan, A. M., Hicks, L., & Midgley, C. (1997). Social goals, academic goals, and avoiding seeking help in the classroom. *Journal of Early Adolescence*, 17(2), 152–171.

Ryan, A. M., & Shim, S. S. (2006). Social achievement goals: The nature and consequences of different orientations toward social competence. *Personality and Social Psychology Bulletin*, 32(9), 1246–1263.

Ryan, A. M., & Shim, S. S. (2008). An exploration of young adolescents' social achievement goals and social adjustment in middle school. *Journal of Educational Psychology*, 100(3), 672–687.

Schneider, F. W., & Green, J. E. (1977). Need for affiliation and sex as moderators of the relationship between need for achievement and academic performance. *Journal of School Psychology*, 15, 269–277.

Schultheiss, O. C. (2008). Implicit motives. In O. P. John, R. W. Robins, & L. A. Pervin (Eds.), *Handbook of personality: Theory and research* (3rd ed., pp. 603–633). New York: Guilford.

Schwartz, S. H. (1992). Universals in the content and structure of values: Theoretical advances and empirical tests in 20 countries. In M. Zanna (Ed.), *Advances in experimental social psychology* (Vol. 25, pp. 1–65). New York: Academic Press.

Schwartz, S. H. (1999). A theory of cultural values and some implications for work. *Applied Psychology*, 48, 23–47.

Schwartz, S. H. (2004). Mapping and interpreting cultural differences around the world. In H. Vinken, J. Soeters, & P. Ester (Eds.), *Comparing cultures: Dimensions of culture in a comparative perspective* (pp. 43–73). Leiden: Brill.

Sheldon, K. M., Ryan, R. M., Deci, E. L., & Kasser, T. (2004). The independent effects of goal contents and motives on well-being: It's both what you pursue and why you pursue it. *Personality and Social Psychology Bulletin*, 30, 475–486.

Sheeran, P. (2002). Intention–behavior relations: A conceptual and empirical review. *European Review of Social Psychology*, 12, 1–36.

Shim, S. S., Cho, Y., & Wang, C. (2013). Classroom goal structures, social achievement goals, and adjustment in middle school. *Learning and Instruction*, 23(0), 69–77.

Shim, S. S., & Finch, W. H. (2013). Academic and social achievement goals and early adolescents' adjustment: A latent class approach. *Learning and Individual Differences*.

Shim, S. S., & Fletcher, K. L. (2012). Perfectionism and social goals: What do perfectionists want to achieve in social situations? *Personality and Individual Differences*, 52(8), 919–924.

Shim, H., & Ryan, A. (2012). How do young adolescents cope with social problems? An examination of social Goals, coping with friends, and social adjustment. *Journal of Early Adolescence*, 32(6), 851–875.

Shim, S. S., Ryan, A. M., & Anderson, C. J. (2008). Achievement goals and achievement during early adolescence: Examining time-varying predictor and outcome variables in growth-curve analysis. *Journal of Educational Psychology*, 100, 655–671.

Shim, S. S., Wang, C., & Cassady, J. C. (2013). Emotional well-being: The role of social achievement goals and self-esteem. *Personality and Individual Differences*, 55(7), 840–845.

Spera, C., & Wentzel, K. R. (2003). Congruence between students' and teachers' goals: Implications for social and academic motivation. *International Journal of Educational Research*, 39(4–5), 395–413.

Steinberg, L., Dornbusch, S. M., & Brown, B. B. (1992). Ethnic differences in adolescent achievement: An ecological perspective. *American Psychologist*, 47, 723–729.

Tao, V. Y. K., & Hong, Y.-Y. (2013). When academic achievement is an obligation: Perspectives from social-oriented achievement motivation. *Journal of Cross-Cultural Psychology*, 45(1), 110–136.

Tian, L., Liu, B., Huang, S., & Huebner, E. S. (2013). Perceived social support and school well-being among Chinese early and middle adolescents: The mediational role of self-esteem. *Social Indicators Research*, 113, 991–1008.

Tuominen-Soini, H., Salmela-Aro, K., & Niemivirta, M. (2008). Achievement goal orientations and subjective well-being: A person-centered analysis. *Learning and Instruction*, 18, 251–266.

Urdan, T. C., & Maehr, M. L. (1995). Beyond a two-goal theory of motivation and achievement: A case for social goals. *Review of Educational Research*, 65, 213–243.

Urdan, T., & Mestas, M. (2006). The goals behind performance goals. *Journal of Educational Psychology*, 98, 354–365.

Usher, E., & Pajares, F. (2008). Sources of self-efficacy in school: Critical review of the literature and future directions. *Review of Educational Research*, 78, 751–796.

van de gaer, E., De Fraine, B., Pustjens, H., Van Damme, J., De Munter, A., & Onghena, P. (2009). School effects on the development of motivation toward learning tasks and the development of academic self-concept in secondary education: A multivariate latent growth curve approach. *School Effectiveness and School Improvement*, 20, 235–253.

van de Vijver, F., & Leung, K. (1997). *Methods and data analysis for cross-cultural research*. Thousand Oaks, CA: Sage.

Vansteenkiste, M., Lens, W., & Deci, E. L. (2006). Intrinsic versus extrinsic goal-contents in self-determination theory: Another look at the quality of academic motivation. *Educational Psychologist*, 41, 19–31.

Vansteenkiste, M., Soenens, B., & Duriez, B. (2008). Presenting a positive alternative to materialistic strivings and the thin-ideal: Understanding the effects of extrinsic relative to intrinsic goal pursuits. In S. J. Lopez, (Ed.) (Vol.4, pp. 57–86). *Positive psychology: Exploring the best in people*. Westport, CT: Greenwood Publishing Company.

Walker, C. O., Winn, T. D., & Lutjens, R. M. (2012). Examining relationships between academic and social achievement goals and routes to happiness. *Education Research International. Article ID 643438, 7 pages. , 2012(2012)*.

Wang, Q., & Pomerantz, E. M. (2009). The motivational landscape of early adolescence in the United States and China: A longitudinal investigation. *Child Development*, 80, 1272–1287.

Watkins, D. A., McInerney, D. M., & Lee, C. (2002). Assessing the school motivation of Hong Kong students. *Psychologia*, 45, 144–154.

Wentzel, K. R. (1989). Adolescent classroom goals, standards for performance, and academic achievement: An interactionist perspective. *Journal of Educational Psychology*, 81, 131–142.

Wentzel, K. R. (1991). Relations between social competence and academic achievement in early adolescence. *Child Development*, 62(5), 1066–1078.

Wentzel, K. R. (1991a). Social and academic goals at school: Achievement motivation in context.In M. Maehr, & P. Pintrich (Eds.), *Advances in motivation and achievement* (vol. 7, pp. 185–212). Greenwich, CT: JAI.

Wentzel, K. R. (1994). Relations of social goal pursuit to social acceptance, Classroom behavior, and perceived social support. *Journal of Educational Psychology*, 86, 173–182.

Wentzel, K. R. (1996). Social and academic motivation in middle school: Concurrent and long-term relations to academic effort. *The Journal of Early Adolescence*, 16, 390–406.

Wentzel, K. R. (1997). Student motivation in middle school: The role of perceived pedagogical caring. *Journal of Educational Psychology*, 89, 411–419.

Wentzel, K. R. (1998). Social relationships and motivation in middle school: The role of parents, teachers, and peers. *Journal of Educational Psychology*, 90, 202–209.

Wentzel, K. R. (2000). What is it that I'm trying to achieve? Classroom goals from a content perspective. *Contemporary Educational Psychology*, 25, 105–115.

Wentzel, K. R. (2002). Are effective teachers like good parents? Teaching styles and student adjustment in early adolescence. *Child Development*, 73(1), 287–301.

Wentzel, K. R. (2003). Sociometric status and adjustment in middle school: A longitudinal study. *The Journal of Early Adolescence*, 23, 5–28.

Wentzel, K. R., Barry, C. M., & Caldwell, K. A. (2004). Friendships in middle school: Influences on motivation and school adjustment. *Journal of Educational Psychology, 96,* 195–203.

Wentzel, K. R., Battle, A., Russell, S. L., & Looney, L. B. (2010). Social supports from teachers and peers as predictors of academic and social motivation. *Contemporary Educational Psychology, 35,* 193–212.

Wentzel, K. R., Filisetti, L., & Looney, L. (2007). Adolescent prosocial behavior: The role of self-processes and contextual cues. *Child Development, 78,* 895–910.

Winell, M. (1987). Personal goals: The key to self-direction in adulthood. In M. E. Ford & D. H. Ford (Eds.), *Humans as self-constructing living systems: Putting the framework to work* (pp. 261–287). Hillsdale, NJ: Erlbaum.

Wirthwein, L., Sparfeldt, J. R., Pinquart, M., Wegerer, J., & Steinmayr, R. (2013). Achievement goals and academic achievement: A closer look at moderating factors. *Educational Research Review, 10,* 66–89.

Woodworth, R. S. (1918). *Dynamic psychology.* New York: Columbia.

Wolters, C., Denton, C., York, M., & Francis, D. (2013). Adolescents' motivation for reading: Group differences and relation to standardized achievement. *Reading and Writing,* 1–31.

Yablon, Y. B. (2012). Social goals and willingness to seek help for school violence. *International Journal of Educational Research, 53,* 192–200.

Zweig, D., & Webster, J. (2004). Validation of a multidimensional measure of goal orientation. *Canadian Journal of Behavioural Science/Revue Canadienne Des Sciences Du Comportement, 36,* 232–248.

PART II
Social Goals

PART II

Social Goals

3

ACADEMIC OR SOCIAL FOCUS TOWARD SCHOOL

Martin H. Jones, Alexandra Tonigan and Gülay Güler

Recent reports in both the popular media and academic journals signify increased interest in the effects of students' focusing on the social aspects of schooling instead of focusing on academic pursuits (Chow, 2013; Kuchment, 2013; Wang, Eccles, & Kenny, 2013a; Wang, Eccles, & Kenny, 2013b). These reports build upon the extant literature suggesting that social interactions inside school can enhance students' motivation and school engagement (Kindermann, 1993, 2007; Ryan, 2000, 2001). Other times, having a social focus in school decreases students' academic performance (Wentzel & Wigfield, 1998) and lowers academic regulation skills (Grund, Brassler, & Fries, 2014). A social focus in school involves the degree to which students center their attention, behaviors, and motivation toward non-academic pursuits in school, such as friends, extracurricular activities, and peer relationships. A social focus in school is in contrast toward having an academic focus in school. Students with an academic focus pursue and value learning and increasing academic performance instead of attuning to the social aspects of school. Having more of an academic or social focus toward schooling can align and predict students' academic motivation, school engagement, and academic achievement (Jones & Mueller, 2017; Jones, Mueller, & McCutchen, 2019).

As students spend increasing amounts of their time in school and engage in school-related pursuits, their choices about whether to engage in academically or socially driven activities becomes increasingly important and is influenced by a range of intrapersonal, interpersonal, and contextual factors. Many times, these types of choices are difficult to make and, in many cases, often conflict. For students the choice is between whether to attend class or skip school, to pay attention during a boring lecture rather than worry about the upcoming football game, or to sacrifice academic performance in order to gain social standing (Wentzel & Wigfield, 1998). Furthermore, the consequences of these choices can have long-lasting implications for students' academic motivation, academic achievement, and peer social acceptance (Grund, Brassler, & Fries, 2014; Wentzel & Wigfield, 1998). While the impacts of these decisions are well understood, there is still much to be discovered about the reasoning behind why students choose between academic or social aspects of school when these opportunities arise. Further, past findings only partly address the short and long-term consequences of having an academic or social focus in school. This omission becomes particularly important as the mix of academic and social foci inside school can affect students' motivational self-beliefs, scholastic performance, and peer relations in school (Kindermann, 1993, 2007; Ryan, 2000, 2001).

A student's academic or social focus toward school is likely a function of the student's sociocultural norms and values as well as the students' agentic decisions. In this way, students' foci in school build from past theoretical work in psychology that incorporates both personal beliefs and the role of environment, such as social cognitive theory (Bandura, 1986; Jones, Mueller, & McCutchen, 2019). Social cognitive theory suggests reciprocal interactions between the self, behavior, and the environment. This might explain how students hold a focus toward school (self) that helps predict school engagement and academic performance (behavior), and how these self-beliefs interact with other classmates and teachers (environment). Social cognitive theory provides a theoretical basis for explaining how students' focus in school might help explain academic performance and social interactions. Before discussing more about the academic and interpersonal effects of students' focus in school, a greater understanding may be warranted of what is, and is not, an academic or social focus toward school.

Defining Academic or Social Focus toward School

An academic or social focus toward school can be operationally defined as whether students perceive school as a place to learn or a place for non-academic/interpersonal interactions (e.g., friends, pursue romantic relationships). It is called a focus toward school because students hold a general outlook, or perception, as to whether school is, or is not, a place to learn. In this way, a students' focus in school may serve as a more superordinate theory over other social goals. That is, one's focus could drive the student toward a variety of other beliefs about schooling, learning, and the process of learning. Students with an academic focus toward school may develop a belief that learning is important, going to school will help their current or future lives, and they may enjoy learning new and interesting topics. Students with a social focus toward school perceive school to be a place for social interactions, avoiding academic work, and enjoying school clubs or activities. For a social focus toward school, the driving motivation is not learning, but rather engaging in non-scholastic activities or social encounters.

A social focus in school does not mean the student is an extrovert or only wants to participate in activities with other students (just as having an academic focus is not a function of being more introverted). Indeed, a social focus may mean that the student enjoys sitting in the school library alone instead of going to class, going to the music room to practice an instrument, or simply "hanging-out" in the school's main office without really engaging with anyone. A student with a social focus may be physically present within a learning space, but the student's focus and intention is not engaged in learning or academic pursuits. For example, a student may be excited to talk with teachers in the school counselor's office (social focus). In contrast, students who go to the school counselor's office to talk about which classes might help them get into college would have an academic focus. The core difference between social and academic focus is the question of whether a student more generally perceives and approaches school as a place to participate in non-academic activities versus the student who more often perceives and approaches school for intellectual pursuits.

The juxtaposition of the academic and social foci in school is often observable in asking a student why they are going to school today. Naturally, a child or adolescent may first answer, "Because I have to" or "Because my parents make me." The second answer could be a bit more illuminating into the student's motives for the day or how they perceive the value of schooling. A student with an academic focus may respond with something like, "I'm going to school because I'm excited about the upcoming science fair" or "My teacher said we are going to learn about why the dinosaurs went extinct." In contrast, a student with a social focus may state, "I have to be in class today in order to perform in the class play tonight" or "I want to talk to my friends about what happened at the party last weekend." The academic or social focus toward school motivates the student toward a series of behaviors and interactions that may aid learning or focus on non-academic activities.

An academic or social focus toward school are on separate ends of a single continuum, with a focus on academics on one side and a social focus to school on the opposite side of the continuum. The continuum between an academic and social focus is probably a better way of understanding focus in school instead of being and either/or situation (i.e., either an academic focus or a social focus). Most students likely hold a complex mixture of school being both a place to learn and to engage in social activities.

Evidence for Academic and Social Focus toward School

There is still much to be learned about the way in which having an academic focus versus a social focus in school relates to each other and other variables. This may be due to the relatively new interest in the idea of social focus in school, as well as the difficulty in measuring the construct itself. The following sections illustrate the measurement of the social and academic focus toward school constructs. Then, we discuss relationships between academic and social focus, achievement goals, and student engagement, specifically, teacher– student relationships, peer support for learning, and control and relevance of school work.

Data came from a study of 410 urban American students from 7 elementary schools. This included 210 females and 200 males, ranging from 7 to 13 years of age (M = 9.7 years, SD = 1 year, 2 months). Students' ethnicities were predominately African American (65%) and Hispanic (16%). As this was a low socioeconomic area, all students were eligible for free or reduced lunches.

Students answered several surveys as part of this study in the fall of 2011 and the spring of 2012. First, six items from the Academic Social Motivation Scale measured student focus as either academically focused (three items) or socially focused (three items), with greater scores indicating more of an academic or social focus on each scale, respectively (Jones & Mueller, 2017; Jones, Mueller, & McCutchen, 2019). Second, achievement goal measurement came from the Achievement Goals Questionnaire-Revised (AGQ-R; Elliot & Murayama, 2008). Three items measured each of the four goals, which include mastery approach, mastery avoid, performance approach, and performance avoid. Third, the Student Engagement Instrument (SEI; Appleton et al., 2006) is a self-reported measure designed to capture student engagement in school. The SEI consists of 35 items divided into two main dimensions: cognitive engagement and affective engagement. Affective engagement consists of three subscales, which includes Peer Support at School (PSL), Teacher–Student Relationships (TSR), and Family Support for Learning. Cognitive engagement consists of two subscales: Control and Relevance of School Work (CRSW) and Future Aspirations and Goals (FG). Finally, academic achievement came from the Iowa Test of Basic Skills national exam with NCE scored collected in September 2011 for math, language, and reading (Hoover, Dunbar, & Frisbie, 2007).

We used these scales in several different analyses. First, we outline measurement of social and academic focus using confirmatory factor analysis. Second, we look at how an academic and social focus in school aligns with achievement goals. Third, results test whether foci toward school corresponds with students' school engagement.

Measurement of academic and social focus in school

Confirmatory factor analysis tested item factor loadings of social foci and academic foci from the Academic Social Motivation Scale using data from the spring of 2012. Academic and social foci items were loaded onto two respective factors: academic and social focus. The final global fit model tests using maximum likelihood suggested the model to have an acceptable fit, χ^2 (8, N = 410) = 16.02, p = 0.04, CFI = .99, RMSEA= .05 [.009, .09]. Estimation converged after 24 iterations. While the global fit tests suggest an acceptable fit, local fit tests were also considered. In reviewing the modification index (MI), relaxation of item 7 for social focus, as well as item 10 for academic focus might improve fit. The expected parameter change (EPC), on the other hand, suggests minimal reductions in chi-square based on relaxing these items. The Standardized Root Mean Square Residual (SRMR), which measures the difference between predicted and observed correlations, was found to be .04, and therefore does not present cause for concern.

In the correlation matrix in Table 3.1, we see a few key things. First, results suggest a relationship between social focus measured in fall 2011, and spring,

Academic or Social Focus toward School **41**

TABLE 3.1 Age and Academic and Social Focus in Fall 2011 and Spring 2012: Correlations and Descriptive Statistics

Variables	1	2	3	4	5
1. Age					
2. Social Focus 2011	−.06				
3. Social Focus 2012	−.06	.20★★★			
4. Academic Focus 2011	−.04	−.001	.05		
5. Academic Focus 2012	−.10★★★	.05	.25★★★	−.08	
M	9.72	3.34	3.17	3.32	
SD	1.20	.68	.76	.79	

★ $p < 0.05$
★★★ $p < 0.001$

2012, r (410) = .20, $p < .001$, but not for academic focus. From this, we might infer that characteristics which "define" to be socially focused, such as wanting to go to school to talk with friends, are more stable than characteristics which "define" what it means to be academically focused, perhaps due to changing course subjects from the fall to spring semesters.

Academic and social focus and achievement goal orientation in school

Now that we have a basic understanding of academic and social focus associations, we can begin to consider their correspondence with other measures, such as achievement goal orientation. Results from correlational analyses in Table 3.2 confirm what previous studies have found and what theory has suggested. Results suggest achievement goal orientations correspond with both academic and social focused students measured in fall, 2011. Academic focus related more than social focus, especially mastery-approach orientations, r (410) = .50, $p < .001$. This aligns with the notion that students who have an academic focus are likely to be mastery-approach oriented. We also see a positive relationship between social focus and mastery approach, r (410) = .16, $p < .001$, but this is less than for the relationship between academic focus and mastery-approach goals. Performance avoid was positively associated with social focus, r (410) = .12, $p < .05$.

Academic and social focus and student engagement in school

Results from the multiple regression models found school engagement associated with both academically and socially focused students, with results varying by each subscale of school engagement in fall, 2011. Peer support for learning accounted for approximately 12% of the variance in predicting students with a social focus,

42 Martin H. Jones et al.

TABLE 3.2 Student Reports of Academic and Social Foci and Achievement Goal Orientations in School from Fall 2011: Correlations and Descriptive Statistics

Variables	1	2	3	4	5	6
1. Social Focus						
2. Academic Focus						
3. Mastery Approach	.16***	.50***				
4. Mastery Avoid	−.07	−.17***	−.03			
5. Performance Approach	.04	.14**	.39***	.03		
6. Performance Avoid	.12*	−.01	.25***	.20***	.18***	
M	3.34	3.17	4.51	2.75	4.33	3.78
SD	.68	.76	.72	1.18	.85	1.12

* $p < 0.05$
***$p < 0.001$

$F (1, 408) = 58.5$, $p < .001$, $R^2 = .12$, whereas only 2% accounted for students with an academic focus, $F (1, 408) = 6.72$, $p = .009$, $R^2 = .01$. In other words, we might infer that students whom report high levels of peer support for learning are students with a social focus in school. In contrast, teacher–student relationships significantly related to those reporting an academic focus in the fall, 2011 and spring, 2012. For students with a social focus, reports of the teacher–student relationship were not significant for fall, 2011, but were significant for spring, 2012, $F (1, 408) = 40.03$, $p < .001$, $R^2 = .09$. Unsurprisingly, control and relevance of school work was best predicted by students with an academic focus, $F (1, 408) = 205.2$, $p < .001$, $R^2 = .33$) in comparison to social focus, $F (1, 408) = 4.64$, $p < .05$, $R^2 = .08$.

TABLE 3.3 Student Reports of Academic and Social Foci and Achievement Goal Orientations in School from Fall 2011: Linear Regression

Variable	Social Focus		Academic Focus	
	SE	β	SE	β
Mastery Approach	.05	.14	.05	.57
Mastery Avoid	.03	−.05	.03	−.08
Performance Approach	.04	−.03	.04	−.04
Performance Avoid	.03	.06	.03	−.07
R^2	.03		.28	
F	4.29***		40.63***	

***$p < 0.001$

Academic or Social Focus toward School **43**

TABLE 3.4 Academic and Social Focus and Student Engagement Fall 2011: Correlations and Descriptive Statistics

Variables	1	2	3	4	5
1. Social Focus 2011					
2. Academic Focus 2011	−.01				
3. TSR 2011	.08	.48***			
4. CRSW 2011	.11*	.58**	.61***		
5. PSL 2011	.35***	.13***	.37***	.28***	
M	3.34	3.17	3.17	3.40	3.04
SD	.68	.76	.60	.52	.71

$\star\, p < 0.05$
$\star\star\star p < 0.001$

Taken in sum, these results suggest several findings. First, academic and social focus in school can be measured with some accuracy, but additional work is needed to improve instrumentation. While measurement of social foci is more difficult, analysis of academic foci is more straightforward. Thus, direct comparison between the two types of foci can be imprecise. Second, students with an academic focus in school may also have a greater propensity for mastery-approach goals than students with a social focus toward school. Third, students with a social focus are more likely engaging in the non-academic facets of school (e.g., peer relationships and teacher–student relationships later in the school year). These findings align with past work suggesting how foci toward school correspond with academic performance and interpersonal relationships.

TABLE 3.5 Academic and Social Focus and Student Engagement Fall 2011: Regression

	Social Focus		Academic Focus	
Variable	SE	β	SE	β
PSL	.16	.37	.05	.12
R^2	.12		.01	
F	58.46***		6.72**	
TSR	.06	.09	.05	.61
R^2	.004		.23	
F	2.76		122.2***	
CRSW	.04	.08	.03	.39
R^2	.01		.33	
F	4.64*		205.2***	

$\star p < 0.05$
$\star\star\star p < 0.001$

Academic Performance and Focus toward School

Focus toward school is a relatively new construct, but with a longer past (Birch & Ladd, 1996; Dweck, 1996; Ladd, 1990). Building from this past work, current literature provides evidence for the academic outcomes of students' focus toward school. Past and current work suggests that students with an academic focus toward school have greater academic motivation, achievement, and performance (Birch & Ladd, 1996; Jones & Mueller, 2017; Jones, Mueller, & McCutchen, 2019; Wentzel & Wigfield, 1998). In contrast, students with a social focus toward school often have less optimal academic motivation and lower achievement (Dweck, 1996; Jones & Mueller, 2016; Jones, Mueller, & McCutchen, 2019). More deeply examining each focus and their outcomes helps highlight the nuanced aspects of either focus toward school.

Students who perceive school to be a place for learning also hold several self-beliefs associated with greater academic motivation, such as achievement goals and school engagement. For example, elementary students with an academic focus toward school can have a more mastery approach toward learning (Jones, Mueller, & McCutchen, 2019). Mastery-approach goals are students' self-beliefs that the purpose or goal of learning is developing self-competency, which often leads to higher academic achievement and greater understanding (Ames, 1992; McGregor & Elliot, 2002). Students' goal of developing self-competency (mastery approach) may stem from a larger belief that school is a place to learn (academic focus; Jones & Mueller, 2017). As students belief school is a place to learn, then they focus more on learning that helps develop their self-competency. In this way, an academic focus toward school helps students have an optimal motivational belief.

Students with a social focus toward school usually do not have a mastery-approach goal (Jones, Mueller, & McCutchen, 2019). Instead, a social focus toward school is more associated with performance-approach goals. Performance-approach goals emerge as students hold a desire to demonstrate ability or outperform other students (Hulleman, Schrager, Bodmann, & Harackiewicz, 2010). Performance-approach goals are inherently social as students focus on the performance of classmates or demonstrating their competency to others. Performance-approach goals can help motivate students to learn, but this motivation wanes when the student reaches their performance goal, or when students realizes they cannot achieve their goal (Ames, 1992). In this way, performance-approach goals are generally not motivationally optimal, but the social aspects of performance-approach goals align with a social focus toward school. Perhaps not surprisingly, students who perceive school as a place for friends and social interactions may also hold more of a goal to outperform or demonstrate competency to others (Jones, Mueller, & McCutchen, 2019). Thus, a student with a social focus toward school is more likely to hold a performance goal instead of a mastery-approach goal.

Students with an academic focus toward school can hold more optimal academic motivation, but an academic focus toward school likely does not directly relate to academic performance (Jones, Mueller, & McCutchen, 2019). Instead, an academic focus toward school orients the student toward mastery-approach goals, which then leads to academic achievement. Additional research is needed to see what specific motivational factors align with an academic focus toward school to enhance academic performance, such as mindset and self-efficacy (Dweck, 1999; Bandura, 1997). Mindset, or whether one believes their abilities can grow and change, may also align with an academic focus toward school, such that students who focus on improving learning each day may also believe their intellectual abilities can change. In a similar way, students with greater self-efficacy, or the degree to which they see themselves as competent, could correspond with an academic focus. Students who believe they are academically competent and have mastery academic experiences in school may be more likely to believe the school is a place for learning. In turn, having a growth mindset and higher self-efficacy leads to higher academic achievement (Dweck, 1999; Bandura, 1997).

Interpersonal Interactions and Focus toward School

Having an academic or social focus toward school alters interpersonal relationships in school. A social focus toward school aligns with multiple different interpersonal outcomes ranging from enhancement of positive relationship to associating with delinquent peers. Students with a social focus attune to other people and their social relationships. Students with an academic focus attune less to social relationships in school than students with a social focus, but are not immune to interpersonal interactions.

An academic focus in school suggests that students believe school is a place to learn, and this focus may coincide with academic benefits (Jones & Mueller, 2017; Jones, Mueller, & McCutchen, 2019). Students with an academic focus also likely associate with other students having a similar focus (Jones & Ford, 2014; Ryan, 2001). In this way, a student with an academic focus, who also has friends with an academic focus, could benefit from their social interactions as the friends socialize each other about how to be successful in school (Jones & Ford, 2014; Jones, Alexander, & Estell, 2010). That is, students with an academic focus in school likely have riendships and peer groups that may help each other become academically successful in school. The extant literature is less clear on other outcomes.

Extant research is not clear on how such social consequences as popularity might correlate with having an academic focus in school. Popularity consists primarily of students who are well known by other students (perceived popularity) and the degree to which classmates like, or dislike, the given student (sociometric status; Gest, Graham-Bermann, & Hartup, 2001). Students who are socially isolated in school often lack social skills, are socially rejected by peers and classmates, and are not well liked by classmates (Asher & Coie, 1990). It may seem that students with an academic focus could be susceptible to this isolation as they are not focused on the social aspects of schooling, and could therefore be rejected. This isolation is unlikely as students with an academic focus likely associate with others having similar beliefs (Ryan, 2001). That is, having an academic focus is unrelated to social skills, peer acceptance, and peer rejection. Rather, having an academic focus, unto itself, likely neither helps or hinders students in their perceived popularity and sociometric status.

The perceived popularity of students with a social focus in school is also not fully understood, but some outcomes are likely. First, students with a social focus in school may be more conscience of the social relationships in a classroom (e.g., which students are friends and enemies of each other) as well as their own popularity and social acceptance inside school. Some students may even be willing to sacrifice their own academic pursuits in order to help gain status with other peers (e.g., Wentzel & Wigfield, 1998).

Students with a social focus toward school can use their focus to develop greater social skills, have strong interpersonal relationships, and hold deep and meaningful friendships (Dweck, 1996; Wentzel, 1996). Students with a social focus toward school may also have more negative social interactions and outcomes in school because they focus on relationships. For example, a student focused on social relationships could choose a friendship based upon skipping school and partaking in delinquent behaviors instead of building friendships with students focused on school. This may occur as students seek approval from certain friends and avoid rejection from others (Dweck, 1996). A student with a social focus can spend more time in developing friendships that help the student succeed in school, or they may befriend students that encourage more negative behaviors.

The interpersonal ramifications of having an academic or social focus in school are less clear and direct than the academic consequences of having an academic or social focus in school. Whereas an academic focus aligns with greater academic motivation, an academic focus does not mean the student will have negative social consequences. Students with a social focus in school generally have less optimal academic motivation, but their social focus does not guarantee greater popularity or whom the student associates with in school. Much more additional research would illuminate how having an academic and social focus helps and hinders the learning and interpersonal relationships of students in school.

Future Areas of Research

Having an academic or social focus toward school is in the early stages of development as a psychological concept. Past work suggests that students hold an academic or social focus (Jones & Mueller, 2017; Jones, Mueller, & McCutchen, 2019), and that having an academic or social focus toward school affects educational and interpersonal outcomes (Grund, Brassler, & Fries, 2014; Wentzel & Wigfield, 1998). Still, there is much unknown about students' foci toward school. Maybe most noticeably, there are persistent issues in the measurement of students' foci in school, the development and change of students' foci across time, the antecedents of school foci, and interventions surrounding students' foci toward school.

Measuring students' focus toward school

As a relatively new psychological construct, the current measurement of students' foci in school is murky at best. The measurement issues center around several factors. Some of these are direct measurement issues, whereas other surrounds the issues of still defining the confines of the construct. For example, the past measurement of the academic focus toward school centered on a potentially singular facet of learning (e.g., "Coming to school today, I was excited about something I might learn today."). Yet, students might interpret the word "learn" in different ways, such as the distinction between mastery and performance learning goals. A student might mean learning is the comprehension or acquisition of a given concept, whereas another student might associate learning with academic performance.

Expanding upon this issue, students might understand that learning is being physically present inside a learning setting (e.g., "I'm excited about coming to class today."), but that does not mean that the student is interesting in cognitively engaging with learning. That is, a student may enjoy being inside the classroom, but not interested in learning inside the classroom. Instead, it may be more accurate to state that the aforementioned child has more of a social focus if they enjoy being present around others in class than a learning focus. The enjoyment of being in class one day (whether to learn or to be with other students) may not continue into the next day, which suggests an additional measurement issue regarding how students' foci in school develop and change over time.

Development and change of students' foci

Current research does not speak to whether a student's focus in school pertains to a specific developmental period. It remains an open question as to whether having an academic or social focus in school is more or less associated with different developmental periods. This question arises as adolescents usually pursue more social interactions than children (e.g., Brown) and children have greater academic motivation than adolescents do (Lepper, Corpus, & Iyengar, 2005). Therefore, a child may have more of an academic focus toward school than an adolescent. The opposite may also be true as children still have complex social interactions in early elementary school (Abrams, Rutland, Pelletier, & Ferrell, 2009; Estell, Cairns, Farmer, & Cairns, 2002), such that a social or academic focus toward school may depend on the student's stage in life and learning context.

The frequency and types of social activities inside school often parallels the students' developmental stages. Elementary schools may offer a select number of sporting events and some extracurricular activities, whereas high schools typically provide a larger number of sports and both a greater amount and wider variety of clubs and organizations for students to join. Further, the opportunity for extracurricular activities varies by the financial capabilities of a given school (or school

48   Martin H. Jones et al.

district) and cultural values of the school/community (e.g., school dances may be prohibited by certain cultural groups). The capacity for a school to offer additional social interactions makes measuring social focus more difficult as wording of items needs to reflect the social possibilities of a given school. For example, the use of wording that references extracurricular activities may not be applicable to all schools.

The consideration of differences across developmental stages would partially address the issue of how foci toward school evolve across the lifespan. Longitudinal analyses could help answer this question, but the use of longitudinal analyses brings forth the question of how frequent should measurements of students' foci toward school occur. It may be that students' foci change across days or even within a given day. It may be that a focus toward school remains generally stable across time, or that it fluctuates regularly. The stability and malleability of student's foci toward school remains an unanswered question in need of additional empirical research. Providing empirical results would help better explain the fluidity of students' focus toward school.

The antecedents of school foci

The psychological antecedents are not fully understood in how students acquire and change their focus toward school. Building from social cognitive theory (Bandura, 1986), there are likely a combination of environmental and personal factors that affect students' focus toward school. Friends, parents, and teachers each contribute to how a student feels toward school. That is, through modeling, direct instruction, and vicarious experiences (Bandura, 1986), students acquire beliefs from others about whether school is more of a place to learn, or more of a place for social interactions. A simple example may be when parents regularly tell their child, "Learn a lot at school today," whereas another parent reminds their child, "Remember about the football game on Friday." Over time, students internalize these messages about what aspects of schooling should be valued and focused upon. Similar message are also being conveyed by friends, teachers, and other parts of an individual's environment (e.g., "The whole town is counting on you at the game on Friday."). Social cognitive theory provides theoretical support that multiple sources from an individual's environment affects having an academic or social focus toward school, but these theoretical relationships are not yet empirically tested. Further research needs to test the degree of influence that each environmental factor has on foci toward school, which environmental factors are more influential than other sources, and whether levels of influence change as students develop across the lifespan.

Interventions for students' foci toward school

There are many avenues of future research for understanding how students acquire an academic or social focus toward school. After understanding how students acquire a given foci, then a potential next line of research includes developing interventions that optimize students' foci toward. The interventions include both helping students' develop an academic focus toward school as well as developing a social focus toward school, which are dependent upon the student's needs.

For many students, the development of an academic focus toward school may be more desirable if the student's academic performance or academic motivation is less than optimal. The use of situational interest that temporarily enables intrinsic motivation may be one way to build an academic focus. Another approach is having parents and teachers regularly discuss the benefits of schooling with the student. The development of personal interest in schooling may take time, but should have a longer-lasting effect on the student's focus toward school than more short-term interventions (e.g., rewarding academic performance with money or punishing poor academic performance). Clearly, how to develop a student's academic focus toward school needs much additional research before any empirical conclusions can be made.

A greater academic focus toward school may not be the goal for all students. A greater social focus toward school may be desired for students experiencing several different personal or social issues. For example, students having special needs, for which the special need affects the student's social relationships, could develop their social focus in such a way to aid their social interactions. A student with a social anxiety disorder or on the autism spectrum disorder could use school as a forum for developing social relationships, improving social skills, and building friendships. The inherent social interactions of schooling provide opportunities for developing these social skills, and a greater focus toward school may direct the student to practicing and acquiring those social skills. Another potential benefit of a greater social focus toward school is for students who are overly focused on academics in school to the detriment of personal relationships and well-being. This may be seen in students who sacrifice their personal relationships with others or develop high levels of stress because of an excessive concentration on learning and academic performance. Developing more of a social focus toward school could help balance the relationship between academic success and holding healthy social relationships with peers or others.

The need for a variety of interventions to help students succeed in school highlights the larger need for future research examining the many facets of students' foci toward school. The need for future research ranges from how to better measure academic and social foci toward school to how to help students develop a given focus toward school. The future areas of research will help establish and clarify the psychological role that students' focus toward school has on academic performance, academic motivation, and interpersonal relationships in school.

Conclusion

The notion that students focus more on academic pursuits or on their social lives in school is not a particularly novel concept, but approaching the notion as a distinct psychological phenomenon is a more recent development. Anecdotally, parents and teachers seem to have near endless conversations with their children and students about focusing on what might be the most important reasons for schooling. These are sometimes for the individual to focus more on academics and not so much on extracurricular activities, whereas some of these conversations are about having the student develop greater friendships in school. These conversations indirectly highlight that students regularly approach school as a place to learn or a place for more social encounters. The antecedents, development, and long-term consequences of such foci are only beginning to be understood. The future may provide greater empirical insight that how students perceive schooling could be another avenue for explaining how students fail or succeed in their learning experiences.

References

Abrams, D., Rutland, A., & Pelletier, J., & Ferrell, J. M. (2009). Children's group nous: Understanding and applying peer exclusion within and between groups. *Child Development*, 80, 224–243.

Ames, C. (1992). Classrooms: Goals, structures, and student motivation. *Journal of Educational Psychology*, 85, 261–271.

Appleton, J., Christenson, S., Kim, D., & Reschly, A. (2006). Measuring cognitive and psychological engagement: Validation of the Student Engagement Instrument. *Journal of School Psychology*, 44, 427–445.

Asher, S. R., & Coie, J. D. (1990). *Peer rejection in childhood*. New York: Cambridge University Press.

Bandura, A. (1986). *Social foundations of thought and action: A social cognitive theory*. Englewood Cliffs, NJ: Prentice-Hall.

Bandura, A. (1997). *Self-efficacy: The exercise of control*. New York: W. H. Freeman and Co.

Birch, S. H., & Ladd, G. W. (1996). Interpersonal relationships in the school environment and children's early school adjustment: The role of teachers and peers. In J. Juvonen & K. R. Wentzel (Eds.), *Social motivation: Understanding children's school adjustment* (pp. 181–195). New York: Cambridge University Press.

Chow, L. (Producer). (2013, September 11). *Why women (like me) choose lower-paying jobs* [Audio broadcast]. Retrieved from www.npr.org/blogs/money/2013/09/11/220748057/why-women-like-me-choose-lower-paying-jobs.

Dweck, C. S. (1996). Social motivation: Goals and social-cognitive processes: A comment. In J. Juvonen & K. R. Wentzel (Eds.), *Social motivation: Understanding children's school adjustment* (pp. 181–195). New York: Cambridge University Press.

Dweck, C. S. (1999). *Self-theories: Their role in motivation, personality, and development*. Philadelphia, PA: Psychology Press.

Elliot, A. J. & Murayama, K. (2008). On the measurement of achievement goals: Critique, illustration, and application. *Journal of Educational Psychology*, 100(3), 613–628.

Estell, D. B., Cairns, R. B., Farmer, T. W., & Cairns, B. D. (2002). Aggression in inner-city early elementary classrooms: Individual and peer-group configurations. *Merrill-Palmer Quarterly*, 48, 52–76.

Gest, S. D., Graham-Bermann, S. A., & Hartup, W. W. (2001). Peer experience: Common and unique features of number of friendships, social network centrality, and sociometric status. *Social Development*, 10, 23–40.

Grund, A., Brassler, N. K., & Fries, S. (2014). Torn between study and leisure: How motivational conflicts relate to students' academic and social adaption. *Journal of Educational Psychology*, 106, 242–257.

Hoover, H. D., Dunbar, S. B., & Frisbie, D. A. (2007). *Iowa test of basic skills*. Rolling Meadows, IL: Riverside Publishing.

Hulleman, C. S., Schrager, S. M., Bodmann, S. M., & Harackiewicz, J. M. (2010). A meta-analytic review of achievement goal measures: Different labels for the same constructs or different constructs with similar labels? *Psychological Bulletin*, 136(3), 422–449.

Jones, M. H., & Ford, J. M. (2014). Social achievement goals, efficacious beliefs, and math performance in a predominately African American high school. *Journal of Black Psychology*, 40(3), 239–262.

Jones, M. H., & Mueller, C. E. (2017). The relationship among achievement goals, standardized test scores, and elementary students' focus in school. *Psychology in the Schools*, 54 (9), 979–990.

Jones, M. H., Alexander, J. M., & Estell, D. B. (2010). Homophily among peer groups members' perceived self-regulated learning. *Journal of Experimental Education*, 78(3), 378–394.

Jones, M. H., Mueller, C. E., & McCutchen, K. L. (2019). School foci and their potential ramifications in urban high schools. *Youth and Society*, 51(4), 484–503.

Kindermann, T. A. (1993). Natural peer groups as contexts for individual development: The case of children's motivation in school. *Developmental Psychology*, 29(6), 970–977.

Kindermann, T. A. (2007). Effects of naturally existing peer groups on changes in academic engagement in a cohort of sixth graders. *Child Development*, 78(4), 1186–1203.

Kuchment, A. (2013, April 16). To attract more girls to STEM, bring more storytelling to Science. *Scientific American*. Retrieved from: http://blogs.scientificamerican.com/bud ding-scientist/2013/04/16/to-attract-more-girls-to-stem-bring-storytelling-to-science/.

Ladd, G. W. (1990). Having friends, keeping friends, making friends, and being liked by peers in the classroom: Predictors of children's early school adjustment? *Child Development*, 61, 1081–1100.

Lepper, M. R., Corpus, J. H., Iyengar, S. S. (2005). Intrinsic and extrinsic motivational orientations in the classroom: Age differences and academic correlates. *Journal of Educational Psychology*, 97(2), 184–196.

McGregor, H. A., & Elliot, A. J. (2002). Achievement goals as predictors of achievement-relevant processes prior to task engagement. *Journal of Educational Psychology*, 94(2), 381–395.

Ryan, A. M. (2000). Peer groups as a context for the socialization of adolescents' motivation, engagement, and achievement in school. *Educational Psychologist*, 35(2), 101–111.

Ryan, A. M. (2001). The peer group as a context for the development of young adolescent motivation and achievement. *Child Development*, 72(4), 1135–1150.

Wang, M., Eccles, J. S., & Kenny, S. (2013a). Not lack of ability but more choice: Individual and gender differences in choice of careers in science, technology, engineering, and mathematics. *Psychological Science*, 24(5), 770–775.

Wang, M., Eccles, J. S., & Kenny, S. (2013b, March 27). What exactly is drawing young women away from STEM fields? *The Huffington Post*. Retrieved from: www.huffing tonpost.com/mingte-wang/women-stem-education_ b_2967180.html.

Wentzel, K. R. (1996). Social goals and social relationships as motivators of school adjustment. In J. Juvonen & K. R. Wentzel (Eds.), *Social motivation: Understanding children's school adjustment* (pp. 181–195). New York: Cambridge University Press.

Wentzel, K. R., & Wigfield, A. (1998). Academic and social motivational influences on students' academic performance. *Educational Psychology Review*, 10(2), 155–175.

4

SOCIAL ACHIEVEMENT GOALS

Sungok Serena Shim and Allison M. Ryan

We live in a web of social relationships. With advances in mobile technology, social networking, and online communities, people engage in social interactions even when they are alone. The amount of time people spend on social media is rapidly increasing and, on average, people around the world spend more than two hours per day on social networking on the Internet (www.statista.com). Forging and managing meaningful and satisfying social relationships is directly linked to human's basic psychological needs and thus, being able to connect to and effectively interact with others is critical to individuals' overall psychological well-being and adjustment (Baumeister & Leary, 1995; Ryff & Keyes, 1995; Ryan & Deci, 2000).

Understanding what contributes to social relationships is an important endeavor. Guided by social-cognitive theory (Bandura, 1986; Dweck & Leggett, 1988), an achievement goal perspective on social motivation postulates that different orientations to social competence are an important factor for understanding social adjustment. When entering a social situation or interacting with others, people vary in the extent to which they focus on *developing* their relationships and improving their competence *or* they are concerned about *demonstrating* their social competence to others. Differences in orientations to social competence put individuals on distinctly different patterns of cognitive, affective, and behavioral processes and are important for their social outcomes (Ryan & Shim, 2006, 2008).

Before the introduction of social achievement goal theory in the mid-2000s, a social content goal approach was the predominant approach to social motivation. A social content goal approach focuses on the specific outcomes that an individual aspires to obtain. Thus, this approach focuses on the "what" aspect of the goals. Research on social goals has a long history, and a wide variety of goals have been investigated, such as affiliation, companionship, responsibility, nurturance, intimacy, fun, revenge, and domination or control over others (Anderman, 1999; Chung &

Asher, 1996; Ford, 1992; Jarvinen & Nicholls, 1996; McAdams, 1987; Rose & Asher, 1999; Sanderson, Rahm, & Beigbeder, 2005; Wentzel, 2001). The research on these goals has shed light onto children and adolescents' motivation and adjustment (see Crick & Dodge, 1994). However, the sheer number and the diversity of the goals that are examined across research programs make it difficult to synthesize the literature. In contrast to the social content goal approach, an achievement goal theoretical approach zeros in on the "why" aspect of the goals. An achievement goal framework focuses on orientations to competence which transcend specific goals and thus provides parsimony without oversimplification. An individual's purpose in social situations reflects different orientations to social competence.

Most of the extant social achievement goal studies have utilized a three-factor model of social achievement goals proposed by Ryan and Shim (2006, 2008). This model differentiates three types of goals: a social development goal, a social demonstration-approach goal, and a social demonstration-avoid goal. These goals mirror mastery, performance-approach and performance-avoidance goals in the academic domain. Since the introduction of these constructs in the mid-2000s, the social achievement goal literature has been growing steadily. The majority of existing studies on social achievement have examined the correlates of the goals, aiming to identify the implications of these goals for individuals' social, psychological, and academic functioning. These studies have been very instrumental in establishing the function of different social achievement goals. In addition, there has been increasing attention to apply the social achievement goal framework to different cultural groups by testing the statistical properties of the social achievement goal scales translated into local languages. Social achievement goal scales are now available in nine different languages including Chinese, English, Greek, Hebrew, Indonesian, Iranian, Japanese, Turkish, and Korean. Many studies on children or adolescents have been conducted and have added support for the importance of peer interaction and relationships during this developmental stage (e.g., Madjar, 2017; Ryan & Shim, 2008; Shim & Finch, 2014; Shim, Cho, & Wang, 2012). With the increasing volume of social achievement goal research, it is timely to offer an up-to-date review of the research to inform and guide future research.

In this chapter, we provide a brief overview of the theory and definitions of social achievement goals and review what is known about the nature and implications of social achievement goals for adjustment. We consider social, psychological, and academic adjustment. We discuss possible mechanisms that may explain why social achievement goals hinder or promote adjustment. We conclude with a discussion of future directions. We used Ryan and Shim's terms throughout this chapter for consistency (i.e., social development goals; social demonstration-approach goals; social demonstration-avoid goals), though a few studies have used different terminology (e.g., social mastery goals, social performance-approach goals, social performance-avoidance goals, Kuroda & Sakurai, 2011), but given the definitions are almost identical, we do not make such distinctions.

Achievement Goal Theory and Social Achievement Goals: An Overview

Goals are generally defined as "cognitive representations of the end outcomes that individuals aim to acquire" (Austin & Vancouver, 1996; Elliot, 2005; Pintrich, 2000; Pintrich & Schunk, 2002). Achievement goal theory emphasizes overarching goal orientations that provide qualitatively distinct perspectives with different implications for individual's cognitions, affect, and behavior. Two distinct orientations (i.e., a mastery goal focus on developing competence vs. a performance goal focus on demonstrating competence) were contrasted by early goal theorists (Ames, 1992; Dweck & Leggett, 1988; Maehr & Nicholls, 1980; Nicholls, 1984). Later, in addition to the goal type dimension (mastery vs. performance goal dimension), a valence dimension (approach-avoidance dimension) was added to the theory to improve the predictive power of achievement goals. Individuals with approach goals aspire to obtain potential positive outcomes, whereas individuals with avoidance goals aim to avoid potential negative outcomes. Given both mastery and performance goals can take approach or avoidance form, there can be four different types of achievement goals. Mastery-approach (e.g., personal improvement and task mastery), mastery-avoidance (e.g., not losing the current skill, not doing the task inaccurately, not understanding), performance-approach (e.g., doing better than others), and performance-avoidance goals (e.g., not being the worst) (see Elliot & McGregor, 2001 for more information).

Extending achievement goal theory into social domain, Ryan and Shim (2006, 2008) proposed a social development goal, a social demonstration-approach goal, and a social demonstration-avoid goal, mirroring mastery, performance-approach, and performance-avoidance goals in other domains. A social achievement goal analogous to a mastery avoidance goal was not included in Ryan and Shim (2006, 2008), due to its low prevalence in real world situations and weaker relationships with adjustment (see Senko & Freund, 2015 for in-depth discussion on this issue). Since the introduction of a three-factor model of social achievement goals, additional distinctions have been made to academic achievement goals (e.g., Elliot, Murayama, & Pekrun, 2011). We use the three-factor model as proposed in Ryan & Shim (2006) as such distinctions have not been applied to social achievement goals.

The Definitions of Different Types of Social Achievement Goals

A social development goal involves focus on developing social competence. Improvement in social competence means improving social skills and becoming a better friend or conversation partner. Success or failure in social endeavors is determined using internal standards, such as making improvement in social competence. For example, individuals feel successful when they did something to strengthen a relationship or could understand their friends better.

Social development goals are related to the belief that people's core characteristics can be altered through effort (i.e., incremental theory, Dweck, 1999) and thus making mistakes is not threatening. Failure or setbacks signal that more effort or different strategies need to be employed to do better in the future. Such beliefs help students approach novel and challenging social situations without worrying too much about making mistakes, affording the opportunities to learn and grow. With the focus on developing competence, individuals are likely to welcome and approach social contexts. The students with this goal focus are likely to have intimate and satisfying relationships, as they are keen on listening to others, making an effort to gain understanding of others' intentions and desires, and adapting their behaviors to become a better friend or improve their relationships. In other words, social development goals promote sensitive and thoughtful social interactions and prosocial and caring behaviors. In sum, social development goals are expected to lead to adaptive social behaviors.

Social demonstration goals focus on demonstrating social competence. It is important for individuals with social demonstration goals to show others that they possess superior social competence, often by visible and external indicators, such as social status. Social demonstration goals can take an approach or avoidance form. A critical distinction between a social demonstration–approach and –avoid goal is the valence of the outcomes sought after. That is, approach-oriented individuals seek demonstration of positive outcomes (e.g., being seen as "cool" or "popular"), whereas avoidant-oriented individuals seek avoidance of negative outcomes. Individuals with social demonstration–approach goals are particularly interested in gaining positive social reputation. Individuals with social demonstration–avoid goals try to avoid demonstrating inferior social competence (e.g., not being seen as a "geek" or a "loser"). Thus, avoiding a negative reputation such as being socially awkward or ineffective is a critical concern for individuals with demonstration-avoid goals.

Both social demonstration-approach and -avoid goals are related to the belief that human core characteristics are innate and unchangeable (i.e., entity theory, Dweck, 1999). Thus, social failure (e.g., a misunderstanding or faux pas) can be threatening, as they indicate inadequacy or flaws of the *self*. Social demonstration-approach and -avoid goals are likely to encourage disengagement from social interaction, if there is a risk for failure. Despite this similarity shared by approach and avoid goals, they are likely to yield different consequences in terms of social adjustment and well-being. The different valences of these goals (i.e., approach vs. avoidance) are likely to trigger different processes.

With its avoidance focus, individuals are concerned more about avoiding potential negative outcomes, than obtaining potential positive outcomes. The best tactic to achieve this goal is to avoid unfamiliar social situations, which naturally involve uncertainty and thus, a higher chance of mistakes. These individuals are likely to prefer familiar situations over novel or new social situations, to avoid experiencing embarrassment or committing a social faux pas. The concerns over getting negative attention or evaluation from others are likely to increase social anxiety and consequently incite passive behaviors when interacting with peers (e.g., avoidance and withdrawal). Avoidance behaviors and anxiety-laden social interaction hinder the formation of bonding or positive relationships. In addition, a concern about other's judgment is likely to be stressful and the individuals may be vulnerable to psychological ill-being.

Unlike social demonstration-avoid goals, social-approach goals are likely to bring about both adaptive and maladaptive processes. Social-approach goals can simultaneously support and hinder adjustment. Given the focus on obtaining positive outcomes, individuals with social-approach goals are likely to approach (rather than avoid) social situations. In addition, this goal may foster socially desirable behaviors, such as attending to others' needs, helping others, fitting in, or getting along with others, to achieve their goal (i.e., to obtain favorable social status).

However, this goal comes with drawbacks. It is unlikely that the socially desirable behaviors are driven by genuine desire to get to know others better or develop a good relationship. The individuals with this goal focus might be strategic and selective with whom they choose to associate. The behaviors might be calculated and strategically dished out after considering the extent to which these behaviors will help secure prestige and favorable social status. The goal's focus is to look cool or popular, and thus effort will be centered on appearance and impression management. Novel or challenging situations might not be favored, given inherent uncertainty of the outcomes. Prior research has shown that this goal might be related to aggressive behavior, as it is associated with looking cool or popular status during early adolescence (LaFontana & Cillessen, 2002; Parkhurst & Hopmeyer, 1998; Rodkin, Farmer, Pearl, & Van Acker, 2000; Rose, Swenson, & Waller, 2004) and young adults (Shim & Ryan, 2012).

The validity of three-factor social achievement goal model has been confirmed across samples of various developmental stages and different cultures (Horst, Finney, & Barron, 2007 Study 3; Ryan & Shim, 2006 Study 3; Shim & Finch, 2014; Talepasand, Alijani, & Bigdeli, 2010). Three sub-scales used to measure social development, demonstration-approach, and -avoid goals have been found to be reliable among independent samples of Chinese college students (Shim et al., 2017; Zhao, Zhu, & Zhao, 2016), Greek adolescents (Mouratidis & Michou, 2011), Indonesian adolescents (Liem, 2016), Turkish adolescents (Michou, Mouratidis, Ersoy, & Uğur, 2016), American elementary school students (Rudolph, Abaied, Flynn, Sugimura, & Agoston, 2011), American middle school students (Ryan & Shim, 2008; Shim & Fletcher, 2012), American high school students (Jones, Mueller, Royal, Shim, & Hart, 2013; Makara & Madjar, 2015), US college students (Horst et al., 2007; Ryan & Shim, 2006; Shim & Fletcher, 2012; Shim & Ryan, 2012), and Korean adolescents (Lee, 2018). Young children are able to distinguish three social achievement goals (3rd–4th graders in Rodkin, Ryan, Jamison, & Wilson, 2013; 2nd-3rd graders in Rudolph et al., 2011).

Are social achievement goals distinct from academic achievement goals?

Given that social and academic achievement goals have "orientation to competence" as a critical element that differentiates different types of achievement goals, one may question whether there is a sufficient ground for differentiating the achievement goals in academic vs. social domains. Introduction of new labels can be confusing and thus, without a robust justification, the law of parsimony prevails. Does the degree of precision gained by using social achievement goal constructs justify the reduction in the parsimony? If the achievement goals are largely dispositional, high levels of consistency across different domains is expected and introduction of domain-specific achievement goals is not necessary. Endorsement of achievement goals does have dispositional influence, and thus goal profiles across domains overlap to some extent (Jansen in de Wal, Hornstra, Prins, & van der Veen, 2016). Dispositional variables such as implicit theories of intelligence, specific self-schemas, relatively stable individual knowledge structures, dispositional achievement motivation, and fear of failure all contribute to individuals' goal orientations (Dweck, 1986; Dweck & Leggett, 1988; Horst et al., 2007). Yet, empirical data indicate that domain specificity should not be ignored. Students tend to show a substantial degree of variability in achievement goals across subject matters (e.g., math vs. reading, Bong, 2001).

Although only a handful of studies included both academic and social achievement goals, all of them provided evidence that academic and social achievement goals are distinct constructs. See Table 4.1 below for the cross-domain correlations between analogous goals. The correlations between goals in different domains range from .19 (shared variance = 4%) to .65 (shared variance = 42%). It is interesting to note that both highest and lowest correlations were found between performance-approach goals and social demonstration-approach goals. Among the studies listed in the table, some studies have used Elliot and McGregor's measure (2001) and others have used Patterns of Adaptive Learning Survey (PALS; Midgley et al., 2000) for academic achievement goals. All studies used an adapted version of the scale developed by Ryan and Shim (2006) to measure social achievement goals. The average cross-domain correlations for the scores on the corresponding academic and social goals were.37, .40, and .40 for the academic mastery and social development goal dyad, academic performance-approach and social demonstration-approach dyad, and academic performance-avoidance and social demonstration-avoid goal dyad, respectively. The correlations seem to be higher when the PALS measure was used, as compared to when Elliot and McGregor's scale was used. In sum, these studies provide empirical evidence that achievement goals in academic and social domains are related but distinct constructs.

The Implications of Social Achievement Goals for Social, Psychological, and Academic Adjustment

How do social achievement goals relate to social adjustment?

Given that social achievement goals represent the orientation to social situations and interactions, it is not surprising that prior research has examined social outcomes frequently. With respect to social competence, social development goals were positively and social demonstration-avoid goals were negatively related to self-reported social competence (Rudolph et al., 2011; Shim & Ryan, 2012). A similar pattern was found when instructor reports were used: instructors tend to rate social adjustment of the students with high social development goals favorably. Individuals with high

Social Achievement Goals 59

TABLE 4.1 Cross-domain concurrent correlations among goals

Authors	MG-DEV	PAP-DAP	PAV-DAV	Academic goal measure	Participants
Berger & Asher 2016	0.28	0.20	0.24	PALS	130 high school students, Australia
Horst, Finnery, & Barron, 2007, Students	0.25	0.27	0.39	Elliot & McGregor	637 university students, US
Liem, 2016	0.31	0.19	0.31	Elliot & McGregor	356 high school students, Indonesia
Ryan & Shim 2006, study 3	0.34	0.37	0.34	PALS	347 college students, US
Shim & Finch 2012	0.50	0.52	0.53	PALS	442 middle school students, US
Talepasand, Alijani, and Bigdeli, 2010	0.51	0.39	0.37	PALS	403 high school students, Iran
Walker, Winn, & Lutjens, 2012	0.52	0.65	0.61	PALS	132 college students, US
Average Correlation	0.41	0.48	0.42	PALS	
Average Correlation	0.28	0.23	0.35	Elliot & McGregor	
Average Correlation	0.37	0.40	0.40	All	

Note. All correlations are significant. MG=Mastery goals; DEV=Social development goals; PAP=Performance approach goals; DAP= Social demonstration-approach goals; PAV=Performance-avoidance goals; DAV=Social demonstration-avoid goals

development goals enjoy caring and warm relationships with peers and feel less lonely (Liem, 2016; Mouratidis & Sideridis, 2009; Rodkin et al., 2013; Rudolph et al., 2011; Ryan & Shim, 2008; Shim & Ryan, 2012).

Social demonstration-avoid goals were negatively related to self-reported social competence (Rudolph et al., 2011; Shim & Ryan, 2012). Students with social demonstration-avoid goals also tend to believe that it is not worth others' time to be friends with them, reflecting a negative self-view. Although it is not necessarily an indicator of social competence, it is worth noting that social demonstration-avoid goals were also linked to negative perceptions about peers (e.g., other kids can be pretty mean) (Rudolph et al., 2011). Thus, these results indicate that the students with high social demonstration-avoid goals tend to negatively view both themselves and others.

Social demonstration-approach goals showed some mixed results related to social competence. When self-report of social competence was used, social demonstration-approach goals were positively related to self-reported social competence (Liem,

2016; Shim & Ryan, 2012). However, this pattern was not always found. A study reported a null relationship (Rudolph et al., 2011), and another study has found negative relations between peer acceptance and social demonstration-approach goals (Mouratidis & Sideridis, 2009).

The negative relationship between social demonstration-avoid goals and peer ratings of popularity has been consistently found across studies (Rodkin et al., 2013; Ryan & Shim, 2008; Shim & Ryan, 2012). An interesting pattern has been observed regarding the positive relationships that both social development and demonstration-approach goals have with favorable peer ratings (Rodkin et al., 2013; Ryan & Shim, 2008; Shim & Ryan, 2012). Although both hold positive relationships, each type of goal seems to be related to positive peer ratings of different natures: individuals with high social development goals were broadly liked by their peers (i.e., preference), whereas individuals with social demonstration-approach goals tend to be rated as popular (e.g., being visible, seen as having prestige or high status, but see Mouratidis & Sideridis, 2009 for an exception). The general pattern is not surprising given the relations between peer acceptance and prosocial behaviors (Wentzel, Barry, & Caldwell, 2004; Wentzel & McNamara, 1999)

Social development goals were associated with prosocial behavior (Rodkin et al., 2013; Rudolph et al., 2011; Shim & Ryan, 2012). Social development goals were negatively related to teacher-reported aggression in one study (Rodkin et al., 2013) but showed a null relationship in the other two studies (Rudolph et al., 2011; Shim & Ryan, 2012). Thus, the significant relation between social development goals and prosocial behavior has been more consistently observed, while this has not been the case for aggression.

Prior studies have found that social demonstration-approach goals were linked to high aggression (Rodkin et al., 2013; Rudolph et al., 2011; Shim & Ryan, 2012) and low prosocial behaviors (Rodkin et al., 2013; Rudolph et al., 2011). A social demonstration-avoid goal was not related to prosocial behaviors but was positively related to self- and teacher-reported anxious solitary behavior (Rudolph et al., 2011; Ryan & Shim, 2008). Unlike social demonstration-approach goals, this goal type showed a negative relation (Rudolph et al., 2011; Ryan & Shim, 2008) or a null relationship with aggression (Rodkin et al., 2013). It is worth noting that these relationships were quite robust and found to be significant when peer ratings or teacher ratings of social behaviors were used (e.g., Rodkin et al., 2013; Rudolph et al., 2011; Ryan & Shim, 2008; Shim & Ryan, 2012). These studies have shown that students with different social achievement goals may behave differently in social situations.

How do social achievement goals relate to psychological adjustment?

Social achievement goals have been shown to be linked to the indicators of psychological adjustment: Life satisfaction and positive affect as well as negative indicators like depression, anxiety, and worry have been examined in prior research (Dykman, 1998). A social development goal was found to be related to a wide array of adaptive well-being indicators. Specifically, social development goals were positively related to psychological well-being indicators (Sutton, Stoeber, & Kamble, 2017; Ryan & Shim, 2006), positive affect (Shim, Wang, & Cassady, 2013), and life satisfaction (Shim et al., 2017). This goal buffers individuals from stress, worry, and depression (Shim et al., 2017) and has been found to be especially beneficial for individuals with low self-esteem (Shim et al., 2013).

A social demonstration-avoid goal was associated with a host of maladaptive emotional outcomes like depression, loneliness, fear of negative evaluation, negative affect, and internalizing behaviors (e.g., crying) (Horst et al., 2007; Kuroda & Sakurai, 2011; Mouratidis & Sideridis, 2009; Shim & Ryan, 2012; Shim et al., 2013; Shim et al., 2017; Sutton et al., 2017; Zhao, Zhu, and Zhao, 2016). It was also linked to low sense of personal growth and autonomy (Ryan & Shim, 2006). This goal was particularly detrimental for individuals with low self-esteem (Shim, Wang, & Cassady, 2013).

The effects of social demonstration-approach goals on psycho-emotional outcomes have been inconsistent, ranging from null, to adaptive, and to maladaptive. This goal has null relationships with psychological wellbeing indicators (e.g., Horst et al., 2007; Kuroda & Sakurai, 2011; Ryan & Shim, 2006). Some studies have found benefits like heightened social confidence, frequent experience of positive affect such as joy, and fewer anxious behaviors (Shim & Ryan, 2012; Shim et al., 2013). A social demonstration-approach goal had a significant negative relationship with personal growth, one of the Ryff's (1989) subjective well-being sub-scales. This means that the individuals with this goal type are less likely to feel a sense of continued growth and development as a person or an openness to new experiences (Ryan & Shim, 2006). This goal type was negatively related to self-reported anxiety and depression (Shim & Ryan, 2012; Shim et al., 2017).

Taken together, a social development goal has a clear advantage and a social demonstration-avoid goal has a clear disadvantage in psycho-emotional functioning. The effects of a social demonstration-approach goal seems to vary across different outcomes and tends to have both benefits and drawbacks. However, we noted that the effects were often marginal or weak (Ryan & Shim, 2006; Shim et al., 2013). Such weak or null relationships are likely to reflect the complex nature of social demonstration-approach goals. The pattern also suggests there might be moderators that need to be considered (e.g., the effects of goals vary for individual with different characteristics). Given the frequent null findings and the mixed pattern of findings when significant, we conclude that this goal type does not yield a substantial positive effect on psychological well-being.

How do social achievement goals relate to academic adjustment?

Often, students' engagement, or lack thereof, is determined by social reasons. Social motives play a key role in students' classroom behaviors (e.g., passing notes during class, group formation due to social motive rather than academic reason). In fact, it appears that social goals are equally as prevalent as academic goals. When asked to rank order six academic and social achievement goals by importance, a social development goal was ranked the most important by college students (Horst et al., 2007). As such, our understanding of students' academic adjustment and success cannot be complete without considering their social motives (Covington, 2000; Urdan & Maehr, 1995). To date, there are only a handful of studies investigating the association between social achievement goals and the indicators of academic adjustment. In the section below, we review the studies with outcomes directly related to academic performance, motivation, and engagement. In the following section, we review two studies which focused on the emotional experience related to academic tasks. The emotions in these studies are not defined as indicators of general well-being. Rather, they represent the emotional quality of academic engagement.

In general, a social development goal has shown an adaptive pattern of relationship with indicators of academic adjustment and success in some studies. With enhanced peer relationships in general and a positive outlook on things, development goal-oriented students are likely to show adaptive patterns of classroom behaviors (e.g., high engagement, low disruptive behavior, adaptive learning strategies) and healthy attitudes toward learning and school in general (academic efficacy, intrinsic value, positive affects toward school). As for achievement itself, Liem (2016) reported that a modest relation existed between a social development goal and academic achievement after controlling for academic achievement goals, but this relationship dissipated when other interaction terms were added in the regression. Makara and Madjar (2015) reported a similar positive relationship between GPA and social development goals. They also found a positive relationship between GPA and social demonstration-avoid goals, but another study reported that math achievement was negatively related to social demonstration-avoid goals among predominately Black students (Jones & Ford, 2014). No significant relationship regarding social demonstration-approach goals has been reported. Given the paucity of the prior studies, it is still unclear whether and how social achievement goals have significantly independent relationships with students' achievement.

The pattern of relationship between social development goals and academic adjustment variables is consistent with the effect of mastery goals in academic domain. Social development goals were related to higher effort, engagement, and self-regulation and lower disruptive behavior (Liem, 2016; Shim, Cho, & Wang, 2013; , Zhu, & Zhao, 2016). Social demonstration-avoid goals did not show significant relationships with most of the academic engagement indicators (Liem, 2016; Zhao, Zhu, & Zhao, 2016), but were related to low disruptive behavior (Shim et al., 2013). For avoid goal-oriented students, academic disengagement and withdrawal can serve as good strategies. The desire to be socially invisible and comply seems to prevent disruptive behavior or aggressive behaviors. However, it is hard to consider these effects as benefits because these conditions are necessary, but not sufficient, for learning and achievement.

With respect to social demonstration-approach goals, prior research reported maladaptive patterns including high disruptive behavior, low effort/persistence, low adaptive help seeking behaviors, and low self-regulated learning (Liem, 2016; Ryan & Shin, 2011; Shim et al., 2013). Zhao, Zhu, and Zhao (2016) was an exception, in which this goal type was positively related to work engagement among Chinese college students. Unlike social demonstration-avoid goals, passive behavior does not support the goal attainment for the students with high social demonstration-approach goals. They might engage in disruptive behaviors in contexts where peers condone or encourage such behaviors (Müller, Hofmann, Begert, & Cillessen, 2018), with an intention to gain approval from peers. There has been no prior study that reported the positive association between this goal type and effective learning strategies.

Shim and Finch (2012) included a wide array of indicators of academic adjustment but they used latent class analysis, making it difficult to infer the nature of each type of goal. The inspection of zero order correlations suggested that social development goals were related to adaptive patterns including high engagement and desirable patterns of academic help seeking behavior (high adaptive help seeking, adaptive learning strategies and intrinsic value). The correlational patterns associated with social demonstration-approach goals were more maladaptive (e.g., high expedient help seeking and help avoidance, maladaptive learning strategies) than those with social demonstration-avoid goals, which did not show significant correlations with most of the academic variables included.

A couple of studies have shown that social achievement goals were also related to emotional experiences during task engagement (Mouratidis & Michou, 2011; Walker, Winn, & Lutjens, 2012). Mouratidis and Michou (2011) found desirable patterns related to social development goals such as high enjoyment and low boredom. Social demonstration-avoid goals were linked to high shame and were not related to other emotions. Interestingly, social demonstration-approach goals were related to a wide array of negative achievement emotions including anxiety, anger, boredom, and helplessness. Walker and colleagues (2012) reported that social development goals and demonstration-approach goals were both related to positive emotional experiences during task engagement. Social demonstration-avoid goals showed a null relation with either kind of happiness during task engagement. Note that the social development goals that were related to happiness resulted from meaningful and purposeful engagement, while social demonstration-approach goals were related to hedonistic enjoyment.

In sum, social development goals promote students' academic engagement. Social demonstration-avoid goals tend to make the students withdraw from the learning situation and encourage compliant behaviors when working with others. Social demonstration-avoid goals seem to trigger self-conscious emotions and fear of not meeting the social expectations during task engagement. The effects of social demonstration-approach goals were often null, and if significant, they were weak in magnitude.

What Mechanisms Might Explain Why Social Achievement Goals Matter for Social Adjustment?

Achievement goals are conceptualized to affect individuals' cognitive, behavioral, and affective responses during social encounters by providing qualitatively different interpretative frameworks (Ryan & Shim, 2006, 2008). In this section, we discuss further the advantages of approach goals and the disadvantages of demonstration goals.

Approach goal advantages

The approach vs. avoidance valence of the goals explains why development and demonstration-approach goals are more beneficial than demonstration-avoid goals (Elliot & McGregor, 2001; Horst et al., 2007; Kuroda & Sakurai, 2011). Students with social demonstration-avoid goals worry about potentially negative outcomes (e.g., being ridiculed, excluded, teased, or considered a nerd or geek; Roussel, Elliot, & Feltman, 2011), rather than anticipating or seeking positive outcomes (e.g., being liked, being popular; Horst et al., 2007). Thus, a demonstration-avoid goal leads individuals to focus more on negative events, highlight the importance of them, and discount the frequency and importance of positive events (Kuroda & Sakurai, 2011).

Cognitively, avoidant goal-oriented individuals tend to weigh the potential cost over potential gain of an action that could lead to a good outcome (e.g., thinking about the cost of asking for help rather than the benefit of such strategy, Roussel et al., 2011). Thinking about potential positive outcomes boosts efficacy and alters behavioral patterns. Approach goals foster exploration of new and unfamiliar social situations and persistence after experiencing setbacks. Such approach behaviors enable and serve as a catalyst for success. On the contrary, a demonstration-avoid goal may encourage individuals to resort to avoidant coping strategies, which are not conducive to problem solving (Shin & Ryan, 2012). This may explain the better social adjustment outcomes associated with approach type goals than an avoid goal. Avoidant-oriented students may not be able to employ effective social problem-solving strategies.

Recurring automatic negative thoughts about past events are closely related to emotional ill-being (e.g., Beck & Clark, 1997), while the tendency to attend to positive features of the environment contributes to high levels of psychological well-being (Carstensen, Gross, & Fung, 1998). Such tendencies lead to lessened efficacy and higher vulnerability to negative affect and stress (Horst et al., 2007; Kuroda & Sakurai, 2011; Ryan & Shim, 2006). Through such negative self-focused attention and intrusive negative thoughts (Gaydukevych & Kocovski, 2012; Masicampo & Baumeister, 2007), individuals' self-regulatory capacity can be compromised. Accordingly, it is not surprising that a demonstration-avoid goal was related to lower emotional self-regulation (Shim et al., 2017) and poor psychological well-being indicators (Kuroda & Sakurai, 2011; Ryan & Shim, 2006, 2008; Shim et al., 2017).

Demonstration-goal disadvantages

Demonstration-avoid goals have been consistently linked to maladaptive social and psychological outcomes, with few exceptions (e.g., low disruptive behavior, low aggression). Despite the approach goal advantages, a demonstration-approach goal often turns out to be maladaptive. Below, we describe some mechanisms addressing why demonstration goals, both approach and avoid forms, might have disadvantages over a development goal.

The belief that personality traits can be changed via effort (i.e., incremental theory) and the belief that personality is something innate (i.e., entity theory) are theorized to lead to social development goals and demonstration goals respectively (Dweck & Leggett, 1988; Horst et al., 2007). Such beliefs elicit different views and reactions to setbacks or mistakes. From a social development goal perspective, less than optimal social interactions or relationships simply mean that more effort is needed. However, from a social demonstration-goal standpoint, unfavorable events may indicate incorrigible flaws of the self and thus are threatening (Ryan & Shim, 2006). Failure is a natural part of learning from the former perspective and is something to be avoided from the latter. A constructive interpretation of setbacks associated with development goals fosters persistence and resilience. Withdrawal from the situation or discounting the importance of the event can be a likely resort for individuals with demonstration-approach or -avoid goals (Shin & Ryan, 2012).

The control-value theory of emotion posits that high value and high perception of control and subjectively construed value of the activities and outcomes are the key factors determining emotion (Pekrun, Elliot, & Maier, 2009). According to this theory, a social development goal has a clear advantage. From this goal framework, the aspired end state entails high intrinsic value, such as forming a meaningful social relationship (i.e., becoming a better friend and understanding their friends better). In contrast, from a social demonstration-goal perspective, the social partner or social interaction serves as a means to an end (e.g., securing a favorable status) and thus bears much less intrinsic value. Accordingly, social development goals are likely to be linked to more positive emotional experiences due to the heightened intrinsic value attached to social interactions, as compared to social demonstration-approach and -avoid goals.

Sense of control afforded by different criteria used to define success could be another explanatory mechanism. In the demonstration-goal perspective, the attainment of a social goal is determined by how *others* evaluate the individual. When the attainment of a social goal is determined by how *the individual* grows within interpersonal relationships, then adaptive cognition, affect, and behavior could be triggered due to enhanced sense of control (Erdley, Cain, Loomis, Dumas-Hines, & Dweck, 1997; Kuroda & Sakurai, 2011). Perceived goal difficulty might also play a role. Demonstration goals, both approach and avoid forms, are less advantageous, as demonstrating normative competence is perceived to be more difficult to attain than making improvement (Senko & Hulleman, 2013). Thus, when a goal is harder to obtain, it may lead to a less positive emotional experiences. Considering the elements of value and control, a social

Directions for Future Research

Over the last two decades or so, research on social achievement goals has established the importance of considering social achievement goals. Substantial attention has been paid to social adjustment during childhood and adolescence given the importance of peer relationships and prevalence of the desire to fit in and be popular at this time. Despite the burgeoning number of studies examining social achievement goals, there remain many unchartered and fruitful areas for research.

We organized our review of the importance of social achievement goals in regards to social, psychological, and academic adjustment. For each of these aspects of adjustment, we showed that social goals matter for adjustment. This pattern of findings certainly implicates social achievement goals as important to well-being and social interactions both in and out of the classroom. However, there are many ways in which future research could cast a wider net and garner a fuller understanding of the implications of social achievement goals for peer interactions and social dynamics. There are many aspects of peer relationships that have not been explored. For example, what role might social achievement goals play in bullying and victimization? Given some links between social demonstration-approach goals and aggressive behavior, this is likely to provide insights. Another line of inquiry could examine the role of social achievement goals in cross-sex peer relationships and romantic relationships. Same-sex and cross-sex relationships change a great deal during adolescence, and it would be interesting to see if social achievement goals are related to the stability and fluctuation of these relationships. An additional topic that receives much attention in research on adolescents is peer influence, or how friends socialize each other to become more similar over time. Much of this work examines general patterns with little attention to important individual differences. Social achievement goals could be an important individual characteristic that adolescents bring to social situations that affect the nature and magnitude of peer influence among friends.

In addition to expanding the consideration of outcomes of social achievement goals, attention to the antecedents of social goals is needed. Far more studies have considered the consequences compared to the precursors of social achievement goals. However, research on antecedents of social achievement goals can offer useful vantage points for educators, parents, and policy makers that are interested in developing and implementing interventions. A few studies are looking into individual students' attributes such as implicit beliefs and personality traits (Erdley et al., 1997, Study 2; Horst et al., 2007; Shim & Fletcher, 2012; Stoeber, 2014). Many of the theoretical constructs that are believed to affect achievement goal adoption are not systematically investigated (e.g., self-concept, fear of failure, fear of evaluation, implicit theories of personality, etc.). Further investigation of the antecedents leading to social achievement goal adoption is likely to be helpful. We can identify the groups of individuals that are prone to having social achievement goals and support them through targeted intervention. In addition, such attributes can be targets for intervention, if malleable. Social achievement goals are conceptualized to be sensitive to classroom context. A few studies have shown that social development goals can be promoted in classrooms in which personal progress and task mastery are emphasized over competition among students, and students are cared for and supported by their peers and teachers (Makara & Madjar, 2015; Shim et al., 2013).

Relatedly, there is a large literature in the academic domain investigating how classroom goal structures are related to students' achievement goals and behaviors. Recent years have seen growing attention to differences between classrooms in the nature of peer relations among students in that setting. There is growing evidence that peer experiences vary across classrooms in regard to relatedness and social support. The amount of reciprocated friendships and levels of peer acceptance and rejection vary across classrooms (Shin & Ryan, 2016). In some classrooms, the patterns of peer nominations indicate high levels of cohesion and an equitable spread of affiliations, whereas in other classrooms the nominations indicate a more hierarchical structure that leaves many students marginalized (Ahn, Garandeau, & Rodkin, 2010). Another way that classrooms vary is the nature of social status or what behaviors are correlated with high social status. For example, in some classrooms academic achievement has a higher correlation with being popular compared to other classrooms. In some classrooms, being aggressive is positively related to being popular, whereas in other classrooms it is negatively related (Shin & Ryan, 2016). What is the role of social goals in these different patterns of peer relationships? Goals are central to peer relationships and affected by classroom context. Can teachers orient students to development goals and create a more positive classroom social climate? Are goals an important lever or catalyst for a healthy classroom learning community?

Another fruitful avenue for future research is to extend the social achievement goal research to social interactions occurring online platforms. According to a recent survey by Pew Research Center (Lenhart, 2015), over 90% of teens report going online daily with 24% of the students being online almost constantly. There has been growing concerns that the interactions on social media are often toxic (e.g., rumor spreading, cyber bullying etc.), leading to depression and other psychological problems (Alhassan et al., 2018; Primack et al., 2017; Vannucci, Flannery, & Ohannessian, 2017). Social comparison and competitiveness, putting in extra efforts to obtain "Likes" from their peers, which are signature behaviors of social demonstration-approach goals, are commonly observed on the social platforms, especially on the ones popular among teenagers (e.g., Snapchat and Instagram) (Teo & Collinson, 2018). A systematic investigation of social achievement goals and social behaviors in this context can shed light on the peer relationship dynamics in this context. Alternatively, longitudinal investigations can track the changes in social achievement goals while considering the patterns of students' social media use (type, frequency, duration, interaction pattern, etc.). Students' online social life has implications for their off-line social relationships, as online social media has become an integral part of adolescents' daily lives. Those who intend to develop effective interventions to support positive peer relationships must consider students' social motivation and behaviors in both online and off-line contexts.

Although our knowledge on the nature and the implications of different social achievement goals has been steadily increasing, future research should systematically examine multiple goals (e.g., cross-domain or within domain goal interactions), different contexts (e.g., formal vs. informal learning settings), various research paradigms (e.g., experimental, longitudinal, person-centered approach), diverse samples (gender, ethnic, or cultural groups), and various moderators (e.g., self-related constructs, beliefs, personality traits). Some researchers have begun the investigations in this direction (Jansen in de Wal et al., 2015; Jones & Ford, 2014; Lee, 2018; Liem, 2016; Madjar, Cohen, & Shoval, 2018; Michou et al., 2016; Shim & Finch, 2014; Shim et al., 2013; Shin & Ryan, 2012; Wilson, Rodkin, & Ryan, 2014), but much more empirical data will be needed before we can have a fuller understanding of the function of social achievement goals.

Conclusion

In conclusion, our review of social achievement goal research indicates that these goals have important implications for students' academic, social, and psychological adjustment. Despite the advances made over the last 20 years, many important questions remain for future research. We outlined five different areas for future research: expansion to additional outcomes, attention to antecedents, more attention to classroom structures, consideration of online social interactions, and examination of multiple goals. With the increasing awareness of the importance of social adjustment for personal well-being and academic success, we hope that future work will continue to advance our understanding of the processes and consequences of social achievement goals.

References

Ahn, H.-J., Garandeau, C. F., & Rodkin, P. C. (2010). Effects of classroom embeddedness and density on the social status of aggressive and victimized children. *The Journal of Early Adolescence*, 30(1), 76–101.

Alhassan, A. A., Alqadhib, E. M., Taha, N. W., Alahmari, R. A., Salam, M., & Almutairi, A. F. (2018). The relationship between addiction to smartphone usage and depression among adults: A cross sectional study. *BMC Psychiatry*, 18(1), 148.

Ames, C. (1992). Classrooms: Goals, structures, and student motivation. *Journal of Educational Psychology, 84*(3), 261–271. doi:10.1037/0022-0663.84.3.261.

Anderman, L. H. (1999). Classroom goal orientation, school belonging and social goals as predictors of students' positive and negative affect following the transition to middle school. *Journal of Research and Development in Education*, 32, 89–103.

Austin, J. T., & Vancouver, J. F. (1996). Goal constructs in psychology: Structure, process, and content. *Psychological Bulletin, 120*(3), 338–375. doi:10.1037/0033-2909.120.3.338.

Bandura, A. (1986). *Social foundations of thought and action: A social cognitive theory*. Englewood Cliffs, NJ: Prentice-Hall, Inc.

Baumeister, R. F., & Leary, M. R. (1995). The need to belong: Desire for interpersonal attachments as a fundamental human motivation. *Psychological Bulletin, 117*(3), 497–529. doi:10.1037/0033-2909.117.3.497.

Beck, A. T., & Clark, D. A. (1997). An information processing model of anxiety: Automatic and strategic processes. *Behavior Research and Therapy, 35*(1), 49–58. doi:10.1016/S0005-7967(96)00069-1.

Bong, M. (2001). Between- and within-domain relations of academic motivation among middle and high school students: Self-efficacy, task-value, and achievement goals. *Journal of Educational Psychology, 93*(1), 23–34. http://dx.doi.org/10.1037//0022-0663.93.1.23.

Carstensen, L. L., Gross, J. J., & Fung, H. (1998). The social context of emotional experience. In K. W. Schaie & M. P. Lawton (Eds.), *Annual review of gerontology and geriatrics* (Vol. 17, pp. 325–352). New York: Springer.

Carver, C. S., Lawrence, J. W., & Scheier, M. F. (1996). A control-process perspective on the origins of affect. In L. L. Martin & A. Tesser (Eds.), *Striving and feeling: Interactions between goals and affect* (pp. 11–52). Hillsdale, NJ: Erlbaum.

Chung, T., & Asher, S. R. (1996). Children's goals and strategies in peer conflict situations. *Merrill-Palmer Quarterly, 42*(1), 125–147.

Covington, M. V. (2000). Goal theory, motivation, and school achievement: An integrative review. *Annual Review of Psychology, 51*, 171–200. doi:10.1146/annurev.psych.51.1.171.

Crick, N. R., & Dodge, K. A. (1994). A review and reformulation of social information-processing mechanisms in children's social adjustment. *Psychological Bulletin, 115*(1), 74–101. doi:10.1037/0033-2909.115.1.74.

Dweck, C. S. (1986). Motivational processes affecting learning. *American Psychologist, 41*(10), 1040–1048. doi:10.1037/0003-066X.41.10.1040.

Dweck, C. S. (1999). *Self-theories: Their role in motivation, personality, and development*. New York: Psychology Press.

Dweck, C. S., & Leggett, E. L. (1988). A social-cognitive approach to motivation and personality. *Psychological Review, 95*(2), 256–273.

Dykman, B. M. (1998). Integrating cognitive and motivational factors in depression. *Journal of Personality and Social Psychology, 74*(1), 139–158.

Elliot, A. J. (2005). A conceptual history for the achievement goal construct. In A. J. Elliot & C. S. Dweck (Eds.), *Handbook of competence and motivation* (pp. 52–72). New York: Guilford Publications.

Elliot, A. J., & McGregor, H. A. (2001). A 2 x 2 achievement goal framework. *Journal of Personality and Social Psychology, 80*(3), 501–519. doi:10.1037/0022-3514.80.3.501.

Elliot, A. J., Murayama, K., & Pekrun, R. (2011). A 3 x 2 achievement goal model. *Journal of Educational Psychology, 103*(3), 632–648.

Erdley, C. A., Cain, K. M., Loomis, C. C., Dumas-Hines, F., & Dweck, C. S. (1997). Relations among children's social goals, implicit personality theories, and responses to social failure. *Developmental Psychology, 33*(2), 263–272. http://dx.doi.org/10.1037/0012-1649.33.2.263.

Ford, D. Y. (1992). Self-perceptions of underachievement and support for the achievement ideology among early adolescent African-Americans. *The Journal of Early Adolescence, 12*(3), 228–252. doi:10.1177/0272431692012003001.

Gable, S. L. (2006). Approach and avoidance social motives and goals. *Journal of Personality, 74*(1), 175–221. doi:10.1111/j.1467-6494.2005.00373.x.

Gaydukevych, D., & Kocovski, N. L. (2012). Effect of self-focused attention on post-event processing in social anxiety. *Behavior Research and Therapy, 50*(1), 47–55. doi:10.1016/j.brat.2011.10.010.

Horst, S. J., Finney, S. J., & Barron, K. E. (2007). Moving beyond academic achievement measures: A study of social achievement goals. *Contemporary Educational Psychology, 32*(4), 667–698. doi:10.1016/j.cedpsych.2006.10.011.

Jansen in de Wal, J., Hornstra, L., Prins, F. J., Peetsma, T., & van der Veen, I. (2016). The prevalence, development and domain specificity of elementary school students' achievement goal profiles. *Educational Psychology, 36*(7), 1303–1322. doi:10.1080/01443410.2015.1035698.

Jarvinen, D. W., & Nicholls, J. G. (1996). Adolescents' social goals, beliefs about the causes of social success, and satisfaction in peer relations. *Developmental Psychology, 32*(3), 435–441. doi:10.1037/0012-1649.32.3.435.

Jones, M. H., & Ford, J. M. (2014). Social achievement goals, efficacious beliefs, and math performance in a predominately African American high school. *Journal of Black Psychology, 40*(3), 239–262. doi:10.1177/0095798413483556.

Jones, M. H., Mueller, C. E., Royal, K. D., Shim, S. S., & Hart, C. O. (2013). Social achievement goals: Validation among rural African American adolescents. *Journal of Psychoeducational Assessment, 31*(6), 566–577. https://doi.org/10.1177/0734282913483982.

Kuroda, Y., & Sakurai, S. (2003). Goal orientation in peer relations and depression among preadolescents: "Distress-generation" and "eustress-generation" models. *Japanese Journal of Educational Psychology, 51,* 86–95.

Kuroda, Y., & Sakurai, S. (2011). Social goal orientations, interpersonal stress, and depressive symptoms among early adolescents in Japan: A test of diathesis-stress model using the trichotomous framework of social achievement goal orientations. *Journal of Early Adolescence, 31*(2), 300–322. doi:10.1177/0272431610363158.

LaFontana, K. M., & Cillessen, A. N. (2002). Children's perceptions of popular and unpopular peers: A multimethod assessment. *Developmental Psychology, 38*(5), 635–647. doi:10.1037/0012-1649.38.5.635.

Lee, E. J. (2018). Social achievement goals and social adjustment in adolescence: A multiple-goal perspective. *Japanese Psychological Research*, 60(3), 121–133. https://doi.org/10.1111/jpr.12189.

Lenhart, A. (2015, April 9). Teens, social media & technology overview 2015. www.pewinternet.org/2015/04/09/teens-social-media-technology-2015/.

Liem, G. A. D. (2016). Academic and social achievement goals: Their additive, interactive, and specialized effects on school functioning. *British Journal of Educational Psychology*, 86(1), 37–56. http://dx.doi.org/10.1111/bjep.12085.

Madjar, N. (2017). Stability and change in social goals as related to goal structures and engagement in school. *The Journal of Experimental Education*, 85(2), 259–277. https://doi.org/10.1080/00220973.2016.1148658.

Madjar, N., Cohen, V., & Shoval, G. (2018). Longitudinal analysis of the trajectories of academic and social motivation across the transition from elementary to middle school. *Educational Psychology*, 38(2), 221–247. https://doi.org/10.1080/01443410.2017.1341623.

Maehr, M. L., & Nicholls, J. G. (1980). Culture and achievement motivation: A second look.In N. Warren (Ed.), *Studies in cross-cultural psychology* (Vol. 3, pp. 221–267). New York: Academic Press.

Makara, K. A., & Madjar, N. (2015). The role of goal structures and peer climate in trajectories of social achievement goals during high school. *Developmental Psychology*, 51(4), 473–488. http://dx.doi.org/10.1037/a0038801.

Masicampo, E. J., & Baumeister, R. F. (2007). Relating mindfulness and self-regulatory processes. *Psychological Inquiry, 18*(4), 255–258. doi:10.1080/10478400701598363.

McAdams, S. (1987). Music: A science of the mind? *Contemporary Music Review, 2*(1), 1–61. doi:10.1080/07494468708567053.

Michou, A., Mouratidis, A., Ersoy, E., & Uğur, H. (2016). Social achievement goals, needs satisfaction, and coping among adolescents. *Personality and Individual Differences*, 99, 260–265. http://dx.doi.org/10.1016/j.paid.2016.05.028.

Midgley, C., Maehr, M. L., Hruda, L. Z., Anderman, E., Anderman, L., Freeman, K. E … Urdan, T. (2000). *Manual for the patterns of Adaptive Learning Scales (PALS)*. Ann Arbor, MI: University of Michigan.

Mouratidis, A., & Michou, A. (2011). Perfectionism, self-determined motivation, and coping among adolescent athletes. *Psychology of Sport and Exercise, 12*(4), 355–367. doi:10.1016/j.psychsport.2011.03.006.

Mouratidis, A., & Sideridis, G. (2009). On social achievement goals: Their relations with peer acceptance, classroom belongingness, and perceptions of loneliness. *Journal of Experimental Education, 77*(3), 285–307. doi:10.3200/JEXE.77.3.285–308.

Müller, C. M., Hofmann, V., Begert, T., & Cillessen, A. H. N. (2018). Peer influence on disruptive classroom behavior depends on teachers' instructional practice. *Journal of Applied Developmental Psychology*, 56, 99–108. https://doi.org/10.1016/j.appdev.2018.04.001.

Nicholls, J. (1984). Achievement motivation: Conceptions of ability, subjective experience, task choice, and performance. *Psychological Review, 91*(3), 328–346. doi:10.1037/0033-295X.91.3.328.

Parkhurst, J. T., & Hopmeyer, A. (1998). Sociometric popularity and peer-perceived popularity: Two distinct dimensions of peer status. *The Journal of Early Adolescence, 18*(2), 125–144. doi:10.1177/0272431698018002001.

Pekrun, R., Elliot, A. J., & Maier, M. A. (2009). Achievement goals and achievement emotions: Testing a model of their joint relations with academic performance. *Journal of Educational Psychology, 101*(1), 115–135. doi:10.1037/a0013383.

Pintrich, P. R. (2000). An achievement goal theory perspective on issues in motivation terminology, theory, and research. *Contemporary Educational Psychology, 25*(1), 92–104. https://doi.org/10.1006/ceps.1999.1017.

Pintrich, P. R., & Schunk, D. H. (2002). *Motivation in education: Theory, research, and applications* (2nd ed.). Upper Saddle River, NJ: Prentice Hall.

Primack, B. A., Shensa, A., Escobar-Viera, C. G., Barrett, E. L., Sidani, J. E., Colditz, J. B., & James, A. E. (2017). Use of multiple social media platforms and symptoms of depression and anxiety: A nationally-representative study among US young adults. *Computers in Human Behavior*, 69, 1–9.

Rodkin, P. C., Farmer, T. W., Pearl, R., & Van Acker, R. (2000). Heterogeneity of popular boys: Antisocial and prosocial configurations. *Developmental Psychology, 36*(1), 14–24. doi:10.1037/0012-1649.36.1.14.

Rodkin, P. C., Ryan, A. M., Jamison, R., & Wilson, T. (2013). Social goals, social behavior, and social status in middle childhood. *Developmental Psychology*, 49(6), 1139–1150. http://dx.doi.org/10.1037/a0029389.

Rose, A. J., & Asher, S. R. (1999). Children's goals and strategies in response to conflicts within a friendship. *Developmental Psychology, 35*(1), 69–79. doi:10.1037/0012-1649.35.1.69.

Rose, A. J., Swenson, L. P., & Waller, E. M. (2004). Overt and relational aggression and perceived popularity: Developmental differences in concurrent and prospective relations. *Developmental Psychology, 40*(3), 378–387. doi:10.1037/0012-1649.40.3.378.

Roussel, P., Elliot, A. J., & Feltman, R. (2011). The influence of achievement goals and social goals on help-seeking from peers in an academic context. *Learning and Instruction, 21*(3), 394–402. doi:10.1016/j.learninstruc.2010.05.003.

Rudolph, K. D., Abaied, J. L., Flynn, M., Sugimura, N., & Agoston, A. M. (2011). Developing relationships, being cool, and not looking like a loser: Social goal orientation predicts children's responses to peer aggression. *Child Development, 82*(5), 1518–1530. http://dx.doi.org/10.1111/j.1467-8624.2011.01631.x.

Ryan, A. M., & Shim, S. S. (2006). Social achievement goals: The nature and consequences of different orientations toward social competence. *Personality and Social Psychology Bulletin, 32*(9), 1246–1263. http://dx.doi.org/10.1177/0146167206289345.

Ryan, A. M., & Shim, S. S. (2008). An exploration of young adolescents' social achievement goals and social adjustment in middle school. *Journal of Educational Psychology, 100*(3), 672–687. http://dx.doi.org/10.1037/0022–0663.100.3.672.

Ryan, A. M., & Shin, H. (2011). Help-seeking tendencies: An examination of motivational correlates and consequences for achievement during the first year of middle school. *Learning and Instruction, 21*(2), 247–256. doi:10.1016/j.learninstruc.2010.07.003.

Ryan, R. M., & Deci, E. L. (2000). The darker and brighter sides of human existence: Basic psychological needs as a unifying concept. *Psychological Inquiry, 11*(4), 319–338. doi:10.1207/S15327965PLI1104_03.

Ryff, C. D. (1989). Happiness is everything, or is it? Explorations on the meaning of psychological well-being. *Journal of Personality and Social Psychology, 57*(6), 1069–1081. doi:10.1037/0022-3514.57.6.1069.

Ryff, C. D., & Keyes, C. M. (1995). The structure of psychological well-being revisited. *Journal of Personality and Social Psychology, 69*(4), 719–727. doi:10.1037/0022-3514.69.4.719.

Sanderson, C. A., Rahm, K. B., & Beigbeder, S. A. (2005). The link between the pursuit of intimacy goals and satisfaction in close same-sex friendships: An examination of the underlying processes. *Journal of Social and Personal Relationships, 22*(1), 75–98. doi:10.1177/0265407505049322.

Senko, C. & Freund, A.M. (2015). Are mastery-avoidance achievement goals always detrimental? An adult development perspective. *Motivation and Emotion, 39,* 477–488. https://doi org.proxy.bsu.edu/10.1007/s11031–11015–9474–9471.

Senko, C., & Hulleman, C. S. (2013). The role of goal attainment expectancies in achievement goal pursuit. *Journal of Educational Psychology, 105*(2), 504–521. http://dx.doi.org/10.1037/a0031136.

Shim, S. S., Cho, Y., & Wang, C. (2013). Classroom goal structures, social achievement goals, and adjustment in middle school. *Learning and Instruction, 23,* 69–77. http://dx.doi.org/10.1016/j.learninstruc.2012.05.008.

Shim, S. S., & Finch, W. H. (2014). Academic and social achievement goals and early adolescents' adjustment: A latent class approach. *Learning and Individual Differences, 30,* 98–105. http://dx.doi.org/10.1016/j.lindif.2013.10.015.

Shim, S. S., & Fletcher, K. L. (2012). Perfectionism and social goals: What do perfectionists want to achieve in social situations? *Personality and Individual Differences, 52*(8), 919–924. doi:10.1016/j.paid.2012.02.002.

Shim, S. S., & Ryan, A. M. (2012). What do students want socially when they arrive at college? Implications of social achievement goals for social behaviors and adjustment during the first semester of college. *Motivation and Emotion, 36*(4), 504–515. http://dx.doi.org/10.1007/s11031-011-9272-3.

Shim, S. S., Wang, C., & Cassady, J. C. (2013). Emotional well-being: The role of social achievement goals and self-esteem. *Personality and Individual Differences*, 55(7), 840–845. http://dx.doi.org/10.1016/j.paid.2013.07.004.

Shim, S. S., Wang, C., Makara, K., Xu, X., Xie, L., & Zhong, M. (2017). College students' social goals and psychological adjustment: Mediation via emotion regulation. *Journal of College Student Development*, 58(8), 1237–1255.

Shin, H. Y., & Ryan, A. M. (2012). How do young adolescents cope with social problems? An examination of social goals, coping with friends, and social adjustment. *Journal of Early Adolescence*, 32(6), 851–875. http://dx.doi.org/10.1177/0272431611429944.

Shin, H. Y., & Ryan, A. M. (2016). Friendship processes around aggressive and pro-social behaviors in the classroom: Examining the moderating role of gender and perceived relatedness with teachers. Presented at 16th Biennial Meeting of Society for Research on Adolescence, Baltimore, MD.

Stoeber, J. (2014). Multidimensional perfectionism and the DSM-5 personality traits. *Personality and Individual Differences, 64*, 115–120. doi:10.1016/j.paid.2014.02.031.

Sutton, R. M., Stoeber, J., & Kamble, S. V. (2017). Belief in a just world for oneself versus others, social goals, and subjective well-being. *Personality and Individual Differences, 113*, 115–119. doi:10.1016/j.paid.2017.03.026.

Talepasand, S., Alijani, F., & Bigdeli, I. (2010). Validation of the social achievement goal orientation scale in Iranian students. *Eurasian Journal of Educational Research*, 40, 17–31.

Teo, N. S. Y., & Collinson, S. L. (2018). Instagram and risk of rumination and eating disorders: An Asian perspective. *Psychology of Popular Media Culture*. doi:10.1037/ppm0000205.

Urdan, T., & Maehr, M. L. (1995). Beyond a two-goal theory of motivation: A case for social goals. *Review of Educational Research*, 65, 213–244.

Vannucci, A., Flannery, K. M., & Ohannessian, C. M. (2017). Social media use and anxiety in emerging adults. *Journal of Affective Disorders*, 207, 163–166.

Walker, C. O., Winn, T. D., & Lutjens, R. M. (2012). Examining relationships between academic and social achievement goals and routes to happiness. *Education Research International*, 2012, 7 pages. https://doi.org/10/1155/2012/643438.

Wentzel, K. R. (2001). Social relationships and motivation in middle school: The role of parents, teachers, and peers. *Journal of Educational Psychology*, 90(2), 202–209.

Wentzel, K. R., Barry, C. M., & Caldwell, K. A. (2004). Friendships in middle school: Influences on motivation and school adjustment. *Journal of Educational Psychology, 96*(2), 195–203. doi:10.1037/0022-0663.96.2.195.

Wentzel, K. R., & McNamara, C. C. (1999). Interpersonal relationships, emotional distress, and prosocial behavior in middle school. *The Journal of Early Adolescence, 19*(1), 114–125. doi:10.1177/0272431699019001006.

Wilson, T. M., Rodkin, P. C., & Ryan, A. M. (2014). The company they keep and avoid: Social goal orientation as a predictor of children's ethnic segregation. *Developmental Psychology, 50*(4), 1116–1124. doi:10.1037/a0035040.

Zhao, Y., Zhu, X., & Zhao, G. (2016). Validation of the Chinese version of the Social Achievement Goal Orientation Scale. *Journal of Psychoeducational Assessment*, 34(2), 199–204.

5

SOCIAL DOMINANCE GOALS

Sarah M. Kiefer

Striving for social dominance over peers is a salient yet relatively overlooked social goal in the classroom. This is surprising given that strivings for dominance have been prominent in much research and theorizing on motivation and personality (McAdams, 1988; McClelland, 1985; Murray, 1938; Veroff, 1957; Winter, 1973). Research suggests that aggressive and manipulative behavior among students is prevalent and important to social adjustment in school (Cillessen & Rose, 2005; Hawley, Little, & Rodkin, 2007), and that social dominance goals have implications for social and academic adjustment (Dawes, 2017; Jonkmann, Trautwein, & Ludtke, 2009; Kiefer & Ryan, 2008). This chapter provides a review of research and theory regarding social dominance goals in the classroom, including different theoretical approaches, empirical findings, implications for social and academic adjustment, and future research directions.

Defining Social Dominance Goals: Different Approaches

Various theoretical approaches have been used to investigate students' social goals. Wentzel's (1996) goal content approach defines social goals as what students try to achieve socially in school. Using this approach, researchers have asked students how often they try to do various things (e.g., have fun, follow rules) to describe their social goals with regard to *what specifically* they are trying to accomplish with peers (Ford, 1992; Wentzel, 2000). A second approach is the social achievement goal orientation, which conceptualizes social goals as distinct orientations toward social competence focusing on broad reasons *why* individuals strive to accomplish their goal with peers (e.g., development and demonstration of social competence; Dweck & Leggett, 1988; Erdley, Cain, Loomis, Dumas-

Hines, & Dweck, 1997; Ryan, Kiefer, & Hopkins, 2004; Ryan & Shim, 2006). However, absent from these approaches is attention to social dominance goals.

One approach to conceptualizing social dominance goals is as being representative of one of the three basic motives that energize and direct behavior: power, achievement, and affiliation (McClelland, 1985). The power motive involves the desire to have impact, control, or influence over others. The achievement motive concerns the desire to succeed, whereas the affiliative motive encompasses the desire to be with others and for intimate relationships characterized by warmth and disclosure of personal thoughts and feelings. Other theorists have also drawn attention to the need for power as an important aspect of motivation (McAdams, 1988; Murray, 1938; Winter, 1973; Winter & Stewart, 1978).

Whereas McClelland (1985) conceptualized these basic motives as enduring traits and distinguished these motives from more specific goal strivings, goals are often conceptualized as concrete and situation-specific (Elliot, 1999). As the more situation-specific manifestations of more general motives, goals should be related to situation-specific behaviors of students (i.e., social and academic adjustment in school). Within this approach, social dominance goals are conceptualized as focusing on having power over peers, characterized by a student getting other peers to comply with their wishes, and instilling fear in peers (Kiefer & Ryan, 2008).

To understand implications of social dominance goals, they have been examined in tandem with two other social goals that represent McClelland's (1985) major motive systems: intimacy and popularity goals (Anderman, 1999; Jarvinen & Nicholls, 1996; Kiefer & Ryan, 2008; Kiefer & Wang, 2016; Ryan, Hicks, & Midgley, 1997). These two social goals are viewed as stemming, in part, from individual differences in students' affiliative and achievement motives, although these are not the only social goals that may emanate from these larger motives.

The measurement of social dominance goals along with popularity and intimacy goals often come from items in the Social Goals Questionnaire among early and middle adolescents (Jarvinen & Nicholls, 1996; Kiefer & Ryan, 2008). The stem for all items is "When I'm with people my own age, I like it when," which focuses students on outcomes that would make them feel successful or happy. This feature is unique to Nicholls's goal measures (Nicholls, Cheung, Lauer, & Pataschnick, 1989) compared with other goal measures that use a range of stems (e.g., "My goal is," "I try to," or "I want to"; Anderman, 1999). Items for social dominance goals include "… they worry that I'll hurt them," and "… I make them do what I want." A study conducted by Midgley et al. (1998) in the academic domain provided the validity information by demonstrating strong correlations between among similar goal constructs focused on striving for superiority in academic ability, Nicholl's ego orientation measure and ability-approach goal orientation measure from the Patterns of Adaptive Learning Survey ($r = .63$).

Recent research on agentic and communal goals builds on McClelland's basic motives. Agentic goals focus on gaining status, influence, or power in social relationships (McClelland's power and achievement motives), whereas communal goals focus on attaining and maintaining close relationships characterized by intimacy, connection, and cooperation with others (McClelland's affiliation motive; Wiggins, 1991). Researchers have used the interpersonal circumplex model to examine agentic and communal goals during adolescence (Locke, 2000; Ojanen, Grönroos, & Salmivalli, 2005; Salmivalli, Ojanen, Haanpää, & Peets, 2005). Within the circumplex model, the vertical axis represents agency (i.e., independence, power, dominance) and the horizontal axis represents communal motives (i.e., solidarity, avoiding conflict). Although social dominance goals are included in this model, they are conceptualized as agentic goals. Thus, strivings for achievement and power are not differentiated in this model.

Additional perspectives relevant to the study of social dominance goals are social dominance theory and resource control theory. Informed by an evolutionary perspective, social dominance theory focuses on the adaptiveness of certain behaviors, including aggressive and prosocial actions that allow individuals to control resources and achieve status (Crick, Murray-Close, Marks, & Mohajeri-Nelson, 2009; Hawley, 2003; Savin-Williams, 1987). Resource control theory, an extension of social dominance theory (Hawley et al., 2007), proposes that all social groups, including peer relations, can be organized by relative competitive ability and suggests that individuals who have resource control are the ones who are given social attention and status (Hawley & Bower, 2018). From these perspectives, social dominance is associated with popularity, and provides an alternative proposal for why children and adolescents use aggression as a way to achieve or maintain social power (Pellegrini, Roseth, Van Ryzin, & Solberg, 2011). In fact, perceived popularity is considered analogous to social dominance by some researchers; one mechanism for perceived popular youth to gain status is via coercive, aggressive strategies (Adler & Adler, 1998; Lease, Kennedy, & Axelrod, 2002). However, it is important to note that social dominance goals are not synonymous with aggressive behavior; aggressive behavior is one possible consequence of striving for dominance or power over peers.

Empirical Findings

Despite research suggesting that social dominance goals are prevalent and important in the lives of young adolescents, they have been understudied relative to other social goals. There is much that we do not know regarding developmental changes of social dominance goals during childhood and adolescence as well as potential gender and ethnic differences.

Developmental and contextual changes

There is a scarcity of longitudinal research examining developmental changes in social dominance goals, as most research has used cross-sectional or short-term longitudinal research designs. Children may decrease striving for power over their peers during childhood as they gain social skills and competencies (Bukowski, Laursen, & Rubin, 2018). As children grow older, however, striving for dominance shifts from being associated with aggression to being associated with social status (Wright, Zakriski, & Fisher, 1996). Previous research considered aggressive behavior as a form of social incompetence and associated with peer rejection (operationalized as many do not like nominations and few like nominations from peers). However, recent research has highlighted that, when social status is measured with indicators such as popular or cool nominations instead of sociometric nominations (liked most, liked least), aggressive behaviors are associated with social status during adolescence (Cillessen & Mayeux, 2004; Cillessen & Rose, 2005; Rodkin, Farmer, Pearl, & Van Acker, 2000; Rose, Swenson, & Waller, 2004). This line of research conceptualizes popularity as a type of status characterized by social power, dominance, and prominence among peers (Adler & Adler, 1998; Cillessen & Marks, 2011; Rodkin et al., 2000). Studies indicate positive links between popularity goals and dominance goals (Kiefer, Matthews, Montesino, Arango, & Preece, 2013; Kiefer & Ryan, 2008; Kiefer & Shim, 2016). Thus, in some cases, striving for social dominance may be associated with striving for popularity.

There have been mixed findings regarding mean-level changes in self-reported social dominance goals during early adolescence using short-term longitudinal studies. Research indicates social dominance goals decrease over time, particularly during the transition to middle school (Kiefer & Ryan, 2008). However, other studies have indicated dominance goals increase across the sixth grade, the first year of middle school (Kiefer & Shim, 2016; Kiefer & Wang, 2016). Dominance goals may have benefits, especially in new but not well-established social relationships (resource control and status; Pellegrini, 2008; Pellegrini & Bartini, 2001). Dominance goals also have social costs, especially for established social relationships, including diminished likability and intimacy as well as fewer high-quality friendships (Eder, 1985; Merten, 1997). Taken together, these findings indicate that the salience of social dominance goals may change as students move from elementary to middle school.

Students' perceptions of the classroom context (e.g., perceptions of the classroom and school environment, teacher and peer support) may change across the middle school transition and influence students' strivings for social dominance. In middle school, it is often difficult for students to establish meaningful relationships with teachers and peers (Eccles, 2004). Schooling at the middle level typically involves changing classes, less contact with teachers, disruptions of peer networks, and an increased focus on performance goals in comparison with elementary school (Eccles, 2004). Furthermore, as students respond to a new environment and changing peer context that often promote social status and dominance over peers, dominant behavior increases (Cillessen & Mayeux, 2004; Jonkmann et al., 2009; Pellegrini & Bartini, 2001). Thus, it is likely that school contextual factors shape students' endorsement of social dominance goals. For example, the promotion of performance goals and social interaction among peers in the classroom is positively associated with social dominance goals during the first year of middle school (Kiefer et al., 2013). Students may strive for dominance when interacting with peers on a task-related activity or in a performance-based classroom; social interaction may provide occasions for students to establish a dominance hierarchy in a new school context (Pellegrini & Bartini, 2001). Although research has examined the role of the classroom context in the development of academic goals, little is known about the developmental trajectories of social dominance, as well as *how* aspects of the school, classroom, or peer context shape social goals.

Gender and ethnicity

The findings regarding gender differences in social dominance goals have been fairly consistent and align with previous research and theory, whereas much less is known regarding ethnic differences as prior research has used predominantly White samples. Research indicates that boys endorse social dominance goals more than girls (Jarvinen & Nicholls, 1996; Kiefer et al., 2013; Kiefer & Shim, 2016; Kiefer & Wang, 2016), and that boys tend to endorse more agentic and status-oriented goals than girls (Rose & Rudolph, 2006). These findings are in line with research indicating that boys are socialized to be more competitive and dominant than girls (Ruble, Martin, & Berenbaum, 2006).

Although relatively understudied, findings regarding ethnic and gender differences in social dominance goals align with McClelland's (1985) theorizing about need for power and Majors's (1991) theorizing about identity development. Regarding McClelland's (1985) basic motives (power, achievement, and affiliation), he theorized that a loss of or threat to one's power in society leads to a compensatory increase in striving for power. Thus, members of marginalized or discriminated groups may strive for power more than those who have not had such adverse social experiences. In support of this viewpoint, Veroff, Depner, Kulka, and Douvan (1980) found that African American men had higher power strivings than White men. A similar process is described by Majors's (1991) theorizing on the identity development of adolescent African American males in urban settings. In response to discrimination, African American males assume a cool pose of toughness, strength, and detachment (Cunningham & Meunier, 2004; Majors & Billson, 1992; Stevenson, 2004). This cool pose is characterized as a bravado or macho attitude and not expressing emotions and vulnerability (Majors & Billson, 1992). Aligned with these ideas, research conducted with youth in urban, predominantly low-income schools found African American students were higher on social dominance goals in sixth and seventh grades and lower on intimacy goals in seventh grade compared to White students (Kiefer & Ryan, 2008). Additionally, being male was associated with increased social dominance and decreased intimacy goals in both sixth and seventh grades. Thus, ethnicity and gender may contribute to students' endorsement of social dominance goals. Future research is needed on students in diverse school contexts to further document gender and ethnic differences in social dominance goals, as well as to understand how social dominance goals may be relevant to understanding social and academic adjustment in school.

Social Adjustment

Dominant and aggressive behaviors are prevalent and important to social adjustment in school and play a central role in peer dynamics and social success (Cillessen & Rose, 2005). Given this, research examining social dominance goals has focused on its implications for social adjustment in school, including heterogeneity among socially dominant youth, aggression and social status, as well as help seeking among peers. Research indicates there is considerable variability among socially dominant youth, and that striving for dominance over peers has both benefits and costs for students' social adjustment in school.

Heterogeneity among socially dominant youth

Research has examined heterogeneity among socially dominant adolescents and identified distinct types of socially dominant students with different levels of social adjustment. Lease et al. (2002) used cluster analysis to identify several subtypes of socially dominant students in elementary school (grades 4–6), including socially dominant students who were well-liked and those who were perceived as popular. Well-liked/dominant students were reported by teachers and peers to exhibit more prosocial characteristics (helps others, values schools, fun to hang around with), whereas perceived popular/dominant youth were reported to exhibit more aggressive and salient characteristics (bullies/relational aggression, good at sports, attractive) and were more admired (rated as cool, admired, and having social control; Lease et al., 2002). Informed by the resource control theory, Hawley (2003) contended there are three subtypes of dominant youth, including coercive, prosocial, and bistrategic. Bistrategic youth, who use aggressive and prosocial behaviors to strive for dominance and gain peer status, had positive social adjustment (socially central, peer acceptance, socially skilled), despite their aggressive and disruptive behavior (Hawley, 2003).

Aggression and social status

Research indicates the pursuit of social dominance goals have both benefits and costs for students' social adjustment in school. Social dominance goals are positively related to overt and relational aggression (Caravita & Cillessen, 2012; Ojanen, Findley, & Fuller, 2012; Sijtsema, Veenstra, Lindenberg, & Salmivalli, 2009). Extending prior cross-sectional research examining links between dominance goals and aggression, Ojanen and Findley-Van Nostrand (2014) examined prospective associations among social goals, overt and relational aggression, social preference, and popularity among middle school students. They found that youth with high agentic goals (status, power) use relational aggression to maintain popularity. Additional research indicates that popular-aggressive youth with high agentic and dominance goals may be socially skilled and savvy individuals, using aggression to establish and maintain status (Cillessen & Mayeux, 2004; Sijtsema et al., 2009). Striving for social dominance can have negative implications for peer relationships, as overt aggression undermines intimacy with peers (Ojanen et al., 2012). Prior observational research has found high-status children tend to mitigate social costs and increase social cohesion by using aggressive tactics followed by affiliative strategies (Roseth et al., 2011). However, less is known regarding these processes during adolescence (Pellegrini & Bartini, 2001). Recent longitudinal research conducted by Allen, Schad, Oudekerk, and Chango (2014) may provide insight into the short-term benefits and long-term costs of social dominance strivings among cool youth. Allen and colleagues followed adolescents from ages 13 to 23; early adolescent pseudomature behavior (e.g., minor delinquency and risk-taking behavior) was linked cross-sectionally to striving for popularity and short-term social success. However, longitudinal findings indicated pseudomature behavior was linked to declines in popularity across adolescence and difficulties in close relationships with peers during early adulthood (Allen et al., 2014).

Research suggests that social goals (i.e., popularity goals) moderate relations between social status and aggression (Cillessen, Mayeux, Ha, de Bruyn, & LaFontana, 2014; Dawes & Xie, 2014; Ojanen & Findley-Van Nostrand, 2014), and that social dominance goals also serve as a moderator (Kiefer & Wang, 2016). Kiefer and Wang (2016) examined associations of coolness and social goals (dominance, popularity, and intimacy goals) with aggression and academic engagement across the sixth grade. Social dominance goals moderated associations among coolness and subsequent peer-reported aggression. Specifically, cool boys who highly endorsed dominance goals had the highest levels of later overt aggression and cool youth who highly endorsed dominance goals had higher subsequent levels of relational aggression. These findings are consistent with research indicating links between social dominance and overt aggression, especially for boys (Pellegrini & Bartini, 2001), and links between cool status and relational aggression, especially for girls (Cillessen & Mayeux, 2004; Ojanen et al., 2012). Further research is needed to understand how dominance goals moderate relations of individual and contextual factors with social adjustment.

Help seeking among peers

Although striving for power over peers may have social benefits such as perceived popularity and social status, there are also detrimental consequences on relationships with friends, classmates, and teachers. Striving to establish power over others is inconsistent with the social responsibility, cooperation, and general good citizenship that is promoted in the classroom (Kiefer & Ryan, 2008). Research indicates students who strive for power over peers may interact with peers in non-collaborative, controlling styles (Ojanen et al., 2012) and may not engage in adaptive help-seeking behaviors among peers. Youth who strive for social dominance may be less willing to appear vulnerable and engage in adaptive help-seeking exchanges with classmates and be more willing to engage in expedient help seeking, as it involves completing tasks by delegating others to do the work for them. Research indicates that for boys, social dominance goals are negatively related to adaptive help seeking and positively related to expedient help seeking (Kiefer & Shim, 2016). Boys may also use asserting control and delegating tasks as a means to establish status in the classroom (Pellegrini & Bartini, 2001). Students striving for power over peers may also avoid help exchanges with classmates in order to control the classroom environment and avoid taking risks (Jones & Gerig, 1994).

Academic Adjustment

Although there are some benefits for social dominance strivings in terms of social adjustment (Hawley et al., 2007), there can be serious costs regarding academic adjustment. Social dominance goals are associated with maladaptive forms of engagement and low achievement. When students are focused on establishing power over peers, they are more likely to engage in off-task behavior, act in ways that disrupt classes, and are less likely to put effort into their schoolwork. Thus, social dominance may be a risk factor for academic success.

Engagement and achievement

Social dominance goals are positively associated with self-reported disruptive classroom behavior and peer reports of not following school rules, and are negatively associated with self-reported classroom effort and school-reported GPA (Kiefer & Ryan, 2008). Associations persisted across the school year (last year of elementary and first year of middle school) after controlling for prior adjustment and included early adolescent participants from large, urban schools. Social dominance goals have also been found to moderate relations between coolness and disruptive behavior across the sixth-grade school year (Kiefer & Wang, 2016). Specifically, cool youth who highly endorsed dominance goals reported high levels of later disruptive behavior. Further, boys who had low dominance goals reported higher levels of later involved behavior (Kiefer & Wang, 2016). Thus, not striving for dominance goals may allow youth, especially boys, to be more engaged in learning activities. These findings indicate that dominance goals are related to later off-task behavior and declines in achievement, and highlight the potential risks associated with dominance goals for adolescents' academic engagement.

Heterogeneity among socially dominant youth

It is important to note that not all socially dominant youth are at risk for negative academic adjustment. Research examining heterogeneity among socially dominant adolescents has demonstrated that different subgroups of socially dominant students have different academic profiles. Jonkmann et al. (2009) found four subgroups of socially dominant students, which they conceptualized as "students who were actively involved in establishing peer norms, influence their classmates' opinions, and are often at the center of attention" (p. 338). Highly accepted and model students had social adjustment profiles similar to Hawley's (2003) bistrategic youth (e.g., socially accepted, socially central, and socially skilled), and experienced positive aspects of academic adjustment (high levels of mathematics achievement and GPA). Socially dominant students with a high self-image and those with a poor self-image exhibited the highest levels of peer rejection and disruptive, deviant behaviors (Jonkmann et al., 2009). Students with a poor self-image fared the worst, and exhibited the lowest levels of academic self-concept, mathematics achievement, and GPA (Jonkmann et al., 2009). Further, associations with achievement and disruptive behavior were moderated by how normative social dominance behaviors were in the classroom (Jonkmann et al., 2009). Thus, research indicates there may be considerable variability regarding the social and academic adjustment of socially dominant youth, and that this may be shaped by the classroom context.

For children and adolescents, the classroom is a primary context to gain academic skills and competencies, as well as establish and maintain peer relationships, develop a sense of belonging, and learn norms valued by peers and teachers (Jonkmann et al., 2009; Wentzel, 2001). Although educators dictate the formal rules in school, many of the informal rules and norms are negotiated among peers, including those regarding social status and acceptance (Adler & Adler, 1998; Jonkmann et al., 2009). Students are expected to master increasingly complex academic skills, as well as navigate shifts in social norms among peers (Galván, Spatzier, & Juvonen, 2011) and maintain a position in an expanding and increasingly complex peer world (Adler & Adler, 1998; Giordano, 1995). Additional research is needed to understand how the endorsement of multiple social goals, including dominance goals, may help students adapt to the social ecology and cope with the demands of the school environment (Dawes, 2017).

Future Directions

Social dominance plays an important role in students' lives and has implications for social and academic adjustment in school. Additional research is needed as social dominance goals have been understudied relative to other goals, despite their salience in peer relations and in the classroom. Five areas for future research directions are discussed in this section, including (1) promoting a theoretically integrated approach to social dominance goals, (2) utilizing person- and context-focused approaches, (3) examining the antecedents and consequences of social dominance goals, (4) examining the underlying mechanisms of social dominance goals, and (5) conducting intervention-based research.

Theoretically integrated approach

There are many theoretical approaches to understanding social goals, including but not limited to social achievement goals, social content goals, agentic and communal goals, and social status goals. Social dominance goals are often conceptualized differently across multiple theoretical approaches, if they are included at all. This challenge of having multiple, often disparate theoretical approaches is also faced by the broader field of motivational research (Wigfield et al., 2015) and can result in a fragmented and limited understanding of motivation and its influence on student adjustment in school. Using a theoretically integrated approach that is interdisciplinary in scope may allow researchers to compare various ways social dominance goals are conceptualized and operationalized across multiple fields (e.g., developmental psychology, social psychology, sociology, evolutionary psychology, and others) and encourage a more holistic view. An integrated, interdisciplinary approach may also encourage the use of multiple research designs and methodologies in studying social dominance goals.

Person- and context-focused approaches

Additional research is needed to understand how personal and contextual factors impact the endorsement of social dominance goals and the goal pursuit process. Students most likely strive for multiple social and academic goals in school; further research is needed to understand how children and adolescents pursue social dominance goals in combination with other social and academic goals (Dawes, 2017; Dowson & McInerney, 2003; Urdan & Maehr, 1995; Wentzel, 2000). Given that students' multiple goals interact in conflicting, converging, or compensatory ways to influence adjustment (Dowson & McInerney, 2003), it is important to examine the ways in which social dominance goals may be complementary to some goals (e.g., popularity goals) and in conflict with others (e.g., intimacy/communal goals, academic goals). Recent research has examined students' pursuit of multiple goals using the social achievement approach (Ryan & Shim, 2008), and studies have increasingly adopted person-centered approaches to examine students' academic goals (Jang & Liu, 2012; Wilson, Zheng, Lemoine, Marton, & Tang, 2016). Such person-centered analyses and qualitative techniques (interviews, structured observations) may provide insight into the naturally occurring combinations of multiple goals and the heterogeneity of students' social dominance goals (Dowson & McInerney, 2003; Wormington & Linnenbrink-Garcia, 2017). Future research may examine adjustment among youth with different social goal profiles (e.g., high dominance goals and low intimacy goals vs. high dominance goals and high intimacy goals; Li & Wright, 2014).

Much research examining social goals has not fully considered the various contexts in which individual students pursue social dominance goals. How do students strive for social dominance goals among different peers (e.g., best friends, peer group members, classmates, enemies, romantic partners, and siblings)? How do youth strive for social dominance in various school contexts (e.g., classrooms, hallways, cafeteria, locker room, and bathroom), out-of-school contexts (e.g., extracurricular activities/ sports, leisure activities, and work), and online contexts (e.g., social media and texting)? To what extent does an individual actively pursue a goal around one group of peers and/or context, but not in another? These questions include methodological and measurement challenges, but may provide critical insight into social goals in context (Dawes, 2017). Most goals research has been survey-based; future research may consider incorporating qualitative and mixed-method research designs as well as time- and context-sensitive methodologies such as observations, interviews, and experience sampling methods to gain a more complex and dynamic understanding of student goals (Dowson & McInerney, 2003).

Situated learning – a process-oriented, person-centered approach – may allow researchers to examine *how* individual students adapt goals to specific situations and understand *why* students pursue certain goals in specific context(s) (Turner & Nolan, 2015). Examining social dominance goals using a situative perspective may allow researchers to interpret individuals' beliefs and behaviors in the context of their participation in social, cultural, and historical contexts (Turner & Nolan, 2015) and provide insight into individual and group differences (e.g., gender, ethnicity, and social status) in striving for power and dominance. Considering specific aspects of the individual and context may allow for a deeper understanding of when, where, how, and why students endorse social dominance goals as well as inform a more tailored approach to supporting students' goal strivings and adjustment in school.

Antecedents and consequences

Research has focused primarily on examining aspects of adjustment associated with social goals; less is known regarding possible antecedents and factors that shape social goals. Theoretical perspectives, including McClelland's (1985) theorizing about need for power and Majors's (1991) theorizing about identity development, assume that striving for social dominance stem in part from individual differences in students' power motive as well as features of the social context (e.g., family context, peer dynamics, school climate, teacher behaviors, social norms, and values). According to social information-processing models, trait-like goals may be activated by contextual cues to affect social information processing and social behaviors (Crick & Dodge, 1994). Students attend to and interpret social contextual cues based on their previous social knowledge, select a goal or desired outcome, evaluate and select a response, and enact the chosen response (Crick & Dodge, 1994). Youth striving for social dominance may interpret social cues in a more hostile manner (e.g., hostile attribution bias) or may have different social schema than youth with lower strivings for social dominance. Social dominance goals may also be activated when youth encounter peers whom they perceive to be submissive or threatening and use goal-concordant behavioral strategies like aggression to establish dominance

(Pellegrini & Long, 2002). In addition, classroom contextual factors shape early adolescents' striving for social dominance goals, including the promotion of performance goals and social interaction among peers (Kiefer et al., 2013). Thus, understanding individual differences and social contextual factors that shape social dominance goals may have implications for promoting positive social and academic adjustment.

Further, although research has investigated outcomes associated with dominance goals, most studies have been relatively short-term in nature. Prior research has examined the trajectory of popularity goals during adolescence using cross-sectional (LaFontana & Cillessen, 2010) and longitudinal designs (Dawes & Xie, 2014; Kiefer & Ryan, 2008), as well as social achievement goals (Madjar, 2018). Longitudinal research examining the trajectories of social dominance goals are needed, including examining implications for normative aspects of social and academic adjustment as well as more extreme outcomes related to bullying, violence, and school climate.

Underlying mechanisms

Another promising future research direction is to consider potential mediation and moderation effects of social dominance goals on the associations between personal or contextual factors and adjustment in school. Research has begun to examine popularity goals as moderating relations between status and aggression during early adolescence (Cillessen et al., 2014; Dawes & Xie, 2014; Ojanen Findley-Van Nostrand, 2014). Research has also examined social dominance goals in tandem with popularity and intimacy goals as moderating relations of coolness with aggression and classroom engagement (Kiefer & Wang, 2016). These relations warrant further research as they may involve complex social interactional processes, given that goals and behaviors are contingent on prior contextual cues and peer behavior as well as anticipated future behavior (Cillessen et al., 2011; Crick & Dodge, 1994). Researchers can also consider social dominance goals as a potential mediator. Recent longitudinal research indicates social goals, specifically agentic goals, impacted adolescent substance use through influencing their school belonging (Meisel & Colder, 2017). The findings call attention to agency goals as a potential risk factor for diminished school belonging and heightened substance use. Additional longitudinal research is needed to examine the social cognitive processes related to social dominance and the strategies youth use to attain dominance and power over peers, as well as implications for adjustment.

Intervention-based research

Intervention-based research regarding students' social dominance goals is essential for solving practical problems and informing educational practice (Hamilton, 2015; Stokes, 1997). Previous school-based interventions indicate that educators can modify student goals (decrease antisocial and increase prosocial goals) in order to change aggressive behavior (Frey, Nolen, Edstrom, & Hirschstein, 2005) and shape classroom and peer norms regarding academic effort and achievement (Hamm, Farmer, Lambert, & Gravelle, 2014). Educators who are attuned to students' social dynamics can structure their classroom environment through promoting social interaction, emotional and academic support, effective seating arrangements, and other instructional practices (Gest, Madill, Zadzora, Miller, & Rodkin, 2014; Gest & Rodkin, 2011; Kiefer et al., 2013) to promote social goals and behaviors associated with positive social and academic adjustment (Bukowski et al., 2018). Providing teachers with information regarding students' social and academic motivations, including social dominance goals, may aid their attempts to positively shape classroom norms and peer dynamics (Dawes, 2017; Farmer et al., 2016).

Providing more adaptive social strivings as alternatives to dominance goals may help students achieve their striving for power in a more socially acceptable and adaptive manner and have implications for intervention and educational practice. Dominance goals are not the only goal that may emanate from the power motive; a more positive expression could be striving for leadership among peers (Kiefer & Ryan, 2008; Waasdorp, Baker, Paskewich, & Leff, 2013). Future research is needed to investigate whether students' strivings for power and social dominance can be channeled into more adaptive social goals, such as leadership.

Lastly, future research may provide information regarding how to effectively tailor and target future interventions to enhance student motivation and adjustment by (1) examining the cumulative effects of social dominance goals on adjustment to identify ideal times to trigger interventions, (2) investigating variability in social dominance goals to inform targeted interventions where benefits are concentrated within subgroups and individual differences, and (3) exploring influential factors of social dominance goals to inform contextual supports that sustain meaningful and lasting changes in student motivation and outcomes (Cohen, Garcia, & Goyer, 2017; Hulleman & Barron, 2016).

Conclusion

Social dominance goals are an overlooked yet salient and important social striving among children and adolescents in school. Researchers are just beginning to capture the complex dynamics of social dominance goals, and their implications for students' social and academic adjustment. As more integrated theoretical approaches and more sophisticated methodological strategies are developed, they are likely to provide insight into the critical role social dominance goals play in students' lives in school.

References

Adler, P. A., & Adler, P. (1998). *Peer power: Preadolescent culture and identity*. New Brunswick, NJ: Rutgers University Press.

Allen, J. P., Schad, M. M., Oudekerk, B., & Chango, J. (2014). What ever happened to the "cool" kids? Long-term sequelae of early adolescent pseudomature behavior. *Child Development*, 85, 1866–1880. doi:10.1111/cdev.12250.

Anderman, L. H. (1999). Classroom goal orientation, school belonging and social goals as predictors of students' positive and negative affect following the transition to middle school. *Journal of Research & Development in Education*, 32, 89–103.

Bukowski, W. M., Laursen, B., & Rubin, K. H. (2018). *Handbook of peer interactions, relationships, and groups* (2nd ed.). New York: The Guilford Press.

Caravita, S. C. S., & Cillessen, A. H. N. (2012). Agentic or communal? Associations between interpersonal goals, popularity, and bullying in middle childhood and early adolescence. *Social Development*, 21, 376–395.

Cillessen, A. H. N., & Marks, P. E. L. (2011). Conceptualizing and measuring popularity. In A. H. N. Cillessen, D. Schwartz, & L. Mayeux (Eds.), *Popularity in the peer system* (pp. 25–56). New York: Guilford.

Cillessen, A. H., & Mayeux, L. (2004). Sociometric status and peer group behavior: Previous findings and current directions. In J. B. Kupersmidt & K. A. Dodge (Eds.), *Children's peer relations* (pp. 3–20). Washington, DC: American Psychological Association.

Cillessen, A. H. N., & Rose, A. J. (2005). Understanding popularity in the peer system. *Current Direction in Psychological Science*, 14, 102–105. doi:10.1111/j.0963-7214.2005.00343.x.

Cillessen, A. H. N., Mayeux, L., Ha, T., de Bruyn, E., & LaFontana, K. (2014). Aggressive effects of prioritizing popularity in early adolescence. *Aggressive Behavior*, 40(3), 204–213. http://dx.doi.org/10.1002/ab.21518.

Cillessen, A. H. N., Schwartz, D., & Mayeux, L. (2011). *Popularity in the peer system*. New York: Guilford.

Cohen, G. L., Garcia, J., & Goyer, J. P. (2017). Turning point: Targeted, tailored, and timely psychological intervention. In A. J. Elliot, C. S. Dweck, & D. S. Yeager (Eds.), *Handbook of competence and motivation: Theory and application* (2nd ed., pp. 657–686). New York: Guilford Press.

Crick, N. R., & Dodge, K. A. (1994). A review and reformulation of social information processing mechanisms in children's social adjustment. *Psychological Bulletin*, 115(1), 74–101. http://dx.doi.org/10.1037/0033-2909.115.1.74.

Crick, N. R., Murray-Close, D., Marks, P. E. L., & Mohajeri-Nelson, N. (2009). Aggression and peer relationships in school-age children. In K. H. Rubin, W. M. Bukowski, & B. Laursen (Eds.), *Handbook of peer interactions, relationships, and groups* (pp. 287–302). New York: The Guilford Press.

Cunningham, M., & Meunier, L. N. (2004). The influence of peer experiences on bravado attitudes among African American males. In N. Way & J. W. Chu (Eds.), *Adolescent boys: Exploring diverse cultures of boyhood* (pp. 219–232). New York: New York University Press.

Dawes, M. (2017). Early adolescents' social goals and school adjustment. *Social Psychology of Education*, 20, 299–328. doi:10.1007/s11218-017-9380-3.

Dawes, M., & Xie, H. (2014). The role of popularity goal in early adolescents' behaviors and popularity status. *Developmental Psychology*, 50(2), 489–497. http://dx.doi.org/10.1037/a0032999.

Dowson, M., & McInerney, D. M. (2003). What do students say about their motivational goals? Towards a more complex and dynamic perspective on student motivation. *Contemporary Educational Psychology*, 28, 91–113. https://doi.org/10.1016/S0361-476X(02)00010–00013.

Dweck, C. S., & Leggett, E. L. (1988). A social–cognitive approach to motivation and personality. *Psychological Review*, 95, 256–273.

Eccles, J. (2004). Schools, academic motivation, and stage–environment fit. In R. M. Lerner & L. Steinberg (Eds.), *Handbook of adolescent psychology* (2nd ed., pp. 125–153). New York: Wiley.

Eder, D. (1985). The cycle of popularity: Interpersonal relations among female adolescents. *Sociology of Education*, 58(3), 154–165.

Elliot, A. J. (1999). Approach and avoidance motivation and achievement goals. *Educational Psychologist*, 34, 169–189.

Erdley, C. A., Cain, K. M., Loomis, C. C., Dumas-Hines, F., & Dweck, C. (1997). Relations among children's social goals, implicit personality theories, and responses to social failure. *Developmental Psychology*, 33, 263–272.

Farmer, T. W., Chen, C.-C., Hamm, J. V., Moates, M. M., Mehtaji, M., Lee, D., et al. (2016). Supporting teachers' management of middle school social dynamics: The scouting report process. *Intervention in School and Clinic, 52*, 67–76. doi:10.1177/1053451216636073.

Ford, M. E. (1992). *Motivating humans: Goals, emotions, and personal agency beliefs.* Newbury Park, CA: Sage.

Frey, K. S., Nolen, S. B., Edstrom, L. V. S., & Hirschstein, M. K. (2005). Effects of a school-based social–emotional competence program: Linking children's goals, attributions, and behavior. *Applied Developmental Psychology*, 26(2), 171–200. http://dx.doi.org/10.1016/j.appdev.2004.12.002.

Galván, A., Spatzier, A., & Juvonen, J. (2011). Perceived norms and social values to capture school culture in elementary and middle school. *Journal of Applied Developmental Psychology*, 32(6), 346–353. doi:10.1016/j.appdev.2011.08.005.

Gest, S. D., Madill, R. A., Zadzora, K. M., Miller, A. M., & Rodkin, P. C. (2014). Teacher management of elementary classroom social dynamics: Associations with changes in student adjustment. *Journal of Emotional and Behavioral Disorders, 22*, 107–118. doi:10.1177/1063426613512677.

Gest, S. D., & Rodkin, P. C. (2011). Teaching practices and elementary classroom peer ecologies. *Journal of Applied Developmental Psychology, 32*, 288–296. doi:10.1016/j.appdev.2011.02.004.

Giordano, P. C. (1995). The wider circle of friends in adolescence. *American Journal of Sociology*, 101(3), 661–697. https://www-jstor-org.ezproxy.lib.usf.edu/stable/2781997.

Hamilton, S. F. (2015). Translational research and youth development. *Applied Developmental Science, 19*(2), 60–73. doi:10.1080/10888691.2014.968279.

Hamm, J. V., Farmer, T. W., Lambert, K., & Gravelle, M. (2014). Enhancing peer cultures of academic effort and achievement in early adolescence: Promotive effects of the SEALS intervention. *Developmental Psychology, 50*(1), 216–228. doi:0.1037/a0032979.

Hawley, P. H. (2003). Prosocial and coercive configurations of resource control in early adolescence: A case from the well-adapted Machiavellian. *Merrill-Palmer Quarterly*, 49, 279–309. www.jstor.org/stable/23096057.

Hawley, P. H., & Bower, A. R. (2018). Evolution and peer relations: Considering the functional roles of aggression and prosociality. In W. M. Bukowski, B. Laursen, & K. H. Rubin (Eds.), *Handbook of peer interactions, relationships, and groups* (pp. 106–122). New York: The Guilford Press.

Hawley, P. H., Little, T. D., & Rodkin, P. C. (2007). *Aggression and adaptation: The bright side to bad behavior.* Mahwah, NJ: Lawrence Erlbaum Associates.

Hulleman, C. S., & Barron, K. E. (2016). Motivation interventions in education: Bridging theory, research, and practice. In L. Corno & E. M. Anderman (Eds.), *Handbook of educational psychology* (3rd ed., Chapter 13). New York: Routledge, Taylor & Francis.

Jang, L. Y., & Liu, W. C. (2012). 2× 2 Achievement goals and achievement emotions: A cluster analysis of students' motivation. *European Journal of Psychology of Education*, 27(1), 59–76. https://doi-org.ezproxy.lib.usf.edu/10.1007/s10212-011-0066-5.

Jarvinen, D. W., & Nicholls, J. G. (1996). Adolescents' social goals, beliefs about the causes of social success, and satisfaction in peer relations. *Developmental Psychology*, 32, 435–441. http://dx.doi.org/10.1037/0012-1649.32.3.435.

Jones, M. G., & Gerig, T. M. (1994). Silent sixth-grade students: Characteristics, achievement, and teacher expectations. *The Elementary School Journal*, 95(2), 169–182. https://www-jstor-org.ezproxy.lib.usf.edu/stable/1002067.

Jonkmann, K., Trautwein, U., & Ludtke, O. (2009). Social dominance in adolescence: The moderating role of the classroom context and behavioral heterogeneity. *Child Development*, 80(2), 338–355. https://www-jstor-org.ezproxy.lib.usf.edu/stable/29738619.

Kiefer, S. M., Matthews, Y. T., Montesino, M., Arango, L., & Preece, K. K. (2013). The effects of contextual and personal factors on young adolescents' social goals. *The Journal of Experimental Education, 81*, 44–67. doi:10.1080/00220973.2011.630046.

Kiefer, S. M., & Ryan, A. M. (2008). Striving for social dominance over peers: The implications for academic adjustment during early adolescence. *Journal of Educational Psychology, 100*, 417–428. doi:10.1037/0022-0663.100.2.417.

Kiefer, S. M., & Shim, S. S. (2016). Academic help seeking from peers during adolescence: The role of social goals. *Journal of Applied Developmental Psychology*, 42, 80–88. doi:10.1016/j.appdev.2015.12.002.

Kiefer, S. M., & Wang, J. H. (2016). Associations of coolness and social goals with aggression and engagement during adolescence. *Journal of Applied Developmental Psychology*, 44, 52–62. doi:10.1016/j.appdev.2016.02.007.

LaFontana, K. M., & Cillessen, A. H. N. (2010). Developmental changes in the priority of perceived status in childhood and adolescence. *Social Development*, 19(1), 130–147.

Lease, A. M., Kennedy, C. A., & Axelrod, J. L. (2002). Children's social constructions of popularity. *Social Development*, 11, 87–109.

Li, Y., & Wright, M. F. (2014). Adolescents' social status goals: Relationships to social status insecurity, aggression, and prosocial behavior. *Journal of Youth and Adolescence*, 43, 146–160. http://dx.doi.org/10.1007/s10964-013-9939-z.

Locke, K. (2000). Circumplex scales of interpersonal values: Reliability, validity, and applicability to interpersonal problems and personality disorders. *Journal of Personality Assessment, 75*, 249–267. doi:10.1207/S15327752JPA7502_6.

Madjar, N., Cohen, V., & Shoval, G. (2018). Longitudinal analysis of the trajectories of academic and social motivation across the transition from elementary to middle school. *Educational Psychology, 38*(2), 221–247, doi:10.1080/01443410.2017.1341623.

Majors, B. (1991). Nonverbal behaviors and communication styles among African Americans. In R. L. Jones (Ed.), *Black psychology* (pp. 269–294). Hampton, VA: Cobb & Henry.

Majors, B., & Billson, J. M. (1992). *Cool pose: The dilemmas of Black manhood in America.* New York: Macmillan.

McAdams, D. P. (1988). *Power, intimacy, and the life story: Personological inquiries into identity.* Chicago: Dorsey Press.

McClelland, D. C. (1985). *Human motivation.* New York: Cambridge University Press.

Meisel, S. N., & Colder, C. R. (2017). Social goals impact adolescent substance use through influencing adolescents' connectedness to their schools. *Journal of Youth and Adolescence, 46*(9), 2015–2027. doi:10.1007/s10964-017-0655-y.

Merten, D. E. (1997). The meaning of meanness: Popularity, competition, and conflict among junior high school girls. *Sociology of Education, 70*(3), 175–191. www.jstor.org/stable/2673207.

Midgley, C., Kaplan, A., Middleton, M., Maehr, M. L., Urdan, T., Anderman, L. H., *et al.* (1998). The development and validation of scales assessing students' achievement goal orientations. *Contemporary Educational Psychology, 23*, 113–131. https://doi.org/10.1006/ceps.1998.0965.

Murray, H. A. (1938). *Explorations in personality.* New York: Oxford University Press.

Nicholls, J. G., Cheung, P. C., Lauer, J., & Pataschnick, M. (1989). Individual differences in academic motivation: Perceived ability, goals, beliefs and values. *Learning and Individual Differences, 1*, 63–84.

Ojanen, T., Findley, D., & Fuller, S. (2012). Physical and relational aggression in early adolescence: Associations with narcissism, temperament, and social goals. *Aggressive Behavior, 38*(2), 99–107. doi:10.1002/ab.21413.

Ojanen, T., & Findley-Van Nostrand, D. (2014). Social goals, aggression, peer preference, and popularity: Longitudinal links during middle school. *Developmental Psychology, 50*, 2134–2143. doi:10.1037/a0037137.

Ojanen, T., Gronroos, M., & Salmivalli, C. (2005). An interpersonal circumplex model of children's social goals: Links with peer-reported behavior and sociometric status. *Developmental Psychology, 41*, 699–710. doi:10.1037/0012-1649.41.5.699.

Pellegrini, A. (2008). The roles of aggressive and affiliative behaviors in resource control: A behavioral ecological perspective. *Developmental Review, 28*(4), 461–487.

Pellegrini, A. D., & Bartini, M. (2001). Dominance in early adolescent boys: Affiliative and aggressive dimensions and possible functions. *Merrill–Palmer Quarterly, 47*, 142–163. doi:10.1353/mpq.2001.0004.

Pellegrini, A. D., & Long, J. D. (2002). A longitudinal study of bullying, dominance, and victimization during the transition from primary school through secondary school. *British Journal of Developmental Psychology, 20*, 259–280.

Pellegrini, A. D., Roseth, C. J., Van Ryzin, M. J., & Solberg, D. W. (2011). Popularity as a form of social dominance: An evolutionary perspective. In A. H. N. Cillessen, D. Schwartz, & L. Mayeux (Eds.), *Popularity in the peer system* (pp. 123–139). New York: The Guilford Press.

Rodkin, P. C., Farmer, T. W., Pearl, R., & Van Acker, R. (2000). Heterogeneity of popular boys: Antisocial and prosocial configurations. *Developmental Psychology, 36*, 14–24. doi:10.1037/0012–1649.361.14.

Rose, A. J., & Rudolph, K. D. (2006). A review of sex differences in peer relationship processes: Potential trade-offs for the emotional and behavioral development of girls and boys. *Psychological Bulletin, 132*, 98–131. doi:10.1037/0033-2909.132.1.98.

Rose, A. J., Swenson, L. P., & Waller, E. M. (2004). Overt and relational aggression and perceived popularity: Developmental differences in concurrent and prospective relations. *Developmental Psychology, 40*, 378–387. http://dx.doi.org/10.1037/0012-1649.40.3.378.

Roseth, C. J., Pellegrini, A. D., Dupuis, D. N., Bohn, C. M., Hickey, M. C., Hilk, C. L., & Peshkam, A. (2011). Preschoolers' bistrategic resource control, reconciliation, and peer regard. *Social Development, 20*, 185–211. http://dx.doi.org/10.1111/j.1467–9507.2010.00579.x.

Ruble, D. N., Martin, C. L., & Berenbaum, S. A. (2006). Gender development. In N. Eisenberg (Ed.), *Handbook of child psychology: Social, emotional, and personality development* (pp. 858–932). New York: Wiley.

Ryan, A. M., Hicks, L., & Midgley, C. (1997). Social goals, academic goals, and avoiding seeking help in the classroom. *Journal of Early Adolescence*, 17, 152–171. http://dx.doi.org/10.1177/0272431697017002003.

Ryan, A. M., Kiefer, S. M., & Hopkins, N. B. (2004). Young adolescents' social motivation: An achievement goal perspective. In M. L. Maehr & P. R. Pintrich (Eds.), *Advances in motivation and achievement* (Vol. 13, pp. 301–330). Amsterdam: Elsevier.

Ryan, A. M., & Shim, S. S. (2006). Social achievement goals: The nature and consequences of different orientations toward social competence. *Personality and Social Psychology Bulletin*, 32, 1246–1263. http://dx.doi.org/10.1177/0146167206289345.

Ryan, A. M., & Shim, S. S. (2008). An exploration of young adolescents' social achievement goals and social adjustment in middle school. *Journal of Educational Psychology, 100*, 672–687. doi:10.1037/0022-0663.100.3.672.

Salmivalli, C., Ojanen, T., Haanpää, J., & Peets, K. (2005). 'I'm OK but you're not' and other peer relational schemas: Explaining individual differences in children's social goals. *Developmental Psychology, 41*, 363–375. doi:10.1037/0012-1649.41.2.363.

Savin-Williams, R. (1987). *Adolescence: An ethological perspective*. New York: Springer Verlag.

Sijtsema, J. J., Veenstra, R., Lindenberg, S., & Salmivalli, C. (2009). Empirical test of bullies' status goals: Assessing direct goals, aggression, and prestige. *Aggressive Behavior, 35*, 57–67. doi:10.1002/ab.20282.

Stevenson, H. C. (2004). Boys in men's clothing: Racial socialization and neighborhood safety as buffers to hypervulnerability in African American adolescent males. In N. Way & J. Y. Chu (Eds.), *Adolescent boys: Exploring diverse cultures of boyhood* (pp. 59–77). New York: New York University Press.

Stokes, D. (1997). *Pasteur's quadrant: Basic science and technological innovation*. Washington, DC: Brookings Institution Press.

Turner, J. C., & Nolan, S. B. (2015). Introduction: The relevance of the situative perspective in educational psychology. *Educational Psychologist, 50*(3), 167–172. doi:10.1080/00461520.2015.1075404.

Urdan, T., & Maehr, M. (1995). Beyond a two-goal theory of motivation: A case for social goals. *Review of Educational Research*, 65, 213–244. https://www-jstor-org.ezproxy.lib.usf.edu/stable/1170683.

Veroff, J. (1957). Development and validation of a projective measure of power motivation. *Journal of Abnormal and Social Psychology*, 54, 1–8.

Veroff, J., Depner, C., Kulka, R., & Douvan, E. (1980). Comparison of American motives: 1957 versus 1976. *Journal of Personality and Social Psychology*, 39, 1249–1262.

Waasdorp, T. E., Baker, C. N., Paskewich, B. S., & Leff, S. S. (2013). The association between forms of aggression, leadership, and social status among urban youth. *Journal of Youth and Adolescence, 42*, 263–274. doi:10.1007/s10964-012-9837-9.

Wentzel, K. R. (1996). Social and academic motivation in middle school: Concurrent and long- term relations to academic effort. *Journal of Early Adolescence*, 16, 390–406. https://doi.org/10.1177/0272431696016004002.

Wentzel, K. R. (2000). What is it that I'm trying to achieve? Classroom goals from a content perspective. *Contemporary Educational Psychology*, 25, 105–115. https://doi.org/10.1006/ceps.1999.1021.

Wentzel, K. R. (2001). The contribution of social goal setting to children's school adjustment. In A. Wigfield & J. S. Eccles (Eds.), *Development of achievement motivation* (pp. 221–246). San Diego, CA: Academic Press.

Wigfield, A., Eccles, J. S., Fredricks, J. A., Simpkins, S., Roeser, R. W., & Schiefele, U. (2015). Development of achievement motivation and engagement. In R. M. Lerner (Ed.), *Handbook of child psychology and developmental science* (7th ed., pp. 1–44). New York: John Wiley & Sons.

Wiggins, J. S. (1991). Agency and communion as conceptual coordinates for the understanding and measurement of interpersonal behavior. In D. Cicchetti & W. M. Grove (Eds.), *Thinking clearly about psychology: Personality and psychopathology* (Vol. 2, pp. 89–113). Minneapolis, MN: University of Minnesota Press.

Wilson, T. M., Zheng, C., Lemoine, K. A., Marton, C. P., & Tang, Y. (2016). Achievement goals during middle childhood: Individual differences in motivation and social adjustment. *The Journal of Experimental Education, 84*(4), 723–743. doi:10.1080/00220973.2015.1094648.

Winter, D. G. (1973). *The power motive*. New York: Free Press.

Winter, D. G., & Stewart, A. J. (1978). Power motivation. In H. London & J. Exner (Eds.), *Dimensions of personality* (pp. 391–447). New York: Wiley.

Wormington, S. V., & Linnenbrink-Garcia, L. (2017). A new look at multiple goal pursuit: The promise of a person-centered approach. *Educational Psychology Review, 29*(3), 407–445. doi:10.1007/s10648-016-9358-2.

Wright, J. C., Zakriski, A. L., & Fisher, P. (1996). Age differences in the correlates of perceived dominance. *Social Development,* 5(1), 24–40. https://doi.org/10.1111/j.1467-9507.1996.tb00070.x.

6

PROSOCIAL GOALS

Christi Bergin

Prosocial Goals in the Classroom

> Andrew is a freshman at a largely working-class high school. He tends to finish his classwork faster than classmates. When his work is finished, he helps his classmates with their work. Peers nominated Andrew as one of the most prosocial students in his grade.

School tends to be a highly social context where success requires not only cognitive skills, but also social skills, such as the ability to get along with classmates and please teachers. In this chapter I focus on a specific aspect of social competence known as "prosocial" behavior. Andrew holds prosocial goals, which drive his prosocial behavior, which, in turn, affects his academic achievement and social acceptance at school. Thus, understanding prosocial goals is important for promoting student's success in as social a setting as school.

Definitions

Definition of prosocial behavior

Prosocial behavior is *any behavior that benefits others or builds harmonious relationships with others*. It is called "prosocial" in contrast to "antisocial" behavior. Prosocial behavior promotes the functioning of society, whereas antisocial behavior disrupts it. Prosocial behavior can take many forms. It can be a response to another's distress (e.g., comforting) or a simple act of civility where there is no distress (e.g., saying "thank you"). Prosocial behavior can involve inhibiting behavior (e.g., walking away to avoid a fight) or assertiveness (e.g., standing up to a bully). Some of the most common prosocial behaviors of students, from preschool through high school include the

94 Christi Bergin

following (Bergin, Bergin, & French, 1995; Bergin, Talley, & Hamer, 2003; Galliger, Tisak, & Tisak, 2009):

Making others smile or laugh
Willing to play
Apologizing
Confronting others when wrong
Sharing
Admitting mistakes
Complimenting and encouraging others
Comforting others in distress
Helping others with school work, social skills or sports
Keeping confidences
Settling disagreements
Being inclusive
Standing up for others
Stopping rumors

Students who seek to enact these kinds of prosocial behaviors hold prosocial goals.

Definition of prosocial goals

Definitions of what is a "goal" vary, which makes it challenging to define students' prosocial goals. Some define a goal as *the result toward which effort is directed* (Vansteenkiste, Lens, Elliot, Soenens, & Mouratidis, 2014). Thus, a prosocial goal would be effortfully enacting behavior that benefits others. Some define a goal as any *cognition of a desired consequence* (Ford & Nichols, 1987). Thus, a prosocial goal would be a desire to benefit others. These are somewhat different constructs. To make this difference more concrete, let's revisit Andrew.

> Andrew said he helps his classmates with their school work after he finishes his own because he is bored and wants the time to pass more quickly. He also said that he often helps boys in the neighborhood do their household chores so that they will get done more quickly and can then go out to play with Andrew.

Is Andrew's goal to be helpful to his classmates, or is it to alleviate his boredom? There are at least three answers to this question:

1. Both are goals. Helping classmates is a proximal goal and alleviating boredom is the distal goal.
2. Alleviating boredom is the goal. Helping classmates is simply a means to the goal.
3. Helping classmates is the goal. Alleviating boredom is a "reason" for the goal.

Prosocial Goals **95**

In this chapter I will take the third perspective. That is, *a prosocial goal is defined as the prosocial result — benefiting others or building harmonious relationships — toward which effort is directed.* Anytime a student like Andrew enacts a prosocial behavior, he can be said to hold a prosocial goal.

Students like Andrew may have various reasons for their prosocial goals. Vansteenkiste and colleagues argue that we must separate goals from reasons (Vansteenkiste et al., 2014). Goals indicate the direction of your strivings. A goal is "what" you are trying to accomplish or the direction you are moving in, and a reason is where the goal came from or "why" you are moving in that direction (e.g., Wentzel, 1993b).[1] The same goal can have different underlying reasons for pursuing that goal.

A prosocial goal can have underlying reasons that may be other-serving or self-serving.[2] That is, a student may behave prosocially because the student purposefully seeks to benefit someone else. A student may also behave prosocially to enhance her own well-being. For example, in one study a colleague and I identified six 9th graders who were nominated by peers as the most prosocial students in their grade (Bergin & Talley, in preparation). We asked these prosocial superstars to tell us about incidents in which they behaved prosocially and why they behaved in that way. Most of their reasons were self-serving. For example,

Kylie said she behaves prosocially in the hopes that others will return the favor. For example, she volunteers to help her friends babysit, so that they will help her when she babysits.

Ashley said she behaves prosocially so that others will not think she is a "bad person." Devon said that he behaves prosocially so that others will think of him as "a really nice kid."

One could argue that prosocial behavior typically is self-serving to some extent. This is because most cultures value prosocial behavior. Thus, behaving prosocially can improve your social standing. It can also make you feel better. People have higher self-esteem and sense of belonging and importance when they help others (Orehek, Forest, & Barbaro, 2018). They feel a boost in mood, if their prosocial behavior is freely chosen (Weinstein & Ryan, 2010). Another of our six prosocial superstars shared this perspective,

Michael said he behaves prosocially because helping others makes him happy and feel good about himself. He believes in the rule "treat others as you would want to be treated."

When self-serving motives (e.g., to have a good reputation or to feel good about the self) align with prosocial goals, they amplify the value associated with prosocial behavior and the likelihood of behaving prosocially (Tamir & Hughes,

2018). However, when they clash, students are likely to select the behavior associated with the more valued goal.

Although they may be self-serving, the reasons these highly prosocial students gave for behaving prosocially are benign. It is also possible for students to have less reputable reasons for engaging in prosocial behavior. For example, a small percentage of students wield prosocial behavior as a tool to attain power or get what they want (Estell, Chapter 9 this volume; Hawley, 2014). Using prosocial behavior selectively to get what they want works for highly skilled students. Such students tend to be classified as "controversial" in peer status (i.e., liked by many and disliked by many, presumably based on whether you are the target of their prosocial behavior or their aggression). When less skilled students use prosocial behavior as a tool for social status, it does not work, perhaps because it is too transparently self-serving. For example, 6th graders said that a boy who complimented a "cool kid" in order to be accepted was not viewed as prosocial. Another girl who gave away candy at school was also not viewed as prosocial because "she just does it for attention because she doesn't have very many friends … it is just to get on the good side of someone" (Bergin et al., 2003). Thus, prosocial behavior increases social status, but young adolescents consider the underlying reasons for their classmates' prosocial behaviors and may reject those who behave prosocially for blatantly self-serving reasons. Students who are prosocial in order to feel good about the self may be judged as more moral than students who are motivated by reputational rewards (Crocker, Canevello, & Brown, 2017).

While reasons for prosocial behavior may often be self-serving, some reasons seem primarily other-centered and could be considered altruistic. Altruism is prosocial behavior that is engaged in for the benefit of others, even at cost to the self. Altruism can range from the heroic (e.g., a firefighter rushing into a burning house to rescue someone) to the mundane (e.g., a parent who throws a baseball ad nauseam to the child until the child learns to catch well). There is a philosophical divide between psychological egoism and altruism. The psychological egoism perspective is that at some level we are always acting in our own self-interest. From this perspective altruism is not possible. Yet, examples of altruism among humans and animals exist. Another of our prosocial superstars shared this example,

Carlita said she helped her mother by tending her younger siblings because her mother came home from work looking exhausted. Carlita said she "felt sorry" for her mother. She also told classmates to stop making fun of a boy in her class because she pitied the boy. This was socially risky, and she said she could only do this successfully because she had social clout, so others listened to her.

In summary, we can accept that prosocial goals may often (always?) have some degree of self-serving underlying reasons. But in practice, because the outcome is positive for others, it may not matter what the underlying reasons for prosocial behavior are as long as the apparent reasons tip more toward altruism than egoism. Andrew's reason for behaving prosocially may be somewhat self-serving – to alleviate his boredom – but his reason is "good enough." Andrew could have made other choices to alleviate his boredom, such as stirring up distractions in class or reading a book to himself, but instead he choose to alleviate his boredom in a prosocial way. The definition of a prosocial goal I use in this chapter is function oriented. That is, directing effort toward benefiting others implies a prosocial goal, even if the underlying reason is to some degree self-serving.

Evidence

The relationship between prosocial goals and prosocial behavior in the classroom is presented in Figure 6.1. That is, students who hold prosocial goals are more likely to enact prosocial behavior. This, in turn, leads to increased academic achievement and social acceptance in the classroom. While this linear trajectory over-simplifies human behavior, Figure 6.1 provides us with context for discussion of the research. In this section I will present evidence to support each of the linkages in Figure 6.1.

Prosocial Goals Predict Prosocial Behavior

Research indicates that goals robustly increase motivation and performance by directing attention and action, mobilizing energy, and prolonging effort and persistence (Locke & Latham, 2006). This has been found across many domains, including prosociality. Students who hold prosocial goals are more likely to engage in prosocial behavior. In multiple studies Wentzel and colleagues have directly asked students about the goals they pursue (e.g., Wentzel, 1993b; Wentzel, Muenks, McNeish, & Russell, 2018). They ask students "how often" they attempt to achieve these prosocial outcomes:

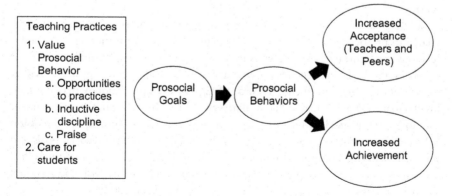

FIGURE 6.1 The Relationship between Prosocial Goals, Behavior, and Student Outcomes

1. Share what you've learned with classmates.
2. Help classmates solve a problem.
3. Be nice to kids when something bad happened to them.
4. Help other kids when they have a problem.
5. Cheer someone up when something is wrong.
6. Help classmates learn new things.
7. Think about how your behavior will affect other kids.
8. Keep promises you make to other kids.
9. Be quiet when others are studying.
10. Do what your teacher asks.

In one study, middle school students who reported more often pursuing these prosocial goals were more likely to share and help classmates and cooperate with the teacher's classroom rules (Wentzel et al., 2018). Students' prosocial behavior toward classmates was measured by peer nomination, so this relationship is not simply a function of shared method (i.e., self-report). Similarly, in two other studies, students who reported more often pursuing prosocial goals were more likely to be nominated by their classmates as prosocial, such as sharing, cooperating, and helping others with problems (Wentzel, 1992, 2002).

Notice that in Wentzel and colleagues' work "Do what your teacher asks" (#10 in the list above) is a prosocial goal. Compliance and social responsibility are components of prosocial behavior. Thus, students' prosocial goals may be manifest as helpful, sharing, and encouraging behavior toward their peers, but they may also be manifest as cooperative and supportive behavior toward their teacher. Conforming to the teacher's agenda in the classroom (e.g., don't talk when others are talking), may convey concern for others, trustworthiness, putting others first, and respect for others, all of which are important for harmonious relationships and social interactions. Prosocial goals are part of what Ford and Nichols calls "integrative social relationship goals" which include social responsibility goals such as complying with classroom rules and norms (Ford, 1992, p. 89).

While goals drive behavior, goals are psychological processes. They can only be related to prosocial outcomes – such as benefiting others or promoting harmonious relationships – through the behaviors they motivate. Whether a goal is pursued and translates into behavior depends on whether regulatory and arousal processes within the student interact with the goal (Ford, 1992). For example, Andrew may not help his classmates if he is lethargic due to illness or sadness. In addition, the same student can hold multiple goals, which may be complementary or conflicting (see discussion below). Thus, although research supports the linkage between prosocial goals and prosocial behavior in Figure 6.1, students with prosocial goals may sometimes "fall off" this trajectory. As a result, the relationship between prosocial goals and prosocial behavior may be modest in size (e.g., r = .21–.25, Wentzel, 2002).

I turn next to the second set of linkages in Figure 6.1; the relationships between prosocial behavior and social acceptance and achievement. However, it is important to note that prosocial behavior is a valued outcome in the classroom for its own sake, regardless of whether it promotes acceptance and achievement. Teachers and students are happier in classrooms characterized by kindness, politeness, honesty and cooperation. In addition, there are many other benefits to prosocial behavior, such as physical and psychological health across the lifespan (Crocker et al., 2017).

Prosocial Behavior Predicts Social Acceptance

Prosocial students are more likely to have positive teacher–student relationships (Jia et al., 2009; Roorda, Koomen, Spilt, & Oort, 2011). This is important because positive teacher–student relationships predict higher grades and test scores, and lower retention and special education referrals. Studies have found this from preschool through high school, as well as in longitudinal studies and intervention studies (e.g., Bergin & Bergin, 2009; Curby, Rimm-Kaufman, & Ponitz, 2009; Jia et al., 2009; Leyva et al., 2015; O'Connor & McCartney, 2007; Roorda et al., 2011). For example, in one study 1st graders who had a positive teacher – student relationship had higher test scores in 3rd grade (Hughes, Luo, Kwok, & Loyd, 2008). For another example, in a high school study when teachers became more sensitive and supportive of students the students learned more (Allen, Pianta, Gregory, Mikami, & Lun, 2011). Students are more engaged and work harder when they believe their teachers care about them (Hughes, Wu, Kwok, Villarreal, & Honson, 2012; Spilt, Hughes, Wu, & Kwok, 2012). The effect size of teacher – student relationships on achievement is substantial for both preschoolers (Mashburn et al., 2008) and school-age students (Cornelius-White, 2007).

Prosocial students are also more likely to be socially accepted by peers and have high-quality friendships. In Chapter 9, Estell describes the difference between preference (i.e., being well-liked) and popularity (i.e., having social power or salience). Prosocial behavior is a key cause of preference. That is, students who are prosocial are widely liked. This is partly because students who facilitate other people's goals are better liked (Orehek et al., 2018). Andrew facilitated his classmates' goals of completing their classwork successfully.

Prosocial Behavior Predicts Increased Achievement

When students like Andrew behave prosocially in the classroom, it has academic consequences both for themselves and for their classmates. Students who are more prosocial tend to have higher academic achievement. This has been documented as early as preschool where children who are more prosocial tend to have better emergent literacy skills (Bierman, Torres, Domitrovich, Welsh, & Gest, 2009). It has also been documented in elementary and high school where students who are more prosocial tend to have higher grades and test scores (Bergin, 2014). For example, Wentzel (1993a) found that 6th and 7th graders who were more prosocial had higher GPA and standardized test scores, after controlling for academic behaviors, IQ and other variables. Similarly, in a study of 452 pre-adolescents in two middle schools, Wentzel (2002) found that prosocial behavior correlated .57 with grades. Prosocial behavior also predicts achievement over time. For example, in a study of high-risk kindergarteners those who were more prosocial were less likely to be retained a grade or placed in special education by the time they reached young adulthood, compared to their less prosocial peers (Jones, Greenberg, & Crowley, 2015).

Not only does students' own prosocial behavior predict their achievement, but students' classmates' prosocial behavior also predicts their achievement. That is, even if Roger is not prosocial, if he is in a class with many prosocial students like Andrew, then Roger is likely to have higher grades and test scores. This has been found in elementary (Molano, Jones, & Willett, 2014) and middle school (Jia et al., 2009). In fact, in one study elementary student's grades were more strongly predicted by their classmates' friendliness than by their teachers' instructional practices (Griffith, 2002).

Furthermore, if non-prosocial Roger is in a class with many prosocial students like Andrew, then Roger is also likely to become more prosocial himself. For example, in a study of 4th graders, those who interacted more with prosocial classmates became more helpful and cooperative toward peers over time (Molano et al., 2014). On the flip side, students who are at risk for developing behavior problems are less likely to actually do so if they have more prosocial classmates (e.g., Griffith, 2002).

The research linking prosocial behavior to academic achievement is primarily correlational. Nevertheless, it is plausible that prosocial behavior causes higher achievement. Four lines of evidence support a causal hypothesis: (1) achievement measures include standardized tests, not just teacher-given grades that could be biased by the student's prosocial behavior, (2) prosocial behavior at time 1 predicts later achievement at time 2, (3) prosocial behavior predicts achievement after controlling for baseline achievement and behaviors, and (4) when teachers implement interventions to increase student's prosocial behavior, the students' academic achievement improves (Durlak, Weissberg, Dymnicki, Taylor, & Schellinger, 2011; Jennings & DiPrete, 2010).

Theory and research support several mechanisms through which prosocial behavior may increase achievement:

Students are happier. When students behave prosocially, or receive prosocial behavior from a classmate, they feel more happiness, gratitude, and affection. According to the broaden-and-build theory, such positive emotions increase learning because they open us to experience (Fredrickson, 2001).

Happy students tend to have higher achievement (Raver, 2004).

Engagement increases. Prosocial students show interest in schoolwork, work independently, pay attention, stay on task and work hard (e.g., Bierman et al., 2009; Matthews, Kizzie, Rowley, & Cortina, 2010; Reyes, Brackett, Rivers, White, & Salovey, 2012).

Students who report that their classmates are more prosocial feel greater engagement and interest in, liking and valuing of the learning activities (Wang, Bergin, & Bergin, 2014; Wentzel, Muenks, McNeish, & Russell, 2017).

Students are more collaborative. Working as a team requires prosocial behaviors such as cooperation, encouragement, turn-taking and supportive helping (Ladd et al., 2014; Watkins & Wentzel, 2008).

Students can provide each other with more valuable resources to promote learning. During collaboration, classmates model academic and social competencies to each other (Wentzel, 1991).

Students are more socially accepted by peers and teachers.

This last mechanism may be particularly important. Feeling socially connected in the classroom is a worthwhile outcome in itself, but it has the added bonus of contributing to higher academic achievement as well. When prosocial behavior increases, there are greater feelings of belongingness and emotional security in students, and as a result, the overall climate of the classroom improves, which leads to increased achievement (Reyes et al., 2012). As discussed above, positive teacher–student relationships predict higher test scores and GPA. One study found that the same student might misbehave to the point they were suspended from class for one teacher, but be prosocial, engaged and cooperative for another teacher. The difference was whether they felt their teacher cared for them (Gregory & Ripski, 2008).

Complementary and conflicting goals

Evidence supports Figure 6.1. That is, holding prosocial goals is linked to increased prosocial behavior which, in turn, is linked to social acceptance and academic achievement. However, the strength of these linkages may vary depending on whether students hold multiple complementary, competing, or unrelated goals.

Students are likely to hold multiple goals at the same time (Wentzel, 2000). For example, Andrew may hold the goals of mastering his class assignments, being the "fastest" or "smartest" in his class, and helping others. When Andrew helps classmates with their assignments after finishing his own quickly, he may deepen his mastery of class assignments. In this case, Andrew's prosocial goals may be *complementary* with his academic goals. On the other hand, if Andrew decides to comfort a friend who is distressed rather than do his class assignment (Phelan, Davidson, & Cao, 1991), Andrew's prosocial goals may be *conflicting* with his academic goals. According to Goal System's Theory when a student has multiple goals, one goal can pull resources away from another goal (Kruglanski et al., 2002). When goals conflict, whether the student pursues one goal or the other depends on the student's relative commitment to the primary goal.

Often prosocial goals and academic goals are complementary. That is, many students who frequently pursue prosocial goals also pursue academic goals (Wentzel, 1993b). However, not all other types of social goals are complementary with academic goals. For example, in another study students' "social interaction" goals – the desire to be with peers rather than by themselves – was not related to their GPAs. Both high- and low-GPA students pursued social interaction goals. Similarly, both high- and low-GPA students pursued goals to "have fun" or "make and keep friendships at school," but these were the primary goals of low-GPA students (Wentzel, 1991). High-GPA students pursued these same social goals, but actively pursued prosocial and other goals as well (e.g., getting things done on time, doing their best, and being a successful student). In addition, the combination of social interaction and prosocial goals was linked to peer status. Students who were well-liked pursued both types of social goals (Wentzel, 1991).

Students who pursue *both* prosocial and academic goals tend to have higher GPAs compared to those who pursue either one or the other (Wentzel, 1993b). Students who pursue only prosocial goals, but not academic goals, tend to earn higher grades than students who do not actively pursue either goal. Thus, prosocial goals contribute to achievement even when students do not actively strive for academic goals, but they may be more powerful when synergistic with academic goals. Having multiple goals probably helps sustain effort over the long term, which is required for academic success (Wentzel, 1992).

One could argue that the more socially skilled students are, the more likely they can pursue both prosocial and academic goals simultaneously. According to Goal System's Theory goals have multifinality in that some means can satisfy multiple goals (Kruglanski et al., 2002). For example, Sara's complimenting and encouraging a teammate may serve both a prosocial goal and a goal for her team to have the winning project. For another example, in class Patrick asks for help on a class assignment that he did not know how to do. Lizzie told him, "I don't know how to do it either, but maybe Lauren can help us. She always knows what to do." Lizzie asks Lauren for help and all three students get their assignment done (Bergin & Bergin, 2018, p. 396). As a cautionary note, Goal System's Theory posits that using the same means to address multiple goals can sometimes dilute the effect. However, in authentic classrooms it is probable that prosocial goals often facilitate academic goals through shared means.

Given that a combination of achievement goals and prosocial goals, rather than either alone, may most strongly predict learning, helping students develop the ability to coordinate multiple goals is important. One way to do this is to create environments that support both types of goals in ways that the goals are mutually facilitative. Students will be more successful to the extent that their multiple goals match the demands of the classroom context. I turn to implications for practice next.

Implications for practice

Goals can come from within the individual, or they can come from the environment. That is, teachers can create environments that may increase the probability that students in their classrooms will hold prosocial goals (Vansteenkiste et al., 2014). A large study found that the effect elementary teachers have on their students' social skills was greater than their effect on students' achievement (Jennings & DiPrete, 2010). Research and theory suggest that teachers can increase their students' prosocial goals and behavior by clearly communicating valuing prosocial behavior and becoming more caring toward students (Bergin, 2014, 2018).

Value prosocial behavior

A value is not the same thing as a goal, but values determine the degree to which a goal is pursued. Teachers who clearly communicate valuing prosocial behavior are more likely to have students who pursue prosocial goals. Teachers vary in how overtly they communicate valuing prosocial behavior. They communicate valuing prosocial behavior in at least three ways. First, they provide opportunities to share, help, and behave prosocially. Students need to have opportunities to care for each other (Noddings, 1992). When students are given opportunities to practice prosocial behavior, they become more prosocial (Mussen & Eisenberg, 2001). Opportunities might include day-to-day events, such as Andrew's teacher encouraging students to help one another with classwork. They might also be part of a formal school program, such as the 4th graders routinely going to the kindergarten room to help their "buddies" read. After behaving prosocially once, children are more likely to behave prosocially again (Chernyak & Kushnir, 2013). Practice helps students build well-rehearsed habits of prosocial behavior.

Second, teachers communicate values during discipline encounters. Teachers promote prosocial goals when they use inductive discipline to correct misbehavior, with emphasis on "victim-centered" induction. In this type of discipline the teacher points out how a student's misbehavior affects others and suggests acts of reparation. Such discipline focuses students' on others' well-being and provides practice of prosocial behavior as students make reparation. Inductive discipline leads to internalization of the disciplinarian's values and communicates caring and respect for students (Bergin & Bergin, 1999).

Third, teachers communicate values by what they reward students for. Praise, a socially powerful form of reward, has been linked to increased prosocial behavior in preschoolers to adolescents (e.g., Carlo, Samper, Malonda, Tur-Porcar, & Davis, 2016; Ramaswamy & Bergin, 2009). Students whose teachers praise them have increased prosocial behavior several months later, after controlling for baseline rates (Reinke, Herman, & Newcomer, 2016). A cautionary note is that rewards can function as "controlling" rather than autonomy supportive (Vansteenkiste et al., 2014), which could undermine adoption of prosocial goals. Indeed, research has found that the use of tangible rewards may decrease prosocial behavior in the long term (Carlo et al., 2016; Martin & Olson, 2015). Praise is processed by students as less controlling than tangible rewards such that the same cautions do not apply to praise.

Care for students

Noddings (1992) argues that prosocial behavior comes from the memory of being cared for. Indeed, in one study students who believed that their teachers and classmates were emotionally supportive tended to pursue more prosocial goals in the classroom (Wentzel et al., 2018). Emotional support was measured with items such as "My teacher cares about how much I learn." "My classmates like me the way I am." The researchers argue that emotional support and connectedness facilitates the adoption of goals that are valued by others in the classroom, particularly goals that contribute to the positive functioning of the classroom. Self-determination theory asserts that a basic human need is belongingness, or a sense that one is important, valued, and part of a classroom community (Deci & Ryan, 2000). Students are more likely to adopt the goals of those who meet their basic needs and are warm toward them.

Caring teacher–student relationships may be especially powerful for at-risk students (e.g., Spilt & Hughes, 2015), yet such students are less likely to have positive relationships with teachers. Teachers can learn to develop positive teacher–student relationships with challenging students (e.g., Allen et al., 2011). They do so by being sensitive to students, perceiving their interests and needs, having warm interactions, praising and encouraging them, greeting them by name, and giving them choice when possible (Bergin & Bergin, 2009). Students feel closer to teachers who do these things.

In addition, students report that they feel cared for when their teachers come to class well prepared and have high expectations for the students (Jeffrey, Auger, & Pepperell, 2013; Wentzel, 1997). Wentzel (2002) found that students' perceptions of their teacher's high expectations (e.g., "my teacher trusts me" or "calls on me to answer questions") predicted students holding prosocial goals. Other teacher behaviors did not predict student's prosocial goals, such as treating all students equitably and clearly communicating rules and consequences. Negative feedback undermined prosocial behavior (e.g., scolding students or making them feel bad for not having the right answer).

There are intervention programs that are designed to increase prosocial behavior in schools. Many of them have small or null effects (Durlak et al., 2011; Social and Character Development Research Consortium, 2010). However, interventions that result in increased valuing of prosocial behavior and caring for students should increase both prosocial behavior and achievement. Two programs that do this are promising. The *Caring School Community* program encourages teachers to use the strategies discussed above – praise prosocial behavior, use inductive discipline, and develop positive relationships with students (Battistich, Schaps, & Wilson, 2004; Battistich, Solomon, Watson, & Schaps, 1997). *The*

Leader in Me program establishes school-wide shared goals around serving others in the school through leadership roles (Bergin, Prewett, Tsai, Jones, & Murphy, 2018). The students all become role models to each other for prosocial behavior. Exposure to role models can increase effort toward shared goals (Orehek et al., 2018). Goal pursuers are not isolated actors. In groups, such as classrooms, where individuals are highly interdependent, they may function more as a goal system than as separate goal pursuers (Fitzsimons & Finkel, 2018). Thus, students in classrooms where prosocial behavior is a shared goal will put more effort into prosocial behavior.

Future Research

Research supports the linkages depicted in Figure 6.1. However, there are gaps in our understanding. While research suggests how to promote prosocial behavior, we do not know whether these approaches alter goals. What classroom- and school-level practices affect whether students hold prosocial goals? What proximal social rewards determine whether prosocial goals actually become manifest as prosocial behavior (Tamir & Hughes, 2018)? How can teachers help students, as a group, coordinate multiple goals that may compete with prosocial goals (Fitzsimons & Finkel, 2018)? More work is needed to answer these questions. In particular, we need to establish causal direction by testing experimental models of the processes through which prosocial goals are developed and how they relate to prosocial behavior, social acceptance and increased academic achievement. The ultimate goal is to provide teachers and administrators with a research-based tool box of effective strategies to enhance prosocial behavior among students.

In conclusion, when students hold prosocial goals they behave in ways that benefit others or build harmonious relationships. This is a worthy outcome in itself, but prosocial behavior has the added bonus that as students enact prosocial behavior they become better liked by their peers and teachers. They also earn higher grades and standardized test scores. Prosocial and academic goals are typically complementary. Students who hold both types of goals tend to have the greatest success in school, probably because holding both helps students sustain long-term effort and because their goals match the demands of the classroom context. Thus, teachers and administrators should work to promote prosocial goals among students. This chapter briefly discussed a few research-based approaches to help in this work.

Notes

1 Not all theorists agree with this perspective. Urdan & Maehr (1995) argue that because Wentzel focuses on what students are trying to do (e.g., she asks "how often do you try to help your classmates?"), but not the underlying reasons, she is not measuring goals per se (p. 216).
2 Some theorists use the terms "communal" and "agentic" to refer to this dichotomy. Students could have communal reasons in which the desire is to help another person feel better or the desire is to improve relationships. Students could also have agentic

reasons in which the desire is social status, to be admired, or avoid being viewed negatively. The desire to "feel better" by behaving prosocially because one's prosocial orientation is internalized as a core value is considered agentic. For example, "I feel better about myself when I am generous or compassionate." There can also be approach and avoidance goals (Elliot & Covington, 2001). Devon has an approach tendency when he wants others to think of him as nice, and Ashley has an avoidance tendency when she wants to avoid being considered a bad person.

References

Allen, J. P., Pianta, R. C., Gregory, A., Mikami, A. Y., & Lun, J. (2011). An interaction-based approach to enhancing secondary school instruction and student achievement. *Science*, 333(6045), 1034–1037.

Battistich, V., Schaps, E., & Wilson, N. (2004). Effects of an elementary school intervention on students' "connectedness" to school and social adjustment during middle school. *Journal of Primary Prevention*, 24(3), 243–262.

Battistich, V., Solomon, D., Watson, M., & Schaps, E. (1997). Caring school communities. *Education Psychologist*, 32(3), 137–151.

Bergin, C. (2014). Educating students to be prosocial at school. In L. M. Padilla-Walker & G. Carlo (Eds.), *Prosocial development: A multidimensional approach* (pp. 279–301). New York: Oxford University Press.

Bergin, C. (2018). *Designing a prosocial classroom: Fostering collaboration in students from pre-K-12 with the curriculum you already use*. New York: Norton.

Bergin, C., & Bergin, D. A. (1999). Classroom discipline that promotes self-control. *Journal of Applied Developmental Psychology*, 20(2), 189–206.

Bergin, C., & Bergin, D. A. (2009). Attachment in the classroom. *Educational Psychology Review*, 21, 141–170.

Bergin, C., & Bergin, D. A. (2018). *Child and adolescent development in your classroom* (3rd ed.). Belmont, CA: Wadsworth Cengage.

Bergin, C., Bergin, D. A., & French, E. (1995). Preschoolers' prosocial repertoires: Parents' perspectives. *Early Childhood Research Quarterly*, 10, 81–103.

Bergin, C., Prewett, S., Tsai, C.-L., Jones, E., & Murphy, B. (2018). The Leader in Me Effectiveness Study. Unpublished manuscript. Retrieve from authors.

Bergin, C., & Talley, S. (in preparation). Prosocial behavior at the transition to high school.

Bergin, C., Talley, S., & Hamer, L. (2003). Prosocial behaviours of young adolescents: A focus group study. *Journal of Adolescence*, 26, 13–32.

Bierman, K. L., Torres, M. M., Domitrovich, C. E., Welsh, J. A., & Gest, S. D. (2009). Behavioral and cognitive readiness for school: Cross-domain associations for children attending Head Start. *Social Development*, 18(2), 305–323.

Carlo, G., Samper, P., Malonda, E., Tur-Porcar, A., & Davis, A. (2016). The effects of perceptions of parents' use of social and material rewards on prosocial behaviors in Spanish and U.S. youth. *Journal of Early Adolescence*, 1–23. doi:10.1177/0272431616665210.

Chernyak, N., & Kushnir, T. (2013). Giving preschoolers choice increases sharing behavior. *Psychological Science*, 24(10), 1971–1979. doi:10.1177/0956797613482335.

Cornelius-White, J. (2007). Learner-centered teacher-student relationships are effective: A meta-analysis. *Review of Educational Research*, 77(1), 113–143.

Crocker, J., Canevello, A., & Brown, A. (2017). Social motivation: Costs and benefits of selfishness and otherishness. *Annual Review of Psychology*, 68, 299–325. doi:10.1146/annurev-psych-010416-044145.

Curby, T. W., Rimm-Kaufman, S. E., & Ponitz, C. C. (2009). Teacher-child interactions and children's achievement trajectories across kindergarten and first grade. *Journal of Educational Psychology*, 101(4), 912–925.

Deci, E. L., & Ryan, R. M. (2000). The "what" and "why" of goal pursuits: Human needs and the self-determination of behavior. *Psychological Inquiry*, 11(4), 227–268. doi:10.1207/S15327965PLI1104_01.

Durlak, J. A., Weissberg, R. P., Dymnicki, A. B., Taylor, R. D., & Schellinger, K. B. (2011). The impact of enhancing students' social and emotional learning: A meta-analysis of school-based universal interventions. *Child Development*, 82(1), 405–432. doi:10.1111/j.1467-8624.2010.01564.x.

Elliot, A. J., & Covington, M. (2001). Approach and avoidance motivation. *Educational Psychology Review*, 13(2), 73–92. doi:10.1023/A:1009009018235.

Fitzsimons, G. M., & Finkel, E. J. (2018). Transactive-Goal-Dynamics Theory: A discipline-wide perspective. *Current Directions in Psychological Science*, 27(5), 332–338. doi:10.1177/0963721417754199.

Ford, M. (1992). *Motivating humans: Goals, emotions, and personal agency beliefs*. Newbury Park, CA: Sage.

Ford, M., & Nichols, C. (1987). A taxonomy of human goals and some possible applications. In M. E. Ford & D. H. Ford (Eds.), *Humans as self-constructing living systems: Putting the framework to work* (pp. 289–311). Hillsdale, NJ: Lawrence Erlbaum.

Fredrickson, B. L. (2001). The role of positive emotions in positive psychology: The broaden-and-build theory of positive emotions. *American Psychologist*, 56(3), 218–226.

Galliger, C., Tisak, M., & Tisak, J. (2009). When the wheels on the bus go round: social interactions on the school bus. *Social Psychology of Education*, 12(1), 43–62. doi:10.1007/s11218-008-9072-0.

Gregory, A., & Ripski, M. B. (2008). Adolescent trust in teachers: Implications for behavior in the high school classroom. *School Psychology Review*, 37(3), 337–353.

Griffith, J. (2002). A multilevel analysis of the relation of school learning and social environments to minority achievement in public elementary schools. *Elementary School Journal*, 102, 349–366.

Hawley, P. H. (2014). The Duality of Human Nature: Coercion and Prosociality in Youths' Hierarchy Ascension and Social Success. *Current Directions in Psychological Science*, 23(6), 433–438. doi:10.1177/0963721414548417.

Hughes, J. N., Luo, W., Kwok, O.-M., & Loyd, L. K. (2008). Teacher-student support, effortful engagement, and achievement: A 3-year longitudinal study. *Journal of Educational Psychology*, 100(1), 1–14.

Hughes, J. N., Wu, J.-Y., Kwok, O.-m., Villarreal, V., & Honson, A. (2012). Indirect effects of child reports of teacher-student relationship on achievement. *Journal of Educational Psychology*, 104(2), 350–365. doi:10.1037/a0026339.

Jeffrey, A., Auger, R., & Pepperell, J. (2013). If we're ever in trouble they're always there: A qualitative study of teacher-student caring. *The Elementary School Journal*, 114(1), 100–117.

Jennings, J., & DiPrete, T. A. (2010). Teacher effects on social and behavioral skills in early elementary school. *Sociology of Education*, 83(2), 135–159.

Jia, Y., Way, N., Ling, G., Yoskihawa, H., Chen, X., Hughes, D …Lu, Z. (2009). The influence of student perceptions of school climate on socioemotional and academic adjustment: A comparison of Chinese and American adolescents. *Child Development*, 80(5), 1514–1530.

Jones, D. E., Greenberg, M., & Crowley, M. (2015). Early social-emotional functioning and public health: The relationship between kindergarten social competence and future wellness. *American Journal of Public Health*, 105(11), e1–e8. doi:10.2105/AJPH.2015.302630.

108 Christi Bergin

Kruglanski, A., Shah, J., Fishbach, A., Friedman, R., Chun, W., & Sleeth-Kepper, D. (2002). A theory of goal systems. In M. Zanna (Ed.), *Advances in experimental social psychology* (Vol. 34, pp. 331–378). San Diego, CA: Academic Press.

Ladd, G. W., Kochenderfer-Ladd, B., Visconti, K., Ettekal, I., Sechler, C., & Cortes, K. (2014). Grade-school children's social collaborative skills: Links with partner preference and achievement. *American Educational Research Journal, 51*(1), 152–183. doi:10.3102/0002831213507327.

Leyva, D., Weiland, C., Barata, M., Yoshikawa, H., Snow, C., Treviño, E., & Rolla, A. (2015). Teacher–child interactions in Chile and their associations with prekindergarten outcomes. *Child Development, 86*(3), 781–799. doi:10.1111/cdev.12342.

Locke, E. A., & Latham, G. P. (2006). New directions in goal-setting theory. *Current Direction in Psychological Science, 15*, 265–268. doi:10.1111/j.1467-8721.2006.00449.x.

Martin, A., & Olson, K. R. (2015). Beyond good and evil: What motivations underlie children's prosocial behavior? *Perspectives on Psychological Science, 10*(2), 159–175. doi:10.1177/1745691615568998.

Mashburn, A. J., Pianta, R. C., Hamre, B., Downer, J. T., Barbarin, O. A., Bryant, D. ..., Howes, C. (2008). Measures of classroom quality in prekindergarten and children's development of academic, language, and social skills. *Child Development, 79*(3), 732–749.

Matthews, J. S., Kizzie, K. T., Rowley, S. J., & Cortina, K. (2010). African Americans and boys: Understanding the literacy gap, tracing academic trajectories, and evaluating the role of learning-related skills. *Journal of Educational Psychology, 102*(3), 757–771. doi:10.1037/a0019616.

Molano, A., Jones, S., & Willett, J. (2014). Peer effects in the elementary school classroom: Socialization of aggressive and prosocial behavior and its consequences for academic achievement. Unpublished doctoral dissertation, Harvard University, Cambridge, MA.

Mussen, P., & Eisenberg, N. (2001). Prosocial development in context. In A. Bohart & D. Stipek (Eds.), *Constructive and destructive behavior: Implications for family, school, and society* (pp. 103–126). Washington D.C.: APA.

Noddings, N. (1992). *The challenge to care in schools: An alternative approach to education*. New York: Teachers College Press.

O'Connor, E., & McCartney, K. (2007). Examining teacher-child relationships and achievement as part of an ecological model of development. *American Educational Research Journal, 44*(2), 340–369.

Orehek, E., Forest, A. L., & Barbaro, N. (2018). A people-as-means approach to interpersonal relationships. *Perspectives on Psychological Science, 13*(3), 373–389. doi:10.1177/1745691617744522.

Phelan, P., Davidson, A. L., & Cao, H. T. (1991). Students' multiple worlds: Negotiating the boundaries of family, peer, and school cultures. *Anthropology & Education Quarterly, 22*, 224–250.

Ramaswamy, V., & Bergin, C. (2009). Do reinforcement and induction increase prosocial behavior? Results of a teacher-based intervention in preschools. *Journal of Research in Childhood Education, 23*(4), 525–536.

Raver, C. C. (2004). Placing emotional self-regulation in sociocultural and socioeconomic contexts. *Child Development, 75*(2), 346–353.

Reinke, W., Herman, K., & Newcomer, L. (2016). The brief student-teacher classroom interaction observation: Using dynamic indicators of behaviors in the classroom to predict outcomes and inform practice. *Assessment for Effective Intervention, preprint*, 1–11. doi:10.1177/1534508416641605.

Reyes, M. R., Brackett, M. A., Rivers, S. E., White, M., & Salovey, P. (2012). Classroom emotional climate, student engagement, and academic achievement. *Journal of Educational Psychology, 104*(3), 700–712. doi:10.1037/a0027268.

Roorda, D. L., Koomen, H. M. Y., Spilt, J. L., & Oort, F. J. (2011). The influence of affective teacher–student relationships on students' school engagement and achievement. *Review of Educational Research, 81*(4), 493–529. doi:10.3102/0034654311421793.

Social and Character Development Research Consortium. (2010). Efficacy of schoolwide programs to promote social and character development and reduce problem behavior in elementary school children (NCER 2011–2001). Washington, DC: National Center for Education Research, Institute of Education Sciences.

Spilt, J., & Hughes, J. N. (2015). African american children at risk of increasingly conflicted teacher-student relationships in elementary school. *School Psychology Review, 44*(3), 306–314.

Spilt, J., Hughes, J., Wu, J.-Y., & Kwok, O.-M. (2012). Dynamics of teacher-student relaitonships: Stability and change across elementary school and the influence on children's academic success. *Child Development, 83*(4), 1180–1195. doi:10.1111/j.1467-8624.2012.01761.x.

Tamir, D. I., & Hughes, B. L. (2018). Social rewards: From basic social building blocks to complex social behavior. *Perspectives on Psychological Science, 13*(6), 700–717. doi:10.1177/1745691618776263.

Urdan, T., & Maehr, M. L. (1995). Beyond a two-goal theory of motivation and achievement: A case for social goals. *Review of Educational Research, 65*(3), 213–243. doi:10.2307/1170683.

Vansteenkiste, M., Lens, W., Elliot, A. J., Soenens, B., & Mouratidis, A. (2014). Moving the achievement goal approach one step forward: Toward a systematic examination of the autonomous and controlled reasons underlying achievement goals. *Educational Psychologist, 49*(3), 153–174. doi:10.1080/00461520.2014.928598.

Wang, Z., Bergin, C., & Bergin, D. A. (2014). Measuring engagement in fourth to twelfth grade classrooms: The classroom engagement inventory. *School Psychology Quarterly, 29* (4), 517–535. doi:10.1037/spq0000050 10.1037/spq0000050.supp (Supplemental).

Watkins, D. E., & Wentzel, K. R. (2008). Training boys with ADHD to work collaboratively: Social and learning outcomes. *Contemporary Educational Psychology, 33*(4), 625–646.

Weinstein, N., & Ryan, R. M. (2010). When helping helps: Autonomous motivation for prosocial behavior and its influence on well-being for the helper and recipient. *Journal of Personality and Social Psychology, 98*, 222–244. doi:98, 222–244. http://dx.doi.org/10.1037/a0016984.

Wentzel, K. R. (1991). Social and academic goals at school: Motivation and achievement in context. In M. L. Maehr & P. R. Pintrich (Eds.), *Advances in motivation and achievement* (Vol. 7, pp. 185–212). Greenwich, CT: JAI Press.

Wentzel, K. R. (1992). Motivation and achievement in adolescence: A multiple goals perspective. In D. Schunk & J. Meece (Eds.), *Student perceptions in the classroom: Causes and consequences* (pp. 287–306). Hillsdale, NJ: Earlbaum.

Wentzel, K. R. (1993a). Does being good make the grade? Social behavior and academic competence in middle school. *Journal of Educational Psychology, 85*, 357–364.

Wentzel, K. R. (1993b). Motivation and achievement in early adolescence: The role of multiple classroom goals. *Journal of Early Adolescence, 13*(1), 4–20.

Wentzel, K. R. (1997). Student motivation in middle school: The role of perceived pedagogical caring. *Journal of Educational Psychology, 89*(3), 411–419.

Wentzel, K. R. (2000). What is it that I'm trying to achieve? Classroom goals from a content perspective. *Contemporary Educational Psychology, 25*, 105–115. doi:10.1006/ceps.1999.1021.

Wentzel, K. R. (2002). Are effective teachers like good parents? Teaching styles and student adjustment in early adolescence. *Child Development, 73*(1), 287–301.

Wentzel, K. R., Muenks, K., McNeish, D., & Russell, S. (2017). Peer and teacher supports in relation to motivation and effort: A multi-level study. *Contemporary Educational Psychology, 49*, 32–45. doi:10.1016/j.cedpsych.2016.11.002.

Wentzel, K. R., Muenks, K., McNeish, D., & Russell, S. (2018). Emotional support, social goals, and classroom behavior: A multilevel, multisite study. *Journal of Educational Psychology.* doi:10.1037/edu0000239.

7

REVENGE GOALS

Kristina L. McDonald

In their everyday lives at school, children face many social challenges that require them to balance competing social goals (Dodge, Asher, & Parkhurst, 1989). Observational studies conducted in classrooms and on playgrounds indicate that instances of provocation are frequent during the school days of youth (Asher, Rose, & Gabriel, 2001; Craig & Pepler, 1998; Craig, Pepler, & Atlas, 2000). When faced with these situations, some youth may choose to react by disengaging, reacting assertively, seeking peer support, or by retaliating against the provocateur (e.g., Dirks, Cuttini, Mott, & Henry, 2017; Tapper & Boulton, 2005; Kochenderfer & Ladd, 1997). Retaliation and desires for revenge may be, in some ways, a very natural way to respond to perceived harm (McCullough, 2008). The fundamental revenge principle of negative reciprocity underlies the institutionalization of laws that are supported in almost all societies (Crombag, Rassin, & Horeselenberg, 2003) and theorists and researchers have suggested several possible rewards that revenge serves for individuals and groups. These functions include restoring feelings of justice and fairness (Gouldner, 1960; Lerner, 1980), changing others' beliefs and teaching moral lessons (Heider, 1958), restoring self-esteem or asserting dominance (Baumeister, 1997; De Castro, Verhulp, & Runions, 2012), and the deterrence of future harm (Frijda, 1988).

Although there may be functional benefits to seeking revenge after harm, research indicates that revenge-seeking in response to minor slights or conflicts may have negative consequences for children's social relationships. The current chapter reviews the evidence of these interpersonal outcomes and hypothesizes about how revenge goals may also have negative implications for academic and school performance. Prior to this discussion, the chapter outlines how revenge goals are defined and reviews research on the social-cognitive and affective processes, as well as the developmental and contextual influences that may explain individual differences in revenge motivations. Throughout the chapter, I also highlight areas of uncertainty and suggest areas that deserve more attention in order to better understand children's revenge motivations.

Definition

Goals are conceptualized as the purpose, reason, or motivation that drives a behavior. Revenge goals have been operationally defined as goals to "get even," "get back," or "hurt" a person who is perceived as responsible for an offense (e.g., McDonald & Asher, 2018; McDonald & Lochman, 2012). Goals are typically studied by presenting children with vignettes depicting various social situations. These social situations vary a great deal. For instance, some have used ambiguous provocations in which it is unclear if a peer meant to hurt the participant (Lochman et al., 1993) or minor conflicts of interest in which the participant is asked to imagine disagreeing with a peer on which activity to do or how to share a resource (McDonald & Asher, 2013; Rose & Asher, 1999). In direct contrast, some researchers have used intentional provocations from peers (McDonald & Asher, 2018) or even relationship transgressions (MacEvoy & Asher, 2012). Participants are then asked to either describe the goals that they would employ in that situation or to indicate, through a Likert-scale rating, the likelihood they would pursue certain goals, such as revenge.

Alternatively, some researchers have also investigated revenge motivations through retrospective reports from youth of stressful incidents or times that they had hurt others or committed retaliatory acts to perceived harms (e.g., Jäggi & Kliewer, 2016; Pasupathi, Wainryb, Bourne, & Posada, 2017). Data generated from these studies are rich in detail and yield important insights and hypotheses about how youth think about retaliatory goals and social provocation situations. This chapter will include findings from both types of studies.

Evidence

Much of the research with children on social cognition and revenge has been implemented by researchers guided by Social Information Processing (SIP) models (Arsenio & Lemerise, 2004; Crick & Dodge, 1994; Dodge, 1986; Lemerise & Arsenio, 2000; McFall, 1982; McFall & Dodge, 1982). SIP models outline a series of cognitive steps hypothesized to influence social behavior during social interaction. Although these processes are likely automatic and reflexive, these steps serve as a guide by which we can understand the variety of cognitive processes that have been linked to revenge motivations. In the first and second steps of the model, individuals encode and interpret cues in the social interaction. The clarification of goals is the third step of the model. Thus, the encoding and interpretation of social cues as outlined in steps 1 and 2 may either enhance or decrease the likelihood that a child would pursue revenge goals in step 3. The fourth, fifth, and sixth steps in the model outline how an individual selects a behavioral response based on the possible consequences, their perceptions of efficacy in enacting the chosen response, and the enactment of the chosen response.

Also, according SIP models, emotional processes and other characteristics of an individual are likely to influence revenge goals and subsequent behavior. Emotional processes, including temperament, emotion regulation, and mood (Lemerise & Arsenio, 2000), may affect any step of social information processing. Furthermore, SIP models also assume that individuals have a "database," which encompasses a wide range of social knowledge structures, including moral reasoning, schemas about others and relationships, scripts for social interactions, and beliefs. This "database" influences how people interpret and respond to social information as well.

This chapter will review the available research on these processes and how they are associated with revenge goals. Ideally, there would be relevant revenge research for each of the steps outlined in the SIP model. However, research is not available for every step, and thus the most attention will be given to the areas with the greatest available literature, including aspects of interpretations and behavioral strategies that have been linked to revenge goals as well as affective processes and aspects of the "database." Research on aggression will also be used to support ideas and provide suggestions for future research. After discussion of SIP and affective processes associated with revenge goals, information on developmental influences and contextual factors that have also been linked to revenge-seeking is discussed.

Encoding and interpretations

Situations involving provocation and retaliation are complex and entail a variety of factors all of which must be attended to, encoded, and interpreted in order to respond appropriately. The first two processing steps that Crick and Dodge (1994) refer to in the SIP model are the encoding of social cues and the interpretation of these cues. There has been relatively little work on the encoding of cues preceding revenge responses. However, there is evidence that children who are prone to aggression may pay attention to different cues within the social situation than other children, either attending to hostile cues more than their non-aggressive peers or failing to attend to relevant details and "falling back" on negative peer schema to choose goals and behavioral responses (Gouze, 1987; Lochman & Dodge, 1994; 1998; Troop-Gordon, Gordon, Vogel-Ciernia, Ewing Lee, & Visonti, 2018).

Compared to encoding, there is more work that has examined how negative attributions or interpretations that are made is social situations are predictive of greater desires for revenge. Attributions about others' intentions are especially important in the selection of revenge and retaliation responses (Vidmar, 2000). In situations where harm is intentionally caused, people are more likely to endorse or support retaliatory responses than in other kinds of situations (e.g. Astor, 1994; Crick & Dodge, 1994; Hewitt, 1975; Shantz & Pentz, 1972; Shantz & Voydanoff, 1973; Smetana, et al. 1999; Tremblay & Belchevski, 2004). It seems likely that individuals who tend to perceive that negative events are intentionally caused may also find themselves more often wanting to get back at their offenders since the perception of harm has been suggested as a precursor to desiring revenge. In order to assess this tendency, investigators typically present children with stimuli, like stories or analog situations, which are purposely ambiguous with regards to the intent of the offender (e.g., a situation where it is unclear whether a peer meant to spill milk on the participant in the lunchroom).

The attribution of negative or malevolent intent in ambiguous situations, otherwise termed the *hostile attribution bias* (Dodge, 1980; Nasby, Hyden, & DePaulo, 1979), has been studied extensively in relation to aggressive behavior. A great deal of work has clearly shown that children who are more likely to attribute negative intent to others are also more likely to be aggressive (de Castro, Veerman, Koops, Bosch, & Monshouwer, 2002). Intervention research has also demonstrated that hostile attributions play a causal role in the genesis of aggressive behavior (Hudley & Graham, 1993). Similar to research focused on aggression, hostile attributions about a provocateur's intent have also been found to be positively related to children's revenge goals (e.g., Peets, Hodges, & Salmivalli, 2013; McDonald, 2008; Smalley & Bannerjee, 2014).

Beyond attributions of intent, however, there are many other attributions that youth may make in social situations that would be associated with revenge goals. McDonald and Asher (2013) studied a variety of positive and negative interpretations that people may make during minor conflicts to see how these interpretations would be related to desires for revenge. They found that interpretations of betrayal, that the other person did not like or respect you, that the other person did something morally wrong, and that the relationship with the person was going to end were all predictive of greater motivations for revenge. In contrast, interpretations that the situation could be easily resolved were negatively related to revenge goals. Similarly, McDonald (2008) found similar associations between these interpretations and revenge goals in a sample of young adolescents, suggesting that a variety of negative attributions and interpretations may give rise to revenge motivations. Thus, there is evidence that youth who make more hostile attributions about others' behaviors and interpret ambiguous or conflictual interactions as having more negative implications for their relationship or how the other person thinks about them are more likely to want to get even.

Strategy generation, selection, and enactment

According to SIP models, the goals that one prioritizes will have implications for the strategies that one pursues. In line with this hypothesis, revenge goals have been consistently linked with aggressive strategies in response to ambiguous situations (Erdley & Asher, 1996; Lochman et al., 1993; Slaby & Guerra, 1988), conflicts of interest (McDonald & Asher, 2013), and in response to clearly intended provocations (McDonald & Asher, 2018). Further, revenge goals have been found to correlate negatively with the strategies of accommodation and compromise (e.g. "I would say that my friend could pick the game if I could pick the game after that" Rose & Asher, 1999; McDonald & Asher, 2013). Thus, it seems that having revenge goals corresponds with pursuing these goals in aggressive, non-prosocial ways.

SIP models also consider that response selection is affected by the evaluation of whether one will be successful enacting the response. Regarding response strategy evaluation, there is evidence that youth who desire revenge after a perceived harm are more likely to think that aggression has benefits and to believe that they will be effective at carrying out the revenge behavior. More specifically, revenge goal endorsement has been linked to beliefs that aggression is a useful way to attain rewards (McDonald & Lochman, 2012), and Erdley and Asher (1996) found that aggressive children felt more efficacious about taking revenge and hurting others than did not aggressive children.

Finally, it does seem that youth who desire to get even with peers are also viewed by teachers and classmates as being aggressive. Lochman et al. (1993) presented adolescent boys with an ambiguous situation vignette, in which the boys were asked to imagine that they were bumped by a new kid at school causing their books to fall to the floor. Subjects then rated a series of goals, including avoidance, dominance, revenge, and affiliation goals. They found that revenge goals were positively associated with aggression; boys who were rated by peers as aggressive rated revenge and dominance goals higher than boys who were not viewed as aggressive (see also McDonald & Asher, 2018). Additionally, Erdley and Asher (1996) found that peer-identified aggressive children were more likely than withdrawn or problem-solving children to endorse the goal of getting back in response to ambiguous provocation. Furthermore, McDonald and Lochman (2012) found that youth who increased in the endorsement of revenge goals between fourth and eighth grade were rated as more reactively aggressive by teachers in eighth grade as well.

Affect and affect regulation

Lemerise and Arsenio (2000) highlighted the importance of studying affective processes and regulation when considering how youth process social information. Negative affective processes are particularly relevant to predicting revenge goals. Berkowitz (1993) defines anger as a feeling that usually occurs after an unpleasant experience, like a peer provocation. Anger arises primarily when people attribute harm to intentional purposeful acts by a perpetrator (e.g. Averill, 1982; Berkowitz, 1993; Betancourt & Blair, 1992). Thus, it would seem that anger, which is caused by perceived intentional harm, may precede revenge responses.

Recent research has corroborated that feelings of anger are highly related to revenge motivations. McDonald and Asher (2013) investigated the emotions and interpretations associated with revenge motivations in conflict-of-interest situations with friends, roommates, and romantic partners. They found ratings of anger were highly correlated with how much participants endorsed wanting to get even with

116 Kristina L. McDonald

these relationship partners. MacEvoy and Asher (2012) also found that feelings of anger in response to hypothetical friendship transgressions positively predicted children's revenge goal endorsement. Finally, McDonald and Asher (2018) found that youth who endorsed revenge goals after peer provocation also reported more anger than youth who were similarly offended by the provocation but did not endorse revenge goals at high levels. Thus, there is ample evidence that revenge goals and feelings of anger in response to a perceived harm are associated experiences (also see de Castro et al. 2012 and Jäggi & Kliewer 2016).

Sadness and hurt feelings may be associated with revenge goals. In contrast to anger leading to revenge, sadness has been hypothesized to lead to disengagement or withdrawing from a situation (Frijda, 1988). In line with this, some research suggests that feelings of sadness may be protective against retaliatory motivations and behaviors. MacEvoy and Asher (2012) found that children's reports of sadness in response to friendship transgression were negatively related to their revenge goal endorsement. However, McDonald and Asher (2018) did not find that reports of sadness differentiated revenge-seekers from youth who did not endorse revenge goals in response to peer provocation.

Research on hurt feelings and revenge goal endorsement is also mixed. Hurt feelings, while a distinct experience, appears to be a form of negative affect that blends sadness and anger, with the latter especially occurring when the offense is seen as unjustified (Leary, Koch, & Hechenbleikner, 2001). Leary, Spring, Negel, Ansell, and Evans (1998) reported that in 62% of episodes in which college students' reported hurt feelings they also reported retaliating with aggressive behavior, suggesting that hurt feelings may be an impetus for revenge. In line with this, McDonald and Asher (2013) found that hurt feelings were positively predictive of revenge goal endorsement in conflict-of-interest situations. However, when comparing adolescents who were offended by peer provocation and endorsed revenge goals to adolescents who were offended but did not seek revenge, hurt feelings did not distinguish between these groups (McDonald & Asher, 2018). Thus, we suggest that the associations of sadness and hurt feelings with revenge responding may be dependent on situational variables such as the relationship with the provocateur or the type of provocation that youth are responding to.

Although it is still unclear how sadness and hurt feelings may predict to revenge goals, it is clear that feelings of anger and revenge goals are closely linked. It is difficult to imagine a revenge response that is not rooted in anger, but it is possible to imagine anger experiences that are not followed by revenge-seeking. Therefore it is important to consider what makes one more or less likely to respond with revenge when angered. Individual differences in emotion regulation may also be important to consider. Emotion regulation is a change associated with activated emotions, including change in the emotion itself, like intensity or duration, as well change in other psychological processes, like memory or social interaction (Cole, Martin, & Dennis, 2004). Children who find it more difficult to regulate anger may react in more hostile ways to provocation. Indeed, children and adolescents who are prone to intense and frequent negative emotions also tend to be more aggressive and have more externalizing problems (Eisenberg, 2000; Eisenberg, Fabes, et al., 1996; Eisenberg, Fabes, Nyman, Bernzweig, & Pinuelas, 1994; Hubbard et al., 2002; Stice & Gonzales, 1998).

McDonald and Lochman (2012) found that youth who endorsed revenge goals in response to ambiguous provocation were more behaviorally and affectively dysregulated than youth who endorsed revenge at lower levels. Further, children who increased in their revenge goal endorsement over four years were more fearfully reactive than were children who decreased in revenge goal endorsement over the same time period. Similarly, McDonald and Asher (2018) found that youth who endorsed revenge goals in response to peer provocation also endorsed the goal of trying to regulate their emotional experiences less than youth who endorsed revenge a low levels.

The idea of poor emotion regulation skills being linked to revenge motivations is also supported by research on anger rumination. Anger rumination has been defined as unintentional and recurrent thinking about experiences that elicit anger (Sukhodolsky, Golub, & Cromwell, 2001). In a sample of adults, McCullough and colleagues (2001) measured rumination by the number of intrusive thoughts an individual had experienced about a past offense. They found that positive attitudes towards revenge and self-reported desires for revenge were positively associated with rumination about offenses. Future research should consider this when studying revenge goals in child samples as well.

In addition to considering anger rumination, it may also prove fruitful for future research on revenge motivations to consider self-conscious emotions, especially the self-conscious experience of shame. According to Lewis (1971), shame is a self-conscious emotion that manifests as hostility toward the self. When a person feels shame, they feel exposed and inferior, are more preoccupied with other people's opinions, and experience more intense feelings of pain. Research with adults suggests that shamed individuals are less likely to attempt reconciliation and are more likely to act aggressively to others (Tangney, 1998; Eisenberg, 2000). There is some preliminary evidence that shame-proneness, or the tendency to feel shame, is associated with anger, aggression, and revenge-seeking in adults and children (Tangney, 1995; Tangney, Wagner, Hill-Barlow, Marschall, & Gramzow, 1996), but more research should be done to examine how experiences of shame and individual differences in the tendency to feel shame may predict to revenge motivations and retaliatory behaviors.

The "database"

Finally, several features of the "database" as outlined by Crick and Dodge (1994) have been conceptualized and examined as predictors of the tendency for youth to endorse revenge goals. First, the "database" likely includes a set of beliefs about the justifiability of revenge and the legitimacy of aggression. Research with both adults and children supports the idea that holding certain beliefs may increase one's likelihood of taking revenge (Eisenberger, Lynch, Aselage, & Rohdieck, 2004; Erdley & Asher, 1998; McDonald & Asher, 2018; Stuckless & Goranson, 1992). For instance, Eisenberger et al. (2004) built on the work of Gouldner (1960) to develop a measure about negative and positive reciprocity beliefs. They found that individuals who more strongly endorsed negative reciprocity beliefs retaliated more when treated unfairly by a confederate compared to participants who did not endorse negative reciprocity as strongly. Building on Eisenberger et al., McDonald and Asher (2018) also found that adolescents who endorsed revenge goals after peer provocation endorsed negative reciprocity beliefs at higher levels than adolescents whose revenge motivations were low.

Beyond beliefs about revenge, beliefs about the legitimacy of aggression also distinguish youth who desire revenge from those who do not. Erdley and Asher (1998) developed a measure of beliefs about the legitimacy of aggression based in part on Slaby and Guerra's (1988) measure about aggression beliefs. Erdley and Asher (1998) found children who more highly endorsed beliefs in the legitimacy of aggression rated retaliatory aggressive strategies in response to ambiguous provocation vignettes more highly than children who were lower in their endorsement of these beliefs. McDonald and Asher (2018) also found that legitimacy of aggression beliefs were the strongest predictor of whether an adolescent chose to seek revenge in response to an offensive provocation. Thus, these belief systems about the proper way to respond to and treat peers deserve more attention in how they predict motivations, like revenge, in social situations.

There are also schema about interpersonal interactions that foster revenge motivations after perceived offenses. In particular, schema of others being rejecting or schema that focus on issues of power and dominance may be particularly likely to prompt revenge responding. For instance, rejection sensitivity, which is the tendency to anxiously or angrily expect rejection, is associated with increased hostile and aggressive behaviors after rejection. (Ayduk, Downey, Testa, Yen & Shoda, 1999; Downey & Feldman, 1996; Downey, Feldman, & Ayduk, 2000; Downey, Lebolt, Rincon, & Freitas, 1998). Preliminary evidence suggests that rejection sensitivity is positively associated with revenge goals after peer provocations and that this effect may be accounted for by increased interpretations of rejection (McDonald, 2008). However, more research should investigate how schema relevant to rejection may foster revenge responding in children.

Schema that reflect concerns about social or interpersonal power may also increase one's tendency to seek revenge. Heider (1958) suggested that revenge may be a way to communicate "you can't treat me like that" and may act as a way to change the offender's beliefs in the relative power, importance, and value of the avenger. Following from this idea, McDonald and Asher (2018) hypothesized that there may be individual differences in adolescents' concerns about being respected (or concerns about relative power) and that youth who were more concerned with being respected by peers may be more likely to want to get even after provocation. These hypotheses were also based off of research done on the "code of honor" and ethnographic research that has described the "code of the streets" (Anderson, 1999; Horowitz, 1983; Fagan & Wilkinson, 1998; Luckenbill & Doyle, 1989; Nisbett & Cohen, 1996). McDonald and Asher (2018) developed a measure to assess this construct, which they called disrespect sensitivity. Disrespect sensitivity was defined as vigilance for signs of disrespect from others and expectations that others will not respect you. They found that revenge-seekers, or youth who endorsed revenge at higher levels after being provoked by peers, also reported more disrespect sensitivity than youth who did not endorse revenge goals when provoked by peers. Thus, it seems that schema that others are disrespecting may be particularly likely to increase desires for revenge among youth.

Finally, beliefs or schema about the ability for others to change also seem to influence how they respond when provoked. Yeager and colleagues (2011; 2103) have found that children's beliefs about personality being fixed or malleable are predictive of their desires for revenge. For instance, beliefs about bullies and victims as being unchangeable were positively related to children's reports of vengeful behavior in response to a time that an acquaintance upset them in or outside of school (Yeager et al., 2011). Yeager et al. (2013) also found that beliefs that personalities being fixed or stable were related to children's desires for vengeance in response to an ambiguous peer provocation. Experimental manipulations of these beliefs have also been found to reduce aggressive responses, including vengeful responses. Youth who were randomly assigned to read materials about how personality is malleable reported fewer vengeful desires and aggressive responses to a hypothetical ambiguous provocation scenario compared to youth in a control group (Yeager et al., 2011; 2013).

Developmental influences

Beyond the study of how cognitive and affective processes are associated with revenge goals after provocation, there are several important developmental processes that may predict individual differences in youth's tendency to want revenge. A great deal about the developmental precursors of aggressive behavior have been studied extensively (e.g., Malti & Rubin, 2018), and it may the developmental precursors of revenge motivations are similar. For instance, preliminary evidence suggests that the parenting behaviors associated with child aggression are similar to those associated with revenge motivations. Heidgerken, Hughes, Cavell, and Willson (2004) found that parent reports of harsh parenting were concurrently and directly related to children's endorsement of dominance and revenge goals in response to ambiguous provocations. McDonald, Baden, and Lochman (2013) also found that child reports of positive parenting, or the use of positive reinforcements for good behaviors, predicted a decrease in revenge goals over a year period.

Second, the neighborhood contexts in which children grow up are also important to consider in understanding revenge motivations. Murphy (2000) wrote that revenge "passions are often felt by those who have been given reason to believe that there are monsters in the world and that they have been forced to fight with them ... (pp. 139–140)." Thus, it may be that revenge motivations are more adaptive for children who grow up in environments that are unsafe or dangerous. In many of these communities, public offenses are viewed as the ultimate transgression, and the only way to protect one's reputation is to retaliate (Kubrin & Weitzer, 2003). As retaliation communicates to the offender that the victim is not to be trifled with (Axelrod, 1984; Crombag et al., 2003), seeking revenge may be a powerful signal in gaining respect and deterring future abuse from peers or authority figures (Bies & Tripp, 1998).

As noted above, the need to enhance one's reputation by retaliatory responding to threats has been noted by several ethnographers (e.g., Anderson, 1999; Fagan &Wilkinson, 1998; Horowitz, 1983). Neighborhood structural factors, in conjunction with these social norms, enhance the likelihood that individuals will take revenge. Lacking trust in the judicial or authority system may increase community member reliance on violence to protect themselves (Huang & Vaghn, 1996; Kubrin & Weitzer, 2003). Furthermore, community violence may also increase beliefs that retaliation and aggression are justified (Schwartz & Proctor, 2000; Guerra, Huesmann, & Spindler, 2003). Jäggi and Kliewer (2016) also observed the urban youth's narratives of revenge experiences stressed the importance of maintaining a "tough" reputation, in part, to prevent future victimization from peers. Adopting the "code of the street" has also been associated with the neighborhood in which a child grows up (Stewart & Simons, 2006). It is not clear, however, what factors may buffer youth who grow up in these contexts from revenge-seeking. Future research should continue to understand individual differences in how these contextual influences affect children's desires for revenge in interpersonal conflict

Situational factors

As much research about children's revenge goals has focused on individual differences, the situational or contextual features that may influence desires for revenge need more attention. There are several features of the context that may either increase or decrease how much someone wants to get even. The first was alluded to when discussing attributions. When it is clear that a provocation was purposely intended by another individual, it is more likely that youth will desire to get even than when it is unclear that the provocation was intentional (e.g. Astor, 1994; Shantz & Voydanoff, 1973). Many of the other factors outlined below have been studied with adults, but more research needs to examine these factors in experimental studies with children.

The relationship context in which the conflict takes place may influence how much individuals want to get even. McDonald and Asher (2013) found that college students endorsed revenge goals in minor conflict-of-interest situations when the conflict was with a romantic partner than with a friend or roommate. However, when studying more substantial transgression situations others have found that children and adults are less likely to make hostile attributions of friends or romantic partners and are less likely to seek revenge with close relationship partners than they are with strangers (e.g., Peets, Hodges, Kikas, & Salmivalli, 2007; Rasmussen, Alibhai, Boon, & Ellard, 2016). It may be that these opposing finding are due to the differences in the types of conflicts that were studied (i.e., minor conflicts of interest vs. more severe provocations); however, it does seem that individuals take the relationship that they have with the other person into account when deciding whether to pursue revenge.

Research by social psychologists has also examined how power imbalances, audiences, apologies, and cultural norms may increase the likelihood of retaliatory aggression. For instance, research has shown that higher status individuals are more likely to take revenge against lower status individuals than vice versa, supposedly because the costs are too high for lower status individuals (e.g. Aquino, Tripp, & Bies 2001; Kim, Smith, & Brigham, 1998). Additionally, an audience may heighten desires for revenge (Baumeister, 1997; Felson, 1978), especially when the audience is perceived as supporting retaliation (e.g., Brown, 1968; Kim et al., 1998). If a transgressor apologizes for their actions, individuals are less likely to desire revenge and more likely to forgive (e.g., Baumeister, Stillwell, & Wotman, 1990). However, there is some evidence that the effects of apologies may depend on attributions of intent. It may be that when offenders intentionally commit offenses forgiveness is less likely following an apology, but when harm is unintentional apologies foster forgiveness (Struthers, Eaton, Santelli, Uchiyama, & Shirvani, 2008). It is also unclear if these factors work in the same way across cultures. There is some evidence that individuals from collectivistic cultures are more hesitant to reciprocate negative treatment, especially when they anticipate future interactions with the provocateur (Chen, Chen, & Portnoy, 2009; Jung et al., 2014). Additionally, it is necessary to examine how these situational or contextual features may affect revenge goals in children. Both avenues are fruitful grounds for further study.

Interpersonal Outcomes

Although there may be several functional reasons that children would want to get even when their peers harm them, research indicates that there are negative consequences for youth who report wanting to get even with peers and friends. Youth who report high desires for revenge are rated as more reactively aggressive by teachers (McDonald & Lochman, 2012), which has been established as a predictor of peer rejection and victimization (Card & Little, 2006). Revenge is also not an effective strategy for decreasing the aggression of the original provocateur. In their study of pre-adolescent girls, Putallaz, Kupersmidt, Coie, McKnight, and Grimes (2004) found that retaliation for aggression was the least effective strategy in yielding positive outcomes. Reactive aggression, which can be considered a form of retaliation, led to continued aggression by other group members 77% of the time. The strategies which led to the most positive outcomes were de-escalation behaviors, such as compromising or using humor in response to aggression.

Researchers have also examined how revenge goals relate to other aspects of children's social competence, such as peer acceptance and features of close relationships (e.g. Erdley & Asher, 1996; Lochman, Wayland, & White, 1993; Renshaw & Asher, 1983; Rose & Asher, 1999; Slaby & Guerra, 1988). Generally, endorsement of revenge goals is negatively associated with high quality peer relationships; youth who endorse revenge-seeking are less liked by peers (e.g., Lochman et al., 1993; McDonald & Asher, 2018; Renshaw & Asher, 1983; Rose & Asher, 1999). Additionally, revenge goals may have negative implications for close relationships. Rose and Asher (1999) presented children with several hypothetical situations which depicted mild conflicts with a friend, such as a disagreement over which game to play. After each hypothetical scenario, children were asked to rate a number of goals and strategies on the likelihood that they would pursue these goals or choose to enact the strategies. Rose and Asher (1999) found that the endorsement of revenge goals was negatively associated with the number of mutual friends a child had as well as negatively related to the quality of the child's best friendship. In other words, the more that children endorsed revenge goals in friendship conflicts, the fewer friends they had, the lower their friendship was in positive qualities, and the more conflict there was in their friendship. McDonald and Asher (2013) also found that college students' endorsement of revenge goals was negatively related to their reports of social support from close others. Thus, although there may be a natural tendency for humans to want to retaliate or seek revenge when provoked, it is clear that it may not be the most effective response for ending aggression or maintaining positive relationships with peers.

Academic Outcomes

In contrast to research on the social implications of revenge-seeking, there is little research examining how revenge goals are directly associated with academic performance. However, it is possible to draw hypotheses about revenge goals and academic performance based on how social dominance goals and aggressive behavior and are associated with achievement. Social goals that are related to social dominance seem to be negatively related to academic performance and academic engagement (Kiefer & Ryan, 2008; Kiefer & Wang, 2016) and youth who are more aggressive tend to perform more poorly in school (e.g., Campbell, Spieker, Burchinal, & Poe, 2006; Hinshaw, 1992). However, it seems as if reactive aggression is more negatively related to academic performance than is proactive aggression (Day, Bream, & Pal, 1992) and that rejection from peers may account for why reactive aggression is related to poor school performance (Fite, Hendrickson, Rubens, Gabrielli, & Evans, 2013). Thus, to the extent that revenge motivations are reactive in nature, and less directed at obtaining rewards, it is likely that youth who pursue revenge goals may also do more poorly in school. It may be that poor regulatory abilities underlie both revenge goals and aspects of poor academic performance, or it may be that poor peer experiences explain the possible association. It will be important for future research to examine the nature of how social goals, like revenge, are related to academic achievement. It seems feasible that poor academic performance may lead peers to treat a child badly and this treatment may increase revenge motivations. Conversely, it may be that revenge motivations and aggressive behavior increase negative interactions with peers which then distract youth from learning.

Future Research

Clearly there is still a great deal to learn about children's revenge motivations. To conclude, I highlight three particularly interesting lines of inquiry. First, it will be important for future studies to consider how much of retaliatory behaviors are driven by affective reactions rather than by reflective, goal-driven processes. De Castro et al. (2012) argued that aggressive behavior is not always goal-oriented. Instead, sometimes youth may retaliate based on their strong emotional reactions to situations and their inability to regulate these emotions. They observed that aggressive boys justified retaliatory behaviors to hypothetical provocations more often with reference to strong feelings of anger and rage, rather than to motivations for revenge. They suggest that revenge motivations may be unconsciously driving these responses, but youth do not recognize these motivations and these retaliatory behaviors are not *experienced* as goal-directed. It is important to understand the distinctions between reflexive versus reflective revenge behaviors because interventions would be designed very differently depending on which process underlies the behavior.

Understanding the moral reasoning and moral justifications behind revenge responding will also be productive for further study. De Castro et al. (2012) noted that aggressive boys used moral imperatives to justify retaliatory responding. Using explanations that resemble ideas about negative reciprocity and preventing future conflicts, these boys did not seem amoral. Instead their moral code directed them to respond with retaliation. Some research investigates individual differences in how children make judgments about retaliation with a focus on age, context, and behavioral differences (e.g., Ardila-Rey, Killen, & Brenick, 2009; Gasser, Malti, & Gutzwiller-Helfenfinger, 2012; Posada & Wainryb, 2008; Smetana et al., 2003). They find that older children judge retaliation to be less morally acceptable, that aggressive children view retaliation as more acceptable than youth lower in aggressive behavior, and that children growing up in violent contexts also judged retaliatory aggression less harshly than youth exposed to less violence. It is not yet clear how moral judgments about retaliation being justified translate into one's own revenge motivations in contexts of interpersonal harm. It seems likely that youth who think retaliation is acceptable may be more likely to want revenge and pursue it when they are harmed. However, it is also likely that youth who judge retaliations to be morally wrong in hypothetical situations may still want revenge when they are harmed, perhaps because they morally disengage and find reasons to justify their revenge behaviors (cf. Bandura, 2016).

Finally, I return to an idea that opened the chapter. Many scholars have described desires for revenge as universal and have considered that revenge may be adaptive, to some extent, in promoting cooperation (Axelrod, 1984; McCullough, 2008). Additionally, many parents encourage retaliating for some provocations because they fear that their child will become a victim if they do not "stand up for themselves" (Jäggi & Kliewer, 2016). Therefore, to fully understand why youth might pursue revenge it would be helpful for researchers to consider when revenge responding is useful in promoting cooperation and protecting oneself versus when it is maladaptive and hurts social relationships. I propose that it may depend on many contextual factors, including the seriousness of the original transgression, the relationship with the provocateur, the proportional strength of the harm for harm pattern, and the way in which retaliation is enacted. For instance, some youth may pursue revenge only under certain circumstances and they may do so in a way that is proportional to the original harm. This pattern differs from a child who retaliates for a minor slight with an overly aggressive response. The way that these children enact their revenge goals may differ as well, with one responding calmly and assertively, and the other with an overemotional and angry response. These are all issues that deserve further consideration.

References

Anderson, E. (1999). *Code of the street*. New York: W. W. Norton.

Aquino, K., Tripp, T. M., & Bies, R. J. (2001). How employees respond to personal offense: The effects of blame attribution, victim status, and offender status on revenge and reconciliation in the workplace. *Journal of Applied Psychology*, 86, 52–59.

Ardila-Rey, A., Killen, M., & Brenick, A. (2009). Moral reasoning in violent contexts: Displaced and non-displaced Colombian children's evaluations of moral transgressions, retaliation, and reconciliation. *Social Development*, 18, 181–209.

Arsenio, W. F., & Lemerise, E. A. (2004). Aggression and moral development: Integrating social information processing and moral domain models. *Child Development*, 75, 987–1002.

Asher, S. R., Rose, A. J., & Gabriel, S. W. (2001). Peer rejection in everyday life. In M. R. Leary (Ed.), *Interpersonal rejection* (pp. 105–142). New York: Oxford University Press.

Astor, R. A. (1994). Children's moral reasoning about family and peer violence: The role of provocation and retribution. *Child Development*, 65, 1054–1068.

Averill, J. R. (1982). *Anger and aggression: An essay on emotion*. New York: Springer-Verlag.

Axelrod, R. (1984). *The evolution of cooperation*. New York: Basic Books.

Ayduk, O., Downey, G., Testa, A., Yen, Y., & Shoda, Y. (1999). Does rejection elicit hostility in rejection-sensitive women? *Social Cognition*, 17, 245–271.

Bandura, A. (2016). *Moral disengagement: How people do harm and live with themselves*. New York: Worth.

Baumeister, R. F. (1997). *Evil: Inside human violence and cruelty*. New York: W. H. Freeman.

Baumeister, R. F., Stillwell, A. M., & Wotman, S. R. (1990). Victim and perpetrator accounts of interpersonal conflict: Autobiographical narratives about anger. *Journal of Personality and Social Psychology*, 39, 994–1005.

Berkowitz, L. (1993). *Aggression: Its causes, consequences, and control*. New York: McGraw-Hill.

Betancourt, H. & Blair, I. (1992). A cognition (attribution)-emotion model of violence in conflict situations. *Personality and Social Psychology*, 18, 343–350.

Bies, R., & Tripp, T. (1998). Revenge in organizations: The good, the bad, and the ugly. In R. Griffin, A. O'Leary-Kelly, & J. Collins (Eds.), *Dysfunctional behavior in organizations: Non-violent dysfunctional behavior* (pp. 49–67). Stanford, CT: JAI Press.

Brown, B. R. (1968). The effects of need to maintain face on interpersonal bargaining. *Journal of Experimental Social Psychology*, 4, 107–122.

Campbell, S. B., Spieker, S., Burchinal, M., Poe, M. D., & NICHD Early Child Care Research Network. (2006). Trajectories of aggression from toddlerhood to age 9 predict academic and social functioning through age 12. *Journal of Child Psychology and Psychiatry*, 47, 791–800.

Card, N. A., & Little, T. D. (2006). Proactive and reactive aggression in childhood and adolescence: A meta-analysis of differential relations with psychosocial adjustment. *International Journal of Behavioral Development*, 30, 466–480.

Chen, Y. R., Chen, X. P., & Portnoy, R. (2009). To whom do positive norm and negative norm of reciprocity apply? Effects of inequitable offer, relationship, and relational-self orientation. *Journal of Experimental Social Psychology*, 45, 24–34.

Cole, P. M., Martin, S. E., & Dennis, T. A. (2004). Emotion regulation as a scientific construct: Methodological challenges and directions for child development research. *Child Development*, 75, 317–333.

Craig, W. M., & Pepler, D. J. (1998). Observations of bullying and victimization in the school yard. *Canadian Journal of School Psychology*, 13(2), 41–59.

Craig, W. M., Pepler, D., & Atlas, R. (2000). Observations of bullying in the playground and in the classroom. *School Psychology International*, 21, 22–36.

Crick, N., & Dodge, K. (1994). A review and reformulation of social information-processing mechanisms in children's social adjustment. *Psychological Bulletin*, 115, 74–101.

Crombag, H., Rassin, E., & Horselenberg, R. (2003). On vengeance. *Psychology, Crime, & Law*, 9, 333–344.

Day, D. M., Bream, L. A., & Pal, A. (1992). Proactive and reactive aggression: An analysis of subtypes based on teacher perceptions. *Journal of Clinical Child Psychology*, 21, 210–217.

De Castro, B. O., Veerman, J. W., Koops, W., Bosch, J. D., & Monshouwer, H. J. (2002). Hostile attribution of intent and aggressive behavior: A meta-analysis. *Child Development*, 73, 916–934.

De Castro, B. O., Verhulp, E. E., & Runions, K. (2012). Rage and revenge: Highly aggressive boys' explanations for their responses to ambiguous provocation. *European Journal of Developmental Psychology*, 9, 331–350,

Dirks, M. A., Cuttini, L. A., Mott, A., & Henry, D. B. (2017). Associations between victimization and adolescents' self-reported responses to peer provocation are moderated by peer-reported aggressiveness. *Journal of Research on Adolescence*, 27, 436–451.

Dodge, K. A. (1980). Social cognition and children's aggressive behavior. *Child Development*, 51, 162–170.

Dodge, K. A. (1986). A social-information processing model of social competence in children. In M. Perlmutter (Ed.), *Minnesota Symposium in Child Psychology* (Vol. 18, pp. 77–125). Hillsdale, NJ: Erlbaum.

Dodge, K. A., Asher, S. R., & Parkhurst, J. T. (1989). Social life as a goal-coordination task. In C. Ames & R. Ames (Eds.), *Research on motivation in education: Goals and cognitions* (Vol. 3, pp. 107–135). San Diego, CA: Academic Press.

Downey, G. & Feldman, S. I. (1996). Implications of rejection sensitivity for intimate relationships. *Journal of Personality and Social Psychology*, 70, 1327–1343.

Downey, G., Feldman, S., & Ayduk, O. (2000). Rejection sensitivity and male violence in romantic relationships.Personal Relationships, 7, 45–61.

Downey, G., Lebolt, A., Rincon, C., & Freitas, A. L. (1998). Rejection sensitivity and children's interpersonal difficulties.Child Development, 69, 1074–1091.

Eisenberg, N. (2000). Emotion, regulation, and moral development.Annual Review of Psychology, 51, 665–697.

Eisenberg, N., Fabes, R. A., Guthrie, I. K., Murphy, B. C., Maszk, P., Holmgren, R., & Suh, K. (1996). The relations of regulation and emotionality to problem behavior in elementary school children.Development and Psychopathology, 8, 141–162.

Eisenberg, N., Fabes, R. A., Nyman, M., Bernzweig, J., & Pinuelas, A. (1994). The relations of emotionality and regulation to children's anger-related reactions.Child Development, 65, 109–128.

Eisenberger, R., Lynch, P., Aselage, J., & Rohdieck, S. (2004). Who takes the most revenge? Individual differences in negative reciprocity norm endorsement.Personality and Social Psychology Bulletin, 30, 787–799.

Erdley, C. A. & Asher, S. R. (1996). Children's social goals and self-efficacy perceptions as influences on their responses to ambiguous provocation.Child Development, 67, 1329–1344.

Erdley, C. A. & Asher, S. R. (1998). Linkages between children's beliefs about the legitimacy of aggression and their behavior.Social Development, 7, 321–339.

Fabes, R. A. & Eisenberg, N. (1992). Young children's coping with interpersonal anger. Child Development, 63, 116–128.

Fagan, J. & Wilkinson, D. (1998). Guns, youth violence, and social identity in inner cities. *Crime and Justice*, 24, 105–188.

Felson, R. B. (1978). Aggression as impression management. *Social Psychology*, 41, 205–213.

Fite, P. J., Hendrickson, M., Rubens, S. L., Gabrielli, J., & Evans, S. (2013). The role of peer rejection in the link between reactive aggression and academic performance. *Child & Youth Care Forum*, 42, 193–205.

Frey, K. S., Pearson, C. R., & Cohen, D. (2015). Revenge is seductive, if not sweet: Why friends matter for prevention efforts. *Journal of Applied Developmental Psychology*, 37, 25–35.

Frijda, N. H. (1988). The laws of emotion. *American Psychologist*, 43, 349–358.

Gasser, L., Malti, T., & Gutzwiller-Helfenfinger, E. (2012). Aggressive and nonaggressive children's moral judgments and moral emotion attributions in situations involving retaliation and unprovoked aggression. *The Journal of Genetic Psychology*, 173, 417–439.

Gouldner, A. (1960). The norm of reciprocity: A preliminary statement. *American Sociological Review*, 25, 176–177.

Gouze, K. R. (1987). Attention and social problem solving as correlates of aggression in preschool males. *Journal of Abnormal Child Psychology*, 15, 181–197.

Guerra, N. G., Huesmann, L. R., & Spindler, A. (2003). Community violence exposure, social cognition, and aggression among urban elementary school children. *Child Development*, 74, 1561–1576.

Heider, F. (1958). *The psychology of interpersonal relations*. New York: Wiley.

Heidgerken, A. D., Hughes, J. N., Cavell, T. A., & Willson, V. L. (2004). Direct and indirect effects of parenting and children's goals on child aggression. *Journal of Clinical Child and Adolescent Psychology*, 33, 684–693.

Hewitt, L. S. (1975). The effects of provocation, intentions and consequences on children's moral judgments. *Child Development*, 46, 540–544.

Hinshaw, S. P. (1992). Academic underachievement, attention deficits, and aggression: Comorbidity and implications for intervention. *Journal of Consulting and Clinical Psychology*, 60, 893–903.

Horowitz, R. (1983). *Honor and the American dream: Culture and identity in a Chicano community*. New Brunswick, NJ: Rutgers University Press.

Huang, W. & Vaughn, M. (1996). Support and confidence: Public attitudes towards the police. In T. Flanagan & D. R. Longmire (Eds.), *Americans view crime and justice: A national public opinion survey*. Thousand Oaks, CA: Sage.

Hubbard, J. A., Smithmyer, C. M., Ramsden, S. R., Parker, E. H., Flanagan, K. D., Dearing, K. F., Relyea, N., & Simons, R. F. (2002). Observational, physiological, and self-report measures of children's anger: Relations to reactive vs. proactive aggression. *Child Development*, 73, 1101–1118.

Hudley, C. & Graham, S. (1993). An attributional intervention to reduce peer-directed aggression among African-American boys. *Child Development*, 64, 124–138.

Jäggi, L., & Kliewer, W. (2016). "Cause that's the only skills in school you need": A qualitative analysis of revenge goals in poor urban youth. *Journal of Adolescent Research*, 31, 32–58.

Jung, Y., Hall, J., Hong, R., Goh, T., Ong, N., & Tan, N. (2014). Payback: Effects of relationship and cultural norms on reciprocity. *Asian Journal of Social Psychology*, 17, 160–172.

Kiefer, S. M., & Ryan, A. M. (2008). Striving for social dominance over peers: The implications for academic adjustment during early adolescence. *Journal of Educational Psychology*, 100, 417–428.

Kiefer, S. M., & Wang, J. H. (2016). Associations of coolness and social goals with aggression and engagement during adolescence. *Journal of Applied Developmental Psychology*, 44, 52–62.

Kim, S. H., Smith, R. H., Brigham, N. L. (1998). Effects of power imbalance and the presence of third parties on reactions to harm: Upward and downward revenge. *Personality and Social Psychology Bulletin*, 24, 353–361.

Kochenderfer, B. J., & Ladd, G. W. (1997). Victimized children's responses to peers' aggression: Behaviors associated with reduced versus continued victimization. *Development and psychopathology*, 9, 59–73.

Kubrin, C. E. & Weitzer, R. (2003). Retaliatory homicide: Concentrated disadvantage and neighborhood culture. *Social Problems*, 50, 157–180.

Leary, M. R., Koch, E., & Hechenbleikner, N. (2001). Emotional responses to interpersonal rejection. In M. R. Leary (Ed.), *Interpersonal rejection* (pp. 145–166). New York: Oxford University Press.

Leary, M. R., Springer, C., Negel, L., Ansell, E., & Evans, K. (1998). The causes, phenomenology, and consequences of hurt feelings. *Journal of Personality and Social Psychology*, 74, 1225–1237.

Lemerise, E. A., & Arsenio, W. F. (2000). An integrated model of emotion processes and cognition in social information processing. *Child Development*, 71, 107–118.

Lerner, M. J. (1980). *The belief in a just world: A fundamental delusion*. New York: Plenum Press.

Lewis, H. B. (1971). *Shame and guilt in neurosis*. New York: International Universities Press.

Lochman, J. E. & Dodge, K. A. (1994). Social-cognitive processes of severly violent, moderately aggressive, and nonaggressive boys. *Journal of Consulting and Clinical Psychology*, 62(2), 366–374.

Lochman, J. E. & Dodge, K. A. (1998). Distorted perceptions in dyadic interactions of aggressive and nonaggressive boys: Effects of prior expectations, context, and boys' age. *Development and Psychopathology*, 10, 495–512.

Lochman, J. E., Wayland, K. K., & White, K. J. (1993). Social goals: Relationship to adolescent adjustment and to social problem solving. *Journal of Abnormal Child Psychology, 21*, 135–151.

Luckenbill, D. F. & Doyle, D. P. (1989). Structural position and violence: Developing a cultural explanation. *Criminology, 27*, 801–818.

MacEvoy, J. P., & Asher, S. R. (2012). When friends disappoint: Boys' and girls' responses to transgressions of friendship expectations. *Child Development, 83*, 104–119.

McCullough, M. E. (2008). *Beyond revenge: The evolution of the forgiveness instinct.* San Francisco: Jossey-Bass.

McCullough, M. E., Bellah, C. G., Kilpatrick, S. D., & Johnson, J. L. (2001). Vengefulness: Relationships with forgiveness, rumination, well-being, and the Big Five. *Personality and Social Psychology Bulletin, 27*, 601–610.

McDonald, K. L. (2008). Interpretations and beliefs associated with children's revenge goals in conflict situations. (Doctoral dissertation). https://dukespace.lib.duke.edu/dspace/handle/10161/667.

McDonald, K. L., & Asher, S. R. (2013). College students' revenge goals across friend, romantic partner, and roommate contexts: The role of interpretations and emotions. *Social Development, 22*, 499–521.

McDonald, K. L., & Asher, S. R. (2018). Pacifists and revenge-seekers in response to unambiguous peer provocation. *The Journal of Youth and Adolescence, 47*, 1907–1925.

McDonald, K. L., Baden, R. E., & Lochman, J. E. (2013). Parenting influences on the social goals of aggressive children. *Applied Developmental Science, 17*, 29–38.

McDonald, K. L., & Lochman, J. E. (2012). Predictors and outcomes associated with trajectories of revenge goals from fourth grade through seventh grade. *Journal of Abnormal Child Psychology, 40*, 225–236.

McFall, R. M. (1982). A review and reformulation of the concept of social skills. *Behavioral Assessment, 4*, 1–33.

McFall, R. M., & Dodge, K. A. (1982). Self-management and interpersonal skills learning. In P. Karoly & F. H. Kanfer (Eds.), *Self-management and behavior change: From theory to practice* (pp. 353–392). New York: Pergamon Press.

Malti, T., & Rubin, K. H. (Eds.) (2018). *Handbook of child and adolescent aggression.* New York: Guilford.

Murphy, J. G. (2000). Two cheers for vindictiveness. *Punishment & Society, 2*, 131–143.

Nasby, W., Hayden, B., & DePaulo, B. M. (1979). Attributional bias among aggressive boys to interpret unambiguous social stimuli as displays of hostility. *Journal of Abnormal Psychology, 89*, 459–468.

Nisbett, R. E. & Cohen, D. (1996). *Culture of honor: The psychology of violence in the south.* Boulder, CO: Westview Press.

Peets, K., Hodges, E. V. E., Kikas, E., & Salmivalli, C. (2007). Hostile attributions and behavioral strategies in children: Does relationship type matter? *Developmental Psychology, 43*(4), 889–900.

Pasupathi, M., Wainryb, C., Bourne, S., & Posada, R. (2017). Narrative construction of morality in adolescence among typically developing and violence-exposed youth. *Imagination, Cognition and Personality, 37*, 178–198.

Peets, K., Hodges, E. V., & Salmivalli, C. (2013). Forgiveness and its determinants depending on the interpersonal context of hurt. *Journal of Experimental Child Psychology, 114*, 131–145.

Posada, R., & Wainryb, C. (2008). Moral development in a violent society: Colombian children's judgments in the context of survival and revenge. *Child Development, 79*, 882–898.

Putallaz, M.Kupersmidt, J. B., Coie, J. D.McKnight, K. & Grimes, C. L. (2004). A behavioral analysis of girls' aggression and victimization. In M. Putallaz & K. L. Bierman (Eds.), *Aggression, antisocial behavior, and violence among girls: A developmental perspective* (pp. 110–136). New York: Guilford Press.

Rasmussen, K. R., Alibhai, A., Boon, S. D., & Ellard, J. H. (2016). Trust as an explanation for relational differences in revenge. *Basic and Applied Social Psychology*, 38, 284–300.

Renshaw, P. D. & Asher, S. R. (1983). Children's goals and strategies for social interaction. *Merrill Palmer Quarterly*, 29, 353–372.

Rose, A. J., & Asher, S. R. (1999). Children's goals and strategies in response to conflicts within a friendship. *Developmental Psychology*, 35, 69–79.

Schwartz, D. & Proctor, L. J. (2000). Community violence exposure and children's social adjustment in the school peer group: The mediating roles of emotion regulation and social cognition. *Journal of Consulting and Clinical Psychology*, 68, 670–683.

Shantz, D. W. & Pentz, T. (1972). Situational effects on the justifiableness of aggression at three age levels. *Child Development*, 43, 274–281.

Shantz, D. W. & Voydanoff, D. A. (1973). Situational effects on relataliatory aggression at three age levels. *Child Development*, 44, 149–153.

Slaby, R. G. & Guerra, N. G. (1988). Cognitive mediators of aggression in adolescent offenders: 1. Assessment. *Developmental Psychology*, 24, 580–588.

Smalley, D., & Banerjee, R. (2014). The role of social goals in bullies' and victims social information processing in response to ambiguous and overtly hostile provocation. *Social Development*, 23, 593–610.

Smetana, J. G., Campione-Barr, N., & Yell, N. (2003). Children's moral and affective judgments regarding provocation and retaliation. *Merrill-Palmer Quarterly*, 49, 209–236.

Smetana, J. G., Toth, S. L., Cicchetti, D., Bruce, J., Kane, P., & Daddis, C. (1999). Maltreated and nonmaltreated preschoolers' conceptions of hypothetical and actual moral transgressions. *Developmental Psychology*, 35, 269–281.

Stewart, E. A., & Simons, R. L. (2006). Structure and culture in African American adolescent violence: A partial test of the "code of the street" thesis. *Justice Quarterly*, 23(1), 1–33.

Stice, E., & Gonzales, N. (1998). Adolescent temperament moderates the relation of parenting to antisocial behavior and substance use. *Journal of Adolescent Research*, 13, 5–31.

Struthers, C. W., Eaton, J., Santelli, A. G., Uchiyama, M., & Shirvani, N. (2008). The effects of attributions of intent and apology on forgiveness: When saying sorry may not help the story. *Journal of Experimental Social Psychology*, 44, 983–992.

Stuckless, N. & Goranson, R. (1992). The vengeance scale: Development of a measure of attitudes toward revenge. *Journal of Social Behavior and Personality*, 7, 25–42.

Sukhodolsky, D. G., Golub, A., & Cromwell, E. N. (2001). Development and validation of the anger rumination scale. *Personality and Individual Differences*, 31, 689–700.

Tangney, J. P. (1995). Shame and guilt in interpersonal relationships. In J. P. Tangney & K. W. Fisher (Eds.), *Self-conscious emotions: Shame, guilt, embarrassment, and pride* (pp. 114–139). New York: Guilford Press.

Tangney, J. P. (1998). How does guilt differ from shame? In J. Bybee (Ed.), *Guilt and children* (pp. 1–18). New York: Academic Press.

Tangney, J. P., Wagner, P. E., Hill-Barlow, D., Marschall, D. E., & Gramzow, R. (1996). Relation of shame and guilt to constructive versus destructive responses to anger across the lifespan. *Journal of Personality and Social Psychology*, 70, 797–809.

Tapper, K., & Boulton, M. J. (2005). Victim and peer group responses to different forms of aggression among primary school children. *Aggressive Behavior*, 31, 238–253.

Tremblay, P. F. & Belchevski, M. (2004). Did the instigator intend to provoke? A key moderator in the relation between trait aggression and aggressive behavior. *Aggressive Behavior*, 30, 409–424. •

Troop-Gordon, W., Gordon, R. D., Vogel-Ciernia, L., Ewing Lee, E., & Visconti, K. J. (2016). Visual attention to dynamic scenes of ambiguous provocation and children's aggressive behavior. *Journal of Clinical Child & Adolescent Psychology*, 47(6), 925–940.

Vidmar, N. (2000). Retribution and revenge. In J. Sanders & V. L. Hamilton (Eds.), *Handbook of justice research in law* (pp. 31–63). New York: Kluwer Academic.

Yeager, D. S., Miu, A. S., Powers, J., & Dweck, C. S. (2013). Implicit theories of personality and attributions of hostile intent: A meta-analysis, an experiment, and a longitudinal intervention. *Child Development*, 84, 1651–1667.

Yeager, D. S., Trzesniewski, K., Tirri, K., Nokelainen, P., & Dweck, C. S. (2011). Adolescents' implicit theories predict desire for vengeance after remembered and hypothetical peer conflicts: Correlational and experimental evidence. *Developmental Psychology*, 47, 1090–1107.

8

COOL GOALS

Rhonda S. Jamison and Travis M. Wilson

Psychosocial growth is dynamic. Studying children's social development involves consideration of myriad internal and external forces operating together in sustaining continuity and driving change. A long-standing approach in developmental research has been to examine the cascading effects of psychological processes at different points in time – for example, how conscious and unconscious cognitions forecast subsequent behavior (Baumeister, Masicampo, & Vohs, 2011). In goal theory, goals are commonly framed as cognitions that set in motion intra-individual emotions and behavior (Dweck, 1992). With this as a basic premise, researchers have accumulated a wealth of knowledge regarding how goals predict a broad range of social, academic, and behavioral *outcomes*, but only limited knowledge of potential intra-individual *precursors* to social goals. In contrast to cascade models, a more dynamic view of psychosocial growth would frame goals as changing *along with* other salient aspects of psychosocial functioning; in this framework, causation is multi-directional, with goals, self-representations, and behavior influencing each other in the short- and long-term. The simplest model would include two salient aspects of psychosocial functioning and examine the bidirectional, *reciprocal effects* between them over time (see Yang, Chen, & Wang, 2015).

In this chapter, we examine longitudinal, reciprocal relations between children's social achievement goals (i.e., their goals for social connection and social standing) and their social status within the classroom peer group. Our approach is based on the premise that internal states and ongoing feedback from peers are mutually contingent and, thus, cannot be understood fully in isolation from each other (Cairns & Cairns, 2005). The developmental age we examine is preadolescence (grades 4 and 5), when youths' comprehension of self-group dynamics becomes more elaborate (Sroufe et al., 2005). Regarding social status, we examine *perceived coolness*, the degree to which youths are viewed by their peers as being cool, an indicator of how they are valued and emulated by others in the peer collective (Graham & Juvonen, 2002; Wilson & Jamison, 2019). We recognize that the peer group is but one source of influence, and that diverse contextual factors bear upon youths' goals in meaningful ways. Nonetheless, our model underscores a key principle: that understanding the stability and change of an individual's internal states (e.g., goals) requires simultaneous consideration of stability and change in how the individual stands in relation to the group in which he or she takes part. Thus, we examine (1) how youths' social goals predict changes in their perceived coolness among peers, and (2) how their perceived coolness among peers simultaneously predicts changes in their social goals.

Definition: Coolness

Coolness is ubiquitous, and the United States is a coolness-valuing culture. Within such an environment, who an individual perceives as cool is in part a reflection of what they value individually and in part a reflection of what is valued in their particular social niche. Despite potential for coolness to manifest differently across settings and social groups, there appears to be discernible patterns in the characteristics commonly associated with being cool. A recent psychological study with a large sample varying widely in age (15–56 years) evidenced two distinct profiles of coolness: cachet coolness and contrarian coolness (Dar-Nimrod et al., 2012). Cachet coolness, the more prevalent form, embodies conventionally prosocial and socially attractive traits like friendliness, competence, trendiness, and desirability. Contrarian coolness embodies more "edgy" or counter-culture traits like rebelliousness, irony, and aloofness (Dar-Nimrod et al., 2012). Though distinct from each other, both forms of coolness share the traits of high social visibility and a sense of social savior faire; whether friendly or aloof, trendy or rebellious, individuals with cachet coolness and contrarian coolness both seem to have a magnetic quality about them, an ability to command attention from others.

Evidence: Coolness

In the child development literature, coolness has been viewed as a type of high social status, operating akin to popularity, another marker of high visibility in the peer group (Rodkin et al., 2006; Wilson & Jamison, 2019; Wilson & Rodkin, 2013). Research has indicated that having high status is a mixed blessing of sorts, as it correlates reliably with both positive and negative developmental outcomes (see Cillessen & van den Berg, 2012). Understanding high status youths has become increasingly complex, as multiple profiles have emerged – some profiles related to positive traits like kindness, and others related to negative traits like relational aggression (Rodkin, Farmer, Pearl, & Van Acker, 2000; Sandstrom & Cillessen, 2006), much like the distinction between cachet coolness and contrarian coolness found among adults (Dar-Nimrod et al., 2012). This appears to be true among preadolescents as well. In a study of elementary school students in grades 1, 3, and 5, coolness was associated with higher levels of prosocial behavior in grade 1 and grade 3, but was associated with both prosocial behavior *and* aggressive behavior among grade 5 students (Wilson & Jamison, 2019). In short, coolness appears to come with a complex behavioral profile (even among pre-adolescents), perhaps an indication that cool youths are controversial characters – variably admired, feared, respected, and disliked – but invariably noticed by peers.

Given the salience of social status in the peer group, do youths develop social goals that lead to discernible changes in social status? To address this question, some researchers have examined unidirectional prospective associations between social goals and status (coolness, popularity) and how these pathways are mediated by social behaviors. For example, prosocial-oriented goals reliably predict prosocial behaviors and subsequent changes in popularity among adolescents (Li & Hu, 2018) and among preadolescents (Rodkin, Ryan, Jamison, & Wilson, 2013). Other researchers have examined the reverse pathway, unidirectional prospective associations between coolness and subsequent social behaviors. For example, studies have shown that, in early adolescence, coolness is associated with increases in aggression (Bellmore, Villarreal, & Ho, 2011; Rodkin et al., 2006), increases in disruptive behavior (Kiefer & Wang, 2016), and decreases in academic reputation (Jamison, Wilson, & Ryan, 2015). Thus, prior evidence indicates that coolness is both a reliable outcome of goal-directed behavior and a reliable predictor of meaningful changes in psychosocial functioning. Based on this evidence, we view coolness not only as an outcome of social goals but also as a characteristic of the individual (in social context) that may foster stability or change in social goals. It is with this rationale that we adopt a reciprocal, bidirectional approach in modeling how goals predict changes in status *and* how status predicts changes in goals over time.

Academic Performance

In addition to the proposed links between coolness and social goals, there are established links between coolness and academic performance across development. In early adolescence, students tend to attribute positive academic qualities to hypothetical high status peers, an indication (though indirect) that coolness and academic performance may be positively associated in the upper elementary grades (LaFontana & Cillessen, 2002). Our research suggests that the relation between coolness and academic achievement changes across school transitions. In a six-month longitudinal study, we found a positive link between students' perceived coolness and academic reputation (albeit for girls only) at the beginning of the first year of middle school but that high baseline levels of coolness predicted declines in African American youths' academic reputation across the school year (Jamison, Wilson, & Ryan, 2015). Additional research on coolness and academic performance is very limited. Although the two empirical studies included in this chapter do not address the link between coolness and academic performance, we consider in the discussion how their relation could be addressed in future work.

Interpersonal Outcomes: Social Achievement Goals

Goal orientations have been studied extensively over the last several decades (see Austin & Vancouver, 1996). Achievement goals assess different attitudes concerning what it means to be competent in a given area (Dweck, 1986; Pintrich, 2000). Social achievement goals help to understand how attitudes concerning social competence vary across individuals (Ryan & Shim, 2006). Two orientations, development and demonstration, emerged from early research establishing social achievement goals. A social development orientation focuses on learning about and improving relationships, whereas a social demonstration orientation focuses on how others perceive or judge one's social competence. The latter orientation has been further subdivided into two distinct goals: demonstration-approach goals, reflecting a desire to appear socially competent; and demonstration-avoid goals, reflecting a desire to avoid the appearance of incompetence (see Shim & Ryan, this volume).

Development and demonstration orientations have been shown to predict important developmental outcomes in the behavioral and academic domains (see Ryan, Jamison, Shin & Thompson, 2012). To our knowledge, research has not yet tested the reciprocal (status – goals) developmental process. However, it is reasonable to conjecture that an individual's status in the peer group may precipitate changes in their social goals as well. The feedback one receives from peers about one's social standing in the group may provoke either self-assuredness or social anxiety, thereby engendering either development or demonstration goals. Indeed, this may be especially true in early adolescence, when youths increasingly value peer status and are learning how to navigate social hierarchies (LaFontana & Cillessen, 2010). Below, we highlight prior research germane to our study hypotheses on reciprocal relations between coolness and each social goal, in turn.

A person high in social development goals focuses on deepening friendships and improving social skills. Studying early adolescents, Ryan and Shim (2008) found social development goals were related to an increase in prosocial behavior and a decrease in aggressive behavior. Social development goals were only associated with higher popularity when they were combined with low social demonstration-avoid goals. In our own previous work with preadolescents (Rodkin et al., 2013), we tested a cascading model (Goals-Behavior-Status) and found that social development goals were indirectly related to increases in being well liked and perceived as popular among peers. Specifically, social development goals were related to increases in prosocial behavior and decreases in aggressive behavior; these behaviors, in turn, were related to changes in social status. Consistent with previous findings, we expect social development goals to predict decreases in coolness, and coolness to predict decreases in social development goals. We hypothesize these relations because the effort and intentionality that are at the core of the development goal are in contradiction to the effortlessness and nonchalance associated with being cool in early adolescence (see Majors & Billson, 1992). That is, individuals who "try hard" in a conventional manner will be perceived as less cool over time, and individuals who are cool at the outset will "try less" over time.

A person with social demonstration-approach goals is concerned with appearing socially skilled and with being perceived as cool or as having a lot of friends (Ryan & Shim, 2006). Both Ryan and Shim (2008) and Rodkin et al. (2013) found that demonstration-approach goals were related to lower levels of prosocial behavior, higher levels of aggressive behavior, and increases in popularity. In the present studies, we expect that espousing demonstration-approach goals will predict increases in coolness (as prior research has found), but that coolness will not necessarily predict changes in approach goals; we posit the latter prediction because stability in approach goals may be necessary to maintain the status one has achieved.

A person with social demonstration-avoid goals is concerned primarily with avoiding the appearance of being socially unskilled and avoiding negative appraisals from others. Thus, demonstration-avoid goals reflect how important it is to an individual to avoid being perceived as uncool or socially awkward. Ryan and Shim (2008) found that demonstration-avoid goals were related to lower levels of aggression and decreases in popularity in a sample of middle school students. Rodkin et al. (2013) found that demonstration-avoid goals predicted decreases in popularity among students in upper elementary school. In the present studies, we expect demonstration-avoid goals to predict decreases in coolness because individuals with this orientation lack the calm self-assuredness that is expected of those who are cool. Considering the reciprocal direction, we anticipate that coolness will be related to decreases in demonstration-avoid goals: Self-assured youths accumulate positive social feedback throughout the school year, which provides a greater sense of security and enables them to worry less about negative judgments from peers.

Individual differences

Although early adolescents universally share some developmental tasks, such as demonstrating competence and autonomy in culturally appropriate ways (Sroufe et al., 2005), other developmental tasks are contingent upon individual characteristics and context-specific social demands. We give consideration to how longitudinal reciprocal associations between social goals and coolness may vary reliably as a function of grade, gender, and ethnicity.

Grade

Children as young as 2nd grade are able to differentiate social achievement goals (Rudolph et al., 2011). By late childhood and early adolescence, peer relationships are much more salient. Youths spend more time with friends (Larson et al., 2002) and increasingly prioritize friendship maintenance (Berndt & Savin-Williams, 1993). Youths' values regarding social success also change across early adolescence, moving toward being less sincere and more disingenuous (Kiefer & Ryan, 2011). In addition to social changes, students are experiencing the onset of puberty. African Americans experience puberty early compared to peers (Slyper, 2006), which may lead them to garner increased attention or status. In the present studies, we examine coolness and social achievement goals in 4th and 5th graders, on the cusp of adolescence, to investigate potential age-related differences in youths' social goals.

Gender

From the achievement goal perspective, performance-approach goals often are more adaptive for boys than for girls (see Midgley, Kaplan, & Middleton, 2001). Conversely, boys with demonstration-avoid goals often have more negative outcomes compared to girls with similar levels of avoid goals (Wilson et al., 2016). In a recent study with a predominantly European-American U.S. sample, boys reported stronger demonstration-approach and lower social development goals relative to girls (Makara & Madjar, 2015). However, in a similar study with a Turkish adolescent sample, boys reported stronger social achievement goals, including stronger social development goals, compared to girls (Bahar, Uğur, & Asil, 2018). Thus, context may play a significant role in gender variations in social achievement goal adherence. Given these mixed findings, we explore gender as a potentially salient moderating factor of the reciprocal relations between social achievement goals and coolness.

Ethnicity

Although coolness is an ubiquitous phenomenon in the U.S., sociologists and historians have made compelling arguments that coolness has long played a unique role in African American culture in particular (Dinerstein, 2017; Majors & Billson, 1992). The historical record indicates that contemporary notions of coolness emanated from African American jazz culture in the early twentieth century and that coolness emerged as a marker of an *alternative success system* in opposition to a materialist and rapidly suburbanizing society (Dinerstein, 2017). Since that time, it has been argued, for many African Americans coolness has been a means of displaying and maintaining dignity against daily oppression experienced in mainstream society (Majors & Billson, 1992).

Over time, cultural notions of coolness have been integrated into and transformed by youth culture to serve youths' particular needs and interests. According to one historical account, the progressive valuation of coolness in youth culture has been subtle but powerful, as "cool [now] embodies the unspoken, unconscious emotional needs that have not yet reached consciousness in young people" (Dinerstein, 2017, p. 15). Contemporary psychologists note that the valuation of coolness in modern society has weighty impact because it socializes individuals to conduct themselves according to behaviors, attitudes, and beliefs deemed cool by the social collective (Dar-Nimrod et al., 2012). Empirical evidence suggests that African American youth may disproportionately benefit in some ways from the cultural capital inherent in the valuation of coolness. In studies of school-aged children, African American students often are viewed as being cooler than their white peers, and being viewed as cool is associated with lower rates of being rejected or victimized by one's peers (Rodkin et al., 2006; Wilson & Rodkin, 2013). Such evidence suggests that coolness may play a protective role for African American youths in particular. Thus, we examine ethnicity as a potential moderator of reciprocal links between social achievement goals and coolness.

Contextual variability

Another aim of this chapter is to examine coolness and social goals in a broader sociocultural context, taking into account the lived experiences of children in two different locales in the U.S. Our analysis rests on the assumption that there is variation within and across cultural communities in what coolness means and what social goals children espouse, depending on the socioeconomic and other daily realities of their lives.

The first locale includes several small cities with populations between 50,000 and 75,000 inhabitants situated in an otherwise sprawling agricultural region of the Midwest. The nine elementary schools from this region selected for this study were situated in four cities located within a 30-mile radius of a large university that is a cultural and economic hub of this region (see Wilson & Rodkin, 2013). Although each of the four small cities has its own distinct character and independent school district, the cities also share important commonalities, including similar histories of manufacturing-based economies, a common regional identity, and populations in which European Americans and African Americans together compose a large majority.

The second locale is a large industrial city situated in the Great Lakes region of the U.S. Historically known as a powerful manufacturing center, the city has experienced considerable economic challenges since the 1960s, similar to many other large cities in this geographic region. The five schools in this city selected for the present study serve predominantly African American, low-income communities. The city's overall unemployment rate is roughly 6%; the average unemployment rate of the neighborhoods that these students live in is more than double this rate, roughly 14%.

Children growing up amid the harsher socioeconomic conditions of a large urban center may be expected to engage with their social worlds differently than their counterparts in smaller cities or suburban areas that are more economically stable. According to Majors and Billson (1992), economically disadvantaged African American youths in large cities may be more likely to manifest coolness as aloofness (vs. social eagerness), a general coping strategy to avoid or neutralize life stressors. In such contexts, being cool may come with various affordances, such as reduced feelings of vulnerability and increased feelings of security. On the other hand, coolness may also have the cost of limiting opportunities to forge new relationships or to deepen one's existing relationships. Given that youths in the two settings face different contextual challenges, we provide a separate analysis for each sample. We address contextual comparisons in the general discussion section of this chapter.

Present studies

Past research has examined the relation between social goals and status primarily in terms of unidirectional, cognition-to-outcome processes. The first goal of the present studies is to move beyond unidirectional models by considering *longitudinal, reciprocal relations* between social achievement goals and coolness; we examine these relations among preadolescent students prior to the transition to middle school (grades 4 and 5). Our second goal is to examine *individual differences* in these longitudinal reciprocal relations in two different samples. Study 1 utilizes a heterogeneous (European-American and African American) sample from four small cities, whereas Study 2 utilizes a largely homogeneous (African American) sample from a large urban center. Thus, in Study 1, we examine whether goal-status associations are moderated by sex, grade, or ethnicity; in Study 2, we examine moderation by sex and grade. Our third goal is to examine *contextual variability* by making holistic cross-study comparisons of the two samples; we highlight these comparisons in the general discussion at the end of the chapter.

Study 1 Method

Study design and procedure

The present research stems from a larger study of children's social development in elementary schools located in four small Midwestern cities (see Rodkin et al., 2013; Wilson & Rodkin, 2013; Wilson, Rodkin, & Ryan, 2014). The study had a longitudinal design with two survey assessments (fall and spring) in one academic year. Participation required parental/guardian consent and individual assent. During each 45-minute survey administration, one member of the research team read each item aloud, while at least two assistants monitored students' progress and addressed individual questions. The order of presentation of measures was randomized for each classroom. (For additional details, see Wilson & Rodkin, 2013).

Participants

Study participation required written parent/guardian consent and student assent. Of all eligible students in grades 4 and 5, 81% participated in the fall and 79% participated in the spring. There were 775 participants in the fall (49% African American, 34% European-American, 17% other ethnicities; 408 girls, 367 boys; 282 in grade 4, 493 in grade 5) and 749 participants in the spring (50% African American, 35% European-American, 15% other ethnicities; 392 girls, 357 boys; 272 in grade 4, 477 in grade 5).

Measurements

Measurements for perceived coolness and social goals were obtained in identical fashion in the fall and spring.

Perceived coolness

Scores for perceived coolness were obtained from an unlimited peer nominations used in prior research with elementary school children (Wilson, Rodkin, & Ryan, 2014; Wilson & Jamison, 2019). Participants were presented with the following item: "These are the COOLEST kids in my class." Below this item was a classroom roster with the name of each student listed alphabetically; participants were asked to circle the names of students who they felt best fit the item description (participants were permitted to nominate other participants as well as non-participants). Self-nominations were excluded from analysis. For each child, a proportion score was calculated as the quotient of nominations received for the cool item divided by the number of nominators in the classroom. The large number of respondents, the unlimited number of nominations permitted, and the face validity of the question ensured robust measurement properties (Cillessen & Marks, 2011).

Social goals

Children completed a measure of social goals adapted from Ryan and Shim (2006, 2008) to be appropriate for elementary school children. Items were rated by children on a 5-point scale (from 1 = *not at all true* to 5 = *very true*). Six social *development goal* items a focus on developing social competence (e.g., "I try to figure out what makes a good friend"). Five social *demonstration – approach goal* items concerned a focus on demonstrating social desirability (e.g., "It is important to me to have 'cool' friends"). Four social *demonstration – avoid goal* items concerned a focus on demonstrating that one is not socially undesirable (e.g., "I try to avoid doing things that make me look foolish to other kids"). Confirmatory factor analysis of these social goals items in previous studies evidenced strong measurement properties (Rodkin et al., 2013; Wilson, Rodkin, & Ryan, 2014).

Study 1 Results

Analytical strategy

Our aim was to examine reciprocal longitudinal relations between coolness and social goals, as well as their variation between grades, sexes, and ethnic groups (African Americans and European Americans only). We followed an analytic procedure similar to one used in prior research (Yang, Chen, & Wang, 2015). First, we tested measurement invariance of social goal latent constructs and coolness across time and subgroups. Second, we calculated the concurrent latent correlations between coolness and each social goal at each time point; we used multiple-group SEM procedures to compare each latent correlation across subgroups (i.e., grades, sexes, and ethnic groups). Third, we conducted SEM analyses to test the reciprocal relations between coolness and social goals. As suggested by Kenny (2005), and as demonstrated by Yang and colleagues (2015), to maintain symmetry in examining longitudinal reciprocal relations between coolness and social goals, the analysis for each social goal was conducted separately. This model tested the stability of coolness and the social goal variable from fall to spring, as well as the two cross-lagged paths, to examine the relations between coolness and the social goal variable.

Analyses were conducted using IBM SPSS Amos 22 (Arbuckle, 2013). Full information maximum likelihood estimation (FIML) was used to account for missing data; all students in the sample (both participants and non-participants) had observed scores for peer-nominated perceived coolness, whereas only participants had observed scores for self-reported social goals. The final data set included 954 children (51% African American, 34% European-American, 15% other ethnicities): 474 boys and 480 girls; 370 in grade 4 and 584 in grade 5.

Measurement models

Measurement invariance

Measurement invariance for coolness and approach, development, and avoid goals was tested across two times of measurement and across subgroups (by grade, by sex, and by ethnicity), using the procedure recommended by Little (2013). Each measurement model had three item parcels for the social goal, and one item for perceived coolness. We tested for strong measurement invariance, which constrains equal item loadings and intercepts across time and subgroups; correlations between latent constructs were freely estimated. There were nine models in all, three per social goal (to compare invariance across grades, sexes, and ethnic groups, respectively). These fully constrained models had excellent levels of fit for all three goals (CFIs: .98–1.00; TLIs: .95–1.00; RMSEAs: .000–.044). These results indicated that the measurements of coolness and the approach, development, and avoid goals were invariant across time and subgroups (i.e., grades, sexes, and ethnic groups), thus permitting valid group comparisons in latent correlations and structural paths (i.e., stability paths and cross-lagged paths).

Latent correlations

Correlations between coolness and each social goal for the full sample (fall and spring) are presented in Table 8.1. In the full sample, thee out of six latent correlations were statistically significant: the approach-cool correlation was reliably positive in the fall (ψ = .09, $p < .05$), but not in the spring (ψ = .04, ns); the development-cool correlation

Cool Goals 141

TABLE 8.1 Study 1: Latent Correlations between Coolness and Social Goals

	Approach - Cool		Development - Cool		Avoidance - Cool	
	Fall	Spring	Fall	Spring	Fall	Spring
Full sample	$-.09^*$	$-.04$	$-.05$	$-.02$	$-.11^{**}$	$-.14^{**}$
Grade 4	$-.10$	$-.07$	$-.01$	$-.01$	$-.13^\dagger$	$-.05$
Grade 5	$-.09^*$	$-.02$	$-.07$	$-.06$	$-.10^\dagger$	$-.21^{**}$
EA	$-.05$	$-.06$	$-.10$	$-.01$	$-.21^{**}$	$-.18^{**}$
AA	$-.09$	$-.03$	$-.06$	$-.04$	$-.03$	$-.12^\dagger$
Boys	$-.11^*$	$-.04$	$-.09$	$-.05$	$-.15^*$	$-.14^*$
Girls	$-.09$	$-.04$	$-.02$	$-.10^\dagger$	$-.06$	$-.13^*$

$^{**}p < .01.$ $^*p < .05.$ $^\dagger p < .10.$

was null in the fall ($\psi = -.05$, *ns*) and in the spring ($\psi = -.02$, *ns*); and the avoid–cool correlation was reliably negative in the fall ($\psi = -.11$, $p < .01$) and in the spring ($\psi = -.14$, $p < .01$). Differences in latent correlations between subgroups were tested one parameter at a time using the method described by Little (2013). Although some estimates appeared to vary moderately between subgroups, no latent correlation differed significantly between grades, sexes, or ethnic groups. Thus, latent correlation parameter estimates in the full sample are most parsimonious.

Structural equations models

Here, our primary interest was to compare subgroups in longitudinal predictive relations between social goals and coolness. To do so, we added structural paths (described below) to the measurement model based on strong factorial invariance, per recommended practice (Little, 2013).

Longitudinal stabilities

For each social goal, we first tested the stability of coolness and the social goal from fall to spring; cross-lagged paths were constrained to zero (see Table 8.2). These models had excellent levels of fit (CFIs: .99–1.00; TLIs: .98–1.00; RMSEAs: .012–.037). Stability coefficients were high and statistically significant for all subgroups (βs: .60–.79, *ps* $< .01$). There was one statistically significant difference between ethnic subgroups ($\chi^2_{(1)} = 14.5$, $p < .01$): The coolness stability was stronger among European Americans ($\beta = .79$, $p < .01$) than among African Americans ($\beta = .65$, $p < .01$). There was one statistically significant difference between sexes ($\chi^2_{(1)} = 15.8$, $p < .01$): The coolness stability was stronger among boys ($\beta = .77$, $p < .01$) than among girls ($\beta = .63$, $p < .01$). There was one statistically significant difference between grade levels ($\chi^2_{(1)} = 4.32$, $p < .05$): The approach stability was stronger in grade 5 ($\beta = .78$, $p < .01$) than in grade 4 ($\beta = .71$, $p < .01$).

142 Rhonda S. Jamison and Travis M. Wilson

TABLE 8.2 Study 1: Longitudinal Stabilities in Coolness and Social Goals

	Coolness	Demonstration-Approach	Social Development	Demonstration-Avoidance
Full sample	$.71_{bc}$**	$.75_a$**	.62**	.68**
Grade 4	.66**	.71**	.65**	.71**
Grade 5	.74**	.78**	.61**	.67**
EA	.79**	.77**	.64**	.62**
AA	.65**	.71**	.60**	.72**
Boys	.77**	.71**	.63**	.66**
Girls	.63**	.77**	.61**	.72**

**$p < .01$. *$p < .05$.

Cross-lagged paths

Next, we tested the full model with longitudinal stabilities and two cross-lagged paths from fall to spring, to examine the relations between coolness and each social goal. These models had excellent levels of fit (CFIs: .99–1.00; TLIs: .98–.99; RMSEAs: .021–.035). In the full sample, two cross-lagged paths were statistically significant: the fall approach goal had a reliably positive effect on spring coolness ($\beta = .06$, $p < .05$), and fall coolness had a reliably negative effect on the spring avoid goal ($\beta = -.10$, $p < .01$). However, there was one statistically significant difference between grade levels ($\chi^2_{(1)} = 10.2$, $p < .01$): fall coolness had a reliably negative effect on the spring avoid goal in grade 5 ($\beta = -.15$, $p < .01$) but not in grade 4 ($\beta = -.01$, *ns*). Although some other estimates appeared to vary moderately between subgroups, no difference was statistically reliable (see Table 8.3).

TABLE 8.3 Study 1: Longitudinal Cross-lagged Paths between Coolness and Social Goals

	Approach → Cool	Cool → Approach	Develop → Cool	Cool → Develop	Avoidance → Cool	Cool → Avoidance
Full sample	**.064***	−.052	−.018	.010	−.054†	**−.100_a****
Grade 4	.053	−.011	−.011	.069	−.011	−.010
Grade 5	.065†	**−.074***	−.032	−.026	**−.083***	**−.153***
EA	.008	**−.099***	.051	.011	−.024	**−.094***
AA	**.090***	.003	−.012	.006	−.019	**−.111***
Boys	**.094***	−.041	−.044	.050	**−.100***	−.066
Girls	.023	**−.058***	.013	−.021	−.007	**−.133***

**$p < .01$. *$p < .05$. †$p < .10$.

Study 1 Discussion

Results from Study 1 indicated significant relations between social achievement goals and coolness. In the full sample, social demonstration-approach goals were positively related to coolness in the fall only. In the bidirectional model, social demonstration-approach goals predicted positive changes in coolness from fall to spring, but coolness was not related to changes in approach goals. As hypothesized, those students who were higher in approach goals were viewed as cool by their peers in the fall and their coolness increased across the course of the school year. Social demonstration-avoid goals were negatively related to coolness in both the fall and the spring. In the bidirectional model, coolness predicted declines in social demonstration-avoid goals from fall to spring in 5th graders only, but avoid goals were not related to changes in coolness. Thus, as 5th grade students' cool status increased in the peer group they were less likely to indicate avoid goals. Contrary to our hypothesis that social development goals would be positively related to coolness, development goals were unrelated to coolness in both latent correlations and the bidirectional model. Although, it is likely that development goals are driving behavior (see Rodkin et al., 2013), we did not find direct relations between development goals and coolness. No other differences related to grade, race, and gender were significant.

Study 2 Method

Study design and procedure

This study is part of a larger investigation of the development of motivation and social adjustment among children attending five schools in a large city in the Great Lakes region. All five schools housed grades k-8 and were predominantly low-income (free or reduced lunch status: $M = 91\%$) and African American ($M = 87\%$). The majority of students attending these schools lived in impoverished neighborhoods; according to 2013 U.S. census tract-level information, the mean unemployment rate was 14.1% and the mean per capita income was $15,200. Here, we focus exclusively on a sub-sample of children in grades 4 and 5.

The study featured student surveys at two time points, one in mid-October (fall semester) and one in mid-April (spring semester). At each time point, students completed questionnaires in a 40-minute session in their respective classrooms; one member of the research team read aloud each questionnaire item, while two or three undergraduate research assistants monitored students as they completed the questionnaire. The order of student questionnaire measures was randomized for each classroom.

Participants

Consent letters describing the study were sent by first-class mail to the parents of children in participating classrooms. An identical copy of the consent letter was distributed to each student to take home to his or her parents two weeks prior to data collection. Parents were informed that if they did not want their child to participate in the study, they were either to return the consent letter to the teacher or to call the school, their child's teacher, or the researchers at the number provided on the letter. Study participation also required written student assent. Of all eligible students in grades 4 and 5, 89% participated in the fall and 87% participated in the spring. There were 264 participants in the fall (87% African American; 144 girls, 120 boys; 140 in grade 4, 124 in grade 5) and 257 participants in the spring (88% African American; 145 girls, 112 boys; 126 in grade 4, 131 in grade 5).

Measurements

Perceived coolness

Fall and spring measurements of perceived coolness were identical to those obtained in Study 1.

Social goals

Fall and spring measurements of social goals (social development, demonstration-approach, demonstration-avoid) were identical to those obtained in Study 1.

Study 2 Results

As in Study 1, here our aim was to examine reciprocal longitudinal relations between coolness and social goals. We followed the analytic procedure described in Study 1; the Study 2 sample permitted comparisons between genders and between grades, but not between ethnic groups. As described in Study 1, full information maximum likelihood estimation (FIML) was used to account for missing data. The final data set included 321 children (88% African American): 177 girls and 144 boys; 165 in grade 4 and 156 in grade 5. Results are presented below in the same order as they were presented in Study 1.

Measurement models

Measurement invariance

Following procedures described in Study 1, we tested for strong measurement invariance, which constrains equal item loadings and intercepts across time and subgroups (i.e., grades and sexes); correlations between latent constructs were freely estimated. To obtain strong measurement invariance for each goal, the intercept for one item was allowed to freely vary; as explained by Little (2013, p. 219), this practice results in "little loss of generality" in the conclusions

Cool Goals **145**

that can be drawn about the latent construct. These models had excellent levels of fit for the social demonstration-approach and social development goals (CFIs: .98–1.00; TLIs: .96–.99; RMSEAs: .018–.042) and adequate levels of fit for the social demonstration-avoid goal (CFIs: .93–.95; TLIs: .87–.91; RMSEAs: .047–.073), indicating that measurements were invariant across time and subgroups, thus permitting valid group comparisons in latent correlations and structural paths.

Latent correlations between coolness and social goals

Correlations between coolness and each social goal for the full sample (fall and spring) are presented in Table 8.4. In the full sample, four out of six latent correlations were statistically significant: the approach-cool latent correlation was reliably negative in the spring ($\psi = -.18$, $p < .01$), but not the fall; the development-cool latent correlation was reliably negative in the fall ($\psi = -.22$, $p < .01$) and in the spring ($\psi = -.35$, $p < .01$); and the avoid-cool latent correlation was reliably negative in the spring ($\psi = -.24$, $p < .01$) but not in the fall. Differences in latent correlations between subgroups were tested one parameter at a time using the method described by Little (2013). There was one statistically significant difference between grades: The fall development-cool latent correlation was reliably negative in grade 5 ($\psi = -.38$, $p < .01$) but not in grade 4 ($\psi = -.08$, ns; $\chi^2_{(1)} = 9.26$, $p < .01$). There also was one statistically significant difference between sexes: The spring approach-cool latent correlation was reliably negative for girls ($\psi = -.29$, $p < .01$) but not for boys ($\psi = -.14$, ns; $\chi^2_{(1)} = 6.78$, $p < .01$).

Structural equations models

Longitudinal stabilities

For each social goal, we first tested the stability of coolness and the social goal from fall to spring; cross-lagged paths were constrained to zero (see Table 8.5). Models with the social demonstration-approach and social development goals had very good levels of fit (CFIs: .97–.98; TLIs: .94–.97; RMSEAs: .043–.056). The model with the social demonstration-avoid goal had acceptable levels of fit (CFIs = .94; TLI = .89; RMSEA = .075). Stability coefficients were reliably positive for all subgroups (βs: .38–.80, $ps < .01$). In the full sample, the coolness stability estimate ($\beta = .77$, $p < .01$) was higher than stability estimates for social goals (βs = .55–.65, $ps < .01$). There was one statistically significant difference between subgroups ($\chi^2_{(1)} = 14.5$, $p < .01$): The approach goal stability was stronger in grade 5 ($\beta = .67$, $p < .01$) than in grade 4 ($\beta = .47$, $p < .01$). Although some other estimates appeared to vary moderately between subgroups, no other statistically significant differences between subgroups were found.

TABLE 8.4 Study 2: Latent Correlations between Coolness and Social Goals

	Approach - Cool			Development - Cool			Avoidance - Cool		
	Fall	Spring		Fall		Spring		Fall	Spring
Full sample	−.05	−.18$_b$**		−.22$_a$**		−.35**	−	−.07	−.24**
Grade 4	.05	−.14	−	−.08	−	−.30**	−	−.05	−	−.24**
Grade 5	.01	−.22**	−	−.38**	−	−.40**	−	−.08	−	−.22**
Boys	−.10	−.05	−	−.28**	−	−.32**	−	−.07	−	−.14
Girls	.02	−.26**	−	−.19*	−	−.38**	−	−.08	−	−.29**

$^{*}p < .05.$ $^{**}p < .01.$

Cool Goals   147

TABLE 8.5 Study 2: Longitudinal Stabilities in Coolness and Social Goals

	Coolness	Demonstration-Approach	Social Development	Demonstration-Avoidance
Full sample	.77*	.57$_a$*	.55*	.65*
Grade 4	.74*	.47*	.38*	.68*
Grade 5	.80*	.67*	.55*	.65*
Boys	.79*	.53*	.49*	.50*
Girls	.76*	.61*	.46*	.75*

*$p < .01$.

TABLE 8.6 Longitudinal Cross-lagged Paths between Coolness and Social Goals

	Approach → Cool	Cool → Approach	Develop → Cool	Cool → Develop	Avoidance → Cool	Cool → Avoidance
Full sample	−.031	−.176**	.046$_b$	−.219$_a$**	−.045	−.232**
Grade 4	−.015	−.095	.006	−.088	−.042	−.136*
Grade 5	−.039	−.240**	.108	−.316**	−.073	−.292**
Boys	−.007	−.167**	.165*	−.221**	.077	−.241**
Girls	−.056	−.183**	−.038	−.227**	−.109	−.214**

**$p < .01$. *$p < .05$.

Cross-lagged paths between coolness and social goals

Next, we tested the full model with longitudinal stabilities and cross-lagged paths from fall to spring to examine the relations between coolness and each social goal (see Table 8.6). Of the six cross-lagged paths (two per achievement goal), three paths were statistically significant in the full sample: fall coolness had a significant and negative effect on the spring approach goal ($\beta = −.18$, $p < .01$), on the spring development goal ($\beta = −.22$, $p < .01$), as well as on the spring avoid goal ($\beta = −.23$, $p < .01$). Fall social goals had no reliable effect on spring coolness in the full sample. However, the fall development goal had a reliably positive effect spring coolness among boys ($\beta = .17$, $p < .05$), though not among girls ($\beta = −.04$, ns; $\chi^2_{(1)} = 4.43$, $p < .05$).

Study 2 Discussion

Results from Study 2 indicated that students' coolness was related to changes in social achievement goals. As students' coolness increased, they were less likely to indicate a focus on social demonstration-approach or social demonstration-avoid goals. Thus, as peers' perceptions of coolness increased, students were less likely to be concerned with appearing cool or avoiding the appearance of being uncool. These findings were true for both 4th and 5th grade students and for both boys and girls. This finding supports our hypothesis that as students receive feedback from their peers about social success they subsequently worry less about how they are being perceived. This is consistent with Majors and Billson's (1992) suggestion that African Americans in particular may feel more security and less anxiety when they are viewed as cool.

In addition, our results showed that as students' coolness increased they were less likely to indicate a focus on social development goals. This differed marginally between 4th and 5th grade students, but not between boys and girls. Thus, as peers' perceptions of coolness increased, 5th grade students were less likely to be concerned with developing friendships. This finding is also consistent with Majors and Billson's (1992) assertion that cool African American students may stop reaching out to forge new or deeper relationships. Conversely, social achievement goals did not appear to have an impact on peers' perception of coolness. One exception was a focus on social development goals was related to an increase in coolness for boys, but not for girls. This is interesting because as boys become cooler they report less of a focus on social development goals, despite our findings indicating that development goals are a pathway for increased status.

General discussion

The present research highlights the need to examine bidirectional relations between youths' social achievement goals and social status, and to examine how these relations meaningfully vary across groups and social contexts. The dominant approach in studying goals has been to examine unidirectional prospective relations between goals and subsequent adjustment outcomes. As our data have shown, adopting a bidirectional approach reveals developmental patterns that would otherwise remain undetected.

First, and contrary to the conventional view that goals engender changes in psychosocial functioning, we found that social achievement goals had only a modest impact on coolness across the school year. Specifically, social demonstration-approach goals had a reliably positive effect on subsequent perceived coolness for all students in Study 1, and social development goals had a reliably positive effect on subsequent perceived coolness for boys in Study 2. These were the only two reliable findings supporting the view that goals engender changes in youths' status; in the absence of a bidirectional approach, our understanding of social goals and coolness would be limited to those insights. By examining the reciprocal relations, we found that it was individuals' levels of perceived coolness that effected changes in social achievement goals. Most noteworthy was that, in both samples, perceived coolness had a reliably negative effect on social demonstration-avoid goals across the school year; this suggests that having a widespread recognition among peers as being cool provides a kind of psychosocial affordance, which may help mitigate social anxiety and worries about looking foolish or dumb. Importantly, this pattern was consistent not only across both study samples but also across grade levels, ethnic groups (Study 1), and sexes. The universality of this pattern raises questions about mediation processes. One possibility is that self-perceptions of social competence mediate the link between having cool status and lower avoid goals. Students may be particularly sensitive to feedback from peers regarding perceptions of coolness; that is, positive feedback may yield more favorable estimations of one's social competence, which, in turn, mitigates anxiety and worry. Examining this possibility, along with other potential mediation processes, is worthy of future research.

Apart from the universal coolness-avoid link, there was meaningful contextual variability in coolness-goals reciprocal associations. Participants from Study 1 were embedded in a racially and socioeconomically heterogeneous peer group of European and African American students, whereas participants from Study 2 were embedded in a predominantly African American and low-SES urban context. Although we did not make explicit statistical comparisons between Study 1 and Study 2, we nonetheless can draw general comparisons between the broader patterns of findings between the two locales.

In the racially heterogeneous Midwest setting (Study 1), fall social demonstration-approach goals had a reliably positive effect on spring coolness. Thus, as students indicated a focus on wanting to be viewed as popular and as having many friends, their peers reported an increase in their coolness. This is consistent with prior reports indicating that approach goals are related to increased status among preadolescents (Rodkin et al., 2013; Ryan & Shim, 2008). However, this finding was not present in the racially homogeneous urban setting (Study 2), where fall social demonstration-approach goals did not reliably predict spring coolness. For the latter students, the bidirectional model showed that coolness reliably predicted changes in approach goals (not vice-versa).

Indeed, for students in the predominantly African American large urban context (Study 2), fall coolness had a reliably negative effect *on all three social goals*. Thus, students who were viewed as cooler in the peer group at the outset were less likely to be concerned with the development of their friendships, less likely to worry about being seen as cool, and less likely to have anxiety about appearing socially incompetent over time. This is consistent with Majors and Billson's (1992) contention that, for many African American youths in urban settings, coolness often manifests as aloofness; this kind of social reserve may be one of a number of adaptive strategies that some youths employ at times in navigating the particular challenges of their daily lives. Our data suggest not only that coolness and social reserve tend to co-occur in these youth at a single point in time but also that having cool status further entrenches this pattern over time.

Future Research

Despite several notable strengths in methodology and sample, the present research also had limitations. First, we did not measure or test for self-reports of perceived social competence. Future research should empirically test whether individuals' self-perceptions of social competence mediate the relation between coolness and decreases in social demonstration-avoid goals. A second limitation was that both studies included just two assessments across a six-month interval in a single academic year. Future research may find additional links between social goals and coolness across longer periods of time or across school transitions, when coolness is susceptible to greater levels of change. In this relatively short period of time, coolness was highly stable. In fact, the stability for coolness was stronger than the stability for social achievement goals, indicating that goal orientations shift across one school year but peers' perceptions of coolness remain relatively stable across one school year. More generally, it must also be acknowledged that we examined social goals vis-à-vis only one aspect of social functioning (status) – and, for that matter, only one *type* of status (coolness). Such a model parsimoniously clarifies narrowly defined growth patterns over time; however, it does not capture the complexity of motives underlying quotidian behaviors, decision making, and striving (Elliot & Niesta, 2009). An intriguing pursuit would be to use qualitative methods to examine *what it is about the social environment of cool youths* (e.g., the nature of verbal feedback from peers) that may spur changes in social goals.

Limitations notwithstanding, there are many ways that a bidirectional approach like the one presented in this chapter can yield insights into the development of students' social achievement goals. Future research can add to our understanding on the precursors of social achievement goals by exploring reciprocal relations of social goals and aspects of psychosocial functioning apart from social status. For example, we know that students with social demonstration-avoid goals are less likely to seek academic help (e.g., Ryan, Hicks, & Midgley, 1997). Might help-seeking behaviors alter (or reaffirm) students' social goals? In addition, future research might examine reciprocal links between coolness and academic performance across development; Research indicates that having social prestige among peers poses risks to academic achievement in adolescence, but it is unclear how this process unfolds (Jamison et al., 2015). Questions like these can be explored using bidirectional models of the co-development of intrapersonal and interpersonal developmental processes.

References

Arbuckle, J. (2013). *AMOS 22: User's guide*. Chicago, IL: Small Waters Corporation.

Austin, J. T., & Vancouver, J. B. (1996). Goal constructs in psychology: Structure, process, and content. *Psychological Bulletin, 120*(3), 338–375.

Bahar, M., Uğur, H., & Asil, M. (2018). Social achievement goals and students' socioeconomic status: Cross-cultural validation and gender invariance. *Issues in Educational Research, 28*(3), 511–529.

Baumeister, R. F., Masicampo, E. J., & Vohs, K. D. (2011). Do conscious thoughts cause behavior? *Annual Review of Psychology, 62*, 331–361.

Bellmore, A., Villarreal, V. M., & Ho, A. Y. (2011). Staying cool across the first year of middle school. *Journal of Youth and Adolescence, 40*(7), 776–785. doi:10.1007/s10964-010-9590-xx.

Berndt, T. J., & Savin-Williams, R. C. (1993). *Peer relations and friendships.* Oxford: John Wiley & Sons.

Cairns, R. D., & Cairns, B. D. (2005). Social ecology over time and space. In U. Bronfenbrenner (Ed.), *Making human beings human: Bioecological perspectives on human development* (pp. 16–21). Thousand Oaks, CA: Sage.

Cillessen, A. H. N., & Berg, Y. H. M. v. d. (2012). Popularity and school adjustment. In A. M. Ryan & G. W. Ladd (Eds.), *Adolescence and education: Peer relationships and adjustment at school* (pp. 135–164). Charlotte, NC: US: IAP Information Age Publishing.

Cillessen, A.H.N., & Marks, P. E. L. (2011). Conceptualizing and measuring popularity. In A. H. N. Cillessen, D. Schwartz, & L. Mayeux (Eds.), *Popularity in the peer system* (pp. 25–56). New York: Guilford.

Dar-Nimrod, I., Hansen, I. G., Proulx, T., Lehman, D. R., Chapman, B. P., & Duberstein, P. R. (2012). Coolness: An empirical investigation. *Journal of Individual Differences, 33*, 175–185.

Dinerstein, J. (2017). *The origins of cool in postwar America.* Chicago, IL: University of Chicago Press.

Dweck, C. S. (1986). Motivational processes affecting learning. *American Psychologist, 41* (10), 1040–1048. http://dx.doi.org/10.1037/0003-066X.41.10.1040.

Dweck, C. S. (1992). Article commentary: The study of goals in psychology. *Psychological Science, 3*(3), 165–167.

Elliot, A. J., & Niesta, D. (2009). Goals in the context of the hierarchical model of approach-avoidance motivation. In G. B. Moskowitz & H. Grant (Eds.), *The psychology of goals* (pp. 56–76). New York: Guilford Press.

Graham, S., & Juvonen, J. (2002). Ethnicity, peer harassment, and adjustment in middle school: An exploratory study. *The Journal of Early Adolescence, 22*(2), 173–199.

Jamison, R. S., Wilson, T., & Ryan, A. (2015). Too cool for school? The relationship between coolness and academic reputation in early adolescence. *Social Development, 24* (2), 384–403.

Kenny, D. A. (2005). Cross-lagged panel design. In B. S. Everitt & D. Howell (Eds.), *Encyclopedia of statistics in behavioral science* (pp. 450–451). New York: Wiley. doi:10.1002/0470013192.bsa1566.

Kiefer, S. M., & Ryan, A. M. (2011). Students' perceptions of characteristics associated with social success: Changes during early adolescence. *Journal of Applied Developmental Psychology, 32*(4), 218–226.

Kiefer, S. M., & Wang, J. H. (2016). Associations of coolness and social goals with aggression and engagement during adolescence. *Journal of Applied Developmental Psychology, 44*, 52–62.

LaFontana, K. M., & Cillessen, A. H. N. (2002). Children's perception of popular and unpopular peers: A multimethod assessment. *Developmental Psychology, 38*, 635–647.

LaFontana, K. M., & Cillessen, A. H. N. (2010). Developmental changes in the priority of perceived status in childhood and adolescence. *Social Development, 19*(1), 130–147. doi:10.1111/j.1467–9507.2008.00522.xx.

Larson, R. W., Wilson, S., Brown, B. B., Furstenberg, J., Frank, F., & Verma, S. (2002). Changes in adolescents' interpersonal experiences: Are they being prepared for adult relationships in the twenty-first century? *Journal of Research on Adolescence, 12*(1), 31–68.

Li, Y. & Hu, Y. (2018) How to attain a popularity goal? Examining the mediation effects of popularity determinants and behaviors. *Journal of Youth and Adolescence*, first online. https://doi.org/10.1007/s10964-018-0882-x.

Little, T. D. (2013). *Longitudinal structural equation modeling*. New York: Guilford Press.

Majors, R., & Billson, J. M. (1992). *Cool pose: The dilemma of Black manhood in America*. New York: Touchstone.

Makara, K. A., & Madjar, N. (2015). The role of goal structures and peer climate in trajectories of social achievement goals during high school. *Developmental Psychology*, 51(4), 473–488.

Midgley, C., Kaplan, A., & Middleton, M. (2001). Performance-approach goals: Good for what, for whom, under what circumstances, and at what cost?. *Journal of Educational Psychology*, 93(1), 77–86.

Pintrich, P. R. (2000). An achievement goal theory perspective on issues in motivation terminology, theory, and research. *Contemporary Educational Psychology*, 25(1), 92–104.

Rodkin, P. C., Farmer, T. W., Pearl, R., & Van Acker, R. (2000). Heterogeneity of popular boys: Antisocial and prosocial configurations. *Developmental Psychology*, 36(1), 14–24.

Rodkin, P. C., Farmer, T. W., Pearl, R., & Van Acker, R. (2006). They're cool: Social status and peer group supports for aggressive boys and girls. *Social Development*, 15(2), 175–204.

Rodkin, P. C., Ryan, A. M., Jamison, R., & Wilson, T. (2013). Social goals, social behavior, and social status in middle childhood. *Developmental Psychology*, 49(6), 1139–1150.

Rudolph, K. D., Abaied, J. L., Flynn, M., Sugimura, N., & Agoston, A. M. (2011). Developing relationships, being cool, and not looking like a loser: Social goal orientation predicts children's responses to peer aggression. *Child Development*, 82(5), 1518–1530.

Ryan, A. M., & Shim, S. S. (2006). Social achievement goals: The nature and consequences of different orientations toward social competence. *Personality and Social Psychology Bulletin*, 32(9), 1246–1263.

Ryan, A. M., & Shim, S. S. (2008). An exploration of young adolescents' social achievement goals and social adjustment in middle school. *Journal of Educational Psychology*, 100(3), 672–687.

Ryan, A. M., Hicks, L., & Midgley, C. (1997). Social goals, academic goals, and avoiding seeking help in the classroom. *The Journal of Early Adolescence*, 17(2), 152–171.

Ryan, A. M., Jamison, R., Shin, H., & Thompson, G. (2012). Social achievement goals and adjustment at school during early adolescence. In A. M. Ryan and G. Ladd (Eds.), *Peer relationships and school adjustment* (pp. 165–186). Charlotte, NC: Information Age Press.

Sandstrom, M. J., & Cillessen, A. H. (2006). Likeable versus popular: Distinct implications for adolescent adjustment. *International Journal of Behavioral Development*, 30(4), 305–314.

Slyper, A. H. (2006). The pubertal timing controversy in the USA, and a review of possible causative factors for the advance in timing of onset of puberty. *Clinical Endocrinology*, 65(1), 1–8.

Sroufe, L. A., Egeland, B., Carlson, E. A., & Collins, W. A. (2005). *The development of the person: The Minnesota study of risk and adaptation from birth to adulthood*. New York: Guilford.

Wilson, T. M., & Jamison, R. S. (2019). Perceptions of same-sex and cross-sex peers: Behavioral correlates of perceived coolness during middle childhood. *Merrill-Palmer Quarterly*.

Wilson, T. M., & Rodkin, P. C. (2013). Children's cross-ethnic relationships in elementary schools: Concurrent and prospective associations between ethnic segregation and social status. *Child Development*, 84(3), 1081–1097.

Wilson, T. M., Rodkin, P. C., & Ryan, A. M. (2014). The company they keep and avoid: Social goal orientation as a predictor of children's ethnic segregation. *Developmental Psychology*, 50(4), 1116–1124.

Wilson, T. M., Zheng, C., Lemoine, K. A., Martin, C. P., & Tang, Y. (2016). Achievement goals during middle childhood: Individual differences in motivation and social adjustment. *The Journal of Experimental Education*, 84(4), 723–743.

Yang, F., Chen, X., & Wang, L. (2015). Shyness-sensitivity and social, school, and psychological adjustment in urban Chinese children: A four-wave longitudinal study. *Child Development*, 86, 1848–1864.

9

POPULARITY/ANTISOCIAL GOALS

David B. Estell

Definitions

Prior to any discussion of goals related to social status, the nature of social status itself needs clarification. Research on social status has its foundations in two different approaches to social functioning: one based more on individual social skills and positive interactions and the other on the functions of social behaviors – prosocial in nature or otherwise – in the complex dynamics of social networks (Estell, Farmer, Pearl, Van Acker, & Rodkin, 2003). The former led to examining social status in terms of how well-liked individuals were among peers, the latter in terms of social power and admiration (Bukowski, 2011; Cillessen & Marks, 2011; Rodkin et al., 2013). These two forms of status have been identified on the one hand as sociometric popularity, likeability, acceptance, or preference and on the other as perceived popularity (Rodkin et al., 2013). For the purposes of this chapter, I will discuss them in their most common current terms: preference and popularity.

Preference

Social preference is measured in a few interrelated ways. Peer nominations for who is most liked, and peer ratings of likeability are two such measures. Sociometric popularity, the most widely used measure of preference, is traditionally defined by peer nominations for whom is liked most and whom is liked least (Coie, Dodge, & Copotelli, 1982). "Popular," i.e., socially preferred, youth are liked by most peers and rarely disliked, while those identified as rejected have the opposite pattern – liked by few, disliked by many. Neglected youth have few nominations for either (i.e., not widely liked nor disliked), and controversial youth many nominations for both (liked by many, disliked by many others).

Popularity

While the study of preference was originally grounded in a social skills approach, other work utilized a more systems approach (Cairns, 1996; Magnusson & Cairns, 1996) to examining the social dynamics of peer relationships. In this view, social status is the product of individual behaviors, characteristics of the group to which individuals belong, and features of the broader social network rather than being driven by any one (Estell, Farmer, Pearl, Van Acker, & Rodkin, 2008). Therefore, though individual abilities and behavior certainly play a key role in social functioning, they cannot be thought of as driving processes, and social status cannot be reduced to an individual characteristic.

Social status has been measured in a number of ways in this approach. These include social network centrality and peer nominations or ratings of who is "cool" and "popular" (Estell et al., 2003, 2008). These latter two are not precisely the same: "cool" kids tend to get attention and admiration from peers, but also are seen as being independent (Jamison, Wilson, & Ryan, 2015; Kiefer & Wang, 2016; Pountain & Robins, 2000), while popularity is a matter of social centrality and prominence (Cillessen, Schwartz, & Mayeux, 2011; Rodkin, Farmer, Pearl, & Van Acker, 2006). These measures, however, are all highly interrelated and index peer admiration, social salience, and social power (Estell et al., 2003, 2008; Rodkin et al., 2006).

Social goals have been classified in two broad ways: as content goals and achievement goals (Ryan & Shim, 2008). A content approach looks at specific goals individuals may have. Content goals relevant to status may include being liked, having a lot of friends, having social power or dominance, and being admired (Dawes & Xie, 2017).

An achievement approach to social goals classifies goals according to broader categories that encompass multiple content goals (Rodkin, Ryan, Jamison, & Wilson, 2013; Ryan & Shim, 2006, 2008). Ryan and Shim (2006, 2008) elucidated a three-factor classification of social achievement goals. Social development goals focus on improving prosocial functioning and relationship quality. Content goals within this include improving interactions with friends or other peers, improving one's understanding of friendship, improving the quality of friendships, bettering one's understanding of peers, and broadly improving social skills. Social demonstration approach goals center on garnering positive social appraisals such as appearing competent, admirable, and influential. Content goals within this domain included wanting to be seen as popular, associating with "cool" and popular peers, having lots of friendships, being admired and thought of as well liked. Finally, Ryan and Shim identified social demonstration avoidance goals, which consist of avoiding negative social judgments. Not being mocked, avoiding embarrassment, and generally avoiding peers saying negative things about oneself are among the content goals that fall under social demonstration avoidance goals.

This same achievement goal structure – development, demonstration approach, and demonstration avoid – has been replicated multiple times in diverse samples

(Jones & Ford, 2014; Jones, Mueller, Royal, Shim, & Hart, 2013; Kiefer & Ryan, 2008; Lopez, Felix, Ruiz, & Ortiz, 2016; Michou, Mouratidis, Ersoy, & Uğur, 2016; Rodkin et al., 2013). Further, parallel work has examined achievement goals in a two-factor structure that parallels Ryan and Shim's construction fairly closely. Specifically, this work has examined social goals in terms of communal and agentic goals (Caravita & Cillessen, 2011; Dawes & Xie, 2017; Dawes, 2017; Ojanen & Findley-Van Nostrand, 2014). Communal goals are those focused on improving relationships, fostering intimacy, and being prosocial, while agentic goals are focused on looking confident, and garnering respect, admiration, social power, and dominance (Dawes, 2017; Dawes & Xie, 2017). These then represent largely the same constructs as social development and social demonstration approach goals respectively.

Evidence

Preference

Socially preferred youth are viewed by their peers as prosocial, cooperative, friendly, sociable, and sensitive (Bukowski & Newcomb, 1984; Cillessen & Mayeux, 2004; Coie, Lochman, Terry, & Hyman, 1992; Dijkstra, Lindenberg, & Veenstra, 2007; Dodge, Coie, & Brakke, 1982; Hartup, 1983; Newcomb & Bukowski, 1983, 1984; Rubin, Bukowski, & Parker, 2006). These individuals also have a good sense of humor, are class leaders, and are rated by peers as being generally well liked and having many friends (Gest, Graham-Bermann, & Hartup, 2001). On the other hand, children who are highly disliked by their peers have been found to have social skills deficits, lack prosocial behaviors and to be withdrawn or aggressive (Asher & Coie, 1990; Cillessen & Mayeux, 2004; Cillessen, van IJzendoorn, van Lieshout, & Hartup, 1992; Coie & Dodge, 1983; Dijkstra et al., 2007; Parkhurst & Asher, 1992). Gest et al. (2001) also reported a negative relationship between measures of peer preference and characteristics including being bossy, hypersensitive, sad, unable to command others' attention, having trouble making friends, being left out, and having a short temper.

Preference is predictive of adjustment for two related reasons. First, it reflects the social competencies individuals bring to daily social interactions (Rubin, et al. 2006). Presumably, socially skilled individuals will remain able to function highly in their psychosocial worlds, while those who initially struggle with social skills may continue to have difficulties with forming positive relationships. Second, early and ongoing peer interactions can affect psychosocial development (Rubin, et al., 2006). If interactions with peers are positive, they can lead to further development prosocial skills, and the establishment and maintenance of close and supportive relationships. Conversely, negative peer relations can inhibit socio-emotional adaptation (Gest, et al., 2001). In effect, then, socially skilled children may have positive interactions with peers that allow them to continue to hone

Popularity/Antisocial Goals **157**

their skills and thrive personally and socially over time. Children who struggle with social skills may withdraw or be excluded by peers, or have negative encounters. In the former case, they may then miss opportunities to develop social skills, and in the latter may in fact learn negative patterns of functioning.

A large body of empirical work supports these assumptions. Specifically, while preference is associated with positive outcomes, such as academic success and a lack of psychopathology, rejected children – particularly aggressive-rejected individuals – have been found to be at risk for a number of negative outcomes. These include losing interest in school (Wentzel & Asher, 1995), early school drop-out (Coie, Dodge, & Kupersmidt, 1990; Hymel, Comfort, Schonert-Reichl, & McDougall, 1996; Parker & Asher, 1987), emotional and behavioral difficulties in adolescence (Coie et al., 1992), and poor adult adjustment (Bagwell, Newcomb, & Bukowski, 1998). Social preference, then, is unambiguously a positive for both those who have it and for others with whom they interact in prosocial ways. Popularity, in contrast, involves both positive and potentially negative functions.

Popularity

In contrast to preference, popularity has been associated with both prosocial and aggressive or manipulative behaviors (Aikins & Litwack, 2011; Caravita & Cillessen, 2011; Cillessen & Mayeux, 2004; Ryan & Shim, 2008). Popular youth are seen as attractive and athletic but also arrogant and aggressive (Cillessen & Mayeux, 2004; de Bruyn & Cillessen, 2006; Dijkstra, Lindenberg, Verhulst, Ormel, & Veenstra, 2009). Resistance to authority and "toughness" were reported in one study of young adolescents as the defining qualities of popular males (Adler, Kless, & Adler, 1992). Others have found that the most influential boys in later elementary classroom social structures tended to acquire their dominant status by bullying less physically able peers, provoking fights, and defying teachers' authority (Adler & Adler, 1995; 1996; Adler, et al., 1992; Pellegrini, 1995; Pepler, Craig, & Roberts, 1998). Further, aggression can be a strategy for garnering status over both members of one's own group and individuals in the larger social network (Adler & Adler, 1995). Aggressive behavior can both help attain popularity through establishing dominance and thus social superiority, and help maintain position through the demotion of others (Adler & Adler, 1995; Atlas & Pepler, 1998; Cairns & Cairns, 1994; Farmer, 2000; Pellegrini, 1995; Salmivalli, Huttunen, Lagerspetz, 1997). Although physically aggressive girls tend to be less popular and influential in the social structure, popular girls tend to become very adept at relational aggression over the elementary school years (Adler & Adler, 1995; Cairns, Cairns, Neckerman, Ferguson, & Gariépy, 1989; Merten, 1997; Xie, Cairns, Cairns, 1999).

Aggression is not the only strategy for becoming popular. When cluster analytic techniques are used, subsets of popular youth emerge (Estell et al., 2003, Estell et al., 2008). One group are marked by low levels of aggressive behavior, are highly academically oriented, and have high social preference. In contrast, other popular youth in these studies were marked by aggressive behavior, lower levels of academic achievement, and were controversial – both liked and disliked – in terms of preference. This latter group matches what Hawley referred to as bi-strategic controllers (2003). That is, individuals who use both prosocial and aggressive techniques to attain social power. They charm and convince some people, while potentially bullying and coercing others.

In summary, preference is a matter of being well liked by peers. Prosocial behavior and a focus on close relationships are fundamental aspects of social preference. In contrast, popularity is a matter of social influence and power. As such, while being liked and convincing others is one form of influence, coercive, dominant, and bullying behaviors can also be a route to attaining and maintaining it. Having one form of status over the other as one's goal may have powerful implications for functioning in school.

Social development goals align with improving the quality of peer relationships via prosocial behavior and social skills, while social demonstration goals – especially social demonstration approach goals – align with social power more broadly (Rodkin et al. 2013). As expected, then, development or communal goals tend to be associated with social preference, while demonstration or agentic goals with popularity (Caravita & Cillessen, 2011; Rodkin et al., 2013). Holding social goals does not necessarily mean one attains those goals (Dawes & Xie, 2014). Aspiring to status may or may not lead to the successful attainment of that status, and the intersection of goals and status is an important area of study (Dawes & Xie, 2014, 2017; Dyches & Mayeux 2015; Kiefer & Wang, 2016). Popularity goals do predict popularity-related behaviors such as altering one's dress to clothes considered more fashionable (Dawes & Xie, 2014). Further, communal goals are associated with higher ratings of likeability (Ojanen, Grönroos, & Salmivalli, 2005) as well as social preference (Ojanen & Findley-Van Nostrand, 2014). Agentic goals, in contrast, predict popularity (Ojanen & Findley-Van Nostrand, 2014).

Status goals and age

The associations among status goals, popularity preference, aggression and prosocial behavior also vary with age. While second and third graders distinguish among social development, social demonstration approach and social demonstration avoid goals (Rudolph, Abaied, Flynn, Sugimura, & Agoston, 2011), agentic and communal goals are negatively correlated in middle childhood, while there is no relationship by early adolescence (Caravita & Cillessen, 2011). That is, in children, one can seek social power or closeness, but not both, whereasthese can be parallel social goals in teens. Similarly, in young children, popular peers are also generally preferred peers (so influence is a product of being liked), while in adolescence there is a split where some popular youth are well liked while others fall into the controversial range on preference measures (Cillessen & Marks, 2011). These findings in teens point to the divergence of routes to popularity noted above.

Status goals in general tend to increase with age, with higher levels of goals being reported among eighth graders as compared to fourth graders (Sijtsema et al., 2009), and the importance of popularity in particular peaks at 13–15 (Cillessen et al., 2011). Further, preference and popularity goals tend to both increase following the transition to middle school, as does the association between popularity goals and dominance (Kiefer, Matthews, Montesino, Arango, & Preece, 2013). After, the transition to middle school, however, popularity goals tend to drop once the middle school social hierarchy becomes more settled (Dawes & Xie, 2017; Kiefer et al., 2013). Overall, these findings indicate that social status becomes more salient from childhood into early adolescence, and when social hierarchies are in flux. Further, while social influence in children tends to be defined by being nice and well liked, by adolescence the issues of social power that differentiate popularity from preference have emerged.

Status goals and sex

While there are no baseline sex differences in prioritizing popularity, valuing popularity is unrelated to actually being popular in females, but modestly so in males (Cillessen et al., 2011). Further, more social interaction with peers is associated with higher popularity goals in females, but lower in males (Kiefer et al., 2013). This may be in part due to the nature of what leads to popularity in males as compared to females. While relational aggression is associated with popularity in female teens (Merten, 1997), they also report that intimacy and sociability are highly important to their popularity (Closson, 2009) or being cool (Kiefer & Wang, 2016), and prosocial behavior is seen as a marker of social success in girls (Kiefer & Ryan, 2011). In contrast, male popularity tends to center more exclusively around dominance (Lease, Kennedy, & Axelrod, 2002), so this aligns more with the nature of popularity as unique from preference. Ongoing friendly interactions may decrease the desire to be dominant, therefore decreasing popularity goals in males. Further, while popular youth with high popularity goals tend to have higher levels of both aggression and leadership, this is especially pronounced among males (Cillessen et al., 2014). Aggression in this context may be in the service of maintaining their valued status. Among females, in contrast, relational aggression is particularly prevalent in those who value popularity but are not themselves popular (Shoulberg, Sijtsema, & Murray-Close, 2011). Combined with the roles of intimacy and prosocial behavior in female popularity cited above, aggression may be a more viable strategy to attain status in females, at which point they change to more prosocial strategies. In males, however, aggression may serve to both achieve and keep popularity.

Other goals that are associated with popularity also differ based on sex. Closson, Hart, and Hogg (2016) found a number of sex differences in the association between conformity goals (wanting to have the clothes, skills, and abilities that are approved of by others) and popularity. Popular girls who hold conformity

160 David B. Estell

goals tend to be victimized and excluded more than popular girls without such goals – perhaps because they are seen as materialistic or superficial (Eder 1985, Merten 1997) and therefore not fulfilling the intimacy and sociability requirements core to ongoing female popularity (Closson, 2009; Kiefer & Ryan, 2011). In contrast, popular boys with conformity goals are less excluded, but unpopular boys with these same goals are at greater risk for exclusion perhaps due to being seen as trying too hard (Closson et al., 2016).

Academic Performance

Most of the research on status goals has examined their association with peer social dynamics rather than academics per se. There are some patterns regarding school involvement and engagement as well academic achievement and motivation. Specifically, those who endorse preference goals (e.g., wanting to make others happy, wanting to be liked) are seen by peers as more academically oriented (Dawes, 2017; Jarvinen & Nicholls, 1996; Li & Wright, 2014). Higher levels of popularity goals, in contrast, are associated with lower levels of school engagement, asking for help when needed, and academic achievement (Anderman, 1999; Gorman et al., 2002; Juvonen & Murdock, 1995; Ryan, Hicks, & Midgley, 1997). This may be due to those with popularity goals tending to view school engagement and academic achievement as not being viable pathways to popularity (Gorman, Kim, & Schimmelbusch, 2002; Juvonen & Murdock, 1995).

Interpersonal Outcomes

Social goals lead to the same kinds of social behaviors associated with each kind of social status. Agentic goals are associated with higher levels of aggression and lower levels of prosocial behavior, while communal goals predict higher levels of prosocial behavior (Ojanen et al., 2005; Ojanen & Findley-Van Nostrand, 2014). Communal goals also have no association with aggression (Ojanen et al., 2005) or a negative relationship (Ojanen & Findley-Van Nostrand, 2014) with antisocial behavior.

Social development goals are associated with higher prosocial behavior, lower levels of aggression higher positive qualities in friendships, while demonstration approach goals correlate with higher aggression, lower prosocial behavior and higher popularity (Ryan & Shim, 2008). Youth who report popularity goals (e.g., wanting to be popular among peers) tend to have higher levels of both physical and relational aggression, desire leadership positions and dominance, and have lower levels of prosocial behavior (Dawes, 2017; Jarvinen & Nicholls, 1996; Li & Wright, 2014). Those who endorse preference goals (e.g., wanting to make others happy, wanting to be liked) are seen as nice, less aggressive, report wanting greater closeness with friends, have higher levels of prosocial behaviors, and the desire to help others (Dawes, 2017; Jarvinen & Nicholls, 1996; Li & Wright, 2014).

Youth identified as bullies have high popularity goals and high popularity, victims have the opposite pattern – neither popularity goals nor popularity – and bully victims have disproportionately low preference (Sijtsema, Veenstra, Lindenberg, & Salmivalli, 2009). These social and behavioral dynamics shift over time, and Dawes and Xie (2014) found multiple pathways to popularity. High popularity goals combined with high popularity was associated with high levels of concurrent relational aggression, and the combination of these three – popularity goals, popularity, and relational aggression – predicted increases in popularity over time. Interestingly, relational aggression also predicted increases in popularity in students with low popularity and low popularity goals, as did physical aggression for these same low-status, low-goal students. However, for students with high goals but low popularity and those with low goals but high popularity, popularity did not change over time regardless of levels of aggression.

Similarly, Kiefer & Wang (2016) found that while all youth with higher popularity goals had high levels of disruptive behavior, among males seen as "cool," those with high popularity goals tended to have higher levels of relational aggression, while those with lower levels of popularity goals tended to be more physically aggressive. Further, agentic goals in combination with relational aggression is associated with higher levels of popularity, and conversely popularity predicts higher aggression only in the presence of high agentic goals (Ojanen & Findley-Van Nostrand, 2014).

Taken together, these studies indicate that intentional aggression, and especially relational aggression, tends to be highest among those who have high popularity goals and have achieved or are achieving those goals. Given that there are prosocial yet popular individuals (Estell et al. 2003, 2008), the intentional seeking of power or dominance may be key youth relying on more aggressive means. Others may be popular because they are admired and liked, but without having social power as a specific goal. This points to the value in considering social goals when examining the behavioral correlates of status in students.

Future Research

The primary focus or research into status goals has been on the social behaviors that lead to and are a consequence of these goals and attained status. Less of an emphasis has, to date, been on academic outcomes. Preference goals tend are associated with prosocial behavior and developing harmonious relationships as well as academic orientation (Dawes, 2017; Jarvinen & Nicholls, 1996; Li & Wright, 2014;), and so align with having a school climate conducive to learning in all students. In contrast, popularity can be associated with a variety of negative behaviors including dominance, aggression more and lower levels of prosocial behavior (Dawes, 2017; Jarvinen & Nicholls, 1996; Li & Wright, 2014; Ryan & Shim, 2008) as well as lower levels of school engagement and academic achievement (Anderman, 1999; Gorman et al., 2002; Juvonen & Murdock, 1995; Ryan et al., 1997). As such, popularity goals may interfere with these other social and academic goals, and prove disruptive to the socioemotional and academic well-being of not only those who hold popularity goals but for other students exposed to their antisocial behaviors. Future research is needed to document to what degree preference goals may enhance the learning environment in school and to what degree high levels of popularity goals among students may be a detriment to school climate.

Research on popular youth has identified two subsets of popular youth – those who are preferred, prosocial, and do well academically and those who are more controversial, aggressive, and less academically oriented (Estell et al., 2003; Estell et al., 2008). Future research into the goals driving these two groups – i.e., does the former hold both preference and popularity goals, or is one form of status perhaps more an inadvertent result of pursuing the other (i.e., seeking preference but are socially charming enough to be popular, or seeking popularity but a reliance on prosocial means leads to co-occurring preference). Disentangling these associations may have powerful implications for shifting the goals and behaviors of the more singularly popularity-oriented, and therefore aggressive and potentially disruptive, students.

Given that prestige, admiration, and social influence are ingrained social desires (Hawley, 1999), efforts to eliminate popularity goals are likely to fail. This opens the question as to how to mitigate the potentially deleterious effects of popularity goals on school climate. As suggested above, one potential avenue from the literature on preference and popularity is to better align these two sets of goals such that social influence and prestige arise from more exclusively prosocial means (Farmer, Lines, & Hamm, 2011). Gest and Rodkin (2011) argue that closer ties among students and less hierarchical peer social structure may promote better student outcomes. Given the findings on the how popularity goals increase when social hierarchies are in flux but decrease when the social structure is more settled (Dawes & Xie, 2017; Kiefer et al., 2013), it is reasonable to assume that diminishing the hierarchical nature of many social networks would place more of an emphasis on creating close social times and less on dominance. The resulting shift from popularity / social demonstration / agentic goals to preference / social development / communal goals should greatly reduce aggression and increase prosocial behavior.

There have been several potential ways in which teachers may affect these changes. Gest and Rodkin (2011) found that teachers who supported rejected and withdrawn students had classrooms where a higher number of students expressed liking for one another. They also found that teacher emotional support of students was associated with more reciprocated friendships. Further, seating charts are a potential way to foster closer social ties among students, as Gest and Rodkin (2011) found they could increase friendship ties, decrease disliking among students, and result in more egalitarian classroom social structures.

As Bierman (2011) notes, these kinds of interventions become much more complicated when students move from the single classrooms of elementary school to multiple classrooms, multiple teachers, and more school-wide social networks in middle school. At this stage, hierarchies exist outside of any given classroom, and so direct efforts by school personnel to promote more egalitarian social structure may be difficult. Social norms among the students themselves may, then, be a more effective way to promote preference goals and prosocial behavior over popularity goals and dominant behavior.

The socioemotional climate modeled by teachers can promote prosocial interactions (Farmer et al., 2011). Given the normative focus on peer relations and status that comes with emerging adolescence, it is extremely doubtful that efforts to change school climate will be successful unless they represent a long-term and ongoing process. This is where social and emotional learning (SEL) curricula may play a vital role, as they have been shown to impact both students directly and by giving teachers skills to help them shape the school peer dynamics (Bierman, 2011). If students can be taught to focus on prosocial behavior and forming friendships throughout their school years, they might not abandon popularity goals as they transition to middle school, but combine popularity goals with preference goals. That is, they may focus on using prosocial strategies to gain social influence by way of admiration rather than domination.

Summary and Conclusion

Social status goals are a subset of social goals focused on one of two areas. First, gaining the approval of and developing close relationships with peers. Alternatively, some goals revolve around attaining admiration, influence, and social power. The former, preference goals, are best attained by developing social skills and using prosocial behaviors to become liked among peers and increase one's number of friendships. The latter, popularity goals, can be achieved via two different but complementary sets of strategies – using social skills, admiration, and charm (the proverbial carrot), and using aggression, coercion, and dominance (the proverbial stick). As such, while preference goals are quite consistent with creating a positive school climate for all, popularity goals have the potential to disrupt feelings of belonging and academic goals not only for those who hold them, but for others exposed to their aggressive behavior. These issues are particularly salient during the transition to middle school due to developmental demands, and for males due to social norms. Social and emotional learning curricula can help shape youth directly as well as inform teacher efforts to promote less hierarchical peer dynamics and encourage those with popularity goals to rely more exclusively on the prosocial strategies for garnering influence, and making these goals more compatible for achieving other social and academic goals that promote healthy development.

References

Adler, P. A., & Adler, P. (1995). Dynamics of inclusion and exclusion in preadolescent cliques. *Social Psychology Quarterly, 58*, 145–162. doi:10.2307/2787039.

Adler, P. A., & Adler, P. (1996). Preadolescent clique stratification and the hierarchy of identity. *Sociological Inquiry, 66*, 111–142. doi:10.1111/j.1475-682X.1996.tb00213.x.

164 David B. Estell

Adler, P. A.Kless, S. J., & Adler, P. (1992). Socialization to gender roles: Popularity among elementary school boys and girls. *Sociology of Education,* 65, 169–187. doi:10.2307/2112807.

AikinsJ. W. & Litwack, S. D. (2011). Prosocial skills, social competence, and popularity. In A. H. N. Cillessen, D. Schwartz, & L. Mayeux (Eds.), *Popularity in the per system* (pp. 140–162). New York: Guilford Press.

Anderman, L. H. (1999).Classroom goal orientation, school belonging and social goals as predictors of students' positive and negative affect following the transition to middle school. *Journal of Research and Development in Education,* 32, 89–103.

Asher, S. R., & Coie, J. (1990). *Peer rejection in childhood.* New York: Cambridge University Press.

Atlas, R. S., & Pepler, D. J. (1998). Observations of bullying in the classroom. *The Journal of Educational Research,* 92, 86–99. doi:10.1080/00220679809597580.

Austin, A. B., & Draper, D. C. (1984). The relationship among peer acceptance, social impact, and academic achievement in middle school. *American Education Research Journal,* 21, 597–604. doi:10.2307/1162918.

Bagwell, C. L., Newcomb, A. F., & Bukowski, W. M. (1998). Preadolescent friendship and peer rejection as predictors of adult adjustment. *Child Development,* 69, 140–153. doi:10.1111/j.1467-8624.1998.tb06139.x.

Bierman, K. L. (2011). The promise and potential of studying the "invisible hand" of teacher influence on peer relations and student outcomes: A commentary. *Journal of Applied Developmental Psychology,* 32, 297–303. doi:10.1016/j.appdev.2011.04.004.

Bukowski, W. B. (2011). Popularity as a social concept: Meanings and significance. In A. H. N. Cillessen, D. Schwartz, & L. Mayeux (Eds.), *Popularity in the per system* (pp. 3–24). New York: Guilford Press.

Bukowski, W. M., & Newcomb, A. F. (1984). The stability and determinants of socio-metric status and friendship choice: A longitudinal perspective. *Developmental Psychology,* 20, 265–274. doi:10.1037/0012-1649.20.5.941.

Cairns, R. B. (1996). Socialization and socio-genesis. In D. Magnusson (Ed.), *The lifespan development of individuals: Behavioral, neurobiological, and psychological perspectives* (pp. 277–295). Cambridge: Cambridge University Press.

Cairns, R. B., & Cairns, B. D. (1994). *Lifelines and risks: Pathways of youth in our time.* Cambridge: Cambridge University Press.

Cairns, R. B., Cairns, B. D., Neckerman, H. J., Ferguson, L. L., & Gariépy, J.-L. (1989). Growth and aggression: I. Childhood to early adolescence. *Developmental Psychology,* 25, 320–330. doi:10.1037/0012-1649.25.2.320.

Caravita, S. C. S., & Cillessen, A. H. N. (2011). Agentic of communal? Associations between interpersonal goals, popularity, and bullying in middle childhood and early adolescence. *Social Development,* 21, 376–395. doi:10.1111/j.1467-9507.2011.00632.x.

Cillessen, A. H. N. & Marks, P. E. L. (2011). Conceptualizing and measuring popularity. In A. H. N. Cillessen, D. Schwartz, & L. Mayeux (Eds.), *Popularity in the per system* (pp. 25–56). New York: Guilford Press.

Cillessen, A. H. N. & Mayeux, L. (2004). From censure to reinforcement: Developmental changes in the association between aggression and social status. *Child Development,*75, 147–163. doi:10.1111/j.1467-8624.2004.00660.x.

Cillessen, A. H. N., Mayeux, L., Ha, T., de Bruyn, E. H., & LaFontana, K. M. (2014). Aggressive effects of prioritizing popularity in early adolescence. *Aggressive Behavior,* 40, 204–213. doi:10.1002/ab.215188.

Cillessen, A. H. N., Schwartz, D. & Mayeux, L. (2011), *Popularity in the per system.* New York: Guilford Press.

CillessenA. H. N., van IJzendoorn, H. W., van Lieshout, C. F. M., & Hartup, W. W. (1992). Heterogeneity among peer-rejected boys: Subtypes and stabilities. *Child Development*, 63, 863–905. doi:10.2307/1131241.

Closson, L. M. (2009). Status and gender difference in early adolescents' descriptions of popularity. *Social Development*, 18, 412–426. doi:10.1111/j.1467-9507.2008.00459.x.

Closson, L. M., Hart, N. C., & Hogg, L. D. (2016). Does the desire to conform to peers moderate links between popularity and indirect victimization in early adolescence? *Social Development*, 26, 489–502. doi:10.1111/sode.12223.

Coie, J. D., & Dodge, K. A. (1983). Continuities and changes in children's social status: A five-year longitudinal study. *Merrill-Palmer Quarterly*, 29(3), 261–282. Retrieved from: http://proxyiub.uits.iu.edu/login?url=https://search-proquest-com.proxyiub.uits.iu.edu/docview/616840468?accountid=11620.

Coie, J. D., Dodge, K. A., & Coppotelli, H. (1982). Dimensions and types of social status: A cross-age perspective. *Developmental Psychology*, 18(4), 557–570. doi:10.1037/0012-1649.18.4.557.

Coie, J. D., Dodge, K. A., & Kupersmidt, J. B. (1990). Peer group behavior and social status. In S. R. Asher and J. D. Coie (Eds.), *Peer rejection in childhood* (pp. 17–59). Cambridge: Cambridge University Press.

Coie, J. D., Lochman, J., Terry, R., & Hyman, C. (1992). Predicting early adolescent disorder from childhood aggression and peer rejection. *Journal of Consulting and Clinical Psychology*, 60, 783–792.

Dawes, M. (2017). Early adolescents' social goals and school adjustment. *Social Psychology of Education*, 20, 299–328. doi:10.1007/s11218-017-9380-3.

Dawes, M. & Xie, H. (2014). The role of popularity goal in early adolescents' behaviors and popularity status. *Developmental Psychology*, 50, 489–497. doi:10.1037/a0032999.

Dawes, M. & Xie, H. (2017). The trajectory of popularity goal during the transition to middle school. *Journal of Early Adolescence*, 37, 852–883. doi:10.1177/0272431615626301.

de Bruyn, E. H. & Cillessen, A. H. N. (2006). Heterogeneity of girls' consensual popularity: Academic and interpersonal behavioral profiles. *Journal of Youth and Adolescence*, 35, 435–445. doi:10.1007/s10964-005-9023-4.

DeRosier, M. E., Kupersmidt, J. B., & Patterson, C. J. (1994). Children's academic and behavioral adjustment as a function of the chronicity and proximity of peer rejection. *Child Development*, 65, 1799–1813. doi:10.1111/j.1467-8624.1994.tb00850.x.

Dijkstra, J. K., Lindenberg, S., & Veenstra, R. (2007). Same-gender and cross-gender peer acceptance and peer rejection and their relation with bullying and helping among pre-adolescents: Comparing predictions from gender-homophily and goal-framing approaches. *Developmental Psychology*, 43, 1377–1389. doi:10.1037/0012-1649.43.6.1377.

Dijkstra, J. K., Lindenberg, S., Verhulst, F. C., Ormel, J., & Veenstra, R. (2009). The relation between popularity and antisocial behavior: Moderating effects of athletic abilities, physical attractiveness, and prosociality. *Journal of Research on Adolescence*, 19, 401–413. doi:10.1111/j.1532-7795.2009.00594.x.

Dodge, K. A., Coie, J. D., & Brakke, N. P. (1982). Behavior patterns of socially rejected and neglected preadolescents: The role of social approach and aggression. *Journal of Abnormal Child Psychology*, 10, 389–410.

Dyches, K. D., & Mayeux, L. (2015). Popularity and resource control goals as predictors of adolescent indirect aggression. *The Journal of Genetic Psychology*, 176, 253–259. doi:10.1080/00221325.2015.1048661.

Eder, D. (1985). The cycle of popularity: Interpersonal relations among female adolescents. *Sociology of Education, 58*, 154–165.

Estell, D. B., Farmer, T. W., Pearl, R., Van Acker, R., & Rodkin, P. C. (2003). Heterogeneity in the relationship between popularity and aggression: Individual, group, and classroom influences. In W. Damon (Series Ed.) & S. C. Peck & R. W. Roeser (Vol. Eds.), *New directions for child and adolescent development: Vol. 101: Person-centered approaches to studying human development in context* (pp. 75–85). San Francisco: Jossey-Bass.

Estell, D. B., Farmer, T. W., Pearl, R., Van Acker, R., & Rodkin, P. C. (2008). Social status and aggressive and disruptive behavior in girls: Individual, group, and classroom influences. *Journal of School Psychology, 46*(2), 193–212. doi:10.1016/j.jsp.2007.03.004.

Farmer, T. W. (2000). The social dynamics of aggressive and disruptive behavior in school: Implications for behavioral consultation. *Journal of Education and Behavioral Consultation, 21*, 194–208. doi:10.1080/10474412.2000.9669417.

Farmer, T. W., Lines, M. M., & Hamm, J. V. (2011). Revealing the invisible hand: The role of teachers in children's peer experiences. *Journal of Applied Developmental Psychology, 32*, 247–256. doi:10.1016/j.appdev.2011.04.006.

Gest, S. D., Graham-Bermann, S. A., & Hartup, W. W. (2001). Peer experience: Common and unique features of number of friendships, social network centrality, and sociometric status. *Social Development, 10*, 23–40. doi:10.111/1467-9507.00146.

Gest, S. D. & Rodkin, P. C. (2011). Teaching practices and elementary classroom peer ecologies. *Journal of Applied Developmental Psychology, 32*, 288–296. doi:10.1016/j.appdev.2011.02.004.

Gorman, A. H., Kim, J., & Schimmelbusch, A. (2002). The attributes adolescents associate with peer popularity and teacher preference. *Journal of School Psychology, 40*, 143–165. doi:10.1016/S0022-4405(02)00092-4.

Hartup, W. W. (1983). Peer relations. In P. H. Mussen (Series Ed.) & E. M. Hetherington (Vol. Ed.). *Handbook of child psychology: Vol. 4: Socialization, personality, and social, development* (pp. 103–196). New York: Wiley.

Hawley, P. H. (1999). The ontogenesis of social dominance: A strategy-based evolutionary perspective. *Developmental Review, 19*, 97–132. doi:10.1006/drev.1998.0470.

Hawley, P. H. (2003). Prosocial and coercive configurations of resource control in early adolescence: A case for the Well-adapted Machiavellian. *Merrill-Palmer Quarterly, 49*, 279–309. Retrieved from: www.jstor.org/stable/23096057.

Hymel, S., Comfort, C., Schonert-Reichl, K., & McDougall, P. (1996). Academic failure and school dropout: The influence of peers. In J. Juvonen & K. R. Wentzel (Eds.), *Social motivation: Understanding children's school adjustment* (pp. 313–345). New York: Cambridge University Press.

Jamison, R. S., Wilson, T., & Ryan, A. (2015). Too cool for school? The relationship between coolness and academic reputation in early adolescence. *Social Development, 24*, 384–403. doi:10.1111/sode.12097.

Jarvinen, D. W. & Nicholls, J. G. (1996). Adolescents' social goals, beliefs about the causes of social success, and satisfaction in peer relations. *Developmental Psychology,32*, 435–441. doi:10.1037/0012-1649.32.3.435.

Jones, M. H. & Ford, J. M. (2014). Social Achievement goals, efficacious beliefs, and math performance in a predominately African American high school. *Journal of Black Psychology, 40*, 239–262. doi:10.1177/0095798413483556.

Jones, M. H., Mueller, C. E., Royal, K. D., Shim, S. S. & Hart, C. O. (2013). Social achievement goals: Validation among rural African American adolescents. *Journal of Educational Assessment*, 31, 566–577. doi:10.1177/0734282913483982.

Juvonen, J., & Murdock, T. B. (1995). Grade-level differences in the social value of effort: Implications for self presentation tactics of early adolescents. *Child Development*, 66, 1694–1705. doi:10.2307/1131904.

Kiefer, S. M. & Ryan, A. M. (2008). Striving for social dominance over peers: The implications for academic adjustment during early adolescence. *Journal of Educational Psychology*, 100, 417–428. doi:10.1037/0022-0663.100.2.417.

Kiefer, S. M., & Ryan, A. M. (2011). Students' perceptions of characteristics associated with social success: Changes over time during early adolescence. *Journal of Applied Developmental Psychology*, 32, 218–226. doi:10.1016/j.appdev.2011.05.002.

Kiefer, S. M. & Wang, J. H. (2016). Associations of coolness and social goals with aggression and engagement during adolescence. *Journal of Applied Developmental Psychology*, 44, 52–62. doi:10.1016/j.appdev.2016.02.007.

Kiefer, S. M., Matthews, Y. T., Montesino, M.Arango, L., & Preece, K. K. (2013). The effects of contextual and personal factors on young adolescents' social goals. *The Journal of Experimental Education*, 81, 44–67. doi:10.1080/00220973.2011.630046.

Ladd, G. W. (2005). *Children's peer relations and social competence: A century of progress*. New Haven, CT: Yale University Press.

Lease, A. M., Kennedy, C. A., & Axelrod, J. L. (2002), Children's social constructions of popularity. *Social Development*, 11, 87–109. doi:10.1111/1467-9507.00188.

Li, Y. & Wright, M. F. (2014). Adolescents' social status goals: Relationships to social status insecurity, aggression, and prosocial behavior. *Journal of Youth and Adolescence*, 43, 146–160. doi:10.1007/s10964–10013–9939-z.

Lopez, M. H., Felix, E. M. R., Ruiz, R. O., & Ortiz, O. G. (2016). Influence of social motivation, self-perception of social efficacy and normative adjustment in the peer setting. *Psicothema*, 28, 32–39. doi:10.7334/psicothema2015.135.

Magnusson, D. & Cairns, R. B. (1996). Developmental science: Toward a unified framework. In R. B. Cairns, G. H. Elder, Jr., and E. J. Costello, (Eds.), *Developmental science* (pp. 7–30). Cambridge: Cambridge University Press.

Merten, D. E. (1997). The meaning of meanness: Popularity, competition, and conflict among junior high school girls. *Sociology of Education*, 70, 175–191. doi:10.2307/2673207.

Michou, A., Mouratidis, A., Ersoy, E., & Uğur, H. (2016). Social achievement goals, needs satisfaction, and coping among adolescents. *Personality and Individual Differences*, 99, 260–265. doi:10.1016/jpaid.2016.05.028.

Newcomb, A. F., & Bukowski, W. M. (1983). Social impact and social preference as determinants of children's peer group status. *Developmental Psychology*, 19, 856–867. doi:10.1037/0012-1649.19.6.856.

Newcomb, A. F., & Bukowski, W. M. (1984). A longitudinal study of the utility of social preference and social impact sociometric classification schemes. *Child Development*, 55, 1434–1447. doi:10.2307/1130013.

Ojanen, T. & Findley-Van Nostrand, D. (2014). Social goals, aggression, peer preference, and popularity: Longitudinal links during middle school. *Developmental Psychology*, 50, 2134–2143. doi:10.1037/a0037137.

Ojanen, T., Grönroos, M. & Salmivalli, C. (2005). An interpersonal circumplex model of children's social goals: Links with peer-reported behavior and sociometric status. *Developmental Psychology*, 41, 699–710. doi:10.1037/0012-1649.41.5.699.

168 David B. Estell

Parker, J. G. & Asher, S. R. (1987). Peer relations and later personal adjustment: Are low-accepted children at risk? *Psychological Bulletin*, 102, 357–389. doi:10.1037/0033-2909.102.3.357.

Parkhurst, J. T., & Asher, S. R. (1992). Peer rejection in middle school: Subgroup differences in behavior, loneliness, and interpersonal concerns. *Developmental Psychology*, 28, 231–241. doi:10.1037/0012-1649.28.2.231.

Pellegrini, A. D. (1995). A longitudinal study of boys' rough-and-tumble play and dominance in early adolescence. *Journal of Applied Developmental Psychology*, 19, 165–176. doi:10.1016/0193-3973(95)90017-9.

Pepler, D. J., Craig, W. M., & Roberts, W. L. (1998). Observations of aggressive and nonaggressive children on the school playground. *Merrill-Palmer Quarterly*, 44, 55–76. Retrieved from: http://proxyiub.uits.iu.edu/login?url=https://search-proquest-com. proxyiub.uits.iu.edu/docview/619179255?accountid=11620.

Pountain, D. & Robins, D. (2000). *Cool rules: Anatomy of an attitude*. London: Reaktion Books Ltd.

Rodkin, P. C., Farmer, T. W., Pearl, R. & Van Acker, R. (2006). They're cool: Social status and peer group supports for aggressive boys and girls. *Social Development*, 15, 175–204. doi:10.1046/j.1467-9507.2006.00336.x.

Rodkin, P. C., Ryan, A. M., Jamison, R., & Wilson, T. (2013). Social goals, social behavior, and social status in middle childhood. *Developmental Psychology*, 49, 1139–1150. doi:10.1037/a0029389.

Rubin, K. H., Bukowski, W. M., & Parker, J. G. (2006). Peer interactions, relationships, and groups. In N. Eisenberg, W. Damon, & R. M. Lerner (Eds.), *Handbook of child psychology: Social, emotional, and personality development* (pp. 571–645). Hoboken, NJ: John Wiley & Sons Inc.

Rudolph, K. D., Abaied, J. L., Flynn, M., Sugimura, N., & Agoston, A. M. (2011). Developing relationships, being cool, and not looking like a loser: Social goal orientation predicts children's responses to peer aggression. *Child Development*, 82, 1518–1530. doi:10.1111/j.1467–8624.2011.01631.x.

Ryan, A. M., & Shim, S. S. (2006). Social achievement goals: The nature and consequences of different orientations toward social competence. *Personality and Social Psychology Bulletin*, 32, 1246–1263. doi:10.1177/0146167206289345.

Ryan, A. M., & Shim, S. S. (2008). An exploration of young adolescents' social achievement goals and social adjustment in middle school. *Journal of Educational Psychology*, 100, 672–687. doi:10.1037/0022-0663.100.3.672.

Ryan, A. M., Hicks, L., & Midgley, C. (1997). Social goals, academic goals, and avoiding seeking help in the classroom. *Journal of Early Adolescence*, 17, 152–171. doi:10.1177/0272431697017002003.

Salmivalli, C., Huttunen, A., & Lagerspetz, K. (1997). Peer networks and bullying in school. *Scandinavian Journal of Psychology*, 38, 305–312. doi:10.1111/1467-9450.00040.

Shoulberg, E. K., Sijtsema, J. J., & Murray-Close, D. (2011). The association between valuing popularity and relational aggression: The moderating effects of actual popularity and physical reactivity to exclusion. *Journal of Experimental Child Psychology*, 110, 20–37. doi:10.1016/j.jecp.2011.03.008.

Sijtsema, J. J., Veenstra, R., Lindenberg, S., & Salmivalli, C. (2009). Empirical test of bullies' status goals: Assessing direct goals, aggression, and prestige. *Aggressive Behavior*, 35, 57–67. doi:10.1002/ab.20282.

Wentzel, K. R. & Asher, S. A. (1995). Academic lives of neglected, rejected, popular, and controversial children. *Child Development, 66,* 754–763. doi:10.2307/1131948.

Xie, H.Cairns, R. B., & Cairns, B. D. (1999). Social networks and configurations in inner-city schools: Aggression, popularity, and implications for students with EBD. *Journal of Emotional and Behavioral Disorders, 7,* 147–155. doi:10.1177/106342669900700303.

PART III

Social Goals in Context

10

SOCIAL GOALS IN CONTEXT
Asian Students

Kara A. Makara

This chapter provides a critical review of Asian students' social goals, including salient cultural values in Asian contexts that may influence students' approaches to social relationships, research on students' social goals across different Asian countries, and differences in Asian and non-Asian students' social goals. This synthesis provides insights into why some Asian students may adopt specific social goals, the complex ways in which Asian students' social goals may be associated with academic goals, and the impact of social goals on academic, interpersonal, and intrapersonal outcomes. The chapter concludes with measurement issues in this area and recommendations for future research.

Schools are highly social settings. Not surprisingly, students may place just as much emphasis on social goals as they do academic goals when in the classroom (Covington, 2000). In fact, students tend to rate social goals, such as wanting to develop friendships with peers, higher than their academic goals (Dowson & McInerney, 2003; Horst et al., 2007; Ryan & Shim, 2006). However, research on social goals is lacking compared to academic goals, and further, research on Asian students' social goals in educational contexts is lacking compared to Western populations. Nearly 60% (4.5 billion) of the current global population lives in Asia. The continent of Asia contains numerous countries, which can be grouped by region: East Asia (e.g., China, Japan), Southeast Asia (e.g., Indonesia, Philippines), Southern Asia (e.g., India, Pakistan), Central Asia (e.g., Uzbekistan, Kazakhstan) and Western Asia/Middle East (e.g., Turkey, Iraq). There are also numerous people of Asian ancestry in Western countries, for example, 5.6% of the United States population and 7.1% of the United Kingdom population identify as Asian (US Census Bureau, 2017; UK Office for National Statistics, 2018). A synthesis of the research on social goals from this significant population

174 Kara A. Makara

can inform researchers and educators around the world who are interested in better understanding and supporting adaptive social motivation for Asian students.

In light of this, the aim of the chapter is to provide a critical review of the research on Asian students' social goals. The first part of this chapter reviews different approaches to how social goals have been defined and conceptualized in the literature. The second part critically examines cultural factors that are salient in Asian contexts that may influence the nature of students' social goals. This part also includes a synthesis of extant research on Asian students' social goals and research on differences in social goals between Asian and non-Asian students. The third part of the chapter reviews research on the implications of Asian students' social goals for academic behaviors and achievement. The fourth part reviews research on the implications of social goals in Asian contexts for interpersonal and intrapersonal outcomes. Finally, the fifth part describes a number of measurement issues within research on Asian students' social goals and proposes recommendations for future research.

Definition of Social Goals

In order to conceptualize social goals within an Asian context, it is necessary to first consider what is meant by social goals. Students' social goals have been defined in multiple ways (e.g., Dweck & Leggett, 1988; Gable, 2006; Jarvinen & Nicholls, 1996; Ryan & Shim, 2006; Urdan & Maehr, 1995; Wentzel, 1994). One approach focuses on social reasons for engaging in academic work (Urdan & Maehr, 1995; Urdan, 1997; Yang & Yu, 1988), such as the desire for approval from parents or teachers. Similarly, King, McInerney, and colleagues (Dowson & McInerney, 2003; King, McInerney, & Watkins, 2010; King & Watkins, 2012) define social goals as "the social reasons students espouse for wanting to achieve in academic situations" (Dowson & McInerney, 2003, p. 100). This approach recognizes that some students strive to do well academically, not just for academic reasons but also for underlying social reasons such as to please one's parents. Importantly, one factor influencing the development of this approach to social goals is a concern that the academic goal construct developed in Western cultures focuses on individual goals, whereas in collectivist cultures, relational goals may be more prominent (King & Watkins, 2012; Urdan & Maehr, 1995; Yang & Yu, 1988).

In contrast, a second approach conceptualizes social goals in terms of "goal content, which are the "cognitive representations of what an individual is trying to achieve" in a given social situation (Kiefer et al., 2013, p. 45). In other words, this is what students are trying to achieve socially when they are with their friends, for example, to be the most popular student, to be helpful to others, to not be alone, or to have meaningful and deep friendships. Wentzel (1994, 1996) has extensively identified and studied various social goals that students strive for in classrooms, including goals to earn approval from others, goals to keep friendships, goals to be socially responsible, or prosocial goals, which involve being dependable, responsible, cooperative, and helpful to others. Similarly, Jarvinen and Nicholls (1996, p. 435) followed a content approach and define social goals as "the types of social outcomes that individuals prefer." These researchers identified six types of social goals: intimacy, nurturance, dominance, leadership, popularity, and avoidance. It is notable that studies using this approach are largely limited to a Western educational context.

A third approach has conceptualized social goals in terms of goal orientations. This approach, based on Achievement Goal Theory, proposes that students have similar orientations towards achievement in the social domain as they do in the academic domain (e.g., Blumenfeld, 1992; Dweck & Leggett, 1988). For example, Ryan and Shim (2006, 2008) framed social goals in a manner parallel to the three-goal Achievement Goal framework typically used to describe academic goals. Social development captures the desire to develop and maintain high-quality friendships; social demonstration-approach represents wanting to be popular and a focus on interpersonal comparisons; and social demonstration-avoidance is a concern with avoiding being made fun of or looking unpopular. As another example of applying achievement goal theory to social goals, Gable (2006) and Elliot, Gable, and Mapes (2006) conceptualized approach and avoidance social goals, which are respectively linked to need for affiliation and fear or rejection, and labeled these as friendship-approach and friendship-avoidance goals. Similar to the goal content approach, the initial studies in this area were largely conducted in a Western educational context.

Research on social goals within Asian contexts

Although the theoretical conceptualizations of social goals are presumed to be universal in nature, the salience of different types of goals, whether certain goals are adaptive or not, and whether these frameworks accurately capture the full nature of social motivation for students in Asian contexts is arguably not certain. This section begins with an examination of cultural factors and influences on the nature of students' social goals in Asian contexts. Next follows a review of research on differences in social goals between Asian countries, including acknowledgment of heterogeneity between and within Asian countries. This section concludes with a review of the research on differences in Asian and non-Asian students' social goals, with particular emphasis on potential differences in avoidance-oriented social goals.

Cultural influences on Asian students' social goals

Traditionally, scholars have used a "collectivist," "interdependent," or "relatedness" paradigm to describe Asian students' approach to social relationships, in contrast to an "individualistic," "independent," or "autonomous" paradigm for Western students. Oyserman and colleagues (2002) provide a thorough review of the concepts of collectivism and individualism. For students who are higher in the cultural orientation of individualism, one's well-being is linked to the attainment of one's personal goals; personal success is valued, judgments or causal inferences about the world are oriented toward the self, and reasoning is decontextualized and not bound to a social context (Oyserman et al., 2002; Markus & Kitayama, 1991). Collectivism, on the other hand, is considered a more diverse construct than individualism, with a focus on group membership as central to one's identity, emphasis on interdependence; well-being is linked to carrying out social roles and obligations, the social context is highly relevant in decision-making, and group memberships are largely permanent (Markus & Kitayama, 1991; Oyserman et al., 2002). Asian countries such as China, India, Japan, and the Philippines tend to have collectivist cultural patterns, in contrast to the US, UK, or Western European countries which tend to have individualistic cultural patterns (Triandis, 1989; Hofstede, 2001).

Given these differences in cultural orientation, it is likely that the social context matters more for students who have a collectivist cultural orientation when deciding what type of goal to pursue, whereas it may be more of a personal decision for students who have an individualistic cultural orientation (Yu & Yang, 1994). For example, a student with an individualistic "construal" (Markus & Kitayama, 1991) may adopt prosocial goals because he or she personally wants this goal and links it to an abstract concept of being a good individual, whereas a student with a collectivist construal may adopt prosocial goals because of expectations from parents and teachers. Not surprisingly, researchers have proposed that social goals should be studied alongside these self-construals (e.g., Urdan & Maehr, 1995). In line with this, researchers developed the concept of "social-oriented achievement motivation," driven by a Confucian emphasis on cooperation in the family (Yu & Yang, 1994), to explain Asian students' motivation. This social-oriented achievement motivation refers to being motivated by one's groups' definition of the "goals, standards, means of goal attainment, and acceptance of achievement outcome" (Bernardo, 2008, p. 887). This is viewed in contrast to "individually-oriented achievement motivation," in which the goals and standards are defined by the students themselves (Yang & Yu, 1988, as cited in Chang & Wong, 2008).

The differences between collectivistic and individualistic cultural patterns also have implications for what types of goals students want to pursue in social situations or their orientations toward social achievement. For example, one may assume that goals to be more prosocial may be more dominant in collectivist cultures, because the focus is on others more than the self. However, this assumption may be too simplistic. Some interesting research has found less prosocial behavior, at least towards adults, among Eastern (Malaysian and Indonesian) children compared to Western (German, Israeli) children (Trommsdorff, Friedlmeier, & Mayer, 2007). The authors explain that Eastern cultures promote interdependence and respect for authority, thus it may be more important in social situations to refrain from helping in order to not risk that the other person loses face (i.e., is embarrassed). Differences in cultural patterns may also have implications for the associations among different social goals. For example, in our study examining Chinese university students' social achievement goals, we noted that the positive correlation between social development (wanting to improve personal relationships) and social demonstration goals (wanting to appear popular to others) was much stronger than those found in Western samples, suggesting that Chinese students may differentiate less between intrapersonal and interpersonal goals (Shim et al., 2017).

Although "collectivism" may be loosely applied to those from Asian countries, it is critical to note that there is great diversity in the national characteristics between different countries in Asia. For example, consider two countries from East Asia: China and Japan. According to cross-cultural comparisons such as those by Hofstede (2001), Japan and China are quite different, with Japan rating lower in power distance, higher in individualism, higher in masculinity, significantly higher in uncertainty avoidance, and higher in indulgence. These differences may have implications for average country-level differences in the social goals that Chinese and Japanese students adopt and how they approach relationships with their peers. For example, Hofstede's dimension of "masculinity" is associated with wanting to be the best, assertiveness, and achievement, whereas "femininity" is associated with cooperation, caring for others, and modesty. Given that Japan rated higher in masculinity compared to China, one could hypothesize that students may report higher levels of demonstration-approach and dominance-related social goals in Japan compared to China. Hofstede's research has limitations (for a discussion of the criticisms see Spector et al., 2001; Baskerville, 2003), so these national differences should be interpreted with some caution.

Differences across nationalities in Asian students' social goals

As stated earlier, Asia contains a large number of countries that vary greatly from one another. However, it appears that much of the research on Asian students' social goals focuses on students primarily from East and Southeast Asia. For example, there have been numerous studies on Chinese students' social goals, including Chinese middle school students (e.g., Cheng & Lam, 2013; Wright, Li, & Shi, 2014), high school students (e.g., Ng, 2018; Nie & Liem, 2013; Wang, King, & Rao, 2018), and university students (e.g., Chang & Wong, 2008; Shim, Wang, & Makara et al., 2017). There have also been several social goals studies on students from the Philippines, including secondary students (e.g., King, McInerney, & Watkins, 2012; King, Ganotice, & Watkins, 2014) and university students (e.g., Bernardo, 2008) as well as on students from Japan, including children (e.g., Nakaya, 1999; Machi & Nakaya, 2014) and early adolescents (e.g., Kuroda & Sakurai, 2011). Other Asian nationalities or republics represented in research pertaining to students' social goals, although to a lesser degree, include South

Korea (Lee, 2018), Indonesia (Liem & Nie, 2008), Hong Kong (Watkins & Hattie, 2012), Singapore (Chang & Wong, 2008), Turkey (Bahar, Uğur, & Asil, 2018), and India (Agarwal & Misra, 1986).

Only a handful of studies directly compare social goals of students from different Asian countries. These studies offer some valuable explanations for why differences may or may not exist, which help to highlight the importance of understanding the interactions between culture and sociocultural, political, and education-system influences on students' social goals. For example, Liem and Nie (2008) exploring differences in Chinese and Indonesian secondary students' individually oriented and socially oriented achievement motivations. Although there were some similarities, differences included that Chinese students rated higher on individual-oriented achievement motivation and academic mastery-approach goals, whereas Indonesian students rated higher on social-oriented achievement motivation, conformity, tradition, and performance-approach goals. The authors note that due to policies in the 1980s, mainland China has increasingly adopted Western individualist values, whereas globalization in Indonesia has been more recent since. Furthermore, Indonesia is more multiethnic and multireligious, and their society values maintaining harmonious social relationships. These interesting differences between countries may explain why Indonesian students in this sample may report greater socially oriented achievement motivations as compared to Chinese students.

As a second example, King, Ganotice, and Watkins (2014) compared Chinese and Filipino students' social goals (affiliation, approval, concern, and social status), academic goals, and self-regulated learning strategy use. The associations uncovered in their study suggest that social goals largely function similarly for both populations, although interestingly, social affiliation goals are not significantly correlated with performance goals for Chinese students from Hong Kong ($r = -.02$), but they are significantly correlated for Filipino students ($r = .31$). In both countries, spending a lot of effort on studying is viewed as a way to improve one's status in society, thus potentially explaining why social status goals predicted self-regulation in both Chinese and Filipino students. However, academic performance goals differed in this study, and the authors suggest the unique competitive nature of testing in Hong Kong may mean that performance goals function differently there than in the Philippines.

Note that comparing individuals by country has limitations, as there is significant variation within countries as well. Many comparative studies indicate that there is more variance within countries than between countries across a range of student outcomes, for example, in motivational-related variables of autonomy, relatedness, and competence (Fischer & Schwartz, 2011) and in cultural values (Taras, Steel, & Kirkman, 2016). It is predicted that with increased globalization, the psychological differences of people will continue to vary more within countries than between countries (Greenfield, 2013). Furthermore, there is recognition of the problems of equating culture with one's nationality (Baskerville, 2003; Matsumoto & Yoo, 2006). Therefore, it is important to be aware that studies comparing one country to another tend to focus on relatively smaller group-level differences rather than on the variance within each population.

It is necessary to fully explore what we mean by culture when trying to interpret cross-country or cross-cultural differences in individuals (Matsumoto & Yoo, 2006). For example, consider the concept of independent and interdependent self-construal and its implication for social goals. One cannot and should not assume that everyone from Asian countries necessarily has interdependent self-construal and thus if this variable is of interest it should be measured. A helpful example of a study acknowledging heterogeneity within a specific Asian population is Cheng and Lam's (2013) study examining the interactions between Chinese students' social goals and their independent versus interdependent self-construals on students' motivation and academic behaviors. These researchers found that social goals (defined as doing well academically in order to please others) led to lower academic avoidance of help seeking and higher willingness to improve after failure, but only for those Chinese students who simultaneously reported an interdependent self-construal. Students in the same sample who reported higher independent self-construal alongside social goals had negative academic behaviors, which was further supported by an experimental study with social goal manipulation.

The review in this section highlights the amount and diversity of research conducted on students' social goals from different Asian countries, while at the same time, the paucity of research on students from particular countries especially those in Southern and Western Asia. Note that India, Indonesia, Pakistan, and Bangladesh are within the top five most populous countries in Asia (after China), yet research on students' social goals from these countries is lacking. Also critical to note is the lack of comparative research specifically on the social goals of Asian students living in Western countries, such as Asian Americans. Findings from comparative research on Asian American students' academic achievement goals (for example, Zusho, Pintrich, & Cortina, 2005) might be useful for informing hypotheses about Asian American students' social goals in the classroom.

Differences between Asian and non-Asian students' social goals

This section focuses on research examining differences in social goals at school between Asian and non-Asian (i.e., largely Western) contexts. One interesting area of comparison between Asian and non-Asian students' social goals are the potential differences in avoidance-oriented social goals. Asian students may be more likely to adopt higher avoidance-oriented goals compared to Western students, due to being motivated more by failure than by success (Heine et al., 2001; Kitayama et al., 1997; Zusho, Pintrich, & Cortina, 2005) and due to the potentially beneficial academic outcomes of avoidance goals for those who are high in collectivism (King, 2016). In line with this prediction, Elliot, Chirkov, Kim, and Sheldon (2001) found that Asian American students adopted more avoidance personal goals compared to non-Asian Americans, and similarly, South Korean and Russian (collectivist) students adopted more avoidance personal goals compared to (individualist) students from the United States.

However, it is unclear whether differences in the level of such goals translates into differences in how avoidance-oriented social goals function. There is substantial evidence in the academic domain that Asian and non-Asian students differ in terms of how avoidance goals function. According to a large meta-analysis, performance-avoidance academic goals are significantly and positively correlated with academic performance outcomes for collectivist Asian samples, and negatively correlated with performance among individualistic Western samples (Hulleman et al., 2010). One noteworthy study explored this phenomenon through measuring within-sample differences in collectivism (King, 2016). King (2016) found that Filipino students' level of collectivism moderates the relationship between avoidance academic goals and adaptive academic outcomes. In contrast, another study found that avoidance academic goals were similarly maladaptive for academic performance for both Asian American and Anglo-American students, although this may be due to the context of a Western school (Zusho et al., 2005). Finally, in a study focusing on personal goals rather than social goals per se, avoidance-oriented social goals negatively predicted well-being in an individualist country but not in two collectivist countries (Elliot et al., 2001).

This interesting cross-cultural difference in performance-avoidance goals in the academic domain leads to the question of whether avoidance motivation in the social domain (e.g., trying to avoid looking unpopular) might similarly be adaptive for Asian students and maladaptive for Western students. There is a lack of cross-cultural research on social goals so comparisons must be made between studies from different countries to explore whether similar patterns emerge, despite limitations of such approaches. Studies of social avoidance goals in Asian contexts suggests that they are harmful for personal outcomes (e.g. Kuroda & Sakarai, 2011; Shim et al., 2017) and neutral for academic outcomes (Zhao, Zhu, & Zhao, 2016). Studies of social avoidance goals in Western contexts suggest they are similarly harmful for personal outcomes (e.g., Gable 2006; Horst et al., 2007; Mouratidis & Sideridis, 2009; Shim, Wang, & Cassady, 2013; Shim & Ryan, 2012). Results of social avoidance goals for Western students' academic outcomes are mixed, as evidenced by social avoidance goals negatively predicting academic help seeking (Roussel Elliot, & Feltman, 2011) and either unrelated to academic achievement (Ben-Eliyahu, Linnenbrink-Garcia, & Putallaz, 2017) or slightly positively related to academic achievement (Makara & Madjar, 2015). Interestingly, then, social avoidance-oriented goals may not be that different in terms of how they function for Asian and non-Asian students. Comparative work in this area is needed as studies vary widely in their measures of social goals, in the age of the participants, and in different academic and social outcomes, so it is difficult to draw strong conclusions.

Another consideration when examining differences between Asian and non-Asian students' social goals is the extent to which the conceptualization of social goals differs, in other words, whether social goals are universal in nature. It is a challenging area to explore because of measurement issues such as applying a social goal measure developed in a Western country in order to examine social goals in Asian countries. Triandis (1989) notes that in individualistic cultures, competition tends to be interpersonal, whereas in collectivist cultures, competition tends to be intergroup. Therefore, arguably, performance-oriented social goals may need to be re-conceptualized for Asian students to distinguish between students' goals for their peer relationships within their friend group and with peers outside of their friend group. It can be hypothesized that perhaps Asian students may only have higher aggression, social status focus, or demonstration-oriented social goals towards peers who are considered in the out-group, whereas non-Asian students may be less likely to differentiate in their social goals for in-group or out-group peers.

Furthermore, there may be a lack of nuance in the direction of performance-focused (i.e., demonstration, competitive, or status-focused) social goals. Most measures of social goals simply ask about one's status in relation to others, but do not ask whom the students are comparing themselves to at school. Research suggests that social comparisons can be made upwards towards students doing better, in parallel with students of relatively equal ability, or downwards by comparing oneself with those who are less skilled (Suls, Martin, & Wheeler, 2002). Research on Chinese adolescent students' academic goals, direction of social comparison, and subjective well-being has found that upwards social comparison is positive for subjective well-being, whereas downwards social comparison is harmful (Tian, Yu, & Huebner, 2017). It is possible that Asian students and Western students differ in the extent to which they engage in upwards, parallel, or downwards comparisons in the social domain as well, which could explain why there may be differences in how adaptive or maladaptive competitive social goals are for Asian and non-Asian students who adopt these goals at school.

There are many opportunities for future research in this area, since in general there is not yet sufficient research to draw strong conclusions between differences in Asian and non-Asian students' social goals. There are several important research questions that can be considered when comparing Asian and Western students' social goals. One is whether students differ in their average level of particular social goals; in other words, do some goals tend to be more dominant than other goals in an Asian context? Two is whether there are some social goals that are quite universal in nature and others that are only specific to Asian and Western contexts? Three is the salience of social goals compared to other types of goals, for example, how important (or differentiated) are Asian students' social goals compared to academic goals and does this differ from students from Western contexts? Four is differences in the function of social goals, for example, whether there are Asian and Western differences in the consequences of adopting particular social goals, such as social avoidance goals. Finally, it is worth considering whether there are cultural differences in the developmental influences and causes of social goals.

Academic Outcomes of Asian Students' Social Goals

Learning at school is part of a social process and therefore it should not be surprising that students' social goals will have implications for their academic outcomes, such as their academic motivation and academic behaviors like use of self-regulated learning strategies and engagement in the classroom. Through focusing on building relationships with others and feeling a sense of belonging at school, students may be more motivated to learn and have more enjoyment at school. In the reverse, students who are not accepted by their peers avoid school and have lower academic achievement. Furthermore, through effectively collaborating with peers, social interactions can directly help students to learn and achieve (King, McInerney, & Watkins, 2012). However, in schools where doing well academically is not a desirable trait among the popular students, students who are concerned with popularity may self-handicap or be less academically engaged (e.g., Ben-Eliyahu, Linnenbrink-Garcia, & Putallaz, 2017). The literature on Asian students' social goals and their academic outcomes is summarized below and suggests that social goals matter for Asian students' academic approaches at school, either in conjunction with or beyond the role of academic goals. However, note that in general there is very little research on the relationship between social goals and academic outcomes, in either Western or Asian populations.

Some initial studies on social goals in Asian contexts have indicated that social goals are associated with students' academic achievement goals. For example, Bernardo's (2008) study on Filipino university students found that parent-oriented motivations were positively associated with students' mastery goals, whereas both parent-oriented and teacher-oriented motivations were positively associated with students' performance goals. As another example, King, Ganotice, and Watkins (2014) found that social goals (approval, concern, affiliation, and status goals) were significantly related to academic mastery and performance goals, although in different patterns for students from Hong Kong and the Philippines. Notably, among Filipino students, all of the social goals were associated with mastery and performance goals although status goals were more strongly related to performance goals, whereas for students from Hong Kong, mastery but not performance goals were correlated with social affiliation goals, performance goals were more strongly correlated with approval and status goals, and mastery was more strongly correlated with social concern goals. Chang and Wong (2008), in a study of Chinese university students, found that a socially oriented goal (i.e., social reasons for studying) was related positively with students' performance goals, mastery goals, and competitive motives; although it was unrelated with mastery motives.

Social goals are also associated with self-regulated learning and use of particular learning strategies at school. Among Chinese students, social status goals had indirect effects on Chinese students' self-regulated learning strategy use, while parent-oriented goals (wanting to do well at school in order to get parents' approval) had direct effects on self-regulated learning strategy use (Wang, King, & Rao, 2018). In students from Hong Kong, a goal for social approval was the strongest predictor of deep learning (compared to mastery and performance goals) and social status goals were the second most powerful predictors for self-regulation for students in both Hong Kong and the Philippines (King, Ganotice, & Watkins, 2014). In an interesting study looking at the interactive effects of Chinese students' social goals with self-construal, Cheng and Lam (2013) found that social goals predicted lower avoidance of help seeking and higher willingness to improve after failure, but only for students who simultaneously had an interdependent self-construal.

Social goals predict Asian students' academic engagement as well. In a study on Chinese university students, both social mastery goals (having high-quality friendships) and social performance-approach goals (being seen as popular) positively predicted students' study engagement (defined as learning-related vigor, dedication, and absorption), whereas social avoidance goals (concern about being unpopular) were not significantly related (Zhao, Zhu, & Zhao, 2016). Among Filipino secondary students, social goals predicted academic engagement at school even after controlling for the influence of students' academic goals (King, McInerney, & Watkins, 2012). Specifically, social concern goals (doing well at school in order to help others), social responsibility goals (doing well at school to show I am a responsible student), and to a lesser extent social status goals (doing well at school so I can appear successful in the future), stood out as positively predicting emotional engagement, behavioral engagement, and cognitive engagement in learning at school. In a comparative study of students from Hong Kong and the Philippines, social goals predicted deep learning, motivational engagement, and effort for both cultures (King, McInerney, & Watkins, 2013).

Interpersonal and Intrapersonal Outcomes of Asian Students' Social Goals

Asian students' social goals also matter for their social behaviors, social outcomes, and their own well-being. The goals that students have for their relationships with others, such as their orientations toward their peers, may affect how individuals interact with those peers. Students with a goal to be prosocial should in turn act more kindly towards their peers. If one has a goal to be aggressive towards peers, it is likely to translate into aggressive behavior towards peers. Aggressive behavior, in turn, might make a student less liked among peers at school. Furthermore, students' social goals may also influence how they interpret and react to social cues and interactions around them, which can influence their own psychological adjustment (Shim et al., 2017). For example, a student who is highly concerned about looking popular may interpret normal disagreements between peers as an attack on their social status, and end up angry or upset after challenging social interactions. Alternatively, a student who wants to be a good friend and understand others may end up more reflective or open to new perspectives after challenging social interactions.

Many researchers characterize students' social behaviors into two types: prosocial behavior and aggressive behavior. For example, Wright, Li, and Shi (2014) investigated how social status goals were related to aggressive and prosocial behaviors among Chinese adolescents. They found that after controlling for each other, students' social preference goals (wanting to be the most liked) were negatively related to self-reported overt aggression, and positively associated with prosocial behaviors as reported by self, peers, and teachers, whereas students' popularity goals (to be the most popular) were not uniquely related to either aggressive or prosocial behaviors. As another example, using a person-centered approach to identify profiles of South Korean students' social achievement goals, Lee (2018) examined differences in a range of social behaviors and found that demonstration-oriented students reported higher aggression, higher social anxiety, and low quality friendships. It is noteworthy, however, that students in this study who rated high on all three goals (development, demonstration-approach, and demonstration-avoidance) fared comparatively well in terms of their social outcomes, thus demonstration goals may not be harmful for South Korean students' friendships if simultaneously paired with high development goals.

Asian students' social goals also matter for various aspects of their well-being and psychological adjustment. In a study on Japanese early adolescents, students with higher social learning goals (similar to social development goals) helped students to have less depression following high interpersonal stress, whereas if they had low social learning goals, then they had a higher increase in depression (Kuroda & Sakurai, 2011). Interestingly, in a sample of Chinese university students, social performance-avoidance goals predicted depressive symptoms, whereas social performance-approach goals negatively predicted depressive symptoms, although the effect sizes were small (Zhao, Zhu, & Zhao, 2016). Among Chinese university students, social development goals positively predicted emotion regulation, whereas social demonstration-approach and -avoidance goals negatively predicted emotion regulation, and in turn, the effects of social goals on students' life satisfaction, depression, stress, and worry were partially or fully mediated via emotion regulation (Shim, Wang, Makara, Xu, Xie, & Zhong, 2017). In summary, Asian students' social goals focused on improving friendships and appearing popular tend to be associated with greater psychological adjustment, whereas social goals focused on avoiding looking unpopular tend to be associated with greater depression.

Recommendations for Future Research

One of the major measurement issues in social goals stems from the need for conceptual clarity. Due to the variety of ways that social goals have been conceptualized, a variety of different measures have been developed and used in the literature on social goals, which makes it difficult to synthesize the research and compare and contrast studies. As noted by Kiefer et al. (2013), these different ways of framing social goals are not meant to be contrasting models, but rather complementary models taking different perspectives. However, more work is needed to systematically explore the different ways social goals are framed – as social reasons for engaging academically, as a content approach to social goals focused on what students are trying to achieve socially at school, and as a goal orientation approach focused on the underlying reasons why students are trying to be socially competent – and the validity of these approaches in Asian contexts. Given the relative lack of research using the content approach to social goals in Asian contexts (Ng, 2018, is an exception), this would be an interesting area to explore in Asian contexts.

A second measurement issue is that the models and measures of social goals are often developed in Western countries and then adapted to Asian contexts. While some of the major scales have been validated in Asian contexts (e.g., Zhao, Zhu, & Zhao, 2016), it does not mean they fully capture everything that is relevant to Asian students' social motivation. There is a need for models and measures to be developed within Asian contexts. One approach is to begin with exploratory qualitative research to identify what Asian students are trying to achieve socially and their reasons for their social behaviors at school, and then use these findings to identify factors and develop new scales. While this can lead to over-proliferation of measures, such approaches may help to highlight which aspects of social goals are universal and which may be unique to the Asian context. In cases where the measure is developed in a Western context and then applied in an Asian context, it would be best practice if part of the translation and adaptation process includes cognitive interviewing to ensure that the meaning of the items and scales is the same across cultures.

A third measurement issue is the lack of diverse statistical methods and limited research approaches for examining social goals. Most of the quantitative research on Asian students' social goals examines the effect of each social goal independently, however, given the intercorrelations among different types of social goals, person-centered approaches may be useful for uncovering profiles of social goals and how they relate to a variety of outcomes. A great example is Lee (2018) who used latent profile analysis to explore South Korean students' social achievement goals. Furthermore, the majority of research conducted on social goals has relied on self-report surveys. There are limitations to such methodological approaches, including socially desirable response bias, and cultural differences in responding to Likert scales (referred to as the reference-group effect) when conducting cross-cultural comparative research (Heine et al., 2002). Expanding to other research approaches (i.e., experiments, interviews) would address some of these limitations. Cheng and Lam (2013) provide an example of one way to manipulate social goals in an experimental design.

A fourth measurement issue is the confounding of broader cultural, political, and historical influences on the educational environment with students' personal culture that they bring to the classroom. There is likely a complex interaction

186 Kara A. Makara

between students and the environment whereby students' personal culture and upbringing influence their social motivation, but the broader culture of the classroom environment can also influence students' social motivation. One approach to explore these issues is through comparing Asian students living in Asian contexts and Western students living in Western contexts with Asian students attending schooling in Western contexts. It would equally be interesting to include Western students who move into or study abroad in Asian contexts to help determine the degree of influence from Asian educational systems, although there is currently less population flow in this direction. Comparing the social goals of Asian students who study abroad in a Western context with Asian students who study in their home countries can help to uncover the role of the educational and social context of the classroom. There are still confounders and limitations of such approaches, such as potentially unique characteristics of students who study abroad, but it would be an interesting area for exploration.

Finally, there are some further areas of research needed in order to better understand Asian students' social goals and to help foster adaptive social goals. As research expands to other populations of Asian students, we can begin to determine the extent to which nuanced differences in culture and educational systems influence students' social goals. More research is also needed regarding individual differences in Asian students' social goals, such as differences by gender, age, level of schooling, or socioeconomic status, so that support can be more appropriately targeted. It is also valuable to understand how Asian students' goals develop. Makara and Madjar's (2015) longitudinal study of Western students' social goals found that despite some stability, social goals were sensitive to perceptions of the educational context and changed over time. For example, we found that students who perceived their classroom as having a performance-avoidant goal structure decreased in their development-focused social goals and increased in their demonstration-focused social goals. However, there is currently a lack of cross-cultural work in this area. It is possible that Asian and Western students differ in how stable their social goals are across time and in the extent to which different social factors (e.g., teachers, parents, peers) impact the adoption of particular social goals. This would be an interesting area for future researchers to explore in order to better understand how to structure educational environments and provide interventions and practices that can effectively encourage students in Asian contexts or in multicultural contexts to adopt adaptive social goals.

Conclusion

The aim of this chapter was to provide a critical review of Asian students' social goals and offer insights for research on students' social goals. This chapter included a review of (1) different conceptualizations of social goals, (2) cultural factors that influence the nature of Asian social goals, research on students' social goals conducted across different Asian countries, and differences in Asian and non-Asian students' social goals, (3) how social goals are associated with a range of academic-related variables in Asian contexts, (4) how social goals are associated with interpersonal and intrapersonal outcomes in Asian contexts, and (5) measurement issues in this area and recommendations for future research. The chapter has two notable limitations, one being that it has only reviewed research that has been published in English, and two that the author is providing an outsider perspective on this field of research rather than a lived experience. However, this chapter aims to make a novel contribution to the literature through providing a critical synthesis of the complex research on social goals in Asian contexts.

The research on Asian students' social goals provides interesting insights regarding why students may adopt particular goals, complex ways in which social goals may be associated with academic goals (such as the social goal behind the academic goal), and how particular goals may or may not be maladaptive for students depending upon the cultural and educational context. As motivation researchers continue to recognize the salience and importance of students' social motivation at school, ideally research in this area will expand to more diverse Asian contexts as well. Throughout the chapter there are recommendations for future research in this area, such as using more diverse and creative methodological approaches to ensure Western-based theories are not limiting our understanding of Asian students' social goals. Finally, it is hoped that this review has accomplished the simultaneous intentions of summarizing findings on Asian students' social goals while also highlighting the rich diversity and complexity of Asian contexts.

References

Agarwal, R., & Misra, G. (1986). A factor analytic study of achievement goals and means: An Indian view. *International Journal of Psychology*, 21(1–4), 717–731.

Bahar, M., Uğur, H., & Asil, M. (2018). Social achievement goals and students' socioeconomic status: Cross-cultural validation and gender invariance. *Issues in Educational Research*, 28(3), 511.

Baskerville, R. F. (2003). Hofstede never studied culture. *Accounting, Organizations and Society*, 28(1), 1–14.

Ben-Eliyahu, A., Linnenbrink-Garcia, L., & Putallaz, M. (2017). The intertwined nature of adolescents' social and academic lives: Social and academic goal orientations. *Journal of Advanced Academics*, 28(1), 66–93.

Bernardo, A. B. (2008). Individual and social dimensions of Filipino students' achievement goals. *International Journal of Psychology*, 43(5), 886–891.

Bernardo, A. B., & Ismail, R. (2010). Social perceptions of achieving students and achievement goals of students in Malaysia and the Philippines. *Social Psychology of Education*, 13(3), 385–407.

Blumenfeld, P. C. (1992). Classroom learning and motivation: Clarifying and expanding goal theory. *Journal of Educational Psychology*, 84(3), 272–281. doi:10.1037/0022-0663.84.3.272.

Chang, W. C., & Wong, K. (2008). Socially oriented achievement goals of Chinese university students in Singapore: Structure and relationships with achievement motives, goals and affective outcomes. *International Journal of Psychology*, 43(5), 880–885.

Cheng, R. W., & Lam, S. (2013). The interaction between social goals and self-construal on achievement motivation. *Contemporary Educational Psychology*, 38(2), 136–148.

Covington, M. V. (2000). Goal theory, motivation, and school achievement: An integrative review. *Annual Review of Psychology*, 51, 171–200. doi:10.1146/annurev.psych.51.1.171.

Dowson, M., & McInerney, D. M. (2003). What do students say about their motivational goals?: Towards a more complex and dynamic perspective on student motivation. *Contemporary Educational Psychology*, 28(1), 91–113. doi:10.1016/S0361-476X(02)00010-3.

Dweck, C. S., & Leggett, E. L. (1988). A social-cognitive approach to motivation and personality. *Psychological Review*, 95(2), 256–273. doi:10.1037//0033–0295X.95.2.256.

Elliot, A. J., Chirkov, V. I., Kim, Y., & Sheldon, K. M. (2001). A cross-cultural analysis of avoidance (relative to approach) personal goals. *Psychological Science*, 12(6), 505–510.

Elliot, A. J., Gable, S. L., & Mapes, R. R. (2006). Approach and avoidance motivation in the social domain. *Personality and Social Psychology Bulletin*, 32(3), 378–391. doi:10.1177/0146167205282153.

Fischer, R., & Schwartz, S. (2011). Whence differences in value priorities? Individual, cultural, or artifactual sources. *Journal of Cross-Cultural Psychology*, 42(7), 1127–1144.

Gable, S. L. (2006). Approach and avoidance social motives and goals. *Journal of Personality*, 74(1), 175–222. doi:10.1111/j.1467-6494.2005.00373.x.

Greenfield, P. M. (2013). The changing psychology of culture from 1800 through 2000. *Psychological Science*, 24(9), 1722–1731.

Heine, S. J., Kitayama, S., Lehman, D. R., Takata, T., Ide, E., Leung, C., & Matsumoto, H. (2001). Divergent consequences of success and failure in Japan and North America: An investigation of self-improving motivations and malleable selves. *Journal of Personality and Social Psychology*, 81(4), 599.

Heine, S. J., Lehman, D. R., Peng, K., & Greenholtz, J. (2002). What's wrong with cross-cultural comparisons of subjective Likert scales?: The reference-group effect. *Journal of personality and social psychology*, 82(6), 903.

Hofstede, G. (2001). *Culture's consequences: Comparing values, behaviors, institutions, and organizations across nations*. Thousand Oaks, CA: Sage Publications.

Horst, J. S., Finney, S. J., & Barron, K. E. (2007). Moving beyond academic achievement goal measures: A study of social achievement goals. *Contemporary Educational Psychology*, 32(4), 667–698. doi:10.1016/j.cedpsych.2006.10.011.

Hulleman, C. S., Schrager, S. M., Bodmann, S. M., & Harackiewicz, J. M. (2010). A meta-analytic review of achievement goal measures: Different labels for the same constructs or different constructs with similar labels?. *Psychological Bulletin*, 136(3), 422.

Jarvinen, D. W., & Nicholls, J. G. (1996). Adolescents' social goals, beliefs about the causes of social success, and satisfaction in peer relations. *Developmental Psychology*, 32, 435–441.

Kiefer, S. M., Matthews, Y. T., Montesino, M., Arango, L., & Preece, K. K. (2013). The effects of contextual and personal factors on young adolescents' social goals. *The Journal of Experimental Education*, 81(1), 44–67.

King, R. B. (2016). Is a performance-avoidance achievement goal always maladaptive? Not necessarily for collectivists. *Personality and Individual Differences*, 99, 190–195.

King, R. B., & Watkins, D. A. (2012). "Socializing" achievement goal theory: The need for social goals. *Psychological Studies*, 57(1), 112–116.

King, R., Ganotice, F., & Watkins, D. (2014). A cross-cultural analysis of achievement and social goals among Chinese and Filipino students. *Social Psychology of Education*, 17(3), 439–455.

King, R. B., McInerney, D. M., & Watkins, D. A. (2010). Can social goals enrich our understanding of students' motivational goals. *Journal of Psychology in Chinese Societies*, 10, 1–16.

King, R. B., McInerney, D. M., & Watkins, D. A. (2012). Studying for the sake of others: The role of social goals on academic engagement. *Educational Psychology*, 32(6), 749–776.

King, R. B., McInerney, D. M., & Watkins, D. A. (2013). Examining the role of social goals in school: A study in two collectivist cultures. *European Journal of Psychology of Education*, 28(4), 1505–1523.

Kitayama, S., Markus, H. R., Matsumoto, H., & Norasakkunkit, V. (1997). Individual and collective processes in the construction of the self: Self-enhancement in the United States and self-criticism in Japan. *Journal of Personality and Social Psychology*, 72(6), 1245–1267.

Kuroda, Y., & Sakurai, S. (2011). Social goal orientations, interpersonal stress, and depressive symptoms among early adolescents in Japan: A test of the diathesis-stress model using the trichotomous framework of social goal orientations. *The Journal of Early Adolescence*, 31(2), 300–322.

Lee, E. J. (2018). Social achievement goals and social adjustment in adolescence: A multiple-goal perspective. *Japanese Psychological Research*, 60(3), 121–133.

Li, X., & Cheung, P. (2001). Academic help-seeking: It's relation to achievement goals, social goals, self-efficacy and academic achievement. *Psychological Science (China)*, 24(1), 54–58.

Liem, A. D., & Nie, Y. (2008). Values, achievement goals, and individual-oriented and social-oriented achievement motivations among Chinese and Indonesian secondary school students. *International Journal of Psychology*, 43(5), 898–903.

Machi, T., & Nakaya, M. (2014). Reciprocal teaching intervention in elementary mathematics classrooms: Children's social goals, interactive processes, and academic achievement. *Japanese Journal of Educational Psychology*, 62, 322–335.

Makara, K. A., & Madjar, N. (2015). The role of goal structures and peer climate in trajectories of social achievement goals during high school. *Developmental Psychology*, 51(4), 473–488. doi:10.1037/a0038801.

Markus, H. R., & Kitayama, S. (1991). Culture and the self: Implications for cognition, emotion, and motivation. *Psychological Review*, 98(2), 224–253.

Matsumoto, D., & Yoo, S. H. (2006). Toward a new generation of cross-cultural research. *Perspectives on Psychological Science*, 1(3), 234–250.

Mouratidis, A. A., & Sideridis, G. D. (2009). On social achievement goals: Their relations with peer acceptance, classroom belongingness, and perceptions of loneliness. *The Journal of Experimental Education*, 77(3), 285–308.

Nakaya, M. (1999). The long-term influence of children's social responsibility goal and their achievement and adaptation to the classroom. *Japanese Journal of Counseling Science*, 32(2), 59–67.

Ng, C. H. C. (2018). High school students' motivation to learn mathematics: The role of multiple goals. *International Journal of Science and Mathematics Education*, 16(2), 357–375.

Nie, Y., & Liem, G. A. D. (2013). Extending antecedents of achievement goals: The double-edged sword effect of social-oriented achievement motive and gender differences. *Learning and Individual Differences*, 23, 249–255.

Oyserman, D., Coon, H. M., & Kemmelmeier, M. (2002). Rethinking individualism and collectivism: Evaluation of theoretical assumptions and meta-analyses. *Psychological Bulletin*, 128(1), 3–72.

Roussel, P., Elliot, A. J., & Feltman, R. (2011). The influence of achievement goals and social goals on help-seeking from peers in an academic context. *Learning and Instruction*, 21(3), 394–402.

Ryan, A., & Shim, S. S. (2006). Social achievement goals: The nature and consequences of different orientations toward social competence. *Personality and Social Psychology Bulletin*, 32, 1246–1263. doi:10.1177/0146167206289345.

Ryan, A., & Shim, S. S. (2008). Young adolescents' social achievement goals: Implications for social adjustment in middle school. *Journal of Educational Psychology*, 100, 672–687. doi:10.1037/0022–0663.100.3.672.

Shim, S. S., & Ryan, A. M. (2012). What do students want socially when they arrive at college? Implications of social achievement goals for social behaviors and adjustment during the first semester of college. *Motivation and Emotion*, 36(4), 504–515.

Shim, S. S., Wang, C., & Cassady, J. C. (2013). Emotional well-being: The role of social achievement goals and self-esteem. *Personality and Individual Differences*, 55(7), 840–845.

Shim, S. S., Wang, C., Makara, K. A., Xu, X., Xie, L., & Zhong, M. (2017). College students' social goals and psychological adjustment: Mediation via emotion regulation. *Journal of College Student Development*, 58(8), 1237–1255.

Spector, P. E., Cooper, C. L., & Sparks, K. (2001). An international study of the psychometric properties of the Hofstede Values Survey Module 1994: A comparison of individual and country/province level results. *Applied Psychology*, 50(2), 269–281.

Suls, J., Martin, R., & Wheeler, L. (2002). Social comparison: Why, with whom, and with what effect?. *Current Directions in Psychological Science*, 11(5), 159–163.

Taras, V., Steel, P., & Kirkman, B. L. (2016). Does country equate with culture? Beyond geography in the search for cultural boundaries. *Management International Review*, 56(4), 455–487.

Tian, L., Yu, T., & Huebner, E. S. (2017). Achievement goal orientations and adolescents' subjective well-being in school: The mediating roles of academic social comparison directions. *Frontiers in Psychology*, 8, 37.

Triandis, H. C. (1989). The self and social behavior in differing cultural contexts. *Psychological Review*, 96(3), 506–520.

Trommsdorff, G., Friedlmeier, W., & Mayer, B. (2007). Sympathy, distress, and prosocial behavior of preschool children in four cultures. *International Journal of Behavioral Development*, 31(3), 284–293.

United Kingdom Office for National Statistics. (2013). Young people by ethnicity in England and UK: Table 2. The proportion of total population by ethnicity, England and UK, APS, Jan - Dec 2017. Retrieved October 18, 2018 from: https://www.ons.gov.uk/peoplepopulationandcommunity/culturalidentity/ethnicity/adhocs/008436youngpeoplebyethnicityinenglandanduk.

United States Census Bureau. (2017). Annual estimates of the resident population by sex, race alone or in combination, and Hispanic origin for the United States, States, and counties: April 1, 2010 to July 1, 2016. Retrieved October 18, 2018 from: https://factfinder.census.gov/faces/tableservices/jsf/pages/productview.xhtml?src=bkmk#.

Urdan, T. C. (1997). Examining the relations among early adolescent students' goals and friends' orientation toward effort and achievement in school. *Contemporary Educational Psychology*, 22(2), 165–191.

Urdan, T. C., & Maehr, M. L. (1995). Beyond a two-goal theory of motivation and achievement: A case for social goals. *Review of Educational Research*, 65(3), 213–243. doi:10.2307/1170683.

Wang, J., King, R. B., & Rao, N. (2018). The role of social-academic goals in Chinese students' self-regulated learning. *European Journal of Psychology of Education*, 1–22.

Watkins, D., & Hattie, J. j. (2012). Multiple goals in a Hong Kong Chinese educational context: An investigation of developmental trends and learning outcomes. *Australian Journal of Education (ACER Press)*, 56(3), 273–286.

Wentzel, K. R. (1994). Relations of social goal pursuit to social acceptance, classroom behavior, and perceived social support. *Journal of Educational Psychology*, 86(2), 173. doi:10.1037//0022–000663.86.2.173.

Wentzel, K. R. (1996). Social goals and social relationships as motivators of school adjustment. In J. Juvonen & K. R. Wentzel (Eds.), *Social motivation: Understanding children's school adjustment* (pp. 226–247). Cambridge studies in social and emotional development.New York: Cambridge University Press. http://dx.doi:10.1017/CBO9780511571190.012.

Wright, M. F., Li, Y., & Shi, J. (2014). Chinese adolescents' social status goals: Associations with behaviors and attributions for relational aggression. *Youth & Society*, 46(4), 566–588.

Yang, K. S., & Yu, A. B. (1988). Social-oriented and individual-oriented achievement motives: Conceptualization and measurement. Paper presented at the Symposium on Chinese Personality and Social Psychology for the XXIVth International Congress of Psychology, Sydney, Australia, August 1988.

Yu, A. B., & Yang, K. S. (1994). The nature of achievement motivation in collectivist societies. In U. Kim, H. C. Triandis, C. Kagitcibasi, S. C. Choi and G. Yoon (Eds.), *Individualism and collectivism: Theory, methods, and applications* (pp. 239–250). London: Sage Publications.

Zhao, Y., Zhu, X., & Zhao, G. (2016). Validation of the Chinese version of the social achievement goal orientation scale. *Journal of Psychoeducational Assessment*, 34(2), 199–204.

Zusho, A., Pintrich, P. R., & Cortina, K. S. (2005). Motives, goals, and adaptive patterns of performance in Asian American and Anglo American students. *Learning and Individual differences*, 15(2), 141–158.

11

SOCIAL GOALS IN CONTEXT

African American Students

James M. Ford, Jr. and Leigh M. Harrell-Williams

As described by many prominent figures in the field of social science, interactions with and observations of the social world provides a foundation for learning social norms, societal expectations, and cultural standards (Bandura, 1986; Bronfenbrenner & Morris, 2006). Aside from the creation and transferring of knowledge, social relationships can afford or inhibit emotional and psychological support (Juvonen & Knifsend, 2016), which in turn can have a profound impact on student's emotional well-being, school attendance, maladaptive behaviors in school, motivation, and engagement (Wentzel, 1999; Rubin et al., 2015). The type and nature of these social relationships is influenced, at least in part, by students' social goals (Dawes, 2017). These include, but are not limited to, social goals such as popularity among peers (Dawes & Xie, 2017), influence, power, or prosocial relationships (Ojanen, Grönroos, & Salmivalli, 2005), and social competence (Ryan & Shim, 2006; 2008). Although the need for social interactions and the utility of social relationships appear to be universal across cultures, the structure, goals of, and the ways in which social relationships impact motivation, engagement, and achievement are perhaps much more nuanced when one considers ethnic group membership (Hamm, 2000; Rivas-Drake et al., 2014; King & McInerney, 2016).

Peer Influences on Academic Outcomes

Regardless of ethnicity, students' academic engagement, motivation and achievement are often influenced by their peers (Kindermann & Skinner, 2009; Dijkstra & Gest, 2015; Rubin et al., 2015). For example, peer support for learning can have a powerful impact on academic interest, prosocial behaviors, classroom engagement, and school belonging (Wentzel, Battle, Russell, & Looney, 2010; Kiefer, Alley, & Ellerbrock, 2015). When considering similarities and differences between African American and European American pre-adolescent students, results from Faircloth and Hamm's (2005) research with middle school students provides some insight. In this study, the authors found a positive relationship between peer support and belongingness and a negative relationship between the emotional risk of making a mistake in class and belongingness for both African American and European American students. Findings such as these suggest that there is at least some universality across African and European American adolescents in terms of the importance and influence of peer support.

When considering African American adolescent students in particular, however, the support, or lack thereof, found in the social environment is especially integral to academic and motivational processes and potentially more so than for European American students (Urdan & Bruchmann, 2018; Usher, 2018). In terms of sense of school belonging, value of education, and value of learning, when comparing the impact of peer social support on these factors across European and African American adolescent students, the influence of peer social support appears to be much greater for African American adolescents (Wang & Eccles, 2012). Graham, Taylor, and Hudley (1998) found that African American male adolescents may value high-achieving male students less than low-achieving male students, potentially suggesting that their male sample perceived underachievement as more socially acceptable than academic success. When Faircloth and Hamm (2005) sought to develop a model to describe the dimensions and mechanisms of motivation and achievement using a diverse adolescent student sample, they hypothesized and assessed a structural equation model where academic efficacy beliefs and valuing of school influenced sense of belongingness in school, which in turn impacted academic success. When the model was compared between African American and European American students, a sense of belongingness mediated the relationship between motivation and academic success for African Americans but this was only partially true for European American students. Given these findings, researcher glean keen insight into not only the significance of social relationships on emotional, psychological, and behavioral factors for African American adolescents but also the need to understand the multifaceted influence of their peers and environment.

Peer Influences on Interpersonal Outcomes

For adolescent African American students, the quality of peer relationships can be predictive of a multitude of interpersonal outcomes. For example, externalizing of behaviors (e.g., aggression; delinquent behavior) has been associated with perceptions of peer support such that the perception of supportive peers can influence African American students' desire to disassociate with maladaptive academic behaviors (Kuperminc, Blatt, Shahar, Henrich, & Leadbeater, 2004). In Padilla-Walker and Bean's (2009) study of peer influence on positive (social initiative, self-esteem, and empathy) and negative (aggression, delinquency, and depression) thoughts and behaviors, they found that for African American adolescent students, peers impacted levels of empathy and aggression. Padilla-Walker and Bean's results suggest that associating with peers who participate in deviant behaviors (e.g., damaging or destroying property) reduces African American adolescent's empathy and increases aggression; however, the silver lining extracted from their study is that affiliating with peers who value activities such as studying and participating in school organizations increases African American adolescent's level of empathy. Furthermore, when pre-adolescent and adolescent African American students' peers hold positive, high academic values, they tend to display greater academic effort in school (Golden, Griffin, Metzger, & Cooper, 2018).

Beyond a simple comparison across ethnicities, interesting results are found when taking into account the ethnic diversity of schools. Regardless of a student's ethnicity, in schools where there are no clear numerical majority or minority ethnic groups, students who reside within schools with greater ethnic diversity, in general, report feeling more integrated into school peer networks (Urberg, Değirmencioğlu, Tolson, & Halliday-Scher, 1995). Jackson, Barth, Powell, and Lochman (2006) found that for African American student who are mathematically in the minority in a classroom reported lower quality friendships than African American students who are in ethnically diverse classrooms. On a larger scale, Goza and Ryabov (2009) found being associated with an ethnically diverse peer network positively affected the GPA of African American high school students in a nationally representative sample. Benner and Graham (2007) conducted a study of the impact of ethnic congruence (i.e., degree of similarity between student ethnicity and the percentage of the school population with the same ethnicity) on the transition from middle to high school. In the study, the authors found a significant difference in sense of belongingness for students who experienced a decline in ethnic congruence (incongruent group), as compared to students who did not experience a change in congruence. Identical results were described in Benner and Graham's (2009) analysis of African American students' sense of belonging. Specifically, African American students who transitioned to incongruent schools displayed significant less belongingness after the transition from middle to high school, whereas school belongingness remained relatively stable for African American students who moved to congruent schools. Results from studies such as these again highlight how vital the social environment is to the academic and social processes for African American students.

Distinctions among types of social goals

A prominent construct in the field of peer influences on academic thinking and behavior is social goals (Ryan, Jamison, Shin, & Thompson, 2012). An in-depth discussion of the many different ways that this construct has been defined can be found elsewhere in this book, but a brief description is warranted before proceeding. For example, Wentzel, Muenks, McNeish, & Russel (2018) studied social goals by attending to *prosocial goal pursuit*, or the desire to assist and share academic and personal problems with peers, and *social responsibility*, or efforts to follow classroom rules or keep interpersonal commitments. Dowson and McInerney (2004) described social goals in the context of school as social-academic goals, which include five rationales for students' focus on academic achievement: *social affiliation*-enhancing a sense of belonging to a group(s) and/or build/maintain relationships; *social approval*-gaining parents,' teachers,' and/or peers' approval; *social concern*-assisting others with personal or academic development; *social responsibility*-adhering to social and moral rules, social role expectations, or relationship commitments; *social status*-obtaining monetary and/or social position in school and/or in the future. Dawes (2017), in a recent review of early adolescents' social goals, gave an account of three overarching social goals: *social status goals, agentic and communal goals*, and *social achievement goals*. Social status goals are aspirations for popularity and/or being well-liked among peers. Agentic goals focus on gaining "status, influence, or power in social relationships," whereas communal goals seek to "maintain positive relationships, intimate connections with others" (p. 304; Dawes, 2017). Social achievement goals, the social goals of primary interest in the present chapter because of the ever growing body of literature with predominately European American samples and the limited research available with predominately African American students, will be discussed in more detail in the following sections.

Social achievement goals

The foundation of Social Achievement Goal Theory is the notion that individuals approach peer relationships with a goal in mind. Clearly, the theory corresponds with tenets of Social Cognitive Theory (Bandura, 1986), which theorizes that the goal a student sets for a task will influence his or her thoughts and actions. For example, a student may seek to feel a sense of mastery over their ability to be a supportive, caring friend or strive to display their social prowess (Wentzel, 1999; Ryan & Shim, 2006; 2008). In Ryan and Shim's research (2006; 2008), the authors identify three social goal orientations: *social development, social demonstration-approach*, and *social demonstration-avoid*. Students who have a social development goal seek to enhance the quality of a friendship and social competence and has been linked to help-seeking from peers, prosocial and non-aggressive behaviors, self-acceptance, personal growth, autonomy, emotional engagement, and social satisfaction (Roussel, Elliot, & Feltman, 2011; Ryan & Shim, 2006, 2008; Shim, Cho, & Wang, 2013). Social demonstration-approach goal is defined as a concern with appearing socially skilled and is associated with disruptive classroom behaviors, social worry, a lack of prosocial behaviors, aggressive behaviors, and perceived popularity (Ryan & Shim, 2006, 2008; Shim, Cho, & Wang, 2013). Individuals holding a social demonstration-avoid goal are trying to avoid appearing socially awkward or undesirable and research has shown a relationship with a lack of aggressive behavior, anxious solitary actions, social worry, low perception of popularity, fear, shame, and sadness (Ryan & Shim, 2006, 2008; Shim, Cho, & Wang, 2013; Shim, Wang, & Cassady, 2013). Based upon the work with social achievement goals, a discernible trend is visible in that one's goal orientation can produce adaptive or maladaptive consequences yet much of the research has been limited to more homogeneous samples.

Social achievement goals and African American adolescents

Much of the scholarly work on social achievement goals has focused predominately on European American, middle class participants (Wentzel, Donlan, & Morrison, 2012). However, several studies within the past ten years have concentrated on social achievement goals and African American students. For instance, Jones, Mueller, Royal, Shim, and Hart's (2013) study was the first to validate the Social Achievement Goal Questionnaire (Ryan & Shim, 2006; 2008) with an African American sample. Utilizing an adolescent sample of rural high school students, the authors found the scale to be valid and reliable, with females reporting higher levels of social development and lower levels of demonstration-approach orientations than male. Jones and Ford (2014), who utilized a predominately African American sample of high school students, reported high scale reliability as well (social development α = .82; social demonstration-approach α = .88; social demonstration-avoid α = .83) and observed an identical gender and development/demonstration-approach orientation pattern to that of the 2013 validation study.

Although much is known of the influence of social relationships on cognition, affect, and behavior for African American youth, very little research is available to inform our knowledge of how social achievement goals impact these factors for this unique population. In the absence of testing for ethnic differences, the social goal literature tends to display somewhat consistent findings. In general, students who seek to develop better friendships typically display more prosocial tendencies, are perceived favorably by peers, report more positive affect, and perform better academically than students whose goal is to either appear socially proficient or to avoid appearing socially inept (Rodkin, Ryan, Jamison, & Wilson, 2013; Mouratidis & Sideridis, 2009; Rudolph, Abaied, Flynn, Sugimura, & Agoston, 2011; Shim, Wang, & Cassady, 2013). However, given the lack of literature on social achievement goals and African American samples, as well as observable differences in how peers and the social environment effects a wealth of outcomes for this distinct group, researchers must continue to delve into the influence of social achievement goals on motivation and academic and interpersonal outcomes for this unique group of students.

Academic outcomes

Jones and Ford's (2014) study provided the first peek into the relationship among social achievement goal orientation, academic beliefs, and academic outcomes for African American adolescent students. As described in the study, male and female students reported relatively high levels of collective efficacy for classmates (M = 3.63 and 3.69 out of 5 respectively) suggesting a culture of perceived high academic ability at this school. In the study, for male students, social demonstration-avoid goal orientation positively predicted students' perceptions of their classmates' academic abilities (i.e., collective efficacy for classmates). For female students, social demonstration-avoid orientation positively predicted their perception of the school and teacher efficacy (i.e., collective efficacy for school). If, as previously discussed, students at this school perceived high levels of academic competence around them, then perhaps focusing on avoiding embarrassment or looking foolish (i.e., social demonstration-avoid) magnified their perceptions of the efficacy of classmates, teachers, and the school. Lastly, for female but not male students, social demonstration-avoid goal inversely predicted math performance. The fear of appearing foolish or of being teased may have paved the way to maladaptive behaviors such as self-handicapping, which, as previous studies have shown, in turn negatively impacts academic performance (Urdan, 2004). Results from this study show a relatively consistent pattern with research with predominately European American samples. Specifically, students who are oriented towards avoiding the appearance of social incompetence may also exhibit emotional and psychological thoughts that are maladaptive to academic thoughts, behaviors, and outcomes. Although development and demonstration-approach goals did not significantly impact academic motivation and achievement in this particular study, as the body of social achievement goals and African American students literature grows so too should a greater understanding of the influence of these factors on not only academic but also interpersonal outcomes.

Interpersonal outcomes

Wilson, Rodkin, and Ryan (2014) pushed the study of social goal orientation and African American students forward by providing the first cross-ethnic comparison of Ryan and Shim's (2006, 2008) social achievement goals and interpersonal outcomes. In their study, the authors examined the social achievement orientation and ethnic diversity of peer groups among 4th and 5th grade African American and European American children. Results from this study showed that male, African American participants were significantly less social development oriented and more demonstration-approach oriented than African American females and European American males and females. The authors also found that holding a social demonstration-approach goal positively predicted increased peer group ethnic-segregation and cross-ethnic dislike for African American students, whereas development goal orientation predicted lower levels of cross-ethnic dislike. On the other hand, for European American students, demonstration-approach goal positively influenced decreases in peer group ethnic-segregation. Based upon these results, it seems that for these African American students appearing socially competent meant avoiding ethnically diverse friendships, while the opposite was true for European American students.

Although the field of social achievement goal research has mostly been hampered by a lack of ethnically diverse samples, the studies previously discussed in this section provide some insight into the importance of social goal orientation for adolescent African American students. In summary, adolescent African American females consistently report greater interest in developing meaningful relationships as opposed to male African American students who tend to focus more so on appearing socially competent. Although these orientations do appear to be relatively indistinguishable to those of European American males and females, it seems apparent that African American males, as comparison to European American males, are much more focused on displaying social acumen. Concentrating on appearing socially competent, unfortunately, traditionally proves to be detrimental to academic engagement, prosocial behavior, foci at school, and ultimately academic performance (Jones, Mueller, & McCutchen, 2017; Jones & Mueller, 2017; Ryan & Shim, 2008). As the field continues grow, alternative factors, especially those that have been historically vital to understanding African American student outcomes, must be considered.

Future Directions

Ethnic identity and African American students

Unfortunately, given the limited empirical knowledge amassed on the social achievement orientations of African American youths and emotional, psychological, and behavioral outcomes, scholars are left to speculate as to how and why social achievement goals may influence the academic behaviors and outcomes of this unique population. However, ethnic identity is one potential avenue of future exploration that has been studied for decades and is a powerful predictor of multiple outcomes for African American studies. Ethnic identity, as described by Phinney (1992), "is an aspect of a person's social identity ... together with the value and emotional significance attached to that membership." (p. 156). Phinney and Ong (2007) stated in their review of the conceptualization and measurement of ethnic identity, "ethnic identity is a multifaceted construct that includes a number of dimensions" (p. 271) such as commitment/attachment, exploration, ethnic behaviors, values and beliefs, and importance/salience. Although ethnic identity has been characterized in many ways (for an overview see Miller-Cotto & Byrnes, 2016), Oyserman, Gant, and Ager (1995) described racial-ethnic identity as being comprised of *connectedness*, or feeling connected to one's racial-ethnic group, *awareness of racism*, or the perception that other individuals may not value your racial-ethnic group, and *embedded achievement*, or believing that academic achievement is a trait of one's racial-ethnic group. In terms of the emotional significance of group membership, Umaña-Taylor, Yazedjian, and Bámaca-Gómez's (2004) indicate that individuals will associate a positive or negative affect with their ethnicity, or *affirmation*, based upon their perception of how others (e.g., social or ethnic groups) view their ethnicity. It is theorized that these factors are influenced by individuals' perceptions of their ethnic group's social status as compared to other ethnic groups, otherwise known as social identity.

In Tajfel and Turner's (1986) Social Identity Theory of Intergroup Behavior, the authors describe a theory of "patterns of individual prejudices and discrimination and on the motivational sequences of interpersonal interaction" (p. 7; Tajfel & Turner, 1986). According to Tajfel and Turner, individuals hold a social identity or "self-image that derive[s] from the social categories to which he perceives himself as belonging" (p. 16). These social categories are mental tools that classify, solidify, and order the social environment (e.g., one ethnic group is superior to another). Social categories also "create and define the individual's place in society" (p. 16; Tajfel & Turner, 1986). Based upon one's perception of the social category to which he or she belongs (i.e., in-group), Tajfel and Turner posit that individuals compare their social identity to members of other social groups. Since in-group membership in certain social groups is more favorable than in-group membership in others (e.g., being a member of the political party of the majority of the population), one's social identity may carry either a positive or negative connotation. For example, as described by Tajfel and Turner, "subordinate groups often seem to internalize a wider social evaluation of themselves as 'inferior' or 'second class'" (p. 10). These connotations can have far reaching implications as an individual's perception of his or her social and ethnic identity will influence numerous psychological constructs, emotions, behaviors, and academic outcomes (Oyserman, Harrison, & Bybee, 2001; Chavous et al., 2003; Altschul, Oyserman, & Bybee, 2006; Rivas-Drake et al. 2014).

For example, ethnic identity affirmation and achievement for African American students has shown to be a positive predictor of lower depressive symptoms concurrently and over time (Mandara, Gaylord-Harden, Richards, & Ragsdale, 2009). According to Buckley and Carter (2005), female adolescent African American students who report more positive Black racial/ethnic identity also display more positive social, emotional, and physical self-concepts. For pre-adolescent African American males, ethnic affirmation appears to have a positive relationship with self-esteem (Mandara, Gaylord-Harden, Richards, & Ragsdale, 2009). Regardless of gender, higher ethnic affirmation also has been linked to higher academic efficacy and school engagement for African American students (Hughes, Witherspoon, Rivas-Drake, & West-Bey, 2009). Oyserman and colleagues have spent over a decade studying the relationship between racial–ethnic identity and academic outcomes and have informed much of the current ethnic identity literature. For example, in a one year longitudinal study of African American eight grade students, those with high levels of racial–ethnic identity did not experience a decrease in school efficacy (Oyserman, Harrison, & Bybee, 2001), a prominent predictor of a wealth of academic outcomes (Zimmerman, 2000). In fact, adolescent African American students who viewed their academic achievement as part of their ethnicity reported improved academic efficacy. When the authors tested for interaction effects, for females, feeling connected to one's ethnic group and believing others perceive this group negatively is harmful only when these students do not view academic achievement as a vital part of their in-group identity. In the same study, feeling connected to one's ethnicity positively predicted improved performance, increased study time, and better attendance for males. For females, embedded achievement also predicts improved grades (Oyserman, Bybee, & Terry, 2003). Moreover, Altschul, Oyserman, and Bybee's (2006) two year longitudinal study of racial-ethnic identity and grades showed that African American youths high in connectedness and embedded achievement out performed students with lower levels. Adelabu (2008) reported ethnic identity significantly predicted grade point average among rural and urban middle and high school African American students.

Chavous et al. (2003) examined racial beliefs of African American students in the 12th grade in order to create profiles of racial identity, which were then used to explore their relationship to educational beliefs, academic performance, and later academic attainment. Findings from their study highlight "that having high centrality, strong group pride (private regard), and positive beliefs about society's view of Blacks (public regard) were related to more positive academic beliefs, supporting the motivational perspective on the role of group identification" (p. 1086; Chavous et al., 2003). Findings from these studies clearly highlight the influence of ethnic identity on the motivational, affective, and academic performance of African American students, yet research focusing on ethnic identity and social relationships of minority students has also yielded thought-provoking results.

Ethnic identity, peers, and where to go from here

Although much is left to be explored in terms of how ethnic identity and social achievement goals are related, several studies have focused on the relationship between ethnic identity and emotional and academic outcomes, peer group membership, and peer similarities. For example, Holmes and Lochman (2009) found that for African American pre-adolescent students who reported high levels of ethnic identity also reported lower levels of dominance and revenge goals in social situations. These findings suggest that stronger ties to African American students' ethnic group offsets the desire to retaliate against or dominate others who may socially harm them. African American student's perception of positive affirmation and belonging to their ethnicity appears to have a positive influence on their ability to resist peer pressure to engage in problem behaviors such as cheating (Derlan & Umaña-Taylor, 2015). Looking beyond the influence of peer pressure, Rivas-Drake, Umaña-Taylor, Schaefer, and Medina (2017) conducted a study to explore if ethnic-racial identity impacted friendship selection and socialization over time for an ethnically diverse sample of pre-adolescent student. In their study, the authors found that friendship selection was not associated with ethnic identity suggesting that peer groups were not formed based upon perceived similarities in ethnic identity, but due to alternative factors. However, over time the ethnic identity of group members became more similar. The authors postulated that the ethnic identity of group members was socialized over the course of the study via the rules and regulations of the group. The authors also found that ethnic identity resolution, or the level in which an individual considers their ethnicity to be a core piece of their identity (Phinney, 1992), at time 1 positively impacted friendship diversity at time 2 for males but not females. Also of note, results showed that friendship diversity at time 2 positively impacted ethnic identity exploration, or engagement in activities to learn more about one's ethnicity (Phinney, 1992), at time 3 for males and females. Although the study of peers and ethnic identity are scarce, these studies provide a general foundation for beginning to understand the impact of peers on the development and perception of student's ethnic identity. However, given that social achievement goal orientation research with African American students is limited to descriptive results and to whether or not students have ethnically diverse friendship groups, we are left to only speculate as to the nature of the relationship between ethnic identity and social achievement goals by leaning on previous research and theory.

As previously discussed, positive ethnic identity is typically associated with positive self-worth, self-esteem, self-efficacy, and peer relationships, lower levels of aggression, and can serve as a buffer to peer pressure (Holmes & Lochman, 2009; Hughes, Witherspoon, Rivas-Drake, & West-Bey, 2009; Rivas-Drake et al., 2014; Derlan & Umaña-Taylor, 2015; Rivas-Drake, Umaña-Taylor, Schaefer, & Medina, 2017). Social achievement goal orientation research has shown similar results, albeit with studies that utilized predominately European American samples, with a few exceptions (Mouratidis & Sideridis, 2009; Ryan, Jamison, Shin, & Thompson, 2012; Rodkin, Ryan, Jamison, & Wilson, 2013; Shim, Wang, & Cassady, 2013; Jones & Ford, 2014). If both concepts (i.e., social achievement goals and ethnic identity) individually impact multiple cognitive, emotional, and relational constructs, then perhaps when considered simultaneously one factor will prove to be a more powerful predictor of academic outcomes. Alternatively, based upon prior research, social cognitive and social group theories (Bandura, 1986; Tajfel & Turner, 1986; Bronfenbrenner & Morris, 2006; Phinney, 1992), an argument could be made that ethnic identity orientation precedes social goals. To this end, researchers may wish to consider building a theoretical model to determine if ethnic identity orientation can predict or inform social achievement goal orientation. However, armed with the knowledge that contextual factors such as the ethnic diversity of schools and friendships, as well as social support have unique effects on African American students, aspects of the environment may also need to be investigated. For example, is positive ethnic identity associated with holding a social development goal but only when interacting with peers of the same ethnicity? Is having a negative ethnic identity associated with a social demonstration-approach or avoid goal but only in schools where other students appear to have positive ethnic identity? How much, if at all, does school local (i.e., rural, urban, or suburban) or geographical region influence these factors? Unfortunately, we are left with many unanswered questions. However, scholars can take some solace in the fact that many studies have provided a foundation to allow others to move social achievement goal orientation research with African American student forward into the future.

References

Adelabu, D. H. (2008). Future time perspective, hope, and ethnic identity among African American adolescents. *Urban Education, 43*(3), 347–360.

Altschul, I., Oyserman, D., & Bybee, D. (2006). Racial-ethnic identity in mid-adolescence: Content and change as predictors of academic achievement. *Child Development, 77*(5), 1155–1169.

Bandura, A. (1986). *Social foundations of thought and action: A social cognitive theory.* Englewood Cliffs, NJ: Prentice-Hall, Inc.

Benner, A. D., & Graham, S. (2007). Navigating the transition to multi-ethnic urban high schools: Changing the ethnic congruence and adolescents' school-related affect. *Journal of Research on Adolescence, 17*(1), 207–220.

Benner, A. D., & Graham, S. (2009). The transition to high school as a developmental process among multiethnic urban youth. *Child Development, 80*(2), 356–376.

Bergman, L. R., & Trost, K. (2006). The person-oriented versus variable oriented approach: Are they complementary, opposites, or exploring different worlds? *Merrill-Palmer Quarterly, 52*, 601–632.

Bronfenbrenner, U., & Morris, P. A. (2006). The bioecological model of human development. In R. M. Lerner & W. Damon (Eds.), *Handbook of child psychology: Theoretical models of human development* (pp. 793–828). Hoboken, NJ: John Wiley.

Buckley, T. R., & Carter, R. T. (2005). Black adolescent girls' self-esteem: Do gender role and racial identity impact their self-esteem? *Sex Roles: A Journal of Research, 53*(9/10), 647–661.

Chavous, T. M., Bernat, D. H., Schmeelk-Cone, K., Caldwell, C. H., Kohn-Wood, L., & Zimmerman, M. A. (2003). Racial identity and academic attainment among African American adolescents. *Child Development, 74*(4), 1076–1090.

Dawes, M. (2017). Early adolescents' social goals and school adjustment. *Social Psychology of Education, 20*(2), 299–328.

Dawes, M., & Xie, H. (2017). The trajectory of popularity goal during the transition to middle school. *The Journal of Early Adolescence, 37*(6), 852–883.

Derlan, C. L., & Umaña-Taylor, A. J. (2015). Brief report: Contextual predictors of African American adolescents' ethnic-racial identity affirmation-belonging and resistance to peer pressure. *Journal of Adolescence, 41*, 1–6.

Dijkstra, J. K., & Gest, S. D. (2015). Peer norm salience for academic achievement, prosocial behavior, and bullying: Implications for adolescent school experiences. *The Journal of Early Adolescence, 35*(1), 79–96.

Dowson, M., & McInerney, D. M. (2004). The development and validation of the Goal Orientation and Learning Strategies Survey (GOALS-S). *Educational and Psychological Measurement, 64*(2), 290–310.

Faircloth, B. S., & Hamm, J. V. (2005). Sense of belonging among high school students representing 4 ethnic groups. *Journal of Youth and Adolescence, 34*(4), 293–309.

Golden, A. R., Griffin, C. B., Metzger, I. W., & Cooper, S. M. (2018). School racial climate and academic outcomes in African American adolescents: The protective role of peers. *Journal of Black Psychology, 44*(1), 47–73.

Goza, F., & Ryabov, I. (2009). Adolescents' educational outcomes: Racial and ethnic variations in peer network importance. *Journal of Youth and Adolescence, 38*(9), 1264–1279.

Graham, S., Taylor, A. Z., & Hudley, C. (1998). Exploring achievement values among ethnic minority early adolescents. *Journal of Educational Psychology, 90*(4), 606–620.

Hamm, J. V. (2000). Do birds of a feather flock together? The variable bases for African American, Asian American, and European American adolescents' selection of similar friends. *Developmental Psychology, 36*(2), 209–219.

Holmes, K. J., & Lochman, J. E. (2009). Ethnic identity in African American and European American preadolescents: Relation to self-worth, social goals, and aggression. *The Journal of Early Adolescence, 29*(4), 476–496.

Hughes, D., Witherspoon, D., Rivas-Drake, D., & West-Bey, N. (2009). Received ethnic–racial socialization messages and youths' academic and behavioral outcomes: Examining the mediating role of ethnic identity and self-esteem. *Cultural Diversity and Ethnic Minority Psychology, 15*(2), 112–124.

Jackson, M. F., Barth, J. M., Powell, N., & Lochman, J. E. (2006). Classroom contextual effects of race on children's peer nominations. *Child Development, 77*, 1325–1337.

Jones, M. H., & Ford, J. M. (2014). Social achievement goals, efficacious beliefs, and math performance in a predominately African American high school. *Journal of Black Psychology, 40*(3), 239–262.

Jones, M. H., & Mueller, C. E. (2017). The relationship among achievement goals, standardized test scores, and elementary students' focus in school. *Psychology in the Schools, 54*(9), 979–990.

Jones, M. H., Mueller, C. E., & McCutchen, K. L. (2017). School foci and their potential ramifications in urban high schools. *Youth & Society.* doi:10.1177/0044118X16685656.

Jones, M. H., Mueller, C. E., Royal, K. D., Shim, S. S., & Hart, C. O. (2013). Social achievement goals: Validation among rural African American adolescents. *Journal of Psychoeducational Assessment, 31*(6), 566–577.

Juvonen, J., & Knifsend, C. (2016). School-based peer relationships and achievement motivation. In K. R. Wentzel & D. B. Miele (Eds.), *Handbook of motivation at school* (2nd ed., pp. 231–248). New York: Routledge.

Kiefer, S. M., Alley, K. M., & Ellerbrock, C. R. (2015). Teacher and peer support for young adolescents' motivation, engagement, and school belonging. *Rmle Online, 38*(8), 1–18, doi:10.1080/19404476.2015.11641184.

Kindermann, T. A., & Skinner, E. A. (2009). How do naturally existing peer groups shape children's academic development during sixth grade? *European Journal of Psychological Science, 3*, 31–43.

King, R. B., & McInerney, D. M. (2016). Culture and motivation: The road traveled and the way ahead. In K. R. Wentzel & D. B. Miele (Eds.), *Handbook of motivation at school* (2nd ed., pp. 275–300). New York: Routledge.

Kuperminc, G. P., Blatt, S. J., Shahar, G., Henrich, C., & Leadbeater, B. J. (2004). Cultural equivalence and cultural variance in longitudinal associations of young adolescent self-definition and interpersonal relatedness to psychological and school adjustment. *Journal of Youth and Adolescence, 33*(1), 13–30.

Mandara, J., Gaylord-Harden, N., Richards, M. H., & Ragsdale, B. L. (2009). The effects of changes in racial identity and self-esteem on changes in African American adolescents' mental health. *Child Development, 80*(6), 1660–1675.

Miller-Cotto, D., & Byrnes, J. P. (2016). Ethnic/racial identity and academic achievement: A meta-analytic review. *Developmental Review, 41*, 51–70.

Mouratidis, A. A., & Sideridis, G. D. (2009). On social achievement goals: Their relations with peer acceptance, classroom belongingness, and perceptions of loneliness. *The Journal of Experimental Education, 77*(3), 285–308.

Ojanen, T., Grönroos, M., & Salmivalli, C. (2005). An interpersonal circumplex model of children's social goals: Links with peer-reported behavior and sociometric status. *Developmental Psychology, 41*(5), 699–710.

Oyserman, D., Bybee, D., & Terry, K. (2003). Gendered racial identity and involvement with school. *Self and Identity, 2*, 307–324.

Oyserman, D., Gant, L., & Ager, J. (1995). A socially contextualized model of African American identity: Possible selves and school persistence. *Journal of Personality and Social Psychology, 69*(6), 1216–1232.

Oyserman, D., Harrison, K., & Bybee, D. (2001). Can racial identity be promotive of academic efficacy. *International Journal of Behavioral Development, 25*, 379–385.

Padilla-Walker, L. M., & Bean, R. A. (2009). Negative and positive peer influence: Relations to positive and negative behaviors for African American, European American, and Hispanic adolescents. *Journal of Adolescence, 32*(2), 323–337.

Phinney, J. (1992). The Multigroup Ethnic Identity Measure: A new scale for use with adolescents and young adults from diverse groups. *Journal of Adolescent Research, 7*, 156–176.

Phinney, J. S., & Ong, A. D. (2007). Conceptualization and measurement of ethnic identity: Current status and future directions. *Journal of Counseling Psychology, 54*(3), 271–281.

Rivas-Drake, D., Seaton, E. K., Markstrom, C., Quintana, S., Syed, M., & Lee, R., Study Group on Ethnic and Racial Identity in the 21st Century. (2014). Ethnic and racial identity in adolescence: Implications for psychosocial, academic, and health outcomes. *Child Development, 85*, 40–57.

Rivas-Drake, D., Umaña-Taylor, A. J., Schaefer, D. R., & Medina, M. (2017). Ethnic-racial identity and friendships in early adolescence. *Child Development, 88*(3), 710–724.

Rodkin, P. C., Ryan, A. M., Jamison, R., & Wilson, T. (2013). Social goals, social behavior, and social status in middle childhood. *Developmental Psychology, 49*(6), 1139–1150.

Rosenzweig, E. Q., & Wigfield, A. (2016). What if reading is easy but unimportant? How students' patterns of affirming and undermining motivation for reading information texts predict different reading outcomes. *Contemporary Educational Psychology.* http://dx.doi:10.1016/j.cedpsych.2016.09.002.

Roussel, P., Elliot, A. J., & Feltman, R. (2011). The influence of achievement goals and social goals on help-seeking from peers in an academic context. *Learning and Instruction, 21*, 394–402.

Rubin, K. H., Coplan, R.Chen, X., Bowker, J. C., McDonald, K. & Heverly-Fitt, S. (2015). Peer relationships in childhood. In M. H. Bornstein & M. E. Lamb (Eds.), *Developmental science: An advanced textbook* (7th ed., pp. 591–649). New York: Psychology Press.

Rudolph, K. D., Abaied, J. L., Flynn, M., Sugimura, N., & AgostonA. M. (2011). Developing relationships, being cool, and not looking like a loser: Social goal orientation predicts children's responses to peer aggression. *Child Development, 82*(5), 1518–1530.

Ryan, A. M., Jamison, R. S., Shin, H., & Thompson, G. N. (2012). Social achievement goals and adjustment at school during early adolescence. In G. W. Ladd & A. M. Ryan (Eds.), *Peer relationships and adjustment at school* (pp. 165–186). Charlotte, NC: Information Age Publishing.

Ryan, A., & Shim, S. S. (2006). Social achievement goals: The nature and consequences of different orientations toward social competence. *Personality and Social Psychology Bulletin, 32*(9), 1246–1263.

Ryan, A., & Shim, S. S. (2008). Young adolescents' social achievement goals: Implications for social adjustment in middle school. *Journal of Educational Psychology, 100*(3), 672–687.

Shim, S. S., Cho, Y., & Wang, C. (2013). Classroom goal structures, social achievement goals, and adjustment in middle school. *Learning and Instruction, 23*, 69–77.

Shim, S. S., Wang, C., & Cassady, J. C. (2013). Emotional well-being: The role of social achievement goals and self-esteem. *Personality and Individual Differences, 55*(7), 840–845.

Smith, T. B., & Silva, L. (2011). Ethnic identity and personal well-being of people of color: A meta-analysis. *Journal of Counseling Psychology, 58*(1), 42–60.

Tajfel, H. & Turner, J. C. (1986). The social identity theory of inter-group behavior. In S. Worchel & L. W. Austin (Eds.), *Psychology of intergroup relations* (2nd ed., pp. 7–24). Chicago: Nelson-Hall.

Umaña-Taylor, A. J., Yazedjian, A., & Bámaca-Gómez, M. (2004). Developing the ethnic identity scale using Eriksonian and social identity perspectives. *Identity: An International Journal of Theory and Research, 4*(1), 9–38.

Urberg, K. A., Değirmencioğlu, S. M., Tolson, J. M., & Halliday-Scher, K. (1995). The structure of adolescent peer networks. *Developmental Psychology, 31*(4), 540–547.

Urdan, T. (2004). Predictors of academic self-handicapping and achievement: Examining achievement goals, classroom goal structures, and culture. *Journal of Educational Psychology, 96*, 251–264.

Urdan, T., & Bruchmann, K. (2018). Examining the academic motivation of a diverse student population: A consideration of methodology. *Educational Psychologist, 53*(2), 114–130.

Usher, E. L. (2018). Acknowledging the Whiteness of motivation research: Seeking cultural relevance. *Educational Psychologist, 53*(2), 131–144.

Vansteenkiste, M., Sierens, E., Soenens, B., Luyckx, K., & Lens, W. (2009). Motivational profiles from a self-determination perspective: The quality of motivation matters. *Journal of Educational Psychology, 101*, 671–688.

Wang, M. T., & Eccles, J. S. (2012). Social support matters: Longitudinal effects of social support on three dimensions of school engagement from middle to high school. *Child Development, 83*(3), 877–895.

Wentzel, K. R. (1999). Social-motivational processes and interpersonal relationships: Implications for understanding motivation at school. *Journal of Educational Psychology, 91*(1), 76–97.

Wentzel, K. R., Battle, A., Russell, S. L., & Looney, L. B. (2010). Social supports from teachers and peers as predictors of academic and social motivation. *Contemporary Educational Psychology, 35*(3), 193–202.

Wentzel, K. R., Donlan, A., & Morrison, D. (2012). Peer relationships and social motivational processes. In A. M. Ryan & G. W. Ladd (Eds.), *Adolescence and education: Peer relationships and adjustment at school* (pp. 79–105). Charlotte, NC: IAP Information Age Publishing.

Wentzel, K. R., Muenks, K., McNeish, D., & Russell, S. (2018). Emotional support, social goals, and classroom behavior: A multilevel, multisite study. *Journal of Educational Psychology, 110*(5), 611–627.

Wilson, T. M., Rodkin, P. C., & Ryan, A. M. (2014). The company they keep and avoid: Social goal orientation as a predictor of children's ethnic segregation. *Developmental Psychology, 50*(4), 1116–1124.

Zimmerman, B. J. (2000). Self-efficacy: An essential motive to learn. *Contemporary Educational Psychology, 25*(1), 82–91.

12

SOCIAL GOALS IN CONTEXT

Latinx Students

Angela M. Labistre Champion and Francesca López

In recent times, studies regarding achievement motivation and its relationship to mastery and performance goals has begun to consider social goals as an additional source of motivation for academic and social outcomes. The varied contexts in which social goals have been studied include focus on students' desire for popularity amongst peers (Ojanen & Findley-Van Nostrand, 2014), as well as investigations of the ways in which academic achievement or performance relates to familial social outcomes (Wing-yi Cheng & Lam, 2013). To further contextualize social goal scholarship, however, some researchers have argued for "culturalization" of achievement goal theory research, including social goals (Zusho & Clayton, 2011). Some researchers have heeded this call, and have conducted work that demonstrates incorporation of cultural concepts utilized in cross-cultural psychology – such as cultural orientation and the related concept of self-construal (King, McInerney, & Pitliya, 2018). Engaging constructs such as these have allowed researchers to consider students' diverse cultural backgrounds and the ways in which the perspectives, values, and roles cultivated in those cultures can motivate students throughout their navigation of formal education (King & McInerney, 2014). However, despite this clear movement toward recognition of cross-cultural differences in the field's understanding of social goals, much of the extant literature provides only a limited representation of Latinx[1] students.

Latinx students exemplify one of the fastest growing student groups in the American K-20 education system (McFarland et al., 2018), but have shown differential rates of academic performance when compared with white peers at nearly every grade level (Gándara & Mordechay, 2017) – spurring urgency for studies seeking to illuminate potential sources for this difference (Gándara, 2015). Decades of researchers have pointed to the importance of understanding Latinx students' cultural values, and have documented their centrality to many Latinx students' identities, as well as the integral role upholding cultural values can play in students' perceptions of, engagement in, and general navigation of the formal schooling system (Corona, McDonald, Velazquez, Rodríguez, & Fuentes, 2017; Guardia & Evans, 2008; Hill & Torres, 2010; Portes & Rumbaut, 2006; Valdés, 1995). Furthermore, Latinx students' achievement goal orientation, specifically in terms of mastery/performance orientations, has been investigated to an extent in existing literature (Stevens, Hamman, & Olivarez, 2007; Witkow & Fuligni, 2007), but has largely left social goals out of the conversation. When considering the oft-noted importance of cultural values in educational research concerning Latinx students, and the burgeoning recognition of cultural constructs in recent social goal work, there remains a paucity of social goal research explicitly centering Latinx students and a lack of exploration of the ways in which Latinx cultural values matter for the social goals held by Latinx students. Thus, this chapter begins with a brief overview of the evolution of social goal work and relevant terminology, as well as existing literature connecting social goals with cultural constructs (e.g., cultural orientation/self-construal). Following this introduction, scholarship describing Latinx students' cultural values will be discussed, as well as the prospective influence of these values on their social goals and related interpersonal and academic outcomes. Lastly, future recommendations for social goals research are explored.

Definitions

Social goals: Diverging definitions and making a case for cultural considerations

Throughout decades of exploration, the definitions of social goals, their operationalization, and their relationships with academic and interpersonal outcomes have evolved in many ways. In general, goals can be understood as "a cognitive representation" for a desired outcome in any given situation (Wentzel, 1999 p. 77; Austin & Vancouver, 1996; Ford, 1992). Though early research focused primarily on mastery and performance achievement goals (King, McInerney, & Watkins, 2013), other scholars felt that other facets of schooling was neglected in existing achievement goal theory work, including social goals (Brophy, 2005). Early research defined social goals broadly – describing them as, "the perceived [social] purposes for trying, or not trying, to achieve academically" (Urdan & Maehr, 1995; p. 214). In addition to this definition, Urdan & Maehr (1995) argued that extant achievement goal literature did not adequately attend to students whose academic achievement was motivated by desired social outcomes – such as to gain approval from peers and teachers or to fulfill the need for affiliation amongst peers – and that students' cultural group membership could be a main source of influence for their various social motives for academic achievement. Regarding acknowledgment of students' cultural backgrounds, they asserted that culturally bound "definition[s] of self," (Urdan &

Maehr, 1995, p. 221) and the values, roles, and perspectives cultivated within students' particular cultural groups could potentially shape the social goals students strive to achieve while in school, and thus were important to consider in future studies of social goals.

Moving beyond the emphasis on social goals' connection with academic achievement, Wentzel (2002) posited that social goals could be understood as "goals people set for themselves to achieve specific social outcomes (e.g., making a friend) or to interact with others in particular ways (e.g., helping someone with a problem)" (p. 222). This content-based definition suggests that academic performance need not always be associated with social goals (though it often is), and that the desires for particular social interactions and outcomes could represent a powerful source of motivation for student behavior alone. In addition to making friends or helping others, Wentzel proposed other social goals, such as to have fun in the classroom (Wentzel, 1999, p. 79), or to behave cooperatively or responsibly with others (Wentzel, Muenks, McNeish, & Russell, 2018). Wentzel and colleagues' extensive contributions to social goal scholarship provide important attention to facets of the schooling experience beyond academic task-related goals – but leave cultural influences that shape how and why students hold and pursue particular social goals relatively unattended.

Further contributing to social goal conceptualization in the academic context, Dowson and McInerney (2003) defined social goals as "the social reasons students espouse for wanting to achieve in academic situations," (p. 100). They uniquely employed an inductive approach to investigating students' most salient academic and social goals – arriving at important differentiations between cognitive, behavioral, and affective components of each type of goal. Further expanding on social goals, Dowson and McInerney (2003) identified five types of social goals for wanting to achieve academically. These included *social concern*, or to be able to help others through their academic/personal development, *social status*, or to obtain/keep some social position later on in life, *social responsibility*, or to fulfill some sense of responsibility or perceived role, *social approval*, or to gain the approval of parents, teachers, and/or peers, and finally, *social affiliation*, or to create a greater sense of belonging within a group/in an interpersonal relationship (p. 100). Also, Dowson and McInerney (2003) emphasized that students could hold multiple social and academic goals simultaneously, and that, in particular, social goals were a powerful source of motivation to achieve academically. Though important foundations were laid in this seminal piece of social goal work, again, the role cultural values can play in the ways in which students define and enact social goals was not explicitly investigated

Focusing on social relationship goals as a necessary addition to academic (or task-related) goals, Ford (1992) outlined the differences between *self-assertive social relationship goals* and *integrative social relationship goals* in the study of person-environment goals, or those goals which are directly influenced by a student's surrounding social environment. Self-assertive social relationship goals included achieving *individuality* in order to feel "unique" and to "avoid similarity or conformity with others," achieving *self-determination* in order to experience "a sense of freedom to act or make choices," achieving *superiority* in order to compare "favorably to others in terms of winning, status, or success," and achieving *resource acquisition* in order to obtain "approval, support, assistance, advice, or validation from others" (p. 89). Conversely, integrative social relationship goals included achieving *belongingness* in order to build or maintain "attachments, friendships, intimacy, or a sense of community," achieving *social responsibility* in order to keep "interpersonal commitments, meetings social role obligations, and conform[*sic*] to social and moral rules," achieving *equity* in order to promote "fairness, justice, reciprocity, or equality," and achieving *resource provision* in order to give "approval, support, assistance, advice, or validation to others" (p. 89). Though not explicitly related to cultural values, Ford's taxonomy of social relationship goals is reflective of cross-cultural psychological constructs of collectivism and individualism, which will be discussed more fully in the following sections.

Though much of the foundational scholarship mentioned in the preceding section only tentatively engages cultural considerations, it nevertheless provides important definitional understanding, as well as a theoretical basis for discussion of social goal studies that exhibit more extensive inclusion of culture. As such, we now turn to scholarship that engages cultural considerations in a more explicit way. In order to properly delineate this work, we also discuss the various construct definitions that are utilized throughout cultural social goal work.

Building upon their previous scholarship, researchers such as McInerney along with other scholars, such as King and Watkins, have continued to delve into the complex nature of social goals, as well as incorporate constructs utilized in cross-cultural psychology. For example, in multiple cross-cultural studies of social goals, (i.e., King, 2017; King & McInerney, 2014; King, McInerney, and Watkins, 2013) investigated the social goals of students (e.g., Chinese, Filipino, and others) who identified as members of cultures that are considered *collectivistic* in terms of their cultural orientations (Triandis, McCusker, & Hui, 1990). They critically established that social goals were significant sources of academic motivation for students who identified with groups associated with collectivistic cultural orientation (King, McInerney, & Watkins, 2013). This finding represents an important contribution to extant social goal work, which mostly centered European American students, and their oft-associated *individualistic* cultural values (King & McInerney, 2014). But what does it mean to be collectivistically or individualistically culturally oriented? What does that mean for notions of the self? And how do those relate to social goals?

Definitions regarding *individualistic* cultural orientation (or *individualism*), like those of social goals, have varied. However, it can be basically understood as a value system which prioritizes "personal goals over the goals of the in-group" (Greenfield & Quiroz, 2013, p. 109). Additionally, individualistic cultural orientation is associated with treating most personal relationships as "impermanent and nonintensive" (Oyserman, Coon, & Kemmelmeier, 2002), and perceiving inter-personal conflict as acceptable interaction (Triandis, McCusker, & Hui, 1990). Conversely, *collectivistic* cultural orientation (or *collectivism*) places the needs of the group before pursuance of one's own goals, and that group membership is central to one's identity (Oyserman, Coon, & Kemmelmeier, 2002). Furthermore, col-lectivistic values often include the view that group harmony must be maintained, through avoidance of conflict, and through enactment of prescribed roles and behaviors which fulfill the group's expectations.

According to Markus and Kitayama (1991), these broader cultural orientations (e.g., individualistic vs. collectivistic) often define group members' respective self-construals, or sense of self in relation to others. In terms of self-construal, col-lectivistically oriented students exhibit more *inter*dependent senses of self, wherein the self is understood as necessarily connected to a network of close or similar others and that motivation is drawn from fulfilling the needs of the collective (Markus & Kitayama, 1991). Furthermore, those who view themselves as *inter*-dependent may more often avoid or amend personal needs and desires if they appear to conflict with the norms of their group (Fuligni, Tseng, & Lam, 1999). An individualistic cultural orientation is more often associated with an *in*depen-dent self-construal – where the normative perspective is to prioritize one's own needs, achievement, and success, rather than being motivated by seeking to fulfill the needs of others (Wing-yi Cheng & Lam, 2013). Additionally, *in*dependent self-construal is more associated with considering the self as "separate or distinct" from all others, rather than as a constituent of a larger social group (Stephens et al., 2012, p. 3).

As is evidenced by the above, some extant social goal work indeed reflects Urdan and Maehr's early insistence for consideration of "definition of self" (1995, p. 221) – which are shaped by cultural orientation. However, now that a basic understanding of cross-cultural constructs used in social goal work has been established, another important question follows – how can findings associated with Chinese, Filipino, or other collectivistically oriented students be utilized to understand Latinx students' cultural values? Bearing in mind the paucity that exists in social goal literature regarding Latinx students, we now attempt to draw inferences from what is known about Latinx cultural values, and the extant social goal work that employs cultural considerations.

Latinx cultural values: A brief overview

First, Latinx cultural groups (in addition to East and Southeast Asian cultural groups), have been strongly associated with collectivistic cultural orientation (Triandis, McCusker, & Hui, 1990; Jabagchourian, Sorkhabi, Quach, & Strage, 2014; Arevalo et al., 2016). Additionally, Latinx students residing in the United States (especially those who have recently immigrated or are children of immi-grants) have been argued to more strongly identify with collectivistic cultural orientations and hold interdependent self-construals despite exposure and navigation of European American, individualistic culture (Marin & Triandis, 1985; Fuligni, Tseng, & Lam, 1999). Some research has linked the Latinx cultural value of familismo to collectivism – arguing that familismo reflects many of the attributes associated with collectivistic cultural orientation (Esparza & Sanchez, 2008). Though the definition of familismo (also referred to as familism) can differ across Latinx individuals and situations (Smith-Morris et al., 2012), extant literature describes this value as placing importance on being closely connected to one's immediate and extended family with an enduring sense of responsibility for and loyalty to them such that one's life and the choices that guide it are ultimately made to support the family and maintain their shared values (Suárez-Orozco & Suárez-Orozco, 2001; Knight et al., 2010). Furthermore, familismo reflects the belief that emotional and problem-solving support is shared reciprocally among family members (Davis et al., 2017). Though familismo has not been readily integrated into social goal studies, Ford's (1992) proposed integrative social relationship goals *social responsibility* (e.g., keeping interpersonal commitments, meeting social role obligations, and conforming to social/moral rules) is clearly reflected, *equity* (e.g., promoting reciprocity), and *resource provision* (e.g., giving support/assistance to others) (p. 83). Additionally, Dowson and McInerney's (2003) *social responsibility* and *social affiliation* goals appear to be reflected as well, though the perceived responsibilities and affiliation may be associated more strongly with the family unit, in addition to peer groups.

Academic Performance Outcomes: Connecting Latinx Cultural Values and Social Goals

In a study of Latinx high school seniors, Esparza and Sanchez (2008) conducted a multiple regression analysis to trace the relationships between parental education level, familismo, and academic achievement. They found that students who reported a strong sense of familismo exhibited greater levels of academic effort, as well as fewer truancies throughout the academic year. Additionally, they found that familism positively predicted students' GPA when mothers' educational attainment was lower, suggesting that Latinx students may view academic achievement as an important component of meeting social role responsibilities in their family. In a study of Latinx college students, some expressed the desire to honor their family's sacrifices made to enable them to pursue higher education (Pérez & Taylor, 2016). Though this study was conducted with a sample of college students, other research has corroborated Latinx students' belief that pursuance of high academic achievement is an important component to fulfilling familial obligations at other levels of development/education as well (Valdés, 1996; Naumann, Guillaume, & Funder, 2012). Thus, it can be argued that Latinx students' upholding of familismo, reflective of social goals described by Ford (1992) and Dowson and McInerney (2003), is significantly related to important facets of academic achievement.

Other studies regarding students' collectivistic cultural values and academic achievement appear to have similar findings. For example, in a cross-cultural study of Chinese and Filipino secondary students, King, McInerney, and Watkins (2013 found that students' social goals positively predicted students' effort – in addition to other important academic outcomes, such as motivational engagement and deep learning (p. 1515). However, King and colleagues chose to utilize peer-centered social goals (e.g., seeking a sense of belongingness and striving to help others), rather than family centered social goals as predictors of academic achievement. Though this adds to issues of generalizability to Latinx students, scholarship regarding Latinx cultural values, has noted that students may prioritize the roles and responsibilities associated with the immediate and extended family, but do not necessarily exclude perceptions of responsibility and commitment to others such as peers and authority figures (Delgado, Ettekal, Simpkins, & Schaefer, 2016; Suárez-Orozco & Suárez-Orozco, 1995; Rodriguez et al., 2003) – especially when those figures are perceived as sharing the student's group membership.

As demonstrated in the preceding discussion, the social reasons Latinx students espouse for academic achievement have the potential to be readily understood using a lens of cultural orientation. Again, existing social goal work has diverged in terms of the emphasis placed on academic outcomes versus "purely social" outcomes. This divergence can also be seen in research concerning Latinx students, therefore representing a paucity that seems greatest in terms of how Latinx students' social goals affect their academic outcomes. Given that Latinx cultural values, especially familismo, are often described in the literature in terms of family connectedness, belonging, and choosing to uphold roles reflecting collectivist perspectives, it is no surprise that much of the research investigating Latinx students' cultural values, and the small amount of social goal work that includes Latinx students, focus on interpersonal outcomes – which are discussed next.

Interpersonal Outcomes

As previously noted, social goals related to interpersonal outcomes can vary. Some of these goals, can include making a friend (Wentzel, 1999), being considered popular, asserting dominance, or building community with others (Ojanen & Findley-Van Nostrand, 2014). Though social goal work regarding Latinx students and interpersonal outcomes is scant, some interesting points can be explored using extant literature that concerns Latinx cultural values. To frame our discussion, we can consider the study conducted by Li and Wright (2014), regarding middle schoolers' social status goals. Though Latinx students did not make up the majority of the study sample, Li and Wright (2014) nevertheless demonstrated important definitions of social status goals, including popularity goals (as evidenced in survey items like, "I want to be well-known among my peers"), and social preference goals (e.g., "I want to be accepted by my peers") (p. 152). In addition to these social goals, Li and Wright (2014) investigated students' relational aggression and prosocial behaviors, as they related to students' differing endorsement of social goals. Interestingly, they found that students who endorsed social preference goals were more likely to report engaging prosocial behaviors, whereas students who endorsed popularity goals were more likely to engage relational aggression. Additionally, Li and Wright (2014) found significant gender difference for some aspects of social status goal/behaviors. Girls differed from boys in their higher endorsement of social preference goals. However, overall, girls exhibited endorsement of popularity goals, as well – which the authors interpreted as girls' increased sensitivity to social relationships overall, when compared with male peers (p. 156). Acknowledging gender differences in the study of social goal work is crucial for understanding the potential for different processes and influences which undergird students' social goal conceptualization and pursuit. Traditional gender norms exhibited in Latinx culture have been identified as a significant source of influence for Latinx identity, resulting in major implications for the lived experiences for Latinx students in both social and academic respects (Cupito, Stein, & Gonzalez, 2015; Sanchez, Smith, & Adams, 2018). For Latinx college women, the cultural value of marianismo has been argued to influence communication with others, expressions of sexuality, and the need to show devotion to family and spirituality (Piña-Watson et al., 2016). Related to these values, Latinx women may express social goals that are more communal in nature, where prosocial behaviors such as helping and collaborating with others are prioritized (Davis et al., 2017), reflective of Li and Wright's (2014) findings. Additionally, marianismo has been found to influence Latinx women's coping strategies and methods of conflict resolution with peers (Sanchez, Smith, & Adams, 2018). Thus, for Latinx women who strongly identify with Latinx cultural values, traditional gender roles such as marianismo, as well as individuals' endorsement of this cultural value, may have important effects for social goals – especially those which beget interpersonal interactions.

Aside from traditional gender roles, extant scholarship regarding the importance of creating a "culture of caring" at schools in which Latinx students perceive that teachers truly care for their well-being and academic success provides some grounds connections to social goal work. For example, Valenzuela (1999) found that Latinx high school students who did not perceive authentic caring from the faculty/staff at their school were more likely to exhibit behaviors that appeared to be defiant of school rules, or adopting a careless attitude toward academia (p. 94). However, she argued that these behaviors demonstrated acts of resistance to the often belittling, dehumanizing ways that teachers who were not familiar with Latinx cultural values treated students. She also argued that authentic mentoring relationships built upon respect and shared cultural values such as those cultivated within students' homes were key to creating a supportive environment for Latinx students.

Though not focused on Latinxs, Wentzel et al. (2018) conducted a two-part study that explored students' perceptions of peer and teacher support – and how those related to students' pursuance social goals for prosocial and socially responsible behavior. Prosocial behaviors were defined in this study as cooperation, respect for others, and positive forms of group participation (p. 612). Socially responsible behavior was defined as behaving consistently with classroom rules for behavior. Participants in this study ranged from grades 5–8, with the majority of the students identified as white. Basically put, students who perceived higher levels of peer and teacher emotional support were more likely to pursue goals related to prosocial and socially responsible behaviors. In other words, creating a learning environment in which students feel emotionally supported by caring others at both the peer and teacher levels is critical for their positive interactions with others, as well as their respect of classroom guidelines for acceptable behaviors. With respect to Valenzuela's research regarding Latinx students' resistance to uncaring learning environments, the opposite side of Wentzel et al.'s findings are exhibited. Though Wentzel et al.'s study did not place cultural values at fore, it nevertheless demonstrated the importance of creating an emotionally supportive environment for adolescents.

Future Research

Attending to Latinx students: Intersectionality and within-group differences

Though a significant portion of extant literature refers to Latinx students as a homogeneous group, recent work has demonstrated more acknowledgment of the vast within-group differences and multi-faceted identities, debunking previous monolithic perspectives of Latinxs (Liang et al., 2017). As an example, Latinx students have been referred to in literature in several different ways (e.g., Latin@, Latina/o, Hispanic) suggesting increased awareness and recognition of the intersectional identities of those who identify as Latinx in addition to other expressions of identity (e.g., sexuality, gender, class, generational status, and more) – each holding potential to influence the social goals Latinx students uphold. Urdan and Bruchmann's recent review of social goal scholarship included the observation that students' intersectional identities were largely ignored, and that this was a major oversight in extant achievement goal literature, along with nearly all other investigations of motivational processes (2018). In particular, we have briefly seen how traditional gender roles associated with Latinx cultural values (e.g., marianismo) can influence students' interpersonal interactions as well as explored how values related to the family (e.g., familismo) can play a role in academically oriented social goals – despite the lack of extant literature clearly connecting these. Though cross-cultural social goal studies provide some indication of work that decenters European American students and their cultural values, to date, none of it emphasizes Latinx students. Therefore, it is of the utmost importance that future social goal work shift its focus to this vastly growing student group in order to understand their experience, and inform educational policy and practice.

Using personal investment theory in social goal work

Again, the existing cross-cultural studies do not explicitly focus on Latinx students, or their cultural values, but have yielded some important findings regarding cultural groups that identify as collectivistic – a cultural orientation that is reflected in Latinx cultural values. As a first step toward amending the paucity of research concerning Latinx social goals, we can turn to personal investment theory (or PI theory). Introduced and utilized in studies by King and colleagues (King & McInerney (2014); King, McInerney, & Nasser (2017), these researchers argue that personal investment theory provides a framework that is much more sensitive to differing cultural values in achievement motivation. The main assumption underlying this framework is that the choice to invest oneself in a particular domain (e.g., school, work, other) differs across three dimensions: 1) sense of self, 2) perceived goals, and 3) facilitating conditions (King & McInerney, 2014, p. 177). With regard to sense of self, this review has shown that Latinx students often hold a sense of self (interdependent) that differs from their peers, especially white, middle class students – who often exhibit independent self-construals. With regard to facilitating conditions, King and McInerney (2014) argue that the environmental context in which a student is navigating (which includes peer interactions, parental support, and other components) matters greatly for investment into any endeavor, and will differ between individuals. Lastly, in terms of social goals, which are included as one of many types of goals that a student could have, King and McInerney (2014) view these as necessarily influenced by each of the other two dimensions. Again, personal investment theory is offered as a theoretical framework for understanding social goals that considers cultural and personal nuance – rather than lumping individuals into groups assumed to be homogeneous. Though there may be other suitable frameworks in existence, this framework may represent a starting point in generating more social goal scholarship that includes Latinx students in a more culturally sensitive capacity than is currently reflected in extant literature.

Remaining critical of the school environment

As evidenced throughout this chapter, a significant portion of research regarding Latinx cultural values seems rooted in, or at least reflective of, cross-cultural notions of collectivism. Additionally, it must be noted that American institutions of education are considered largely oriented toward individualistic cultural values, with multiple scholars arguing that this orientation pervades the K-20 system (Stephens et al., 2012; Cholewa & West-Olatunji, 2008). Some cross-cultural research attends to cross-cultural discontinuity, or cultural clashes/mismatches that occur when Latinx students who uphold collectivistic values navigate educational institutions that promote individualistic cultural values. However, few of these studies critique the issues of power, race, and discrimination that may undergird cultural discontinuity – preferring instead to summarize, rather than critique the facilitating environment surrounding Latinx students.

Related to the dimension of facilitating conditions in personal investment theory, the paucity of research regarding Latinx students' social goals represents a missed opportunity to conduct more critical studies of the educational environment in which Latinx students are living. In particular, it is necessary for social goal scholars to consider the effects of racial discrimination on Latinx students' social goal creation, navigation, and behaviors related to those goals. Many culturally sensitive scholars have highlighted the very real presence of racist interactions and other discriminatory practices that Latinx students experience throughout their navigation of the K-20 schooling system (Valenzuela, 1999; Yosso, Smith, Ceja, & Solórzano, 2009; Gomez, Miranda, & Polanco, 2011; Suárez-Orozco et al., 2015) – which could powerfully shape the goals that Latinx students engage for themselves – whether those goals be to achieve desired academic outcomes, or desired interpersonal outcomes. Additionally, Piña-Watson et al. (2016) warn researchers to avoid adopting deficit-based perspectives when researching Latinx students, especially when considering facets of their identity, such as cultural values. Moving forward, social goal scholarship must pay heed to this warning.

Note

1 Referencing Garcia & Dwyer (2018), we use the term Latinx instead of Latina/o as a more inclusive expression of group identity.

References

Arevalo, I., So, D., & Mcnaughton-Cassill, M. (2016). The role of collectivism among Latino American college students. *Journal of Latinos and Education, 15*(1), 1–9. Retrieved from: https://doi-org.ezproxy3.library.arizona.edu/10.1080/15348431.2015.1045143.

Austin, J. T., & Vancouver, J. B. (1996). Goal constructs in psychology: Structure, process, and content. *Psychological bulletin, 120*(3), 338. doi:10.1037/0033–2909.120.3.338.

Brophy, J. (2005). Goal theorists should move on from performance goals. *Educational Psychologist, 40*(3), 167–176. Retrieved from: https://doi-org.ezproxy1.library.arizona.edu/10.1207/s15326985ep4003_3.

Cholewa, B., & West-Olatunji, C. (2008). Exploring the relationship among cultural discontinuity, psychological distress, and academic outcomes with low- income, culturally diverse students. *Professional School Counseling, 12*(1), 54–61. Retrieved from: http://link.galegroup.com.ezproxy2.library.arizona.edu/apps/doc/A187904848/AONE?u=uarizona_main&sid=AONE&xid=3f8afe18.

Corona, R., Rodríguez, V., McDonald, S., Velazquez, E., Rodríguez, A., & Fuentes, V. (2017). Associations between cultural stressors, cultural values, and Latina/o college students' mental health. *Journal of Youth and Adolescence, 46*, 63–77. doi:10.1007/s10964–10016–0600–0605.

Cupito, A. M., Stein, G. L., & Gonzalez, L. M. (2015). Familial cultural values, depressive symptoms, school belonging and grades in Latino adolescents: Does gender matter?

Journal of Child and Family Studies, 24(6), 1638–1649. doi:4.library.arizona.edu/10.1007/s10826-014-9967-7.

Davis, A., Carlos, G., Schwartz, S., Zamboanga, B., Armenta, B., Kim, S., Opal, D., & Streit, C. (2017). The roles of familism and emotional reappraisal in the relations between acculturative stress and prosocial behaviors in Latino/a college students. *Journal of Latina/o Psychology, 6*, 175–189. doi:10.1037/lat0000092.

Dawes, M. (2017). Early adolescents' social goals and school adjustment. *Social Psychology of Education, 20*(2), 299–328. doi:10.1007/s11218-017-9380-3.

Delgado, M. Y., Ettekal, A. V., Simpkins, S. D., & Schaefer, D. R. (2016). How do my friends matter? Examining Latino adolescents' friendships, school belonging, and academic achievement. *Journal of Youth and Adolescence, 45*(6), 1110–1125. doi:4.library.arizona.edu/10.1007/s10964-015-0341-x.

Dowson, M., & McInerney, D. M. (2003). What do students say about their motivational goals?: Towards a more complex and dynamic perspective on student motivation. *Contemporary Educational Psychology, 28*(1), 91–113. doi:10.1016/S0361-476X(02)00010–00013.

Esparza, P., & Sánchez, B. (2008). The role of attitudinal familism in academic outcomes: A study of urban, Latino high school seniors. *Cultural Diversity and Ethnic Minority Psychology, 14*(3), 193–200. doi:10.1037/1099–9809.14.3.193.

Ford, M. (1992). *Motivating humans: Goals, emotions, and personal agency beliefs.* Thousand Oaks, CA: Sage Publications.

Fuligni, A. J., Tseng, V., & Lam, M. (1999). Attitudes toward family obligations among American adolescents with Asian, Latin American, and European backgrounds. *Child Development, 70*(4), 1030–1044. Retrieved from: http://ezproxy.library.arizona.edu/login?url=http://search.ebscohost.com/login.aspx?direct=true&db=a2h&AN=2163803&site=ehost-live.

Gándara, P. (2015). With the future on the line: Why studying Latino education is so urgent. *American Journal of Education, 121*(3), 451–463. doi:10.1086/680411.

Gándara, P., & Mordechay, K. (2017). Demographic change and the new (and not so new) challenges for Latino education. *The Educational Forum, 81*, 148–159. doi:10.1080/00131725.2017.1280755.

Garcia, G., & Dwyer, B. (2018). Exploring college students' identification with an organizational identity for serving Latinx students at a Hispanic serving institute (HSI) and an emerging HSI. *American Journal of Education, 124*, 191–215. doi:10.1086/695609.

Gomez, J., Miranda, R., & Polanco, L. (2011). Acculturative stress, perceived discrimination, and vulnerability to suicide attempts among emerging adults. *Journal of Youth and Adolescence, 40*(11), 1465–1476. doi:10.1007/s10964–10011–9688–9689.

Greenfield, P. M., & Quiroz, B. (2013). Context and culture in the socialization and development of personal achievement values: Comparing Latino immigrant families, European American families, and elementary school teachers. *Journal of Applied Developmental Psychology, 34*(2), 108–118. doi:10.1016/j.appdev.2012.11.002.

Guardia, J. R., & Evans, N. J. (2008). Factors influencing the ethnic identity development of latino fraternity members at a hispanic serving institution. *Journal of College Student Development, 49*(3), 163–181. Retrieved from http://ezproxy.library.arizona.edu/login?url=https://search-proquest-com.ezproxy4.library.arizona.edu/docview/195184944?accountid=8360.

Hill, N., & Torres, K. (2010). Negotiating the American dream: The paradox of aspirations and achievement among Latino students and engagement between their families and schools. *Journal of Social Issues, 66*, 95–112. doi:10.1111/j.1540-4560.2009.01635.x.

Jabagchourian, J. J., Sorkhabi, N., Quach, W., & Strage, A. (2014). Parenting styles and practices of Latino parents and Latino fifth graders' academic, cognitive, social, and behavioral outcomes. *Hispanic Journal of Behavioral Sciences, 36*(2), 175–194. doi:10.1177/0739986314523289.

King, R. B. (2017). Social goals and well-being. *Journal of Experimental Education, 85*(1), 107–125. doi:10.1080/00220973.2015.1111853.

King, R. B., & McInerney, D. M. (2014) Culture's consequences on student motivation: Capturing cross-cultural universality and variability through personal investment theory, *Educational Psychologist, 49*(3), 175–198, doi:10.1080/00461520.2014.926813.

King, R., McInerney, B., & Nasser, D. (2017). Different goals for different folks: A cross-cultural study of achievement goals across nine cultures. *Social Psychology of Education, 20* (3), 619–642. doi:10.1007/s11218–11017–9381–9382.

King, R., McInerney, D., & Pitliya, R. (2018). Envisioning a culturally imaginative educational psychology. *Educational Psychology Review, 30*, 1031–1065. doi:2.library.arizona.edu/10.1007/s10648-018-9440-z.

King, R. B., McInerney, D. M., & Watkins, D. A. (2013). Examining the role of social goals in school: A study in two collectivist cultures. *European Journal of Psychology of Education, 28*(4), 1505–1523. doi:2.library.arizona.edu/10.1007/s10212-013-0179-0.

Knight, G. P., Gonzalez, N. A., Saenz, D. S., Bonds, D. D., Germán, M., Deardorff, J., & Updegraff, K. A. (2010). The Mexican American cultural values scales for adolescents and adults. *Journal of Early Adolescence, 30*, 444–481. doi:10.1177/0272431609338178.

Li, Y., & Wright, M. F. (2014). Adolescents' social status goals: Relationships to social status insecurity, aggression, and prosocial behavior. *Journal of Youth and Adolescence, 43*, 146–160. doi:10.1007/s10964-013-9939-z.

Liang, C. T. H., Knauer-Turner, E. A., Molenaar, C. M., & Price, E. (2017). A qualitative examination of the gendered and racialized lives of Latina college students. *Gender Issues, 34*, 149–170. doi:10.1007/s12147–12016–9163–9168.

Marin, G., & Triandis, H. C. (1985). Allocentrism as an important characteristic of the behavior of Latin Americans and Hispanics. *Cross-Cultural and National Studies in Social Psychology, 69*, 80.

Markus, H., & Kitayama, S. (1991). Culture and the self: Implications for cognition, emotion, and motivation. *Psychological Review, 98*(2), 224–253. doi:10.1037/0033–295X.98.2.224.

McFarland, J., Hussar, B., Wang, X., Zhang, J., Wang, K., Rathbun, A., Barmer, A., Forrest Cataldi, E., & Bullock Mann, F. (2018). The condition of education 2018 (NCES 2018–2144). U. S. Department of Education. Washington, DC: National Center for Education Statistics. Retrieved from: https://nces.ed.gov/pubsearch/pubsinfo. asp?pubid=2018144.

Naumann, L. P., Guillaume, E. M., & Funder, D. C. (2012). The correlates of high parental academic expectations: An Asian-Latino comparison. *Journal of Cross-Cultural Psychology, 43*(4), 515–520. doi:10.1177/0022022112438398.

Ojanen, Tiina, & Findley-Van Nostrand, Danielle. (2014). Social goals, aggression, peer preference, and popularity: Longitudinal links during middle school. *Developmental Psychology, 50*(8), 2134–2143. doi:10.1037/a0037137.

Oyserman, D., Coon, H., & Kemmelmeier, M. (2002). Rethinking individualism and collectivism: Evaluation of theoretical assumptions and meta-analyses. *Psychological Bulletin, 128*(1), 3–72. doi:10.1037//0033–2909.128.1.3.

Pérez II, D., & Taylor, K. (2016). Cultivando logradores: Nurturing and sustaining Latino male success in higher education. *Journal of Diversity in Higher Education*, 9, 1–19. doi:10.1037/a0039145.

Piña-Watson, B., Lorenzo-Blanco, E., Dornhecker, M., Martinez, A., and Nagoshi, J. (2016). Moving away from a cultural deficit to a holistic perspective: Traditional gender role values, academic attitudes, and educational goals for Mexican descent adolescents. *Journal of Counseling Psychology*, 63, 307–318. doi:10.1037/cou0000133.

Portes, A., & Rumbaut, R. (2006). *Immigrant America: A portrait*. Los Angeles: University of California Press.

Rodriguez, N., Mira, C. B., Myers, H. F., Morris, J. K., & Cardoza, D. (2003). Family or friends: Who plays a greater supportive role for Latino college students? *Cultural Diversity and Ethnic Minority Psychology*, 9(3), 236–250. Retrieved from: https://doi-org.ezproxy3.library.arizona.edu/10.1037/1099-9809.9.3.236.

Sanchez, D., Smith, L., & Adams, W. (2018). The relationships among perceived discrimination, marianismo, gender role attitudes, racial-ethnic socialization, coping styles, and mental health outcomes in Latina college students. *Journal of Latina/o Psychology*, 6 (1), 1–15. doi:10.1037/lat0000077.

Smith-Morris, C., Morales-Campos, D., Castañeda Alvarez, E. A., & Turner, M. (2012). An anthropology of familismo: On narratives and descriptions of Mexican/immigrants. *Hispanic Journal of Behavioral Sciences*, 35, 35–60. doi:10.1177/0739986312459508.

Stephens, N. M., Fryberg, S. A., Markus, H. R., Johnson, C. S., & Covarrubias, R. (2012). Unseen disadvantage: How American universities' focus on independence undermines the academic performance of first-generation college students. *Journal of Personality and Social Psychology*, 102(6), 1178–1197. doi:10.1037/a0027143.

Stephens, N. M., Townsend, S., Markus, H. R., & Phillips, L. T. (2012). A cultural mismatch: Independent cultural norms produce greater increases in cortisol and more negative emotions among first-generation college students. *Journal of Experimental Social Psychology*, 48(6), 1389–1393. doi:10.1016/j.jesp.2012.07.008 www.sciencedirect.com/science/article/pii/S0022103112001424.

Stevens, T., Hamman, D., & Olivarez, A. (2007). Hispanic students' perception of white teachers' mastery goal orientation influences sense of school belonging. *Journal of Latinos & Education*, 6(1), 55–70. doi:10.1207/s1532771xjle0601_4.

Suarez-Orozco, C., & Suarez-Orozco, M. (1995). *Transformations: Migration, family life, and achievement motivation among Latino adolescents*. Stanford, CA: Stanford University Press.

Suárez-Orozco, C., & Suárez-Orozco, M. (2001). *Children of immigration*. Cambridge, MA: Harvard University Press.

Suárez-Orozco, C., Casanova, S., Martin, M., Katsiaficas, D., Cuellar, V., Smith, N., & Dias, S. (2015). Toxic rain in class: Classroom interpersonal microaggressions. *Educational Researcher*, 44, 151–160. doi:10.3102/0013189X15580314.

Sue, D. W., Lin, A. I., Torino, G. C., Capodilupo, C. M., & Rivera, D. P. (2009). Racial microaggressions and difficult dialogues on race in the classroom. *Cultural Diversity and Ethnic Minority Psychology*, 15, 183–190. doi:10.1037/a001419.

Triandis, H., McCusker, C., & Hui, C. (1990). Multimethod probes of individualism and collectivism. *Journal of Personality and Social Psychology*, 59(5), 1006–1020. Retrieved from: https://doi-org.ezproxy3.library.arizona.edu/10.1037/0022-3514.59.5.1006.

Urdan, T., & Bruchmann, K. (2018). Examining the academic motivation of a diverse student population: A consideration of methodology. *Educational Psychologist*, 53(2), 114–130. doi:10.1080/00461520.2018.1440234.

Urdan, T., & Maehr, M. (1995). Beyond a two-goal theory of motivation and achievement: A case for social goals. *Review of Educational Research*, 65(3), 213–243. Retrieved from: www.jstor.org.ezproxy2.library.arizona.edu/stable/1170683.

Valdés, G. (1996). *Con respeto: Bridging the distances between culturally diverse families and schools.* New York: Teachers College Press.

Valenzuela, A. (1999). *Subtractive schooling: U. S.-Mexican youth and the politics of caring.* Albany: State University of New York Press.

Wentzel, K. R. (1999). Social-motivational processes and interpersonal relationships: Implications for understanding motivation at school. *Journal of Educational Psychology*, 91 (1), 76–97. Retrieved from: https://doi-org.ezproxy1.library.arizona.edu/10.1037/0022-0663.91.1.76.

Wentzel, K. R. (2002). The contribution of social goal setting to children's school adjustment. In A. Wigfield & J. S. Eccles, (Eds.). *Development of achievement motivation* (pp. 221–246). Retrieved from: https://ebookcentral.proquest.com.

Wentzel, K., Muenks, K., McNeish, D., & Russell, S. (2018). Emotional support, social goals, and classroom behavior: A multilevel, multisite study. *Journal of Educational Psychology*, 110(5), 611–627. doi:10.1037/edu0000239.

Wing-yi Cheng, R., & Lam, S. (2013). The interaction between social goals and self-construal on achievement motivation. *Contemporary Educational Psychology*, 38, 136–148. doi:10.1016/j.cedpsych.2013.01.001

Witkow, M. R., & Fuligni, A. J. (2007). Achievement goals and daily school experiences among adolescents with Asian, Latino, and European American backgrounds. *Journal of Educational Psychology*, 99(3), 584–596. doi:2.library.arizona.edu/10.1037/0022-0663.99.3.584.

Yosso, T., Smith, W., Ceja, M., & Solorzano, D. (2009). Critical race theory, racial microaggressions, and campus racial climate for Latina/o undergraduates. *Harvard Educational Review*, 79(4), 659–690. Retrieved from: http://ezproxy.library.arizona.edu/login?url=https://search-proquest-com.ezproxy1.library.arizona.edu/docview/212300985?accountid=8360.

Zusho, A., & Clayton, K. (2011). Culturalizing achievement goal theory and research. *Educational Psychologist*, 46(4), 239–260. doi:10.1080/00461520.2011.614526.

13

SOCIAL GOALS IN CONTEXT

Sexuality and Gender Diversity

Tara S. Hackel and Kristopher M. Goodrich

Students' sexual and gender identities can influence their academic experiences in school. Lesbian, gay, bisexual, transgender, and queer (LGBTQ) students often demonstrate low academic achievement, experience minimal social acceptance with peers, and face academic adversities from teachers (Kosciw, Greytak, Giga, Villenas, & Danischewski, 2016). Understanding a school's social landscape for LGBTQ students may offer educators and researchers tools to improve LGBTQ students' academic outcomes. Though much of the extant literature investigates bullying and school belonging for LGBTQ students, to the authors' knowledge, the social goals of LGBTQ people have not been investigated in a dedicated and comprehensive way. Social goals may be important mediators for LGBTQ students' school success and as such are deserving of their own attention.

This chapter aims to be a guide for understanding some of the insights regarding social goals that can be gained from current research about LGBTQ students' academic achievement and interpersonal outcomes. From this point forward, we will refer to these students as sexually and gender diverse students to acknowledge the many different identities that could be held, as well as the fluidity of identity and expression some students might experience while in school. For the purposes of this chapter, we define social goals in relation to how one's understanding of their identity influences their behavior in a variety of contexts (e.g., academic achievement, social achievement goals, social content goals, focus towards school, etc.). This chapter begins with an overview of relevant definitions of sexual and gender identity and concludes with suggestions for researching the relationship between social goals and the school experiences of people with varied sexual and gender identities.

Definitions

To understand social goals with sexually and gender diverse students, it is important to first contextualize sexual and gender identity and describe some of the variations in these identities experienced by students. Many people conflate gender and sexual identity, but all persons have a gender identity as well as a sexual orientation. Gender identity is a person's self-referenced understanding and definition of their gender (Tate, Ledbetter, & Youssef, 2013). Gender identity is contrasted with sex assigned at birth, which is the sex (i.e., male, female, intersex) ascribed to a person based on their anatomy, typically by a medical doctor or another person in authority (Tate et al., 2013). The interaction between sex assigned at birth and gender identity form two major groups: cisgender and transgender (Tate et al., 2013). Cisgender persons are people who identify their gender with the sex assigned to them at birth. For example, a person who was assigned female at birth and identifies as a woman is a cisgender woman. Transgender persons do not identify with the sex assigned to them at birth, but instead see themselves as having a different sex, or living outside the gender binary of male or female. Intersex persons are born with sexual characteristics of both sexes (Intersex Society of North America, 2008). We utilize the term gender diversity to reflect that cisgender and transgender are two major categories of gender identity, although youth have taken many different labels to describe their gendered self (Goodrich & Luke, 2009).

Sexual identity has emotional, cognitive, and behavioral dimensions (Saewyc et al., 2004; van Anders, 2015). Sexual identity generally considers one's gender identity in relation to the gender(s) one is attracted to and/or engages in sexual behaviors with (van Anders, 2015). Sexual identity development takes place during the middle school years for many students (D'Augelli, Grossman, & Starks, 2008; Dubé, 2000; Dubé & Savin-Williams, 1999). Past studies find variation in the onset of awareness of same-gender attraction, engagement in sexual behaviors with the same gender, and adoption of a identity label such as gay or bisexual (D'Augelli et al., 2008; Dubé, 2000; Dubé & Savin-Williams, 1999). Specifically, some students are aware of their attraction to their same gender before nine years of age (Dubé & Savin-Williams, 1999). Other studies find that youth recognize their attraction to same gender youth between ages 10 and 13 years (D'Augelli et al., 2008; Dubé & Savin-Williams, 1999). Further, youth may engage in sexual behaviors with people of their same gender before they adopt a representative identity label (Dubé, 2000), although sexual behavior does not need to occur for one to adopt a sexual identity. As attraction, behavior, and identity label milestones occur at different times across people, considering different aspects of sexual identity (e.g., attraction) outside of or in addition to one's label for their identity may help locate youth who have diverse sexual identities.

LGBTQ is a commonly used acronym referring to people with diverse sexual and gender identities. Each letter in the acronym refers to a particular sexual or gender identity label, but the acronym is often used more broadly to refer to anyone who does not identify as heterosexual and cisgender. Lesbians (L) are women who are intimately, physically, and relationally attracted to other women. Gay men (G) are men who are intimately, physically, and relationally attracted to other men. Bisexuals (B) are persons who are intimately, physically, and relationally attracted to persons who identify as men or women. Heterosexual, or straight persons, are intimately, physically, and relationally attracted to persons with a different gender identity from their own. Asexuals (A) are persons who do not identify as being sexually active with persons of any gender. Each of these categories describe the label a person can take in relation to their sexual identity.

"Queer" and "questioning" (Q) are two other terms that can also be used to describe sexual orientation or gender identity. Questioning reflects a student's exploration, or uncertainty, related to either (or both) their sexual or gender identity. The person is not yet ready to make a commitment to their identity classification. The term queer is an umbrella term, which has some roots in politics or advocacy (Goodrich & Luke, 2015). Queer can be used by students to not allow others to define them precisely, as well as to deviate from established norms or binaries present in our culture (Goodrich & Luke, 2015). Queer can be used to identify one's sexual orientation or gender identity as fluid or undefinable. Queer may also be used to reflect a student's sociopolitical bend, such as using the term queer as a political identity (alongside a potential gender identity). Adopting a queer label may also be a way for the student to understand themselves in the context of a larger culture. Not all queer identified students subscribe to the same political causes, but, for each person, the queer label may speak to an identity that fits outside the traditional cultural norms. Combining these conceptualizations of sexual and gender identities, we use the acronym LGBTQ throughout the chapter to refer to any students outside of heterosexual sexual identities or cisgender gender identities. In instances when a topic only considers diverse sexualities and not diverse genders, we use the acronym LGBQ.

Gender and sexual identity may inform each other, but these identities are distinct. For example, people with non-binary genders (i.e., not a man or a woman) tend to have high rates of LGBQ sexual identities (Katz-Wise & Hyde, 2015). However, one cannot discern one's sexual identity from one's gender identity or vice versa as all combinations of genders and sexual identities are possible. As such, it is possible to identify as cisgender and heterosexual, cisgender and gay, transgender and lesbian, transgender and heterosexual, etc. To fully understand a student, one needs to be conscious that all students have gender and sexual identities, and, even if the identities may seem confusing based on current social norms, they make sense and are congruent identities for students.

Evidence

Though the social goals of LGBTQ people have not been empirically examined, the extant literature can still provide insights about how students' social motivations may shape schooling experiences for LGBTQ students. As specific types of social goals align with certain behaviors (Rudolph, Abaied, Flynn, Sugimura, & Agoston, 2011), inferences can be made about the types of social goals LGBTQ students and their peers hold by analyzing their responses to social situations. Much of the extant literature on LGBTQ students relates to peer aggression, and this chapter draws some of its insights about social goals by considering LGBTQ students' perceptions and behaviors in relation to their experiences of harassment. For example, might LGBTQ related harassment and social isolation provide cues to youth that it is not appropriate or cool to be LGBTQ? Similarly, analyzing LGBTQ students' beliefs and behaviors may provide insight about the social goals held by peers who perpetrate aggression based on sexual or gender identity. Lastly, LGBTQ students' peer interactions could be evidence of students' awareness of school social norms, what it means to be socially competent in a school, and how one's sexual or gender identities influence social status.

Social goals are affected by the environment (Ryan & Shim, 2006) and the social norms of a school (Munoz-Plaza, Crouse Quinn, & Rounds, 2002). Pursuing social goals requires that students understand and consider social norms to obtain their desired social outcomes. School norms vary by school context and shape the quality of a school's environment for LGBTQ youth. We can use social integration of LGBTQ students in the school peer network as a clue about school norms for LGBTQ identities: Social integration of LGBTQ youth may indicate favorable school norms and social isolation could indicate anti-LGBTQ norms. Research indicates that LGBQ youth are more socially isolated than heterosexual peers and LGBQ females have low perceived popularity (Hatzenbuehler, McLaughlin, & Xuan, 2012). Adolescents tend to not accept boys who do not conform to gender norms (Horn, 2007). This lack of social acceptance may suggest anti-LGBTQ social norms, which could provide motivation for students to not associate with LGBTQ students to appear socially competent. Further, Martin-Storey and colleagues (2015) found that LGBQ youth were more socially marginalized in a smaller predominantly White school, but not in a larger, more racially diverse school. These results suggest that norms towards LGBTQ identities in the racially diverse school likely differ from the predominantly White school, but deserve further study. Thus, the actions required to pursue social goals in either school probably differ as well. In sum, school norms about LGBTQ identities may help contextualize what actions are required to pursue different social goals.

Some social goals are concerned with obtaining certain outcomes, such as popularity, coolness, social dominance, and revenge. Students with a popularity goal, for example, strive for high social status among peers (Jarvinen & Nicholls, 1996). Social dominance goals relate to having power over or instilling fear in others (Jarvinen & Nicholls, 1996). If school norms support LGBTQ identities, a student may pursue a popularity goal by being pro-LGBTQ, or intervening in cases of LGBTQ harassment to uphold school norms (e.g., Poteat, 2015). However, if school norms are anti-LGBTQ, students may pursue dominance or popularity goals by perpetrating aggression towards LGBTQ students to gain power or status. Research has supported that students who tolerate social dominance tend to endorse less positive attitudes towards LGBQ peers (Poteat, 2007), however links between holding social dominance goals and LGBTQ acceptance remain untested. Having a lesbian or gay friend aligns with thinking that teasing lesbian and gay peers is wrong (Heinze & Horn, 2009). Thus, having a LGBTQ friend could motivate students to set prosocial goals. Lastly, school norms that do not support the pursuit of prosocial goals and, instead, support bullying might influence rates of perpetration of violence based on a students' gender and sexual identity. Again, extant research has not invested the interaction between prosocial goals and school norms for bullying.

Less than half of LGBTQ students experiencing harassment or assault demonstrate adaptive help-seeking (Kosciw et al., 2016), and social goals may provide insight about what promotes this behavior. A majority of LGBTQ students identify fear of being perceived as a "tattle tale" as one motivation for not reporting victimization to school staff and another 42% were too embarrassed or ashamed to report the harassment (Kosciw et al., 2016). These behaviors could align with a demonstration social achievement goal. A demonstration social achievement goal has both approach and avoid components (Ryan & Shim, 2006). A student holding a demonstration approach social goal is focused on appearing socially competent to others, whereas holding a demonstration avoid goal involves refraining from behaviors that may indicate to others that one lacks social competence (Ryan & Shim, 2006). One reason LGBTQ students may not report harassment is because the student is attempting to avoid looking socially incompetent with reporting (i.e., demonstration avoid) or is trying to demonstrate social competence by not getting other students in trouble (i.e., demonstration approach). Similarly, if school norms for social prestige do not allow for reporting peer harassment, LGBTQ's motivations for not reporting could also be related to pursuing a cool or popular outcome-based goal by upholding the school norms. About a third of LGBTQ students suggest that they do not involve staff in situations of harassment because they handled the harassment themselves, which could indicate a proactive response pattern of instructing the perpetrator to stop, or maladaptive patterns of retaliation (i.e., revenge social goal; Kosciw et al., 2016). About 36% of students did not report harassment because they were afraid of retaliation or violence from the perpetrator (Kosciw et al., 2016), which may indicate that LGBTQ students are worried about their peers acting on revenge goals.

Though studies have not investigated how social goals may be linked to perpetrating violence or harassment against LGBTQ students, some studies have investigated how witnessing teachers or peers intervene in cases of sexuality-based harassment (Wernick, Kulick, & Inglehart, 2013) influenced student behavior. Wernick et al. (2013) found that seeing teachers intervene in cases of harassment did relate to an increased likelihood of students intervening in cases of LGBTQ harassment. Further, seeing other students intervene had a more significant positive effect on a students' likelihood to intervene than seeing teachers intervene (Wernick et al., 2013). Witnessing teacher and peer intervention only partially explained a students' likelihood to intervene, and it is possible that social goals related to norms for demonstrating social competence or how to achieve dominance or popularity might help explain students' propensity to intervene in cases of anti-LGBTQ harassment.

The potential role that social goals could play in illuminating social motivations is clear. Increased understanding of the social norms across schools related to LGBTQ acceptance may help contextualize which actions are required to achieve social goals in specific school contexts and help explain students' behavior. Thus, social goals may be one tool for understanding varied rates of bullying, harassment, and social integration of LGBTQ students among schools as well as the motivations for LGBTQ students' responses to peer victimization.

Academic Performance

LGBTQ students are at risk for poor educational outcomes, which may be due to these students' experiences of harassment, low school belonging, or discriminatory school policies (Kosciw et al., 2016; Rostosky, Owens, Zimmerman, & Riggle, 2003; Toomey, Ryan, Diaz, Card, & Russell, 2010). The majority of LGBTQ students report experiencing verbal harassment and sexual harassment at school due to their sexual orientation or gender identity, with some LGBTQ students also reporting physical harassment or assault because of their identity (Kosciw et al., 2016). Victims of bullying tend to avoid school, feel lonely (Ladd, 1996), become less engaged in school over time (Buhs, Ladd, & Herald, 2006), and earn lower grades (Juvonen, Wang, & Espinoza, 2011). Emotional distress, such as depression and anxiety associated with bullying leads students to avoid school, and frequent absences hinder students ability to stay engaged in school, resulting in poor grades (Nishina, Juvonen, & Witkow, 2005). Further, psychosocial difficulties increase the risk for peer victimization, which can lead to a cyclical pattern of abuse and depression (Nishina et al., 2005). Patterns of victimization and low academic achievement translate to LGBTQ students. LGBTQ students who experience higher rates of victimization tend to disclose higher levels of depression, more absences, lower aspirations for post-secondary education, lower school belonging, and earn lower GPAs than their peers reporting lower levels of victimization (Galliher, Rostosky, & Hughes, 2004; Rostosky et al., 2003).

As school norms and social goals may contextualize students' behaviors in schools, it may be fruitful for researchers to integrate social goals in to investigations about improving LGBTQ students' academic performance. Improving academic performance of LGBTQ students seems directly related to reducing emotional distress from peer victimization and improving feelings of school belonging and school attendance. Understanding whether achieving popularity, dominance, and social achievement goals involves bullying LGBTQ students could clue researchers in to the school climate, and the goals that drive student behavior. Findings from this research could then discuss how teachers or schools may work to shift social goals so as to work to dis-incentivize bullying for LGBTQ students to have a safer and healthier learning environment.

Academic motivation

Academic motivation is understood to be multiple factors that prompt and sustain a desire to pursue educational pursuits (Shell et al., 2010). High academic motivation tends to align with high academic achievement (Wentzel & Miele, 2016). Thus, improving LGBTQ students' academic motivation may be one pathway for improving these students' school achievement and experiences. Multiple motivational constructs are prominent within educational psychology research (Murphy & Alexander, 2000). Yet, most published research on LGBTQ students' motivation relates to belonging and connectedness (Galliher et al., 2004; Kosciw et al., 2016; Murdock & Bolch, 2005; Rostosky et al., 2003). School belonging is students' beliefs that they are respected and valued members of their school community (Finn, 1989). LGBTQ students tend to have lower school belonging than their heterosexual peers (Galliher et al., 2004; Kosciw et al., 2016; Rostosky et al., 2003). Many of these belonging studies utilize survey instruments that ask students about their level of feeling connected to their school (Kosciw et al., 2016). Less optimal social goals relates to lower experiences of school connectedness (Meisel & Colder, 2017). Perhaps, LGBTQ students holding less optimal social goals contribute to lower academic motivation (e.g., belonging) and achievement for LGBTQ students, but this remains untested.

School belonging relates to other motivational constructs such as mindset and self-efficacy (Good, Rattan, & Dweck, 2012; Roeser, Midgley, & Urdan, 1996). Considering the often low reported school belonging of LGBTQ students, we can infer that LGBTQ students may have lower academic motivation than their heterosexual and cisgender peers. A single unpublished empirical investigation of LGBQ middle school students' academic motivation found that sexual identity did not relate with either mindsets for intelligence or self-efficacy (Hackel, Jones, Collins, & St. John, 2019). The authors did not suggest why sexual identity and motivation were unrelated (Hackel et al., 2019). School norms around LGBTQ identities and academic motivation might relate to whether students hold social goals around feeling motivated towards school work. For example, a socially victimized LGBTQ student may still put forth academic effort even if a school's norms do not value scholastic ability, because the LGBTQ student has no social capital to lose by trying in school. Further research should continue investigating the potential relationships between social goals, academic motivation, and diverse gender and sexual identities in various school contexts.

Interpersonal Outcomes

Interpersonal outcomes have been defined in this text as the consequences of the given social goals, such as how the social goal affects relationships with friends, classmates, teachers, or others. From the extant literature, there is clear evidence that LGBTQ students struggle in schools, and those struggles influence LGBTQ students' interpersonal outcomes (Copeland, Wolke, Angold, & Costello, 2013; Fisher, Poirier, & Blau, 2012; Institute of Medicine, 2011; Kosciw et al., 2016). LGBTQ students are more likely than their heterosexual and cisgender peers to face harassment, discrimination and violence in schools (Kosciw et al., 2016), which influences, not only their academic and mental health outcomes, but also interpersonal relationships with others. In the comprehensive 2015 GLSEN study, over half of LGBTQ students (51.6%) reported feeling unsafe at school due to their sexual orientation, and 43.3% because of their gender expression. Further, over a third of students noted they avoided gender-segregated spaces in schools due to feelings of discomfort or lack of safety (39.4% bathrooms and 37.9% locker rooms). This further led students to avoid school functions and extracurricular activities (71.5% and 65.7% respectively) because of similar fears (Kosciw et al., 2016). The avoidance of spaces in school and school activities demonstrates the lack of connection and fear that LGBTQ students can hold with their peers and may lead them to be further estranged from other peers who could be more supportive or friendly. It is therefore unsurprising that research by Hatzenbuehler and colleagues (2012) found that, in general, queer youth were socially isolated and queer females were found to have low popularity in schools.

Victimization and isolation in schools may influence LBGTQ students' persistence and mental health outcomes in schools. Bidell (2014) found that LGBTQ homeless students who dropped out of school had higher mental health outcomes compared to those who persisted to graduation. Although a surprising finding, it appeared that education itself did not serve as a protective factor when mixed with continuous and pervasive harassment and bullying. To preserve one's mental health, queer students had to disengage from their education.

High absenteeism among LGBTQ students not only precludes students from participating in classroom learning, but LGBTQ students also cannot create meaningful social connections with classmates and teachers if they are not at school. Though we do not yet empirically understand which social goals LGBTQ students tend to adopt, it seems reasonable to infer that a student might not be motivated to set social achievement goals to appear socially competent or cool goals in a school setting where they do not feel they belong or avoid. Being competent or cool in a space that does not value you or your identities might require one to be self-destructive. Thus, lack of meaningful social interaction might preclude LGBTQ students from setting social goals or limit the influence of these goals on LGBTQ students' school behaviors. Further, if school is a place where one is harassed, LGBTQ students may not set achievement goals, as schooling and school achievement might be associated with harassment and discrimination, and safety may be seen as more paramount than school achievement. In schools where there are strong social dominance and revenge goals, and anti-LGBTQ behavior is accepted or promoted, some LGBTQ students may find it safer to disengage with the schooling environment than pursue achievement or other social goals.

Additional results from the GLSEN national survey (Kosciw et al., 2016) include that 98.1% of all LGBTQ students reported hearing the term "gay" in a negative way, with 67.4% hearing those remarks frequently or often; 95.8% reported hearing other types of homophobic remarks, with 58.8% hearing those types of remarks frequently or often. In parallel findings, 95.7% of LGBTQ students reported hearing negative remarks about gender expression, 62.9% reported hearing this frequently or often. Additionally, 85.7% of students heard specifically negative remarks about transgender people, 40.5% hearing them frequently or often. Of all the students who heard these remarks, 93.4% reported feeling distressed because of this language.

This type of language further creates a barrier between LGBTQ students and their peers, as well as school staff. That is because students further reported hearing homophobic (56.2%) and negative gender expression (63.5%) remarks from teachers or other school staff, which might further make students feel as if school is an unsafe environment, and build barriers in relating with teachers and other school staff members (Kosciw et al., 2016). Less than two thirds of students could identify at least six supportive school staff members (63.7%), and only 36.8% of students reported that their school administration was supportive of LGBTQ students (Kosciw et al., 2016). In the same study, however, 97% of students could identify at least one staff member supportive of LGBTQ students in their school, which could lead to some form of comfortable and positive relationship building in schools (Kosciw et al., 2016). Supportive relationships with teachers, school staff, and peers may be protective factors against negative academic outcomes of these children (Kosciw et al., 2016; Poteat, Calzo, & Yoshikawa, 2016; Poteat, Heck, Yoshikawa, & Calzo, 2016; Wentzel & Wigfield, 1998).

When LGBTQ students do report instances of victimization to school staff, more than half of students were told to ignore the harassment (Kosciw et al., 2016). Ignoring negative social outcomes is a maladaptive response to aggression (Rudolph et al., 2011). Thus, school staff need more support with how to effectively scaffold LGBTQ students' response to aggression to promote developmental social goals and adaptive student responses to peer victimization (e.g., Goodrich & Luke, 2009; Shi & Doud, 2017; Simons, Beck, Asplund, Chan, & Byrd, 2018). Additionally, the authors found that pre-service teachers' self-reported levels of heterosexism was the strongest predictor for their sense of efficacy in instructing LGBTQ youth (Jones, Hershberger, Goodrich, Hackel, & Love, n.d.). As such, teacher education programs may need to attend to heterosexism and biases towards LGBTQ youth to ensure greater likelihood of effective teaching with these groups of students. Ideally, more effective responses to aggression could lead to less experience of victimization and increased school attendance and achievement for LGBTQ students. Outside of reporting harassment, teachers' having high efficacy for instructing LGBTQ youth could also be one tool for improving LGBTQ students' school experiences (Jones et al., n.d.).

Not all interpersonal outcomes appear negative in schools, as social integration has been found to vary widely among individual schools for LGBTQ students (Chesir-Teran, 2003; Martin-Storey et al., 2015). Factors, including school policies, teachers' beliefs, and the social norms of the school can all influence the social connection of LGBTQ youth (Chesir-Teran, 2003; Poteat, 2007, 2015). Gay Straight Alliances (GSA's; or more recently named Gender Sexuality Alliances to be more inclusive of students' identities) and Acceptance Coalitions (Ax-Co) groups, are emerging in many school environments and have been demonstrated to support overall school climate (Schmidt & Nilsson, 2006) as well as LGBTQ students' experiences, regardless of their participation level in the group (Walls, Kane, & Wisneski, 2010). Though it seems unlikely that a LGBTQ person would set goals to be socially competent within a social network that does not value them, perhaps, LGBTQ students set unique social goals amongst their LGBTQ-identified peer group compared to the social goals they hold in relation to the entire school. Extant research has found that GSA and Ax-Co groups can provide LGBTQ students a sense of belonging and community (Valenti & Campbell, 2009), facilitate personal exploration and self-awareness (Anderson, 1998), and improve relationships with school stakeholders (Lee, 2002). GSAs have also been found as a place where students can practice prosocial behaviors, such as building friendships with peers (Mereish & Poteat, 2015). As such, these types of groups within school can promote social goals and interpersonal outcomes amongst and between LGBTQ students and their heterosexual and cisgender peers to make school a safer place.

Areas of Future Research

There is much opportunity for future research into LGBTQ students' social goals, as currently no research has operationalized or measured LGBTQ person's social goals in the ways described in this chapter. As such, a wide number of research questions exist across conceptualizations of social goals, including how social goals relate to interpersonal relationships, academic achievement, academic motivation, and so forth. First, it would be important to better understand the types of social goals that sexually and gender diverse students might hold. Researchers might consider asking the question: which social goals are most relevant for LGBTQ students? And why might this be so? There are many potential factors that might influence how LGBTQ persons come to adopt a social goal. For example, a factor that may be explored is the influence a students' sexual identity or gender identity may have on their social goals. Does marginalized identity status reflect certain social goals, versus others? Or is the relationship to these variables more complex? Perhaps congruence, or incongruence, with stated gender roles may be a more important than a social goal (e.g., popularity, academic or social achievement), or connections to the binary identity of gender culture. Researchers can investigate whether a shared identity status influences how persons set social goals. LGBTQ persons may be more likely to set social goals for their relationships towards other LGBTQ persons than with cis-gender or heterosexual peers. Conversely, rather than shared identity status, perhaps perceptions around how supportive, or knowledgeable about LGBTQ issues a person is serves as a greater factor than LGBTQ identity status for providing context to the adoption of social goals. An unanswered question is how similar or dissimilar social goals are for LGBTQ persons compared to people from other marginalized identities. This might show us some universality in how marginalized persons understand and live social goals, versus what may be sexual identity, gender identity, or context specific.

A further unanswered question relates to LGBTQ students' focus towards school. Researchers should disentangle whether LGBTQ students tend to be motivated to participate in the schooling experience to learn or to be social. These investigations should consider whether school norms about LGBTQ identity moderate the adoption of a social or academic focus. Does it make sense to focus on academics if school norms preclude you from gaining social status because of your LGBTQ identity?

Advancements in social goals research should be inclusive of gender diverse students by offering expansive gender options to study participants and examining the influence of gender beyond a binary conceptualization. Research often assumes participants' hold a binary gender identity; that is, research methodology only provides opportunities for students to identify as boys and girls and does not allow for transgender or non-binary people to identify themselves within research studies. Without identification, researchers cannot gain insights about these students or how to leverage social goals to improve schooling experiences gender diverse students. Additionally, a large volume of research investigates common gender stereotypes for traditionally gender identifying students (e.g., girls are good at language arts whereas, boys are good at math; girls are relationally aggressive, whereas boys are physically aggressive). These gender stereotypes may influence the social norms and behaviors associated with pursuing social goals in a school. For example, prior research demonstrates that boys who do not comply with gender norms are less accepted by peers (Horn, 2007). Researchers may consider how binary gender stereotypes influence the adoption of social goals of gender diverse students. If a student cannot access social competence and popularity through upholding gender norms, what other factors become more salient to gender diverse students as they pursue social status?

Finally, individual differences in academic achievement, motivation, and social experiences have been found to vary by ethnicity and gender; as such, there may be a possibility that sexual identity could also affect academic and interpersonal outcomes in school. Therefore, it will be important to measure sexual identity when conducting social goals research. Readers should refer to Jones, Hackel, Hershberger, and Goodrich (in press) for a discussion of measuring sexual identity in educational studies and further potential studies that might address this gap in the literature. Additionally, as gender and sexual identity often interact to shape behavior and experience, studies looking to make claims about gender differences might be able to better interpret nuances in behaviors within gender groups if the research does not overlook the influence of sexual identity. People with diverse sexual identities might reflect stereotypical or average academic and social outcomes for their gender group, or researchers might observe challenges to these gendered results.

Another question that should be answered in the literature is how social goals persist or change across the lifespan, especially with LGBTQ persons and their timelines for exploring their sexual and gender identities. Social goals for LGBTQ people and their peers might change from elementary to middle or high school to college as the social norms of a school, geographic area, or nation change. Changes in social goals may also be motivated by one's changing conception or acceptance of their diverse sexual or gender identity. Conversely, perhaps there is some stability in the endorsement of social goal regardless of changing social contexts. Thus, research is needed to determine if social goals change, and what may motivate the change across the lifespan of human development?

Although we see high rates of harassment and discrimination with LGBTQ students, we currently need a more detailed understanding of how social goals influence the ways that LGBTQ students respond to these forms of aggression. Social goals may help illuminate why LGBTQ students confront, ignore, or retaliate against an oppressor. What motivates different responses, social goals or otherwise, and how do LGBTQ students' responses to aggression compare to their heterosexual and cisgender peers? Response patterns across LGBTQ, heterosexual, and cisgender students with congruent social goals may be similar, or LGBTQ students may understand or enact those goals differently compared to their heterosexual and cisgender peers. Further, investigating whether LGBTQ response patterns mimic those of students from other marginalized groups could help disentangle the role of sexual and gender identity in shaping social goals compared to the influence of marginalization within a social context on social goals. Further, it is unclear in the literature whether LGBTQ students seek help from peers or family in response to harassment. Future research understanding LGBTQ students' social goals towards engaging with others who are close to them is warranted.

Conclusion

This chapter explores how social goals may increase understanding of schools' social landscapes for LGBTQ students. School norms related to sexual and gender identity may influence students' adoption of social goals and the behaviors required for pursuing various social goals. Although LGBTQ students' social goals or how social goals shape interactions with LGBTQ peers have not been investigated, this chapter demonstrates that social goals may be a valuable tool for gaining more insight about harassment, academic performance, and social relationships of LGBTQ students. Researchers can increase understanding of LGBTQ students' social goals by first identifying which goals are most salient for LGBTQ students. Then, this work can be expanded to illuminate why these goals are most relevant for LGBTQ students and how adoption of these goals relates to academic outcomes for LGBTQ students. Outside of LGBTQ-specific research, all future social goals research stands to benefit from being inclusive of gender diverse students as well as considering the role of sexual identity in producing social outcomes.

References

Anderson, A. L. (1998). Strengths of gay male youth: An untold story. *Child and Adolescent Social Work Journal*, 15, 5–71.

Bidell, M. P. (2014). Is there an emotional cost of completing high school? Ecological factors and psychological distress among LGBT homeless youth. *Journal of Homosexuality*, 61(3), 366–381. doi:10.1080/00918369.2013.842426.

Buhs, E. S., Ladd, G. W., & Herald, S. L. (2006). Peer exclusion and victimization: Processes that mediate the relation between peer group rejection and children's classroom engagement and achievement? *Journal of Educational Psychology*, 98(1), 1–13.

Chesir-Teran, D. (2003). Conceptualizing and assessing heterosexism in high schools: A setting-level approach. *American Journal of Community Psychology*, 31(3–4), 267–279. doi:10.1023/A:1023910820994.

Copeland, W. E., Wolke, D., Angold, A., & Costello, E. J. (2013). Adult psychiatric outcomes of bullying and being bullied by peers in childhood and adolescence. *JAMA Psychiatry*. Retrieved from: http://archpsyc.jamanetwork.com/.

D'Augelli, A. R., Grossman, A. H., & Starks, M. T. (2008). Gender atypicality and sexual orientation development among lesbian, gay, and bisexual youth. *Journal of Gay & Lesbian Mental Health*, 12(1–2), 121–143. doi:10.1300/J529v12n01_08.

Dubé, E. M. (2000). The role of sexual behavior in the identification process of gay and bisexual males. *Journal of Sex Research*, 37(2), 123–132. doi:10.1080/00224490009552029.

Dubé, E. M., & Savin-Williams, R. C. (1999). Sexual identity development among ethnic sexual-minority male youths. *Developmental Psychology*, 35(6), 1389–1398. doi:10.1037/0012-1649.35.6.1389.

Dweck, C. S., & Leggett, E. L. (1988). A social-cognitive approach to motivation and personality. *Psychological Review*, 95(2), 256–273. doi:10.1037/0033-295X.95.2.256.

Finn, J. D. (1989). Withdrawing from school. *Review of Educational Research*, 59(2), 117–142. doi:10.2307/1170412.

Fisher, S. K., Poirier, J. M., & Blau, G. M. (2012). *Improving emotional and behavioral outcomes for LGBT youth: A guide for professionals*. Baltimore, MD: Brookes Publishing.

Galliher, R. V., Rostosky, S. S., & Hughes, H. K. (2004). School belonging, self-esteem, and depressive symptoms in adolescents: An examination of sex, sexual attraction status, and urbanicity. *Journal of Youth and Adolescence*, 33(3), 235–245. doi:10.1023/B: JOYO.0000025322.11510.9d.

Good, C., Rattan, A., & Dweck, C. S. (2012). Why do women opt out? Sense of belonging and women's representation in mathematics. *Journal of Personality and Social Psychology*, 102(4), 700–717. https://doi:10.1037/a0026659.

Goodrich, K., & Luke, M. (2015). *Group counseling with LGBTQI persons across the life span.* Hoboken, NJ: John Wiley & Sons.

Goodrich, K. M., & Luke, M. (2009). LGBTQ responsive school counseling. *Journal of LGBT Issues in Counseling*, 3(2), 113–127.

Hackel, T. S., Jones, M. H., Collins, A. S., & St. John, J. M. (2019, April). *Middle school students' sexual identities do not relate to their academic motivation.* Poster presented at the annual meeting of the American Educational Research Association, Toronto, Canada.

Hatzenbuehler, M. L., McLaughlin, K. A., & Xuan, Z. (2012). Social networks and risk for depressive symptoms in a national sample of sexual minority youth. *Social Science & Medicine*, 75(7), 1184–1191. doi:10.1016/j.socscimed.2012.05.030.

Heinze, J. E., & Horn, S. S. (2009). Intergroup contact and beliefs about homosexuality in adolescence. *Journal of Youth and Adolescence*, 38(7), 937–951. doi:10.1007/s10964-009-9408-x.

Horn, S. S. (2007). Adolescents' acceptance of same-sex peers based on sexual orientation and gender expression. *Journal of Youth and Adolescence*, 36(3), 363–371. doi:10.1007/s10964-006-9111-0.

Institute of Medicine. (2011). The health of lesbian, gay, bisexual, and transgender people: Building a foundation for better understanding. Retrieved from: www.iom.edu.

Intersex Society of North America. (2008). What is Intersex?www.isna.org/faq/what_is_intersex.

Jarvinen, D. W., & Nicholls, J. G. (1996). Adolescents' social goals, beliefs about the causes of social success, and satisfaction in peer relations. *Developmental Psychology*, 32(3), 435–441.

Jones, M. H., Hackel, T. S., Hershberger, M. A., & Goodrich, K. M. (published online September 24, 2018). Queer youth in educational psychology research. *Journal of Homosexuality*, doi:10.1080/00918369.2018.1510262.

Jones, M. H., Hershberger, M. A., Goodrich, K. M., Hackel, T. S., & Love, A. M. A. (n.d.). Preservice teachers' self-efficacy for teaching LGBQ youth.

Juvonen, J., Wang, Y., & Espinoza, G. (2011). Bullying experiences and compromised academic performance across middle school grades. *The Journal of Early Adolescence*, 31(1), 152–173.

Katz-Wise, S. L., & Hyde, J. S. (2015). Sexual fluidity and related attitudes and beliefs among young adults with a same-gender orientation. *Archives of Sexual Behavior*, 44(5), 1459–1470. doi:10.1007/s10508-014-0420-1.

Kosciw, J. G., Greytak, E. A., Giga, N. M., Villenas, C., & Danischewski, D. J. (2016). *The 2015 national school climate survey: The experiences of lesbian, gay, bisexual, transgender, and queer youth in our nation's schools.* New York: GLSEN.

Lee, C. (2002). The impact of belonging to a high school gay/straight alliance. *The High School Journal*, 85(3), 13–26.

Martin-Storey, A., Cheadle, J. E., Skalamera, J., & Crosnoe, R. (2015). Exploring the social integration of sexual minority youth across high school contexts. *Child Development*, 86(3), 965–975. doi:10.1111/cdev.12352.

Meisel, S. N., & Colder, C. R. (2017). Social goals impact adolescent substance use through influencing adolescents' connectedness to their schools. *Journal of Youth and Adolescence*, 46(9), 2015–2027doi:10.1007/s10964-017-0655-y.

Mereish, E. H., & Poteat, V. P. (2015). A relational model of sexual minority mental and physical health: The negative effects of shame on relationships, loneliness, and health. *Journal of Counseling Psychology*, 62(3), 425–437. doi:10.1037/cou0000088.

Munoz-Plaza, C., Crouse Quinn, S., & Rounds, K. A. (2002). Lesbian, gay, bisexual and transgender students: Perceived social support in the high school environment. *The High School Journal*, 85(4), 52–63.

Murdock, T. B., & Bolch, M. B. (2005). Risk and protective factors for poor school adjustment in lesbian, gay, and bisexual (LGB) high school youth: Variable and person-centered analyses. *Psychology in the Schools*, 42(2), 159–172. doi:10.1002/pits.20054.

Murphy, P. K., & Alexander, P. A. (2000). A motivated exploration of motivation terminology. *Contemporary Educational Psychology*, 25(1), 3–53. doi:10.1006/ceps.1999.1019.

Nishina, A., Juvonen, J., & Witkow, M. R. (2005). Sticks and stones may break my bones, but names will make me feel sick: The psychosocial, somatic, and scholastic consequences of peer harassment. *Journal of Clinical Child & Adolescent Psychology*, 34(1), 37–48. doi:10.1207/s15374424jccp3401_4.

Poteat, V. P. (2007). Peer group socialization of homophobic attitudes and behavior during adolescence. *Child Development*, 78(6), 1830–1842.

Poteat, V. P. (2015). When prejudice is popular: Implications for discriminatory behavior. *Social Development*, 24(2), 404–419.

Poteat, V. P., Calzo, J. P., & Yoshikawa, H. (2016). Promoting youth agency through dimensions of gay–straight alliance involvement and conditions that maximize associations. *Journal of Youth and Adolescence*, 45(7), 1438–1451. doi:10.1007/s10964-016-0421-6.

Poteat, V. P., Heck, N. C., Yoshikawa, H., & Calzo, J. P. (2016). Greater engagement among members of gay-straight alliances: Individual and structural contributors. *American Educational Research Journal*, 53(6), 1732–1758. doi:10.3102/0002831216674804.

Roeser, R. W., Midgley, C., & Urdan, T. C. (1996). Perceptions of the school psychological environment and early adolescents' psychological and behavioral functioning in school: The mediating role of goals and belonging. *Journal of Educational Psychology*, 88(3), 408–422. doi:10.1037/0022-0663.88.3.408.

Rostosky, S. S., Owens, G. P., Zimmerman, R. S., & Riggle, E. D. B. (2003). Associations among sexual attraction status, school belonging, and alcohol and marijuana use in rural high school students. *Journal of Adolescence,* 26(6), 741–751. doi:10.1016/j.adolescence.2003.09.002.

Rudolph, K. D., Abaied, J. L., Flynn, M., Sugimura, N., & Agoston, A. M. (2011). Developing relationships, being cool, and not looking like a loser: Social goal orientation predicts children's responses to peer aggression: Responses to peer aggression. *Child Development,* 82(5), 1518–1530. doi:10.1111/j.1467-8624.2011.01631.x.

Ryan, A. M., & Shim, S. S. (2006). Social achievement goals: The nature and consequences of different orientations toward social competence. *Personality and Social Psychology Bulletin*, 32(9), 1246–1263.

Saewyc, E. M., Bauer, G. R., Skay, C. L., Bearinger, L. H., Resnick, M. D., Reis, E., & Murphy, A. (2004). Measuring sexual orientation in adolescent health surveys: Evaluation of eight school-based surveys. *Journal of Adolescent Health,* 35(4), 345.e1–345.e15. doi:10.1016/j.jadohealth.2004.06.002.

Schmidt, C. K., & Nilsson, J. E. (2006). The effects of simultaneous developmental processes: Factors relating to the career development of lesbian, gay, and bisexual youth. *The Career Development Quarterly,* 55, 22–37.

Shell, D. F., Brooks, D. W., Trainin, G., Wilson, K. M., Kauffman, D. F., & Herr, L. M. (2010). *The unified learning model*. Dordrecht: Springer Netherlands. Retrieved from: http://link.springer.com/10.1007/978-90-481-3215-7.

Shi, Q., & Doud, S. (2017). An examination of school counselors' competency working with lesbian, gay, bisexual and transgender students. *Journal of LGBT Issues in Counseling, 11*(1), 2–17. doi:10.1080/15538605.2017.1273165.

Simons, J. D., Beck, M. J., Asplund, N. R., Chan, C. D., & Byrd, R. (2018). Advocacy for gender minority students: recommendations for counselor counselors. *Sex Education.* doi:10.1080/14681811.2017.1421531.

Social Perception, Attitudes, Mental Simulation Laboratory. (n.d.). Complete list of gender-related terms. Retrieved August 6, 2018, from: http://online.sfsu.edu/ctate2/genderterms.html.

Tate, C. C., Ledbetter, J. N., & Youssef, C. P. (2013). A two-question method for assessing gender categories in the social and medical sciences. *Journal of Sex Research, 50*(8), 767–776.

Toomey, R. B., Ryan, C., Diaz, R. M., Card, N. A., & Russell, S. T. (2010). Gender-nonconforming lesbian, gay, bisexual, and transgender youth: School victimization and young adult psychosocial adjustment. *Developmental Psychology, 46*(6), 1580–1589. doi:10.1037/a0020705.

Valenti, M., & Campbell, R. (2009). Working with youth on LGBT issues: why Gay–Straight Alliance advisors become involved. *Journal of Community Psychology, 37*(2), 228–248. doi:10.1002/jcop.20290.

van Anders, S. M. (2015). Beyond sexual orientation: Integrating gender/sex and diverse sexualities via Sexual Configurations Theory. *Archives of Sexual Behavior, 44*(5), 1177–1213. doi:10.1007/s10508-015-0490-8.

Walls, N. E., Kane, S. B., & Wisneski, H. (2010). Gay-straight alliances and school experiences of sexual minority youth. *Youth & Society, 41*, 307–332. doi:10.1177/0044118X09334957.

Wentzel, K. R., & Miele, D. B. (2016). *Handbook of motivation at school* (2nd ed.). New York: Routledge.

Wentzel, K. R., & Wigfield, A. (1998). Academic and social motivational influences on students' academic performance. *Educational Psychology Review, 10*(2), 155–175. doi:10.1023/A:1022137619834.

Wernick, L. J., Kulick, A., & Inglehart, M. H. (2013). Factors predicting student intervention when witnessing anti-LGBTQ harassment: The influence of peers, teachers, and climate. *Children and Youth Services Review, 35*(2), 296–301. doi:10.1016/j.childyouth.2012.11.003.

14

SOCIAL GOALS IN CONTEXT
Social Media

Gaëlle Ouvrein, Karen Verswijvel and Lies De Kimpe

The Internet and related technologies are a central element in the lives of teens and young adults (Boyd, 2007; Lenhart, Duggan, Perrin, Stepler, Rainie, & Parker, 2015; Lenhart, Purcell, Smith & Zuckuhr, 2010; Kowalski, Giumetti, Schroeder, & Lattanner, 2014). Research conducted by the Pew Research Center indicates that, in the United States, 92% of the adolescents go online on a daily basis (Lenhart et al., 2015). A considerable number of these adolescents are active on social media, namely 68% of the younger adolescents (13–14 years old) and 81% of the older adolescents (15–17 years old) (Lenhart et al., 2015). Given the high importance of peers in adolescents' lives (Furman & Collins, 2008; Steinberg 1996; Steinberg & Morris, 2001), the most important reason for them to turn to those platforms is the connection and re-connection with friends (Lenhart et al., 2010; Katzer, Fetchenhauer, & Belschak, 2009; Subrahmanyam, Reich, Waechter, & Espinoza, 2008). Many different activities help to achieve these social goals, such as group chatting, sending private messages and commenting on pictures and friends' walls (Lenhart et al., 2010; Subrahmanyam et al., 2008).

Existing research confirms the added value of maintaining friendships on social media. Compared to face-to-face interactions, social media enable stronger feelings of distance in online interactions, which makes adolescents feel less self-conscious and allows these connections to obtain a higher level of intimacy (Blais, Craig, Pepler, & Connolly, 2008; Valkenburg & Peter, 2007; Valkenburg & Peter, 2009). The consequences of this might be translated to the school context, with an increase in well-being and stronger feelings of fitting-in at school (Haythornthwaite & Kazmer, 2002; Ko & Kuo, 2009; Valkenburg & Peter, 2007). Moreover, maintaining friendships on social media may enhance learning by fostering social support, help, and feedback among adolescents and their peers (Deng & Yuen, 2011; Hrastinski & Aghaee, 2012).

Although social media are attractive and interesting tools to contribute to both adolescents' interpersonal and academic outcomes, some scholars expressed concerns about the potential negative impact of social media use. Several scholars point to the negative correlation between the time spent on social media and academic performance (e.g., Jacobsen & Forste, 2011; Junco, 2012b). According to these authors, spending time online is related with a lack of sleep and concentration, missing lessons, and fewer hours spent on studying (Kirschner & Karpinski, 2010; Kubey, Lavin, & Barrow, 2001). The risks of social media use are not restricted to the academic level. On the interpersonal level, the use of social media might not always be a positive experience, as these platforms can also be used to socially exclude or even (cyber)bully peers (Konishi, Hymel, Zumbo, & Li, 2010).

This chapter aims to offer a literature overview on how social goals in the classroom "play out" in the context of social media. More specifically, we will start by defining the central concept of this work, namely social media, and what those media and their functionalities mean within the lives of adolescents. Existing research will be supplemented with data from our large-scale survey study on adolescents' social media use, conducted among 1,300 adolescents (49.3% female) from 13 Flemish schools (i.e., the Dutch-speaking part of Belgium) (M_{age}= 16.06; SD = 1.45 years). Thereafter, we will describe how social media might be related with academic performance, and which interpersonal consequences might originate from the use of these platforms. Finally, directions for future research will be discussed.

Definitions

Nowadays, many social media platforms are available for adolescents, who are generally allowed to use these channels from the age of 13 (Anderson & Jingjing, 2018). In general, six types of social media can be identified, including collaborative projects (e.g., Wikipedia), blogs and microblogs (e.g., WordPress), content (created) communities (e.g., YouTube and Instagram), social network sites (e.g., Facebook), virtual game worlds (e.g., World of Warcraft), and virtual social worlds (e.g., Second Life) (Baruah, 2012; Kaplan & Haenlein, 2010; Vanwynsberghe, 2014) Results of our large-scale study indicated that adolescents mostly make use of the social media platforms YouTube (97.23%), Facebook Messenger (92.15%), Facebook itself (90.31%), Snapchat (84.08%), and Instagram (78.23%). The Pew Research Center also indicated that these are the platforms that are most popular among adolescents (Anderson & Jingjing, 2018). The popularity of the platforms differs based on the specific functionalities they offer. One way to describe these different functionalities is through the honeycomb model, as developed by Kietzmann and colleagues (2011). This widely used model distinguishes seven functional blocks, namely *sharing, conversations, relationships, groups, identity, reputation* and *presence* (Kietzmann et al., 2011). The blocks are neither mutually exclusive, nor are they all necessarily present in one social media context (Kietzmann et al., 2011; Kietzmann, Silvestre, McCarthy, & Pitt, 2012).

The first block we will discuss is *sharing*. This block stands for the extent to which users exchange, distribute, and receive content, such as pictures (e.g., WeHeartIt), videos (e.g., YouTube), and comments (e.g., Twitter) (Bolton et al., 2013; Kietzmann et al., 2011). In this case, social media are used by people who are connected by a shared object (Kietzmann et al., 2011). The term "social" comes from the objects that mediate ties between people (Engeström, 2005). Kietzmann and colleagues (2011) emphasize that sharing behavior is a way of interacting, but that it does not always leads to strong social relationships or even conversations.

Apart from sharing, many social media platforms also provide users with the opportunity to send messages among individuals and groups themselves (Lenhart & Madden, 2007). This brings us to the second block, namely *conversations*. This block represents the extent to which users communicate with each other (Kietzmann et al., 2011). Mostly, social media users have the option to make use of both private (e.g., private messages) and public ways (e.g., wall posts) of online communication (Lenhart & Madden, 2007). Within these communication options, each social medium has different conversation features. For instance, Twitter is a form of micro-blogging (i.e., short messages), whereas Facebook allows users to write more extensive posts (Kaplan & Heanlein, 2011).

By using conversations, people connect with each other. Kietzmann and colleagues (2011) described the phenomenon of connection and re-connection in the third block *relationships*. This block stands for the extent to which users relate to each other. Some social media platforms are characterized by more formal social relationships (e.g., LinkedIn), whereas other platforms are especially known for their informal connections (e.g., Facebook) (Kietzmann et al., 2011). Through these social relationships, adolescents may increase their social capital (Ellison, Steinfield, & Lampe, 2011). According to Putnam (2000), two forms of social capital can be distinguished. The first one is bonding social capital, which is the benefit adolescents will derive from close relationships or strong ties (e.g., family members and best friends). The second one is bridging social capital, which describes the benefit adolescents will experience from loose relationships or weak ties. Analogous to the study conducted by Ellison and colleagues (2007), results of our large-scale survey study indicated that Facebook use has a strong connection with both bonding social capital and bridging social capital.

Besides the difference between formal and informal social relationships on social media, a second distinction can be made according to the origin of these social relationships. It is stated that three different types of social relationships can be distinguished: (1) social relationships that originated offline but extend on social media (i.e., offline-to-online), (2) social relationships that originated on social media but do not extend offline (i.e., exclusively online), and (3) social relationships that developed on social media and extend ofline (i.e., online-to-offline) (Verswijvel, Heirman, Hardies, & Walrave, 2018). Results of our large-scale study (see Table 14.1) indicated that adolescents mostly use Facebook to stay connected with people they already know from the offline world ($M = 4.38$; $SD = .76$). Facebook mostly appeared to be a tool for maintaining existing friendships. This is in line with research conducted by Ellison and colleagues (2014). They found that adolescents made more use of Facebook in order to stay connected with offline contacts, rather than to meet new people.

As adolescents might have many social relationships on social media, they are often provided with the opportunity to use *groups*, which is the fourth block we will describe. This block represents the extent to which users can form communities and sub-communities to organize their social relationships (Kietzmann et al., 2011). These communities might be self-created and can have different privacy-settings (i.e., open to anyone, closed (approval is needed), and secret (by invitation only); Kietzmann et al., 2011). This strategy appeared to be popular among adolescent users. Results of our large-scale study indicated that 76.45% of the adolescents already use groups to structure their connections on Facebook.

The fifth block is *identity*, representing the extent to which users reveal their identities in a social media setting (Kietzmann et al., 2011). Kietzmann and colleagues (2011) emphasized that users can develop their online identity through self-disclosure and subjective information such as likes and dislikes. By disclosing personal information on social media platforms, users may also receive feedback from their social relationships. This might help them to explore their "self" (Burhmester & Prager, 1995). The disclosure preferences and aims may differ among social media platforms as well as among individual users (Kietzmann et al., 2011). Compared to adults, adolescents disclose more personal information on social media (Christofides, Muise, & Desmarais, 2012; Walrave, Vanwesenbeeck, & Heirman, 2012). Moreover, adolescents disclose information about a broader range of personal topics (Walrave et al., 2012). Results of our large-scale study for instance, indicated that a substantial number of the adolescents had already posted something about their personal opinions and ideas (45.40%), and about personal feelings (29.69%) since they were active on social media (see Table 14.2).

The sixth block is referred to as *reputation*. This block stands for the extent to which users know the social standing of others and themselves (Kietzmann et al., 2011). On each social media platform, reputation can have different meanings, but mostly it is connected with trust. On Instagram, for example, the number of followers is an indication of someone's reputation, whereas on LinkedIn endorsements determine a user's reputation (Kietzmann et al., 2011; Kietzmann et al., 2012). Reputation may also be related to the content which is shared on social

TABLE 14.1 Types of Social Relationships (five-point Likert scale)

I use Facebook to ...	M	SD
... stay connected with people I know from the offline world	**4.38**	**.76**
... meet new people online	1.77	.95
... meet new people online and to meet them afterwards in the offline world	2.06	1.06

TABLE 14.2 Self-disclosure

I have already posted ...	%	I have already posted ...	%
... personal feelings	**29.69**	... feelings of love	11.90
... personal opinions and ideas	**45.40**	... things I am shamed for	4.06
... things I am worried about	14.87	... information about	6.10
... personal secrets	.58	my love and sex life	

media (Kietzmann et al., 2011). On Twitter, for instance, the reputation of a tweet depends on the retweets.

The last block is *presence*, representing the extent to which users know if others are available at a specific time (and where they are in the virtual and/or real world) (Kietzmann et al., 2011; Kietzmann et al., 2012). Therefore, some social media platforms make use of status lines like "available" or "hidden" (e.g., Facebook) or provide users with the opportunity to check in (e.g., Foursquare) (Kietzmann et al., 2011).

Although these different functionalities are available to adolescents, it seems like there are clear differences in the extent to which they use these different features. Results of our large-scale study further indicated that adolescents use social media most often just to see what is happening online. By doing this, they get updates of their friends, family, and things that interest them. Our results indicated that 84.31% of the adolescents check their social media at least twice a day. Posting messages, pictures, videos, and music is something that happens less frequently among adolescents. A total of 79.01% post something less than once a day on their own profile or someone else's profile. These findings are in line with research conducted by Pempek and colleagues (2009). They found that looking at other people's profiles or photos and reading newsfeeds or walls posts was more common on a weekly basis than posting something on their own profile or someone else's profile. Also, Walrave and colleagues (2012) indicated that 54% of the adolescents checked their profile at least once a day, whereas only 17% of the adolescents posted messages at least daily.

Social Media in Adolescents' Daily Lives

As adolescents grew up in a digital world and use social media for several different functionalities, social media have become a common aspect of their daily lives (Center for Digital Future and the USC Annenberg School, 2010; Lenhart et al., 2015). Consequently, social media are also integrated in adolescents' educational context. In our survey, 794 (61.08%) out of 1,300 adolescents indicated that they use social media at their school. This raises questions on the potential impact social media might have on adolescents' academic performances and how this might translate to the interpersonal level. In the next two sections, we will discuss how social media use is related to academic performance and interpersonal outcomes.

Social Media and Academic Performance: A Two-Sided Story

Scholars have started questioning how the use of social media platforms relate to students' academic performance (Doleck & Lajoie, 2018). Existing research has looked at the relationship between social media use and, among others, time spent on homework and studying (e.g., Kirschner & Karpinski, 2010), grades (e.g., Junco, 2012b; Leung, 2015), performance in class (e.g., Wood et al., 2012) and student engagement (e.g., Junco, 2012a). Findings remain rather inconclusive as to whether a negative or positive relationship exists between social media use and the performance of pupils at school (Doleck & Lajoie, 2018; Marker, Gnambs, & Appel, 2017).

On the one hand, considerable support exists for the argument that there is a negative relationship between spending time on social media and academic achievement (Glass, Li, & Pan, 2014; Jacobsen & Forste, 2011; Paul, Baker, & Cochran, 2012). A study by Kirschner and Karpinski (2010) on Facebook use and academic performance, for example, shows that Facebook users have lower mean Grade Point Averages (GPAs) and spend fewer hours studying per week, compared to non-Facebook users. In a study observing middle school, high school, and university students, students accessing Facebook while studying had lower GPA scores than those who avoided this social media platform (Rosen, Carrier, & Cheever, 2013). Scholars have suggested several explanations for these findings, one is the *time displacement perspective* (Junco, 2012b; Marker et al., 2017). From this point of view, it is argued that time spent on social media takes away time that could otherwise be spent on academic tasks and knowledge acquisition. Another possible explanation for these results is related to *multitasking* behavior, which is defined as performing two or more activities simultaneously or switching very quickly between the tasks (Kirschner & Karpinski, 2010). In this specific context, it would mean using social media during other activities, such as studying or following classes (Marker et al., 2017). The negative results found could thus also be an indication of the detrimental effect multitasking might have on adolescents' effectiveness and efficiency while studying or taking courses.

Other studies provided more clarity into the validity of the multitasking and time displacement perspectives. For example, it was shown in several studies by Junco (2012a, 2012b) that there is only a weak relationship between time spent on Facebook and time spent preparing for class. This indicates that time displacement might actually not play a big role in explaining the existing negative link between general Facebook use and GPAs (Marker et al., 2017). Significant relationships were found between engaging in Facebook chat and time spent preparing for class. This suggests that it is not necessarily Facebook use in general, but only certain specific activities performed on online social platforms that might have a negative effect on academic performance, an idea that was confirmed for activities such as using Facebook Messenger (Leung, 2015; Wood et al., 2012) and MSN (Wood et al., 2012). These instant messaging services slow students when performing a task as the interruptions caused by the pop-up messages probably derail students' attention or force them to redo some parts of the initial task they were working on (Bowman, Levine, Waite, & Gendron, 2010).

It should be noted that up until now, the relationship between social media use and academic performance has been discussed as being unidirectional (Doleck & Lajoie, 2018). However, Michikyan, Subrahmanyam and Dennis (2015b), showed that it could be valuable to also take into consideration another perspective, as they studied the way academic performance might have an influence on Facebook use, instead of the other way around. Their research shows that social media are sometimes used for academic disclosure, because in that way students can update friends and family about their experiences at school. Participants with lower GPA scores showed greater level of Facebook activity, which might indicate that those experiencing some trouble at school might look for distraction or support on Facebook. Still, this study again stresses the negative link between social media use and academic performance.

Not all studies on this topic agree upon the fact that the use of social media and academic achievement are negatively related. Online social platforms can also be seen as tools to support learning. For example, social media can be used as tools to link the formal learning environment with more informal learning environments, where students can connect to larger communities, fellow students, teachers, and multimedia content, which has the potential to result in more engagement in the learning process (Chen & Bryer, 2012). Studies on student-student interactions show that even though face-to-face communication is still the most popular type of interaction between students for school-related topics, email, instant messaging and social media are supplementing these interactions in a substantive way (Hrastinski & Aghaee, 2012; Van Cleemput, 2010). As social media allow students to connect with each other at all times, the platforms are most often used for quick questions and to coordinate group collaborations (Hrastinski & Aghaee, 2012). Moreover, a study by Leung (2015) shows that heavy Facebook use in fact has a positive instead of a negative effect on changes in overall grades over the course of one year. A possible explanation for this result is that students might have formed communities on the social media platforms, where people help each other with school assignments and offer each other comfort and social support. Also personal development might benefit from social media (cf. infra), which in turn has positive effects on adolescents' academic success and learning outcomes (Yu, Tian, Vogel, & Kwok, 2010). Social media can thus serve as a mediator between socialization and academic performance (Ainin, Naqshbandi, Moghavvemi, & Jaafar, 2015).

Even though both positive and negative results can be found in studies on social media use and academic achievement, they do not necessarily contradict each other. A meta-analysis conducted by Marker and colleagues (2017) points out that especially the way "social media use" is defined and measured, is crucial. When looking at studies that focus on school-related social media use (e.g., using social media to communicate with other students about school), a positive relationship could be found between social media use and the grades obtained by the students, whereas social media are related to lower academic achievement when consulted while studying (i.e., multitasking activity) or for non-academic purposes. This highlights the fact that social media use is not necessarily a bad thing for the academic performance of adolescents. How and when social media are used is a more important aspect to consider when discussing this topic.

Interpersonal Outcomes: A Complex Relation between Opportunities and Risks

Social media have not only established a central place in adolescents' educational lives but also play a central role in the development of their identity and social relationships (Livingstone, 2008). The public response to these processes are mixed, with some people admiring the great potential of communication through social media for developing and maintaining contacts, self-expression, and sociability (Livingstone, 2008), whereas others express concerns regarding potential risks associated with the (excessive) use of these platforms (Best, Manktelow, & Taylor, 2014; Livingstone, 2008). Research on the interpersonal outcomes of social media for adolescents' social goals can then be classified into two groups. The first group of scholars has pointed out the contribution of social media to the developmental processes and general well-being during adolescence (Allen, Ryan, Greay, McInerney, & Waters, 2014; Davis, 2012; Livingstone, 2008; Michikyan, Dennis, & Subrahmanyam, 2015a). More specifically, Spies Shapiro and Margolin (2014) distinguished two ways in which social media can foster adolescents' identity development.

Firstly, social media make it easier to connect with like-minded peers across time and boundaries (Davis, 2012; Spies Shapiro & Margolin, 2014). In that way, social media enhance adolescents' sense of belonging to certain peer groups (Quinn & Oldmeadow, 2013). A sense of belonging refers to one's feelings of being part of a certain social group (Allen et al., 2014; Quinn & Oldmeadow, 2013). Thanks to social media, these social groups can be quite specific, such as ethnic or sexual minority groups (Larson, Wilson, Brown, Furstenberg, & Verma, 2002). Such connections can broaden and deepen adolescents' identity development (Spies Shapiro & Margolin, 2014).

Secondly, social media offer adolescents a playground for experimenting with self-disclosure and self-presentation (Livingstone, 2008; Michikyan et al., 2015a; Spies Shapiro & Margolin, 2014). By creating their own profiles, managing their own networks and commenting on others' posts (Davis, 2011; Steinberg & Morris, 2001), adolescents build an online image they like and want to live up to (Allen et al., 2014; Livingstone, 2008; Michikyan et al., 2015a; Spies et al., 2014). The advantage of building a self-representation through social media lies in its asynchronous character, allowing adolescents to take more time to reflect on their communication compared to face-to-face situations (Valkenburg & Peter, 2011), and to revise their identity representation when necessary (Livingstone, 2008). These online representations will also be the subject of evaluation and feedback coming from peers in the form of likes, comments and in- or exclusion of certain social groups (Davis, 2012; Spies Shapiro & Margolin, 2014).

There are mixed ideas on whether the online interactions and friendships that result from social media are good or bad for adolescents' social development. One study by Valkenburg and Peter (2007) therefore tested both the *stimulation hypothesis* and *the social deprivation or reduction hypothesis* (Locke, 1998) using an online survey among teenagers between 10 and 17 years old. Whereas the *stimulation hypothesis* describes how adolescents can more easily self-disclose online and experience more freedom online compared to face-to-face situations, (McKenna & Bargh, 2000), the *social deprivation hypothesis* (Locke, 1998; Valkenburg & Peter, 2007) states that online friendships are of low quality and are a threat for offline friendships because people spend more time online and less with their offline friends (Locke, 1998; Valkenburg & Peter, 2007). The authors found that time spent on instant messaging was positively associated with the time spent on offline friendships. Moreover, the quality of the friendships mediated the relationship between time spent on instant messaging and well-being. The authors interpreted these results as a confirmation of the *stimulation hypothesis*, whereas the *social deprivation hypothesis* was not confirmed.

The positive versus negative effects might also differ based on personality characteristics. Lonely and socially anxious adolescents benefit from online communication, as it encourages them to self-disclose in a more comfortable way and enhances their feelings of connection (Bonetti, Campbell, & Gillmore, 2010; Spies Shapiro & Margolin, 2014). The perception of more freedom can be attributed to the stronger feelings of anonymity and the absence of real-time cues, which help adolescents to talk about difficult and personal topics (Blais et al., 2008; Valkenburg & Peter, 2007; Valkenburg & Peter, 2009). In this way, social media can bring peer conversations to a higher level of intimacy (Blais et al., 2008; Valkenburg & Peter, 2007; Valkenburg & Peter, 2009), resulting in stronger friendships (Blais et al., 2008; Valkenburg & Peter, 2007; Valkenburg & Peter, 2009), which more easily involve the sharing of "secrets" compared to purely offline friendships (Blais et al., 2008). Higher quality friendships and greater intimacy are generally associated with increased self-esteem (Gross, 2009; Valkenburg, Peter, & Schouten, 2006) and higher well-being (Nezlek, 2000). The strength of online communication lies in the fact that these interactions are not a replacement for phone calls and offline meetings, but should rather be seen as supplementary, with adolescents using online channels to make plans offline (Bargh & McKenna, 2004; Jacobsen & Forste, 2011) or to continue their offline conversations (Jacobsen & Forste, 2011). Interactions with well-known peers not only facilitate adolescents' social development and conversations with strangers, but also help adolescents to socialize in the current society (boyd, 2007).

Moreover, online chatting with unfamiliar peers seems to help adolescents to restore their self-esteem when previously being confronted with social exclusion (Gross, 2009).

A second group of scholars has focused on a broad range of risks associated with social media use. Given their limited experience in the online space and their susceptibility to peer pressure (Best et al., 2014), adolescents might easily become the victims of social media risks such as sleep disturbance (Levenson, Shensa, Sidani, Colditz, & Primack, 2016; Spies Shapiro & Margolin, 2014), depression (O'Keeffe & Clarke-Pearson, 2011; Selfhout, Branje, Delsing, Ter Boght, & Meeu, 2009) and Internet addiction (Song, Laroze, Eastin, & Lin, 2004; Spies Shapiro & Margolin, 2014). Furthermore, despite the numerous opportunities for social media to contribute to adolescents' social connections and sense of belonging (Davis, 2012; Livingston, 2008), online contacts among peers do not always have a positive character. As adolescents easily disclose information (Best et al., 2014), play around with their online representation and respond more emotionally empathic compared to adults (Siriaraya, Tang, Ang, Pfeil, & Zaphiris, 2011), they might become the subject of critical responses from others (Allen et al., 2014; Livingstone, 2008) or more serious issues such as cyberbullying (Smith et al., 2008), online insulting (Vandebosch & Van Cleemput, 2008) and sexting (boyd, 2014; Lenhart, 2009; O'Keeffe & Clarke-Pearson, 2011).

Cyberbullying refers to "an aggressive, intentional act carried out by a group or individual using electronic forms of contact, repeatedly and over time, against a victim who cannot easily defend him or herself" (Smith et al. 2008, p. 376). Meta-analyses on cyberbullying indicate that prevalence rates differ widely based on the measurement and population, with an average of 24% of adolescents being involved as a victim (Kowalski et al., 2014; Patchin & Hinduja, 2012; Tokunaga, 2010), between 3 and 44% as a perpetrator (Kowalski et al., 2014; Patchin & Hinduja, 2012) and 33% as a bystander (Vandebosch & Van Cleemput, 2009). The consequences of cyberbullying can be very intense for adolescents, struggling with a lack of self-esteem, anxiety and isolation (Hinduja & Patchin, 2007). In some cases, the experiences contribute to the development of depression or suicidal intentions (Hinduja & Patchin, 2007).

One specific subform of cyberbullying that is very common among adolescents is *negative online commenting*. In a qualitative study on how adolescents perceive and define cyberbullying, negative commenting via instant messaging was mentioned as one of the first behaviors that comes to mind when thinking about cyberbullying (Vandebosch & Van Cleemput, 2008). Several survey studies further confirmed the frequency of exchanging rude online comments among adolescents (e.g., Chang et al., 2013; Ybarra, Diener-West, & Leaf, 2007). Adolescents who are regularly being confronted with negative online comments might experience feelings of lower self-esteem, shame, and anger (Kowalski et al., 2014). Moreover, these feelings might disturb future peer interactions, which makes even close peer relations problematic (Davila, La Greca, Starr, & Landoll, 2008).

Sexting refers to "the interpersonal exchange of self-produced sexualized texts and above all images (photos, videos) via cell phone or the Internet" (Döring, 2014). According to recent research, involvement rates among adolescents are situated around 1 out of 5 (18%) (Dake, Price, Maziarz, & Ward, 2012; Walrave, Ponnet, Van Ouytsel, Van Gool, Heirman, & Verbeek, 2015). Sexting becomes a problem when adolescents are being pressured to participate in it (Walker, Sanci, & Temple-Smith, 2013), or when pictures are being shared without one's permission (Mitchell, Finkelhor, Jones, & Wolak, 2012). The consequences for a victim's reputation can be far-reaching, as the victims can be confronted with negative comments, harassment or even bullying (Dake et al., 2012).

Based on the existing literature, it must be recognized that adolescents might experience both benefits as well as pitfalls of their social media use on the interpersonal level. In a literature review, Best and collegues (2014) tried to explain the contradictory findings by referring to the importance of potential mediators and moderators. According to the *"rich get richer" hypothesis* (Kraut, Kiesler, Boneva, Cummings, Helgeson, & Crawford, 2002), for instance, the positive versus negative effects of online communicative activities depend on the quality of one's offline friendships, with adolescents enjoying high quality offline friendships experiencing more benefits from online contact compared to adolescents with less high quality offline friendships (Davis, 2012; Gross, 2009).

Conclusion and Directions for Future Research

Throughout the last decade, social media have become an integrated part of adolescents' life (Lenhart et al., 2015). Our large-scale survey which was referred to several times in this literature overview showed that social media are not only used during adolescents' leisure time but that the majority (61.08%) of young people also consult social media while at school. This situation has raised concern about the potential academic and interpersonal drawbacks linked to social media use. Several studies support the claim that time spent on social media has a negative effect on students' academic performance (Glass et al., 2014; Jacobsen & Forste, 2011; Paul, Baker, & Cochran, 2012). Also the connections made with peers through social media do not always have a positive nature, as the platforms can be used for cyberbullying (Smith et al., 2008), negative commenting (Vandebosch & Van Cleemput, 2008), and sexting (Walrave et al., 2015). Still, it should be stressed that even though there are certain risks and downsides related to the use of social media, not all types of social media use have detrimental effects on the life of its young users. When social media are used for school-related purposes, for example, this can actually have a positive influence on the grades obtained by students (Marker et al., 2017). On an interpersonal level, social media might also serve the development of adolescents' identity and connection with peers (Livingstone, 2008). The greater intimacy and stronger friendships that are created through social media platforms are linked to increases in well-being (Nezlek, 2000) and self-esteem (Gross, 2009; Valkenburg et al., 2006). Moreover, social media use mediates the relationship between social acceptance and academic performance (Ainin et al., 2015).

Going forward, it is essential to stimulate the positive ways in which these platforms can be used, while at the same time warning users for the potential pitfalls. For instance, adolescents should be warned about the risks related to certain forms of online self-disclosure, such as sexting. Moreover, non-school-related social media use should be discouraged during classes and study activities. Social media should not be banned completely, as these platforms might also help adolescents to find social support and help with school assignments and build interpersonal relationships. To improve our insights into this matter, it would be useful for future research to look into the different ways schools, teachers, and parents could contribute to finding the right balance.

Moreover, we suggest future research to focus on a broader range of pupils and students, as children are connected to the Internet and social media at an increasingly younger age. More than half of the children between 9 and 12 already have their own smartphone and/or tablet, and between 27% and 46% of 11–12-year-old children use social media like Instagram, Facebook, Snapchat, and Tik Tok (Apestaartjaren, 2018). Therefore it would be useful to include more middle school and younger high school students in future studies (9–13 years old), to check whether the findings for older high school and university students still hold true for their younger counterparts. At the same time, these future studies should take into account that the online environment is continuously changing. New features (e.g., Instagram TV; Instagram Stories, memories on Facebook) and platforms (e.g., Tik Tok) cause shifts in the popularity and functionalities of the social media that are used by adolescents. The research field should therefore evolve together with the social media landscape. Lastly, a longitudinal approach in future studies is highly encouraged. Existing cross-sectional research gives us an indication of the relationships that exist between concepts like social media use, academic performance, social capital, quality of friendships, self-esteem, and well-being, but does not allow us to make conclusions about causality. Increasing and updating our understanding of the exact relationship between these elements would help us to make sure that adolescents can make the most out of their time spent on social media, both inside and outside the classroom.

References

Ainin, S., Naqshbandi, M. M., Moghavvemi, S., & Jaafar, N. I. (2015). Facebook usage, socialization and academic performance. *Computers & Education*, 83, 64–73.

Allen, K. A., Ryan, T., Gray, D. L., McInerney, D. M., & Waters, L. (2014). Social media use and social connectedness in adolescents: The positives and the potential pitfalls. *The Australian Educational and Developmental Psychologist*, 31(1), 18–31.

Anderson, M., & Jingjing, J. (2018). Teens, social media & technology 2018. Pew Internet & American Life Project.

Apestaartjaren. (2018). Apestaartjaren: de digitale leefwereld van kinderen en jongeren. Gent. Retrieved from: https://www.apestaartjaren.be/onderzoek/apestaartjaren-2018.

Bargh, J., & McKenna, K. (2004). The Internet and social life. *Annual Review of Psychology*, 55(1), 573–590.

Best, P., Manktelow, R., & Taylor, B. (2014). Online communication, social media and adolescent wellbeing: A systematic narrative review. *Children & Youth Services Review*, 41(9), 27–36.

Blais, J. J., Craig, W. M., Pepler, D., & Connolly, J. (2008). Adolescents online: The importance of internet activity choices to salient relationships. *Journal of Youth and Adolescence*, 37(5), 522–536.

Bolton, R. N., Parasuraman, A., Hoefnagels, A., Migchels, N., Kabadayi, S., Gruber, T., ... Solnet, D. (2013). Understanding generation Y and their use of social media: A review and research agenda. *Journal of Service Management*, 24(3), 245–267.

Bonetti, L., Campbell, M. A., & Gilmore, L. (2010). The relationship of loneliness and social anxiety with children's and adolescents'online communication. *Cyberpsychology, Behavior, and Social Networking*, 13(3), 279–285.

Bowman, L. L., Levine, L. E., Waite, B. M., & Gendron, M. (2010). Can students really multitask? An experimental study of instant messaging while reading. *Computers & Education*, 54(4), 927–931.

boyd, d. (2007). "Why youth (heart) social network sites". In D. Buckingham (Ed.), *MacArthur foundation series on digital learning: Youth, identity, and digital media volume* (pp. 119–142). Cambridge: MIT Press.

boyd, d. (2014). *It's complicated: The social lives of networked teens*. New Haven, CT: Yale University Press.

boyd, d., & Ellison, N. B. (2007). Social network sites: Definition, history, and scholarship. *Journal of Computer-Mediated Communication*, 13(1), 210–230.

Burhmester, D., & Prager, K. (1995). Patterns and functions of self-disclosure during childhood and adolescence. In K. J. Rotenberg (Ed.), *Disclosure processes in children and adolescents* (pp. 10–56). New York: Cambridge University Press.

Center for the digital future at the USC Annenberg school. (2010). The 2010 digital future report. Retrieved from: www.digitalcentrer.org.

Chang, F., Lee, C., Chiu, C., His, W., Huang, T., & Pan, Y. (2013). Relationships among cyberbullying, school bullying, and mental health in Taiwanese adolescents. *Journal of School Health*, 83, 454–462.

Chen, B., & Bryer, T. (2012). Investigating instructional strategies for using social media in formal and informal learning. *The International Review of Research in Open and Distributed Learning*, 13(1), 87–104.

Christofides, E., Muise, A., & Desmarais, S. (2012). Hey mom, what's on your Facebook? Comparing Facebook disclosure and privacy in adolescents and adults. *Social Psychological and Personality Science*, 3(1), 48–54.

Dake, J. A., Price, D. H., Maziarz, L., & Ward, B. (2012). Prevalence and correlates of sexting behaviour in adolescents. *American Journal of Sexuality Education*, 7(1), 1–15.

Davila, J., La Greca, A. M., Starr, L. R., & Landoll, R. (2008). Anxiety disorders in adolescence. In J. G. Beck (Ed.), *Interpersonal processes in the anxiety disorders: Implications for understanding psychopathology and treatment*. Washington, DC: American Psychological Association.

Davis, K. (2011). Tensions of identity in a networked era: Young people's perspectives on the risks and rewards of online self-expression. *New Media & Society*, 14(4), 634–651.

Davis, K. (2012). Friendship 2.0: Adolescents' experiences of belonging and self-disclosure online. *Journal of Adolescence*, 35(6), 1527–1536.

Deng, L., & Yuen, A. H. K. (2011). Towards a framework for educational affordances of blogs. *Computers & Education*, 56(2), 441–451.

Doleck, T., & Lajoie, S. (2018). Social networking and academic performance: A review. *Education and Information Technologies*, 23(1), 435–465.

Döring, N. (2014). Consensual sexting among adolescents: Risk prevention through abstinence education or safer sexting? *Cyberpsychology: Journal of Psychosocial Research on Cyberspace*, 8(9).

Ellison, N. B., Steinfield, C., & Lampe, C. (2007). The benefits of Facebook "friends": Social capital and college students' use of online social network sites. *Journal of Computer-Mediated Communication*, 12(4), 1143–1168.

Ellison, N. B., Steinfield, C., & Lampe, C. (2011). Connection strategies: Social capital implications of Facebook-enabled communication practices. *New Media & Society*, 13(6), 873–892.

Ellison, N. B., Vitak, J., Gray, R., & Lampe, C. (2014). Cultivating social resources on social network sites: Facebook relationship maintenance behaviors and their role in social capital processes. *Journal of Computer-Mediated Communication*, 19(4), 855–870.

Engeström, J. (2005). Why some social network services work and others don't – Or: The case for object-centered sociality. Retrieved from: www.zengestrom.com/blog/2005/04/why-some-social-network-services-work-and-others-dont-or-the-case-for-object-centered-sociality.html.

Furman, W., & Collins, W. A. (2008). Adolescent romantic relationships and experiences. In K. H. Rubin, W. Bukowski, & B. Laursen (Eds.), *Peer interactions, relationships, and groups* (pp. 341–360). New York: Guilford Press.

Glass, R., Li, S., & Pan, R. (2014). Personality, problematic social network use and academic performance in China. *Journal of Computer Information Systems*, 54(4), 88–96.

Gross, E. (2009). *Logging on, bouncing back: An experimental investigation of online communication following social exclusion.* Los Angeles: University of California.

Haythornthwaite, C., & Kazmer, M. M. (2002). Bringing the internet home: Adult distance learners and their internet, home, and work worlds. In B. Wellman & C. Haythornthwaite (Eds.), *The internet in everyday life* (pp. 429–463). Oxford: Blackwell Publishers.

Hinduja, S., & Patchin, J. (2007). Offline consequences of online victimization: School violence and delinquency. *Journal of School Violence*, 6(3), 89–112.

Hrastinski, S., & Aghaee, N. M. (2012). How are campus students using social media to support their studies? An explorative interview study. *Education and Information Technologies*, 17(4), 451–464.

Jacobsen, W. C., & Forste, R. (2011). The wired generation: Academic and social outcomes of electronic media use among university students. *Cyberpsychology, Behavior, and Social Networking*, 14(5), 275–280.

Junco, R. (2012a). The relationship between frequency of Facebook use, participation in Facebook activities, and student engagement. *Computers & Education*, 58(1), 162–171.

Junco, R. (2012b). Too much face and not enough books: The relationship between multiple indices of Facebook use and academic performance. *Computers in Human Behavior*, 28(1), 187–198.

Kaplan, A. M., & Haenlein, M. (2011). The early bird catches the news: Nine things you should know about micro-blogging. *Business Horizons*, 54(2), 105–113.

Katzer, C., Fetchenhauer, D., & Belschak, F. (2009). Cyberbullying: Who are the victims? A comparison of victimization in internet chatrooms and victimization in school. *Journal of Media Psychology*, 21(1), 25–36.

Kietzmann, J. H., Hermkens, K., McCarthy, I. P., & Silvestre, B. S. (2011). Social media? Get serious! Understanding the functional building blocks of social media. *Business Horizons*, 54(3), 241–251.

Kietzmann, J. H., Silvestre, B. S., McCarthy, I. P., & Pitt, L. F. (2012). Unpacking the social media phenomenon: Towards a research agenda. *Journal of Public Affairs*, 12(2), 109–119.

Kirschner, P. A., & Karpinski, A. C. (2010). Facebook and academic performance. *Computers in Human Behavior*, 26(6), 1237–1245.

Ko, H. C., & Kuo, F. Y. (2009). Can blogging enhance subjective well-being through self-disclosure? *CyberPsychology & Behavior*, 12(1), 75–79.

Konishi, C., Hymel, S., Zumbo, B. D., & Li, Z. (2010). Do school bullying and student-teacher relations matter for academic achievement? A multilevel analysis. *Canadian Journal of School Psychology*, 25(1), 19–39.

Kowalski, R. M., Giumetti, G., W., Schroeder, A. N., & Lattanner, M. R. (2014). Bullying in the digital age: A critical review and meta-analysis of cyberbullying research among youth. *Psychological Bulletin*, 140(4), 1073–1137.

Kraut, R., Kiesler, S., Boneva, B., Cummings, J., Helgeson, V., & Crawford, A. (2002). Internet paradox revisited. *Journal of Social Issues*, 58(1), 49–74.

Kubey, R. W., Lavin, M. J., & Barrow, J. R. (2001). Internet use and collegiate academic performance decrements: Early findings. *Journal of Communication*, 51(2), 366–382.

Larson, R., Wilson, S., Brown, B. B., Furstenberg, F. F.Jr., & Verma, S. (2002). Changes in adolescents' interpersonal experiences: Are they being prepared for adult relationships in the twenty-first century? *Journal of Research on Adolescence*, 12(1), 31–68.

Lenhart, A. (2009). Adults and social network websites. Pew Internet and American Life Project. Retrieved from: www.pewinternet.org/2009/01/14/adults-and-social-network-websites/.

Lenhart, A. (2010). Cyberbullying: What the research is telling us. Retrieved from: www.pewInternet.org/Presentations/2010/May/Cyberbullying-2010.aspx.

Lenhart, A., & Madden, M. (2007). Teens, privacy and online social networks: How teens manage their online identities and personal information in the age of MySpace. Pew Internet & American Life Project. Retrieved from: www.pewinternet.org/files/old-media//Files/Reports/2007/PIP_Teens_Privacy_SNS_Report_Final.pdf.pdf.

Lenhart, A., Duggan, M., Perrin, A., Stepler, R., Rainie, L., & Parker, K. (2015). Pew Research Center: Teens, social media and technology overview 2015. Retrieved from www.pewinternet.org/2015/04/09/teens-social-media-technology-2015/.

Lenhart, A., Purcell, K., Smith, A., & Zickuhr, K. (2010). Social media & mobile internet use among teens and young adults. Pew Internet & American Life Project. Retrieved November 5, 2010 from: http://pewinternet.org/Reports/2010/Social-Media-and-Young-Adults.aspx.

Leung, L. (2015). A panel study on the effects of social media use and internet connectedness on academic performance and social support. *International Journal of Cyber Behavior, Psychology and Learning (IJCBPL)*, 5(1), 1–16.

Levenson, J. C., Shensa, A., Sidani, J. E., Colditz, J. B., & Primack, B. A. (2016). The association between social media use and sleep disturbance among young adults. *Preventive Medicine*, 85, 36–41.

Livingstone, S. (2008). Taking risky opportunities in youthful content creation: Teenagers' use of social networking sites for intimacy, privacy and self-expression. *New Media and Society*, 10(3), 393–411.

Locke, J. L. (1998). *The de-voicing of society: Why we don't talk to each other anymore*. New York: Simon & Schuster.

Marker, C., Gnambs, T., & Appel, M. (2017). Active on Facebook and failing at school? Meta-analytic findings on the relationship between online social networking activities and academic achievement. *Educational Psychology Review*, 30, 651–677.

McKenna, K. Y. A., & Bargh, J. A. (2000). Plan 9 from cyberspace: The implications of the Internet for personality and social psychology. *Personality and Social Psychology Review*, 4(1), 57–75.

Michikyan, M., Dennis, J., & Subrahmanyam, K. (2015a). Can you guess who I am? Real, ideal, and false self-presentation on facebook among emerging adults. *Emerging Adulthood*, 3(1), 55–64.

Michikyan, M., Subrahmanyam, K., & Dennis, J. (2015b). Facebook use and academic performance among college students: A mixed-methods study with a multi-ethnic sample. *Computers in Human Behavior*, 45, 265–272.

Mitchell, K. J., Finkelhor, D.Jones, L. M., & Wolak, J. (2012). Prevalence and characteristics of youth sexting: A national study. *Pediatrics*, 129(1), 1–8.

Nezlek, J. B. (2000). Themotivational and cognitive dynamics of day-to-day social life. In J. P. Forgas, K.Williams, & L.Wheeler (Eds.), *The social mind: Cognitive and motivational aspects of interpersonal behaviour* (pp. 92–111). New York: Cambridge University Press.

O'Keeffe, G. S., & Clarke-Pearson, K. (2011). Council on communications and media. Clinical report: The impact of social media on children, adolescents, and families. *Pediatrics*, 127(4), 800–804.

Patchin, J. W., & Hinduja, S. (2012). Cyberbullying: An update and synthesis of the research. In J. W. Patchin & S. Hinduja (Eds.), *Cyberbullying prevention and response: Expert perspectives* (pp. 13–36). New York: Routledge.

Paul, J. A., Baker, H. M., & Cochran, J. D. (2012). Effect of online social networking on student academic performance. *Computers in Human Behavior*, 28(6), 2117–2127.

Pempek, T. A., Yermolayeva, Y. A., & Calvert, S. L. (2009). College students' social networking experiences on Facebook. *Journal of Applied Developmental Psychology*, 30(3), 227–238.

Putnam, R. (2000). *Bowling alone: The collapse and revival of American community*. New York: Simon & Schuster.

Quinn, S. V., & Oldmeadow, J. A. (2013). Is the iGeneration a 'We' generation?: Social networking use and belonging in 9–13 year olds. *British Journal of Developmental Psychology*, 31(1), 136–142.

Rosen, L. D., Carrier, L. M., & Cheever, N. A. (2013). Facebook and texting made me do it: Media-induced task-switching while studying. *Computers in Human Behavior*, 29(3), 948–958.

Selfhout, M. H. W., Branje, S. J. T., Delsing, M., ter Bogt, T. F. M., & Meeu, W. H. J. (2009). Different types of internet use, depression, and social anxiety: The role of perceived friendship quality. *Journal of Adolescence*, 32(4), 819–833.

Siriaraya, P., Tang, C., Ang, S., Pfeil, U., & Zaphiris, P. (2011). A comparison of empathic communication pattern for teenagers and older people in online support communities. *Behaviour & Information Technology*, 30(5), 617–628.

Smith, P. K., Mahdavi, J., Carvalho, M., Fisher, S., Russell, S., & Tippett, N. (2008). Cyberbullying: Its nature and impact in secondary school pupils. *Journal of Child Psychology and Psychiatry*, 49(4), 376–385.

Song, I., LaRose, R., Eastin, M. S., & Lin, C. (2004). Internet gratification and internet addiction: On the uses and abuses of new media. *Cyber Psychology & Behavior*, 7(4), 385–395.

Spies Shapiro, L. A., & Margolin, G. (2014). Growing up wired: Social networking sites and adolescent psychosocial development. *Clinical Child and Family Psychology Review*, 17(1), 1–18.

Steinberg, L. (1996). *Adolescence* (4th ed). New York: McGraw-Hill Humanities.

Steinberg, L., & Morris, A. S. (2001). Adolescent development. *Annual Review of Psychology*, 52(1), 83–110.

Subrahmanyam, K., Reich, S. M., Waechter, N., & Espinoza, G. (2008). Online and offline social networks: Use of social networking sites by emerging adults. *Journal of Applied Developmental Psychology*, 29(6), 420–433.

Tokunaga, R. S. (2010). Following you home from school: A critical review and synthesis of research on cyberbullying victimization. *Computers in Human Behavior*, 26(3), 277–287.

Valkenburg, P., & Peter, J. (2007). Online communication and adolescent well-being: Testing the stimulation versus the displacement hypothesis. *Journal of Computer-Mediated Communication*, 12(4), 169–182.

Valkenburg, P. M., & Peter, J. (2009). Social consequences of the internet for adolescents: A decade of research. *Current Directions in Psychological Science*, 18(1), 1–5.

Valkenburg, P. M. & Peter, J. (2011). Online communication among adolescents: An integrated model of its attraction, opportunities, and risks. *Journal of Adolescent Health*, 48 (2), 121–127.

Valkenburg, P. M., & Peter, J., & Schouten, A. (2006). Friend networking sites and their relationship to adolescents' well-being and social self-esteem. *CyberPsychology & Behavior*, 9(5), 584–590.

Van Cleemput, K. (2010). "I'll See You on IM, Text, or Call You": A Social network approach of adolescents' use of communication media. *Bulletin of Science, Technology & Society*, 30(2), 75–85.

Vandebosch, H., & Van Cleemput, K. (2008). Defining cyberbullying: A qualitative research into the perceptions of youngsters. *CyberPsychology & Behavior*, 11, 499–503.

Vandebosch, H., & Van Cleemput, K. (2009). Cyberbullying among youngsters: Profiles of bullies and victims. *New Media and Society*, 11(8), 1349–1371.

Verswijvel, K., Heirman, W., Hardies, K., & Walrave, M. (2018). Designing and validating the friendship quality on social network sites questionnaire. *Computers in Human Behavior*, 86, 289–298.

Walker, S., Sanci, L., & Temple-Smith, M. (2013). Sexting: Young women's and men's views on its nature and origins. *Journal of Adolescent Health*, 52(6), 697–701.

Walrave, M., Ponnet, K., Van Ouytsel, J., Van Gool, E., Heirman, W., & Verbeek, A. (2015). Whether or not to engage in sexting: Explaining adolescent sexting behaviour by applying the prototype willingness model. *Telematics and Informatics*, 32(4), 796–808.

Walrave, M., Vanwesenbeeck, I., & Heirman, W. (2012). Connecting and protecting? Comparing predictors of self-disclosure and privacy settings use between adolescents and adults. *Cyberpsychology: Journal of Psychosocial Research on Cyberspace*, 6(1).

Wood, E., Zivcakova, L., Gentile, P., Archer, K., De Pasquale, D., & Nosko, A. (2012). Examining the impact of off-task multi-tasking with technology on real-time classroom learning. *Computers & Education*, 58(1), 365–374.

Ybarra, M., Diener-West, M. D., & Leaf, P. (2007). Examining the overlap in internet harassment and school bullying: Implications for school intervention. *Journal of Adolescent Health*, 41, S42–S50.

Yu, A. Y., Tian, S. W., Vogel, D. R., & Kwok, R. C.-W. (2010). Embedded social learning in online social networking. Paper presented at the Thirty First International Conference on Information Systems, St. Louis, MO.

PART IV
In Conclusion

15

SOCIAL GOALS

Conclusions and Future Directions

Martin H. Jones

This book hoped to summarize and advance the current research on students' social goals in school. The first half of the book focused on specific social goals, whereas the second half focused on the contextual application of social goals. Together, these chapters hope to examined our understanding of which social goals students employ, provide evidence of the social goals, and then describe the academic and interpersonal consequences of social goals.

In summarizing the book, three important and distinct factors emerge. First, there are unintentional, but seemingly coherent, themes that each chapter's authors came to independently of the other authors. These themes range from the popularity of certain theories (e.g., social achievement goals) to the many gaps in the literature of the academic and interpersonal consequences of social achievement goals. Second, there are many areas of future research to help solidify the theoretical and empirical issues surrounding current social goals research. There is much additional work needed from how many social goals exist to which goals are most important in determining students' academic performance and interpersonal relationships. Third, the chapters help lay the groundwork for what topics the field might be researching in 20 years. In 2040, social goals may look very different as new research and theories within the field, as well from other fields, concurrently and independently develop our understanding of social goals.

Thus, this final chapter hopes to summarize the themes of the book, discuss areas of future research, and describe how the field of social goals research may appear in the upcoming decades. In doing so, this final chapter might propel future researchers to undertake why students pursue their social interactions in school. By understanding students' social motives, we may find better ways of reaching students to help them succeed in school.

Themes

Over the course of the book, several themes seemingly emerged across chapters. These themes were not intended in the creation of the book, but emerged independently as authors wrote chapters apart from each other. Theses themes are rather subjectively created as I noticed them appear. The first theme is the popularity of certain social goals. The second theme is the need for additional research across nearly all social goals. The third theme is the importance of understanding how social goals affect the learning process.

Popularity of Social Achievement Goals and Prosocial Goals

The book includes seven different social goals and five chapters describing how social goals might operate in context. Still, two social goals appeared across multiple chapters and contexts: social achievement goals and prosocial goals. Social achievement goals appeared as a means of explaining what social goals are and what social goals can do. For example, in Chapter 9, Estell discusses how the goal of gaining social status aligns with social achievement goals. In Chapter 10, Makara discusses how social achievement goals might operate differently between Asian and Western students. That is, Chinese students' social development and social demonstration goals were more correlated than Western students' social achievement goals. These chapters highlight that the work of Shim and Ryan (Chapter 4) in developing social achievement goals continues to impact social goal researchers across the globe. In a similar way, prosocial goals continue to impact the work done by social goal researchers.

Chapter 12 discusses how prosocial goals might overlap with the values of community and communal support in Latinx communities. The prosocial goal of helping other students aligns with many Latinx communities' values of helping those who are in need. These same values also appear in helping LGBTQ students feel socially supported in school (Chapter 13). When classmates exhibit a sense of caring and helping for others, then students who feel socially ostracized or vulnerable may feel more supported by their classmates. LGBTQ students may feel safer in school because their classmates want to help each other and build a climate of respect for students' sexual identities. In this way, the popularity of prosocial goals (Chapter 6) spans across cultures, and continues to build from the extant literature on how powerful, and popular, prosocial goals are in educational research.

Need for More Research

It may be cliché to say that future research is needed, but the need is apparent across the chapters in this book and in the field of social goal research. Most

Conclusions and Future Directions **259**

chapters in this book, including this chapter, mention a need for additional work in understanding social goals. This need partly comes from the relative youth of several social goal theories. For example, revenge goals and school foci are only beginning to appear in the literature as specific social goals, though there is historical work on both constructs. Their youth means that there are many future opportunities for exploring revenge goals, school foci, and other social goals. The need for future research is more fully described later in this chapter.

Social Goals in the Learning Process

Another theme across the book is how social goals embed themselves within the learning process. Each chapter includes discussion on how social goals affect students' academic performance. This may include such things as academic achievement, motivation to learn, or school engagement. More globally, the chapters situate social goals within the learning setting and the learning process. That is, students hold social goals concurrently with their learning goals, and these social goals can affect their learning outcomes. Much past work on students' learning processes excludes social goals in describing which factors affect what students learn and how students perform academically. The work in this book demonstrates that social goals play an important role in students' learning, and should therefore be included in research understanding how students learn in school or other educational settings.

The role of social goals in the learning process suggests that future work should consider how social goals interplay with students' academic motivation and academic achievement. For example, how do students co-regulate their motivation and their social goals? Students' academic pursuits and their social pursuits occur in parallel with each other, so it may be that students must alter or change their social goals in line with their academic goals, or vice versa. The interplay of social goals and the learning process suggests that self-regulated learning researchers and situated learning researchers should consider how students' social goals interrupt, improve, or change how students learn. That is, social goals are not ancillary to the learning process, but, instead, are a core tenet to how students learn in any social setting.

Future Research

Each chapter in this book concludes with areas of future research. Instead of summarizing each chapter's writing on future research here, it might be best to discuss future areas of research for all social goals. While not an exhaustive list, there are several larger questions that social goal research can begin to address in the forthcoming years. Three promising areas are the frequency, type, and interactions of social goals. Further, future research can consider interventions for

260 Martin H. Jones

social goals and determining which goals might best help students' academic and social functioning.

Frequency, Type, and Interactions of Social Goals

The number of different social goals presented in this book demonstrates the breadth of purposes for which a child or adolescent could pursue interpersonal interactions in learning settings. Social goals range from developing friendships to seeking revenge to gaining social prominence. The breadth of social goals as well as the relative short period for which these goals emerged in research calls to question whether researchers uncovered the full number and scope of all social goals. This is a largely empirical question examining whether the extant literature encapsulates all social goals. Additional research should examine any and all potential future social goals.

Without any empirical evidence, it is difficult conjuring the frequency or type of yet uncovered social goals. How many social goals and what these goals entail will require researchers to observe students in the classroom, ask teachers about their experiences, and having researchers be perceptive enough to uncover the subtle, and not so subtle, social desires that learners hold. Some potential areas for deeper consideration are which and how many social goals that learners hold in their classroom. There are potentially many social goals to consider. These social goals might involve why students might avoid social interactions in school (i.e., introversion, avoiding bullying). A student may only build a few social relationships due to a natural tendency for limited social interaction or as a goal for limiting harassment from peers. Another area for potential social goals is why learners can hold a desire to change their appearance to peers, such as building a new identity or image. A student may want to appear more athletic, artistic, or try different gender identities, but how this desire to change from a past to new identity affects academic and personal interactions is not understood as a potential social goal. An additional area is the use of humor in social interactions in school. The social goal of appearing funny to classmates and teachers may come with greater social acceptance as people desire to associate with others who are funny, but how the goal of appearing funny affects learning and interpersonal interactions needs additional research. These are only a few possible future social goals. There are likely much more social goals for students. There are also many understudied possible social goals held by teachers.

The social motives an instructor holds may appear when instructing students, interacting with learners in the school hallways and in extracurricular activities, speaking with other teachers, chatting with parents, and having conversations with administrators. The social goals of instructors and administrators are currently greatly understudied, but it may be that why instructors interact with students and others may have direct and indirect consequences for students' learning and peers' behaviors. For example, it may be that teachers with cool goals may interact with

Conclusions and Future Directions **261**

students and colleagues quite differently than teachers with a social development goal. How this, or any , social goal sets forth a series of behaviors among educators and their learners is in need of additional research. Further, the number of social goals and when teachers employ them need much more investigation.

The frequency and multiplicity of social goals for teachers and students are not yet known. That is, little extant research examines how many goals are used at any given time in school. A student likely holds multiple social goals in a learning setting, and these social goals may be even seem somewhat contradictory. A student may hold a social development goal and a popularity goal, such that a student wants to build greater social relationships with peers, but is willing to concede this goal in order to gain popularity in school. Thus, the question arises of how many, which, and to what consequence do learners hold multiple social goals.

Further, the degree to which a student holds a given goal will come into play when considering multiple social goals. A student with competing multiple social goals could hold one social goal to a greater degree than the other social goal. In this way, a students' social interactions may be greater swayed by a given social goal instead of another. This may even occur when one social goal (popularity goal) seems contradictory to others social goals (social development goals). This suggests that there may also be interactions among social goals.

Interactions among social goals build from the possibility that multiple social goals can co-occur. Then, it may be that certain social goals interact with each other, such that a prosocial goal and a cool goal describes students who are altruistic with classmates, but do so in a somewhat aloof way. The interactions of social goals might better explain academic performance or interpersonal interactions than a single social goal. Students with popularity goals and revenge goals may spend more time focusing on hurting others for social benefits. These social interactions might lead researchers to develop profiles of students' social goals, which can help practitioners predict which students could struggle or succeed in school. Thus, a series of research questions remain as to what happens when students hold multiple goals as well as the number of existing possible goals and the intensity of each goal.

Which Goals Matter Most?

Each social goal mentioned in this book has academic and interpersonal outcomes. Some of these goals may directly or indirectly align with academic performance, whereas each social goal directly affects learners' interpersonal interactions. Multiple social goals may combine to better explain academic performance and interpersonal outcomes, though not yet understood. Future work may begin disentangling which social goals are the most important for academic performance and which goals are the most influential for different interpersonal interactions.

262 Martin H. Jones

It may be that certain social goals are more adaptive for specific academic outcomes. In a similar way, different social goals may correspond with very different interpersonal outcomes. Revenge goals may be used in school settings and encouraged by peers, but revenge goals likely will not have the same effect on developing friendships as a social development goal. Revenge goals may result in a lower social status if revenge is sought from the wrong peer, but successful revenge could lead to gained social status. In turn, a social development goal may not improve student's social standing as much as would a popularity goal. Though a social development goal should improve the quality of a friendship, this does not mean the improved friendship leads to greater social status. These outcomes demonstrate that a variety of social outcomes stem from specific different social goals.

The variety of social and academic outcomes makes it difficult to suggest that a certain social goal might be the most important, or that one social goal is more important than the other. Rather, the researcher or practitioner must decide what is the desired outcome for the student, and then select a social goal(s) that aids the desired outcome. For example, wanting to improve a students' social status and academic achievement may mean using popularity and social demonstration-approach goals, whereas decreasing aggression could include social dominance goals and revenge goals. By understanding the desired outcome(s) associated with social goals, the researcher or educational practitioner can begin to help the student. This makes the development of interventions for social goals a more complicated task.

Interventions

Once social goals are better understood, then the next step will be developing interventions to help students enhance or reduce the presence of a given social goal. What these interventions look like, what is required of those involved, and the efficacy for any given intervention are yet to be understood. Who should be involved with the interventions (teachers, students, parents) is also to be determined. What is likely to occur is that interventions will attempt to enhance students' social skills, build friendships, and strengthen relationships with teachers in school. Enhancing these social relationships begins with knowing which social goal needs to be changed in order to acquire the given outcome. The efficacy of these interventions will likely depend on the context of the student and the values of the student's school community.

Context will be very important in understanding which social goals should be changed. The cultural values and community norms of a given school will guide teachers and parents to examine which social goals should be addressed for interventions. If a teacher or parent believes that one particular social goal is maladaptive or hurting the child in some way, then that social goal will become the target for intervention. Which social goal(s) are maladaptive will depend on the cultural values of the child's community, such that certain goals (e.g., popularity) in specific contexts (social media) may not be as negative as other social goals (e.g., revenge goals) in social media. This is seen with cyberbullying where revenge is generally viewed as inappropriate, but using social media to enhance one's social status is considered socially appropriate. In a similar way, context will matter for minority students and students with diverse sexual identities.

Interventions that target minority students must understand cultural context. Whether an intervention should teach "appropriate" social goals will depend on the cultural and ethnic context of those involved. After considering the context of those involved with the intervention, future interventions will need to examine which actors will take part in the intervention. It may be that teachers, peers, and parents would need to be involved for some social goal interventions, whereas other interventions will only need to focus on peers or teachers. This may require teachers and classmates working together to intervene on a student's social goals (e.g., revenge goals), but a different social may just focus on friends (e.g., social development goal). The level(s) of social interactions inherent to social networks will need to be examined for which persons are most appropriate for involving in interventions.

Interventions will be one of the exciting future areas of research, but the future for social goal research is bright in many areas. The final section of this chapter will be devoted to predicting where the field of social goal research might be in 20 years. This may be a way for researchers to begin developing studies today that impact the field for the next several decades.

In 2040

Social goal research started appearing in academic journals in a somewhat regular fashion a few decades ago. Over time, the frequency and types of social goals published began to grow. This growing interest in which social goals students pursue, and the consequences of pursuing these social goals, suggests that the future of social goal research is open to great exploration. This exploration may lead to what the future of social goal research entails in the year 2040. In particular, I anticipate that social goal research in 2040 will be increasingly more complex.

In 20 years, the field of social goal research will likely be using different methodologies that stem from theoretical improvements, new analytical techniques, and greater interdisciplinary work. Theoretical improvements will include the use of complex systems theory to explore social interactions (Hilpert & Marchand, 2019; Jacobson, Kapur, & Reimann, 2016). Complex systems theory suggests that multiple systems (i.e., schools, school districts, communities) overlap with each other. Social goal research will change as the fields of psychology and sociology better explain how multiple and layered systems concurrently operate with each other, and interact with individual students. The pursuit of students' social goals within complex systems necessitates that the systems will change because of students' goals, but the systems will also affect students' social goals. The reciprocal relationships across systems and students' social goals will push forward which goals are most important to different student outcomes (i.e., academic performance and interpersonal relationships).

The methodological advancement of understanding how multiple systematic players relate with student's social goals will coincide with the evolution of social network analyses. There are currently several different methods of analyzing social networks (e.g., social network analysis, RSiena, social cognitive mapping), with more likely emerging in future years. Currently, there is not much agreement on which social network analysis techniques are the most accurate, but this may converge as more analytical techniques come forward. These analytical techniques may also make analyzing data faster as current techniques are usually quite laborious in entering names into software. As social network analyses becomes faster and more accurate, there should be greater ability to assess how social goals affect dyadic relationships and peer groups in a given student's social network.

Social network analyses techniques will likely change as new technologies emerge involving social media, and the pushback against social media. Student's use their social goals within a variety of social media platforms (see Chapter 14). Social goal research will likely follow these trends to use social media and other technologies to examine how students use social goals, and to what effect having social goals effects relationships within social media. There will also be pushback against social media as some students reject electronic social relationships. The seemingly ubiquitous nature of social media may actually cause some people to avoid or reject social media platforms for more face-to-face contact or seek areas without social media (i.e., nature, the outdoors). Whether future students use or reject social media, future social media platforms and technologies will need to consider the role of students' social goals to better understand why users interact with each other.

The greater application of social media with social goals highlights the interdisciplinary nature of social goal research. Several different fields of research are currently seeking an understanding of why individuals pursue social interactions, and the consequences of these social goals. Businesses and business researchers may want to know why their customers engage with a company or a brand's social media, why employees socially engage with each other, and how employees might develop better social relationships with customers. Sociologists may want to understand the motives for how larger groups pursue social goals with each other and within particular social groups. Anthropologists and historians can also use social goals to understand the motives behind cultural shifts among a given sociocultural group or within a historical period. Hence, interdisciplinary research may provide a deeper understanding of how social goals work and cross-pollinate ideas across each other's research areas.

Conclusion

Social goals include a variety of reasons behind why students pursue social interactions inside school. Each social goal provides distinct academic and interpersonal outcomes. The future for social goal research is wide and varied. The current crossroads of social goal research serves as the "jumping-off" point for the next generation of social goal work. This work will ultimately be more expansive that past work and only deepen our understanding of which and how social goals matter. It is only in understanding how social goals operate that we begin to help students succeed.

References

Hilpert, J. C., & Marchand, G. C. (2019). Complex systems research in educational psychology: Aligning theory and method. *Educational Psychologist*, 53(3), 185–202.

Jacobson, M. J., Kapur, M., & Reimann, P. (2016). Conceptualizing debates in learning and educational research: Toward a complex systems conceptual framework of learning. *Educational Psychologist*, 51(2), 210–218.

INDEX

academic motivation *see* motivation
academic performance 4, 11, 37, 38, 43, 44, 45, 47, 49, 58, 62, 122, 123, 133, 150, 160, 178, 180, 197, 198, 200, 206, 208, 211, 226, 238, 241, 242–44, 247, 248, 259, 261, 264
achievement goals 8, 10–1, 12, 17, 18, 23, 24, 39, 40, 44, 55, 57–8, 67, 102, 134, 155, 156, 179, 182, 207, 228
adolescence 20, 57, 66, 76, 77, 80, 85, 131, 133–34, 135, 150, 157, 158, 159, 163, 244
African American 62, 78, 133, 135–37, 148, 149, 192–05
aggression 60, 65, 76, 77, 79–80, 84, 85, 96, 113, 114, 115, 117–19, 121, 123, 132, 133, 135, 157–61, 162, 181, 184, 193, 194, 201, 213, 224, 229, 230, 232, 262,
antisocial 85, 93, 154, 160, 162
Asia *see* Asian students
Asian students 173–91, 210, 258
Black *see* African American

bullying 4, 66, 67, 85, 157, 158, 221, 225, 226, 238, 246, 247, 260, 263

childhood 66, 76, 77, 135, 158, 159
classmates 3, 4, 6, 7, 38, 44, 45, 80, 81, 82, 93, 94, 96, 98, 100, 101, 102, 104, 105, 115, 197, 228, 258, 260, 261, 263
collective efficacy 23, 197

collectivism 21, 121, 174–77, 179, 180, 212, 209, 210, 211, 215
collectivist culture *see* collectivism
cool goals 6, 8, 56, 57, 77–81, 85, 96, 131–53, 155, 159, 161, 224, 225, 228, 260, 261
culture 21, 136, 178, 179, 185, 186, 197, 209, 211, 213, 223, 231
cyberbullying *see* bullying

delinquent 20, 45, 46, 193
delinquency 80, 193
dominance goals 4, 6, 11, 74–92, 111, 115, 118, 119, 122, 155, 156, 157, 159–62, 163, 175, 177, 200, 212, 224, 225, 226, 229, 262
drive theory 9–10,

ethnic diversity 68, 76, 78, 79, 192, 194, 197, 201, 244, 263
ethnic identity 193, 198–201

friendships 4, 6, 16, 46, 50, 67, 77, 99, 102, 134, 148, 155, 160, 162, 163, 174, 183, 184, 194, 196, 197, 201, 209, 230, 237, 240, 245, 247, 248, 260, 262

gender differences 78, 135, 136, 199, 213,
gender diversity 213, 221–36, 260

homophily 6
Hispanic students *see also* Latinx 214

interventions 48–9, 66, 68, 85, 86, 100, 104, 123, 162, 186, 259, 262–63

Latinx (Latino/a) students 206–20, 258
LGBTQ 221–36

mindset 45, 227
motivation 15, 37, 44, 46, 49, 86, 182, 197, 209, 227, 259

peer groups 6, 45, 83, 131, 132, 133, 134, 197, 200, 201, 211, 230, 244, 264
perceived popularity 45, 46, 76, 80, 154, 195, 224
popular *see* perceived popularity *or* sociometric status
power 9, 75–76, 77, 78, 80, 84, 86, 96, 99, 103, 118, 119, 121, 154, 155, 156, 158, 161, 163, 177, 192, 195, 215, 224, 225
prosocial goals 4, 8, 12, 14, 18, 19, 23, 56, 60, 76, 79, 85, 93–110, 115, 132, 133, 134, 135, 154–57, 159, 160, 162, 163,174, 176,183, 184, 192, 194, 195,198, 213, 214, 225, 230, 258, 261

self-concept 66, 82, 199
self-determination theory 16–17, 19, 21, 25, 104
self-efficacy 15, 19, 23, 45, 201, 227
social achievement goals 12, 18–19, 22, 53–73, 74, 83, 85, 134, 135, 136, 138, 147, 148, 150, 155, 177, 184, 185, 195–98, 200, 201, 221, 225, 226, 228, 257, 258
social cognitive theory 38, 48, 53, 195
social media 53, 67, 84, 237–54, 263, 264
social network 6, 155, 157, 224, 230, 238, 264
socioeconomic status 137, 186,

Queer *see* LGBTQ

revenge goals 4, 53, 111–30, 200, 224, 225, 229, 259, 260, 261, 262, 263
teachers 3–4, 7, 17, 38, 46, 48, 49, 50, 67, 77, 79, 80, 82, 86, 93, 99, 100, 101, 103, 104, 105, 115, 121, 157, 162, 163, 174, 176, 184, 186, 197, 207, 213, 221, 225, 227, 228, 229, 230, 243, 248, 260–63

victim 103, 120, 124, 246

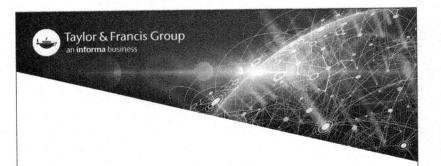